W9-ASQ-153

case	pronoun case (373–377)
coh	coherence (300–302, 323–324)
comp	comparison (389)
cs/cf/fs	comma splice, comma fault, fused sentence (402–403)
d	diction (341–359)
def	define
div	word division (427–428)
doc	documentation (195–200)
dm	dangling modifier (385, 387–388)
emph	emphasis (326–330)
fn	note form (200–204)
form	format, manuscript style (443 and inside the back cover)
frag	fragment (420)
jarg	jargon (352)
lc	lower case (438–440)
ll	language level (356–357)
log	logic (121–136)
mm	misplaced modifier (387–388)
nos	numbers (395, 421)
P	punctuation (402–420)
ref	pronoun reference (378)
rep	repetition (324–326)
sp	spelling (423–426, 429–436)
t	tense (381–384)
trans	transition (302–304, 310)
t switch	tense switch (354–355)
v switch	voice switch (355–357)
w	wordiness (325)
ww	wrong word (341–342)

THE WRITER'S WORK

DEAN MEMERING
Central Michigan University

FRANK O'HARE
The Ohio State University

Guide to effective composition

PRENTICE-HALL, INC.
Englewood Cliffs, New Jersey 07632

DOWNS-JONES LIBRARY
HUSTON-TILLOTSON COLLEGE

THE WRITER'S WORK

PE 1408
M463

DEAN MEMERING
FRANK O'HARE

The Writer's Work: Guide to Effective Composition

© 1980 by Prentice-Hall, Inc., Englewood Cliffs, New Jersey 07632

*All rights reserved. No part of this book may be reproduced
in any form or by any means without permission in writing from
the publisher. Printed in the United States of America.*
10   9   8   7   6   5   4   3   2   1

LIBRARY OF CONGRESS CATALOGING IN PUBLICATION DATA

MEMERING, DEAN (date)
　　The writer's work.
　　Includes index.
　　1. English language—Rhetoric.　I. O'HARE,
FRANK, joint author.　II. Title.
PE1408.M463　　　808'.042　　　79-23573
ISBN 0-13-969865-5

Prentice-Hall International, Inc., LONDON
Prentice-Hall of Australia Pty. Limited, SYDNEY
Prentice-Hall of Canada, Ltd., TORONTO
Prentice-Hall of India Private Limited, NEW DELHI
Prentice-Hall of Japan, Inc., TOKYO
Prentice-Hall of Southeast Asia Pte. Ltd., SINGAPORE
Whitehall Books Limited, WELLINGTON, NEW ZEALAND

Interior and cover design: BETTY BINNS GRAPHICS
Drawings: VANTAGE ART, INC.
Editorial and production supervision: JOYCE FUMIA PERKINS
Manufacturing coordination: RAY KEATING

TO THE INSTRUCTOR

Composition instructors of the 1980s are heirs to a complex history and stewards of an uncertain future. The 1960s were a decade of unrest and experimentation; in many schools where it had been traditionally taught as a mechanical skill, composition became self-expressive writing, a change some found refreshing and others disturbing. In the 1970s there has been much public and professional concern about an alleged loss of direction in composition and a presumed deemphasis of basic skills in composition courses. As SAT scores have fallen, critics of the profession have insisted that composition has become dichotomized, divorcing content from style, invention from expression, the larger issues of composition from the lesser. The skills of writing have always been difficult to teach, more difficult to learn, and—especially when divorced from more creative aspects of writing—they are often the least rewarding components of the writing process. Yet writers themselves seldom view the skills as trivial. The dichotomy between ideas and skills of expression does not exist in the work of experienced writers, most of whom hold that the quality of an idea is limited by the writer's power of expression. The notion that style and substance are separable creates a hardship for our students if this notion means that they are being offered a choice between ideas and language skills: between large, important matters in one composition course and small, unimportant matters in another composition course. Because we believe this split between form and content is false, and contrary to both the theory and the practice of good writing, we have attempted to present both and to show the interaction between them in *The Writer's Work.*

Chapter by chapter, as they move through a progression of increasingly formal writing tasks from personal to expository to critical to research writing, students will see how these choices of style and substance work together regardless of the writing task. The nonfiction

v

81015

writer's commitment to truth, accuracy, and integrity in writing requires not only factual honesty but dedication to accuracy of expression. Even such mundane matters as spelling and punctuation are seen as a writer's tools, the means of precise expression. Because of the special nature of the relationship between the writer and the reader of nonfiction, all accidents of expression both interfere with the intended message and send another message about the author's view of self and attitudes toward the reader and the subject. After more than a decade of controversy over form and substance, it is time to replace the dichotomy with a unified theory of composition.

Part of the impulse behind *The Writer's Work* has been the discovery that inexperienced writers are capable of dedication to their craft. We have discovered, for example, that students can move from the inherently rewarding pleasures of personal writing and autobiographical narratives to the more demanding work of other kinds of writing. The "term paper," or research paper, is not beyond inexperienced writers and need not be a routine and uninspired collection of footnotes. Class testing of the materials in *The Writer's Work* has demonstrated that students can succeed at academic writing. Leading students through increasingly more demanding writing tasks and building into those tasks an accumulation of skills that develop into formal and impersonal kinds of writing, the text provides a natural bridge from free writing to research writing.

Chapter 1, "The Composing Process," first presents the writer's choices and then describes the stages of writing in which the choices operate. All writing is governed by the writer's purpose, but having said that, we must go on to explore the choices a writer makes as a part of that purpose: choices about audience, experience, self, and especially choices about code—the language a writer selects. These elements must unite in the writer's overall design, either through conscious decision or writer's intuition, to produce the concept and the expression of that concept, which we call composition. Decisions about each of these aspects must be made during all four phases of the writing process: prewriting, writing, rewriting, and proofreading. Chapter 1 explains and illustrates the composing process with both student and professional writing and provides activities to help students understand and practice the process.

Chapter 2, "Personal Writing," offers students a variety of writing situations, starting with the least structured and most self-expressive—free writing and journal writing—and progressing to more structured personal-experience writing. The chapter ends with a ghost-writing assignment that requires students to search beyond themselves for materials for composition. The chapter contains student and professional examples, activities, and principles for effective personal writing.

Chapter 3, "Strategies of Exposition," moves from the personal to a focus on subjects in the world outside the self. The chapter begins with more formalized invention procedures than those in Chapter 2:

students are shown several ways to find material and analyze subjects for expository writing, including field analysis and Burke's *pentad*. There are many opportunities for writing, including the thesis and support paper, the comparison and contrast paper, the classification paper, the process paper, and the definition paper, with examples from student and professional writers.

Chapter 4, "Reasoned Writing," extends the progression into structured writing with evaluative and persuasive writing. The chapter features critical writing; a full treatment of logic, including syllogistic reasoning and the fallacies; and the techniques of argumentation involved in writing that seeks to convince the reader of the writer's reliability and authority. In addition to illustrative compositions, there are many specific suggestions for writing activities.

Chapter 5, "Writing with Sources," describes an introduction to the library, including a library-search assignment that will help to familiarize students with the contents and organization of their school library, and writing assignments leading to the full research paper: the objective summary, the critical summary, and the comparison of sources. There is a comprehensive treatment of the research paper entailing finding and limiting a researchable thesis, finding and evaluating data, and using evidence to develop a research concept. The chapter provides a stylesheet based on the *MLA Handbook* and also an example of APA documentation style. Students are given a step-by-step guide through the research paper, a complete model paper, and a selection of popular research topics. Chapter 5 is the culmination of the progression from unstructured, informal, personal writing to structured, formal, and impersonal writing.

Chapter 6, "Sentence Combining," contains exercises based on the signal system developed by O'Hare, as well as new unsignaled and creative exercises in exploring prose. While we view sentence-level problems as just one of many difficulties in writing, students often view sentence problems as the chief difficulty in writing. Students who tediously write one word at a time (like those who read one word at a time), students who labor to produce a sentence and then discover that the sentence is incomprehensible—students who lack syntactic fluency—are often not able to attend to larger problems of composition. The sentence-level barrier is absolute for them. As most instructors know, efforts to drill grammar into these students have usually failed. But the new research incorporated into *The Writer's Work* should make this kind of language handicap a thing of the past for most students. O'Hare's work, *Sentence Combining: Improving Student Writing without Formal Grammar Instruction*, NCTE Research Report No. 15, 1973, demonstrated that syntactic fluency is a discrete skill and that most students can acquire an ease with sentences characteristic of mature writers. Based on O'Hare's research and the subsequent revisions and adaptations of that work for the college classroom by Memering and O'Hare, sentence combining makes possible the dedication to skills required by the view that composition is a union of thought and expression. With periodic exercises throughout a semester, students will first lose their "scribal stutter," and second, acquire something of the grace and maturity of the professional writers whose prose illustrates this chapter.

Chapter 7, "Effective Paragraphs," presents principles of paragraph composition and demonstrates the application of topic sentence, development, unity, and coherence in mature paragraphs. The chapter introduces a number of approaches to paragraph structure, including Christensen's generative rhetoric of the paragraph. The chapter includes various approaches to such problem paragraphs as the introductory and concluding paragraphs of formal nonfiction. "Effective Paragraphs" is illustrated with student and professional writing and contains many suggestions for writing activities at the paragraph level.

Chapter 8, "Effective Sentences," covers rhetorical and stylistic considerations of effectiveness in sentence structure based on principles of clarity, economy, emphasis, and variety. The chapter demonstrates flaws to be avoided as well as the many options available to writers. Chapter 8 complements Chapter 6; together they offer students comprehensive treatment of sentence options, and they allow teachers flexibility in determining how much of each they wish to emphasize with students. The chapter is profusely illustrated with professional and student examples of effective prose contrasted with less effective sentences.

Chapter 9, "Effective Diction," highlights the vocabulary choices writers make, as well as those they avoid, based on the overall purpose and stance of the writer who is interested in clear, concise, and accurate writing. This chapter contains a dictionary section discussing entries and connotative and denotative definitions. As in Chapter 8, the choices are presented in pairs exemplifying effective diction contrasted with less effective writing. The chapter uses many examples of professional and student writing and contains review exercises to help students distinguish between effective writing and poor.

Chapter 10, "Usage," describes grammatical choices and problems. As we use the term, "grammar" is restricted to such things as agreement of subjects and verbs, the reference of pronouns to their antecedents, and so forth—what is frequently called "usage." Since usage questions can involve minority dialects, linguistic prejudice can become a real problem in any classroom in which instructors teach a "standard English." But the nonfiction writer's task is to affect his or her audience; the reader-writer relationship is created and controlled through the language the writer uses. The writer cannot ignore the usage expectations of readers. Educated readers expect subjects and verbs to "agree," pronouns to refer clearly to antecedents, and so forth. Thus, for the writer, usage choices become a means of fulfilling the expectations of the reader. The more intimate and self-expressive the writing is, the less the reader expects the writer to conform to conventional usage;

but as the writing becomes more formal, less focused on self, readers have greater expectations of conventional usage. Chapter 10 explains and illustrates with effective prose the usage choices typically found in formal writing today. The chapter includes a Dictionary of Usage Problems and abundant exercises, to help students familiarize themselves with conventional usage.

Chapter 11, "Mechanics," provides a reference guide to punctuation, spelling, and capitalization. Mechanics rules and principles are explained and illustrated, as are significant options and variations. The spelling section contains a guide to trouble spots in spelling and a dictionary of frequently misspelled words.

The Glossary of Language Terms amounts to a twelfth chapter—an extensive glossary of grammatical, linguistic, rhetorical, and lexicographical terms that students may encounter in *The Writer's Work*, and elsewhere, as they study composition and undertake research for writing assignments. This glossary and the comprehensive index complete the text and make of it not only a classroom guide but a reference work for students, writers, and others who may have questions about nonfiction writing.

TO THE STUDENT

There is little about writing that all writers will agree to, except, perhaps, that all writers are different. You may approach writing one way; your friend may do just the opposite. Some writers compose standing up, some make endless notes and preliminary outlines, some work very fast, others are very slow. Despite these differences, many writers—especially inexperienced writers—share a common fear: the fear of writing. You may be one of those who feel writing is too complex, too subjective, too mysterious to learn. There are even some writers who fear that writing requires some special talent or genius they lack.

Our experiences with writers have shown that these fears are usually unfounded. Most people can learn to write. Writing is not mysterious. We cannot promise that you can learn to write with the artistry of a great author, but we do promise that most inexperienced writers can learn to write well. We are certain you will be able to understand what effective writing is. We believe that anything important to writers can be explained in simple language, and we rely on examples to help explain and illustrate every concept and problem in writing. We have drawn on the work of many published authors—some famous, some not so famous—to demonstrate the power and variety of modern writing. All the writing assignments are illustrated with student examples.

Through these examples and plain-English explanations, we have attempted to focus on the work of the writer. The nonfiction writer uses data, information, facts. These have to be collected and arranged.

While work is not necessarily easy, most work has procedures and guidelines you can follow. The key to work is practice; the more you do of it, the better you get at it. Writers too have methods and techniques in their work, and for writers too, practice is the key. We have tried to show how writers do their work, and for that reason we have titled our book *The Writer's Work*.

Because writers are different, some need to start with free writing and journal writing to help themselves gain confidence and a degree of fluency before moving on to more structured assignments. Most writers enjoy personal writing and gain insight into their writing techniques through it. In both fiction and nonfiction writing, storytelling is very popular. But in nonfiction writing there are other forms the writer should explore too. Beyond narrative writing there are equally rewarding forms of expository and critical writing. Eventually nonfiction writers should be able to use any form or technique appropriate to their purpose, including research writing. How much you do of any one kind of writing depends a lot on you. Some writers need a good deal of work in personal writing before they feel ready to move on. Others may be ready to start immediately with expository or critical writing. Some inexperienced writers have felt that research writing is too difficult to attempt at all. But sooner or later research becomes a primary tool for the nonfiction writer, and we have attempted to go beyond mere footnote advice to show you how to find data, how to evaluate evidence, and how to put together a research paper step by step. Research writing needn't be mechanical or uninspired. Since few nonfiction writers can get along without research, we have attempted to show some of the interest, the challenge, and the reward of research writing. Still, how much research any given writer is ready for depends on the writer. Some may be ready for it immediately; others may need preparatory work first.

A writer must have ideas to write about, of course, and the first half of *The Writer's Work* is devoted to the writing process and invention procedures that will help you find your own ideas. To further help you, we have included many of the ideas our students have suggested. But a writer must have skills too. Very few professional writers are indifferent to spelling, punctuation, grammar. To help you review your skills, we have provided many exercises. We don't mean to imply that the second half of the book should be used like a workbook nor even that you should wait until you have finished the first half of the book before turning to "Skills." Some writers need to review when problems come up in their own writing. Others may need to do some of the exercises. In some cases your instructor may wish to go over some of the exercises in class. We do not think writers learn skills merely by drilling away at them, and we have not provided exercises for that purpose. Our experience has been that limited, periodic review of skills is most effective with inexperienced writers.

Nothing in writing can be approached in a mechanical and unthinking way, and nothing in writing can be seen as too trivial to bother with. Some writers make the most improvement in the quality of their writing when they gain control over their skills. Sometimes it is the lack of skills that gets in the way and prevents a writer from finding his or her ideas: "I know what I mean; I just can't say it!" It is as if a barrier to expression is formed at the skills level, and it is this barrier that is removed when students improve in skills. It is true that when you have your ideas clearly in mind, writing is easier than when your ideas are not clear. It is also true that when you can express yourself clearly and easily, your ideas will flow with greater ease.

Our students have been pleased to discover the relative ease with which they have been able to turn their sentences into mature and effective writing. One of the best techniques for untangling sentence problems is sentence combining, a creative exercise in which writers experiment with different ways to write sentences. With sufficient practice in generating well-formed sentences, most writers gain surprising strength and effectiveness in writing. The aim of sentence combining is to give you flexibility and control so that you can easily produce long, short, simple, complex, or any other kind of sentences that suit your purpose, and without struggling with grammar or traditional advice about when to do what in writing.

The Writer's Work is a complete guide to all the skills. There are two attitudes about modern usage. One is that there are correct and incorrect language choices. (Most of us were taught that "ain't" was incorrect.) The other is that there is no such thing as "correct" or "incorrect" language. All language must be judged on its suitability to the author's purpose. Language should be appropriate to the context. We think appropriateness is the best guide for language choices. But we also think that inexperienced writers need more guidance and more to hang on to than the concept of appropriateness. Therefore, throughout *The Writer's Work* we have attempted to specify the contexts of appropriateness. In general we suggest a middle-level style stressing clear, concise, and accurate English. And we show the changes in appropriateness as writers move from informal, personal writing to formal, impersonal writing.

To make it easier to find answers to your questions about how best to express what you want to write, the pages of Chapters 6–11 are colored—one color for Chapters 6–9, in which the larger issues of paragraphs, sentences, and words are discussed, and a different color for Chapters 10 and 11, in which you will find guidelines on usage and mechanics. The table of contents is especially helpful, too, for locating specific information about documentation (Chapter 5), usage (Chapter 10), and mechanics (Chapter 11).

You may wonder, as others have, whether writing is worth the effort it requires. What is the point of writing anyway? There are two very good answers to that question. Nonfiction writing is a salable skill.

Business, science, law, medicine, education—all modern careers have heavy demands for writers. And the demand is growing. Reports, proposals, letters, speeches, and dozens of other writing tasks arise today in all sorts of jobs. Try to imagine the numbers of writers required in a visual and oral medium like television: everything you see and hear on television must first be written by someone. Quite an astonishing percentage of the work in our so-called oral world is conducted through the written word.

But the best answer is that, for many writers, writing is fun. Writing is a totally involving and demanding activity, calling upon all your inner resources. It is a means of self-expression and a means of communication. Even for the nonfiction writer, writing is creative work. It can produce something as functional and simple as a straight news item, or it can produce something meaningful and artistic like a nonfiction novel. Nonfiction writing today need not be mere drudge work, pointless exercises in formula writing. As you can see from the examples throughout *The Writer's Work*, the people with whom we have worked over the years have enjoyed writing (even though there may have been a lot of hard rewriting and polishing to produce the final version). And from the many enjoyable pieces our students have provided for examples, we believe you can see that there can be a tremendous feeling of satisfaction in writing. Like other forms of self-fulfillment, writing leaves many writers pleased and proud of a job well done. Our students have said so. We think you will agree with them.

ACKNOWLEDGMENTS

We have benefitted from generous suggestions and helpful criticism from many people at many stages in writing this book. Special thanks to the following: Douglas Butturff, *University of Central Arkansas;* John Fenstermaker, *Florida State University;* Vincent Gillespie, *Kansas State University;* Melinda Kramer, *Purdue University;* Richard L. Larson, *Lehman College, City University of New York;* Cleo McNelly, *Rutgers College, Rutgers University;* David B. Merrell, *Abilene Christian University;* James C. Raymond, *University of Alabama;* Ken Symes, *Western Washington University;* Joseph Trimmer, *Ball State University.*

DEAN MEMERING

FRANK O'HARE

Preface, v

THREE   STRATEGIES OF EXPOSITION   54

FOUR   REASONED WRITING   112

SKILLS

xviii

ELEVEN   MECHANICS   *400*

THE WRITER'S WORK

RITING

I suffer as always from the fear of putting down the first line. It is amazing the terrors, the magics, the prayers, the straightening shyness that assails one.

JOHN STEINBECK, *The Journals of a Novel: The East of Eden Letters*

CHAPTER ONE
THE COMPOSING PROCESS

GOOD WRITING

As a beginning writer, you should be aware of one important fact about writing: *good* writing isn't the same as *great* writing. It is possible to have a well-written children's story, a well-written humor piece in a magazine, a well-written editorial in a newspaper; but none of these is necessarily "great" writing. Masterpieces of literature are well written, but they are also significant and beautiful and a number of other things that we call "great." Naturally, we would all like to turn out writing that is both well written and great; however, it is important to remember from the start that the two things are not the same.

You are bright enough and well educated enough to become a good writer. Good writing can be learned, and there is nothing very mysterious about it. Writing is a craft, and those who practice it enough can become good at it. And nearly everyone of average ability and experience can tell the difference between something that is well crafted and something that isn't. For example, which of the following two paragraphs is well written?

Somebody asked Picasso why did he choose to be an artist but he got mad and said that if he would have to ask a question like that he would stop being one. I asked some scientists the same thing. They didn't get mad, but they didn't really give me reasons why. They just said they liked it. They couldn't describe it any better than why a young guy falls in love with some girl but not with another one. Most scientists know they won't get rich. They know they won't be successful, really. So why do they do it?

Picasso, when asked why he chose to be an artist, lost his temper and retorted that when a man finds himself asking why he is doing what

5

he is doing, it is time for him to give it up. The men of science whom I questioned kept their tempers; still, what they gave me were not reasons at all but only statements of preference. These highly analytical men were no more able to describe precisely what had captured their minds than is any young lover able to explain why he is deeply in love with a particular girl and not with her sister. They knew there would never be wealth as the world measures it, nor even success in the popular sense. Why, then, do they do it? They don't know.

Most people would agree that the second paragraph, which is by Mitchell Wilson ("On Being a Scientist," *Atlantic Monthly,* Sept. 1970), is well written and the first is not so well written. Both passages are about the same idea; the information in them is quite similar. Yet almost any reader can see that Wilson is expressing it better.

Wilson handles language better; he expresses himself better; and this is what is meant by "well written." Wilson's paragraph has no difficult language, no hard words, and the idea itself is quite simple: neither artists nor scientists know why they choose their careers. Good writing, therefore, can be crafted from very humble language and simple ideas. What is good about such writing lies precisely in the craftsmanship, the skill with which the writer puts together words and ideas. And this skill can be learned.

Learning to write well means becoming fluent in written English. All native speakers of English are, by definition, fluent in spoken English. But these same fluent *speakers* have shown a surprising tendency to "stutter," falter, become inarticulate when they write. It is specifically, and *only,* in the process of writing English that inexperienced writers tend to lose their natural fluency with language. Therefore, your goal should be to perfect the skills of writing to the degree that anything you can *think,* you can express in writing with the same fluency you have in oral English. It is very easy to say that good writing comes from one *or* the other—good ideas or good language skills—but few things in life work on this either/or principle. Ideas without language skills are apt to sound like the paragraph that tries to express Wilson's ideas without his command of language: inarticulate, immature. On the other hand, smooth-sounding language that doesn't say anything is just as bad, and thinking people will not accept it. Thus, there really is no choice; there is no either/or to it. Good writing must have both: good ideas and good language skills.

Fortunately, another fact about writing—perhaps the most important one—is that although writing is difficult, you are equal to the challenge. If you continue to think of "real writing" as something you will have to do *after* you've completed your education, that assumption will work against you. Students can and do become skilled writers *while* they are in school, as the following paragraph reveals:

As he sat tightly strapped to the chair, the young man listened while the warden read the execution order and then asked the condemned man if he had anything to say. The riflemen who were to be his executioners were hidden from the man, behind a dark-colored curtain, and he gazed for a long moment at the ceiling and then back at the warden, uttering a brief sentence. There was a loud explosion, and the five bullets that tore through Gary Gilmore's heart ended not only his life, but also the uneasy moratorium on the death penalty that had begun nearly ten years before.
MICHAEL G. KNAPP

This is good writing by adult standards, and it was written by a student *in* college.

Moreover, much of this book is the result of important research in composition, research showing that inexperienced writers can write mature sentences without conscious reliance on traditional grammar systems. The writer in the preceding example has learned the simple art of combining many short sentences into longer ones. His first sentence, for example, could be composed of several shorter sentences such as the following:

The young man sat tightly strapped to the chair. He listened. The warden read the execution order. Then the warden asked him a question. Did he have anything to say?

It doesn't take any knowledge of grammatical terminology or any extraordinary talent to revise these sentences into one longer, more mature sentence. What used to take years of complex grammar study can now be accomplished relatively quickly through sentence combining, and this means you can soon be writing the sentences of an experienced writer—even if you are one of those people for whom "English was always my worst subject."

SPEAKING AND WRITING

It should be reassuring to know that you already have a skill that will help you learn to write well: your ability to speak. Writing developed as a means of recording speech. Ancient peoples evolved methods for keeping records of the seasons, harvest yields, who owed what to whom, and so on. From these beginnings grew the world's writing systems.

Nearly every human being learns to speak his or her native language almost without effort. Many people who find writing quite difficult have no difficulty communicating orally. Perhaps we should not be surprised that most people are better at speaking than writing; still, if writing is only a way to record speech, it is not clear why people who speak fluent English should have so much trouble writing the language.

Part of the answer lies in the fact that written languages are not identical with spoken languages. We can only imperfectly record speech. The written language is voiceless; it does not very well convey *tone* of voice, rising and falling *pitch,* loud or soft *volume,* rapid or slow *pace,* nor other things we can do with our voices. We attempt to make up some of the deficiencies in written language through punctuation and other conventions of print.

But speakers take shortcuts with the language. They speak in fragments and silences that cannot be translated into written English. They are able to do so because, in addition to the words of the language, speakers have nonverbal feedback systems that supplement their words. A nod of the head, a lift of an eyebrow, a hand gesture or facial expression, or a snort, sniff, or chuckle— with these, speakers and listeners have the means to understand messages that would appear incoherent in print. Thus, in addition to differences between voiced and unvoiced communication, there is an important difference between communicating directly (talking) with a present audience and communicating indirectly (writing) with an absent audience. Facial expressions as well as outright complaints indicate to a speaker that the audience isn't understanding the message. The speaker can immediately repeat or rephrase and keep on doing so until the audience does understand. But as a writer you have no such opportunities. You must try to estimate beforehand how readers will react, but once the words are written and sent on to the reader, there is nothing more you can do.

If all writing were only simple, factual communications— How many cows are in the meadow? Whose turn is it to go to market? When must we plant corn?—you would not have to be too concerned with audience. Simple information can be given on a take-it-or-leave-it basis. In most cases, such information-dominated writing is reader-initiated. That is, the reader starts the communication process by requesting or seeking information.

In these situations, your task is straightforward: to write the facts when readers ask for them.

But most of the world's writing is initiated by the writer, not the reader. Letters, stories, news accounts, advertisements, business documents, and so on, are writing tasks undertaken when a writer perceives the need to reach out to a reader. The need to reestablish lines of communication with a friend, the wish to share a story or an experience, the compulsion to involve others in a crusade—writing happens most often because a writer wants or needs to create some response in a reader.

For most writing, then, you aren't just supplying requested information. Indeed, in some cases you may be offering *unwanted* information, and the written word may actually be received with hostility, contempt, or indifference. The telephone, television, radio, recorded music, and films—not to mention the demands of family, friends, and work—all vie for people's attention. Imagine the task, in that case, of trying to get people to donate money to your favorite charity by means of what you are able to write in a letter or brochure. How can you get anyone to pay attention instead of just throwing your writing into the wastebasket? Effective writing is writing that moves your reader to react in some way you intend. Written communication is very much a transaction between reader and writer, and in most cases the transaction is aimed at getting the reader to do something: to learn, to share, to laugh . . . to react in some way.

You can *control* every aspect of writing except the reader's reaction. Fortunately, though you may not always know who will read your works, you can *imagine* an audience and aim your writing at an *intended* audience. And to the degree that you can imagine *speaking* to such an audience, you can take advantage of the speaking-writing relationship. In short, you can use your fluency in oral English to help yourself become equally fluent in written English, as long as you use your imagination to make up for the lack of audience-feedback in writing.

THE WRITER'S CHOICES

The first step in learning to write well is to understand that writing involves a series of interrelated choices. Think of what happens when you write. Sometimes your *purpose* is to entertain; at others to argue or persuade; at others to discover what you think ("How do I know what I think until I see what I said?").

Your *audience* is just as variable; it may be your closest friend on one occasion, a group of nameless, faceless strangers on the next. To these, add choices (conscious and subconscious) from every facet of your *experience*, about the *self* you present in your writing, and about the structure and language, which we call *code*, you use to convey your written *message*. (See Figure 1.1.) Writing *is* choice.

FIGURE 1.1

The thinking you do about each of these elements, together with the decisions you make about each of them, shapes and controls your writing. Most of the ills of writing can be traced to underemphasizing or overemphasizing any of these elements. A finished piece of writing appears to the reader as one thing, a unified composition. In order for all these elements to blend together so that nothing appears to be missing and nothing sticks out and draws too much attention to itself, you must consider each of them and orchestrate them all into the finished product, just as notes, rhythm, pace, and lyrics must be blended together to make a pleasing song. A closer look at each of these components will help explain why this is so.

THE WRITER'S PURPOSE

The word "purpose" means, in part, the writer's intention, *why* the writer is writing. It also means the unifying principle of any written work: not only what the writer is attempting to do, but what the composition is attempting to do.

If the question is, What prompts you to write? you may give reasons such as to entertain, to inform, to persuade, to impress, to evaluate, or to express yourself. There are many possibilities. Quite possibly, you may not always have a clear notion of why you are writing when you start out. And it can happen that you sometimes have more than one motive.

If you ask yourself, What is my purpose? you will realize that you must think about all the components of the writing process before you can answer. A good writer will not settle for mere surface analysis. What are your *true* motives? Furthermore, there is no way to deny that writing is aimed at an audience. If you have a purpose, it must be a purpose aimed at the reader, at least in any writing that someone is actually going to read. Some analysis of the audience you are writing to is inevitable. And if you are selecting elements from your experience to write about, you must be aware that your selection is not random. Analysis of your experiences, your audience, and your view of self all become factors in your purpose. Even the code you use—whether you use street slang or formal English, for example—depends on all the other factors.

We can summarize purpose as the overall controlling set of decisions in a piece of writing. It includes your view of self and your motives; your attitudes and decisions about your experiences; your decisions and attitudes toward audience or projected audience; and your decisions about the code to be used to carry the message to the reader. Since all these factors interrelate and are mutually dependent upon each other, like the pieces in a design, the harmony among them or the pattern among them becomes the unifying principle of the written work. Change any one of them and you change all of them.

THE WRITER'S AUDIENCE

Writing that is directed at no one in particular usually fails. A keen sense of audience helps you refine your purpose, select a self, and use your experience appropriately. Without a clear sense of audience it is impossible to gauge the effect of a whole composition or a single word. You will discover that who you write to powerfully influences what and how you write. Is your audience the instructor? What does the instructor expect? Is your audience the "general reader"? Can you imagine anything about such a person? Are you your own audience (as in a diary that only you may read)? Must you adapt yourself to the audience? Or can you make the audience accept you "as you are"? What do you know about the audience? What do they know about you?

What do they know about the subject of your paper? How do they feel about this topic? Will they react favorably to your point of view? Will they be persuaded more by emotion than cold fact?

Answering questions like these creates an audience model to whom you can "speak" directly. You can assess whether you need to define your terms for this audience, whether they will understand a comparison you want to draw, whether you need to quote other people to be believable. In short, what you decide about your readers influences the writing strategies you choose to make your writing effective.

For most college writing, it is a good idea to imagine a composite general audience, such as the people in your composition class. You can assume that such a group will probably understand and appreciate many of the things you know and enjoy. And if you're ever in doubt as to their opinions on a particular subject, you can always ask them.

THE WRITER'S SELF

Every writer's attitude toward self and outlook on life in general are fundamental to his or her motives. And every writer must try to *find* his or her self. Only when you've developed a sense of self can you begin to communicate with your audience. People are complex, multifaceted, many-layered. Are you an optimist or a pessimist, a mystic or a realist, a believer or a nonbeliever? Each of you will discover several selves. And a particular view of self is similar to a role you project to suit a specific writing purpose.

When you consider your attitude toward your self and your subject, you have an important decision to make: what self do you want to show your reader? Suppose you've been assigned a serious paper for an academic audience. You are very interested in the topic, but you realize that you are easygoing and very informal. Your "natural" writing style (as in letters to friends) is also informal, sprinkled with slang. Suppose you tend to be short-tempered, however, and this topic makes you angry. Realizing that lack of control, informality, and inappropriate language will cause you to fail to convince your audience, you must select from among the many different selves that make up your multifaceted character the one that is genuinely serious about and interested in the topic. You decide a formal style and tone are right for the self you have chosen to help persuade your audience of the reasonableness of your position.

There is nothing artificial about discovering a self, then consciously projecting that self when you write. There is no way to avoid *having* self and no way to avoid expressing it, either. Consequently, it makes sense to show in your writing the self that is best suited to your purpose.

Aristotle said, "The unexamined life is not worth living." We should add to this, the unexamined life is not worth writing about. Once you begin questioning yourself, be prepared to be surprised. Within your many-layered personality you can find a self for most writing purposes.

Writing activity

Write a paragraph or two in which you project a character who is trying to persuade a particular audience to act or think in a certain way. Try to project a self who will be viewed sympathetically by the audience. Then, in a paragraph or two, project a second self whose purpose is the same but whose writing personality will almost certainly alienate the audience.

What effect did the change in self have on the piece of writing? How did you show the two different selves? Describe each self in a few words.

THE WRITER'S EXPERIENCE

The word "experience" means every instant of your life—everything you have done, everything that has happened to you, everything you know. But experience is more than that, because what you know also defines what you don't know. Suppose you have been asked to write a story or an essay about a subject of your own choosing. You think over your experiences, or maybe you go to the library and start looking for something that sparks your interest. Thus you begin to explore subject matter. Finally, you decide to tell about wrecking the family car. What can you tell about it? It was all over in a flash; how can you fill up two or three pages? You must try to understand the subject just as you try to understand yourself. In fact, the subject and your view of it should fuse so that your writing does more than report the facts. Why *this* story? What does the subject mean to you personally? It is not a good idea just to start numbering the different details of a car accident. (If that's what your readers wanted, they'd read the police report.) What happened means nothing until it interacts with the human nervous system to which it happened. We learn very little from a chronological analysis of an accident. It isn't just the *what* about anything that people care to know but also the *so what* about it—the way the accident entered and affected your store of experience.

You may feel that your experience is limited at this stage in your life. It's not. Count as experience all the incidents, events, people, places, and objects you've seen; all the books, journals, magazines, and newspapers you've read; all the films and television programs you've watched; all your daydreams and daily existence. The section called "Prewriting: The First Stage" later in this chapter will show you that your experience is a far richer store than you may imagine.

THE WRITER'S CODE

Having interesting ideas is only a beginning; writers must be able to express these ideas clearly and efficiently. Knowing what to say is not enough; you must also know *how*. This *how* skill, the language writers use to express their ideas, we call *code*. Code includes not only the language—words, phrases, and sentences— but also the overall structure of a composition, including the interrelationships (coherence) governing sentences, paragraphs, and the whole work. Also involved in code are style, tone, and various methods of developing a piece of writing. We shall have more to say about these elements of code throughout this book. For now, it is enough for you to understand that code signifies the relationship between language and idea in writing.

Any writing you do creates a set of expectations you must fulfill for your readers. If you start out to prove a point, the reader expects you to try to prove it. If you set out to be logical, you aren't free to use faulty reasoning, propaganda, or emotional language. If you address a learned audience on a formal topic but use a very informal tone and style in a rambling, ill-organized paper, you'll probably fail to establish much credibility with that audience. All these matters of language and form and thought comprise code. And decisions about the code you choose become part of your decisions about purpose.

Writing activity

Try to recall or imagine an unpleasant incident in your life: a car accident; an argument with your boss that ended with your being fired; an upsetting encounter in school or on a trip; the time when you came home at five o'clock in the morning in bad shape; and so on. Write a letter explaining what happened to you to someone in a position of authority: a school official, parents, police officer, or judge. Then write another letter recounting the same incident to your best friend.

After you have written the letters, look at the code you have used in each. Does the code differ? What about sentence length? Sentence structure? Vocabulary?

Discussing each of these choices individually suggests that writers decide their purpose, determine their audience, select a self, choose relevant and informative experience, and then use a code to achieve that purpose. But in the real world of writing, things aren't that simple. Indeed, for many writers, writing— especially the initial stages—is confusing, disorderly, even chaotic. How are the choices we've been talking about really made? Let's see what can happen when you have to write a typical college paper.

Suppose that you have just heard a lecture given by a renowned scientist on the future of organ and limb transplants. You decide that this topic might make an interesting paper, but you cannot decide whether to write it for your biology class or your composition class. You begin jotting down informal notes from past experiences—what you know about people who have lost limbs and about organ donors and recipients—from books, magazines, newspapers, scientific journals, films, and radio and television programs. Next, you skim through several articles from *Time, Redbook,* and *Harper's;* two or three from scientific journals recommended by your biology instructor; and the relevant sections of Alvin Toffler's *Future Shock.* You take detailed notes, especially from the scientific journals, because they cover territory you aren't familiar with. A quick look at all your notes shows you that they're sketchy, unorganized, and that there are striking differences in the level of formality of these notes. Some summarize scientific concepts in complex language; others, like the ones about your grade-school classmate who had a kidney disease, are informal and anecdotal.

At this point, perhaps you decide to write the paper for your composition course, partly because you have a paper due in that class and partly because you are more interested in the human side of your topic than its scientific aspects. You select the composition class as your audience and decide that your purpose will be not only to inform but to entertain them. You may even impress them with your scientific knowledge. A too formal tone will be forbidding and dull; so you decide to try for a relaxed, reasonable tone, somewhere between the familiar and the formal.

You begin making careful notes, most of which expand on the jottings you have about your classmate. You quickly write out a page and a half describing how difficult it was for her to keep up in school when she spent so much time in the hospital undergoing dialysis treatment. As you reread these pages, you realize that focusing on your classmate's school problems has turned out to be depressing, not entertaining. What you've written sounds too personal and emotional when you had intended to sound relaxed and informative. And with this emphasis, you haven't a way to include any of the ideas you heard at the lecture that got you interested in the subject in the first place.

As you look back over all your notes, you become convinced that a better approach is to use a historical perspective. You'll compare and contrast today's techniques for kidney transplants, about which you've become fairly knowledgeable from your reading, with treatment for kidney disease in the past. You'll illustrate the situation in the past by bringing in two or three brief anecdotes about your classmate's experience with dialysis. You'll then connect these perspectives with your sense of the way kidney disease will be treated in the future, as described by the lecturer. You sketch out a rough outline to keep your ideas straight, then begin to write a first draft.

It should be clear now that we are not describing a sequential process like baking a cake, in which each step follows in prescribed order and, once completed, need not be thought about again. Disorder, during which multiple purposes, audiences, selves, experiences, and codes have to be sifted and selected, weighed and evaluated, reconsidered and reworked, is normal. Writing is like painting or sculpting or composing music; all evolve from a complex of decisions that must mesh together and contribute harmoniously to an outcome that may or may not have been foreseen at the start. The stone lion that is the sculptor's finished product may have started simply as an exploration in stone, with the outcome ultimately determined by an ongoing process of decisions, choices, reconsiderations, and changes. So too the compositions you write.

Writing activity

Select a real or imagined event—a news report, a family incident, a sports report, a fashion show—and relate the incident in a paragraph or two to a particular audience. Your purpose should be to present the event in a favorable light. Then, using the same incident, write a paragraph or two in which your purpose is to present the same incident in an unfavorable light.

Have different purposes evoked different selves, different audiences, different codes, and so on, in the two pieces of writing?

THE WRITING PROCESS

All these matters about the components of writing are general, but how does the process work in practice? Granted that the composing process is made up of purpose, self, audience, experience, and code—all generating the message—how do you get the process going? Processes usually have steps or stages in them; what are the stages in writing?

PREWRITING: THE FIRST STAGE

Prewriting refers to all those activities that can go on when you are in the early stages of your work—the stage during which you make your first decisions about purpose, audience, code, and so on. It will help you greatly to understand that for most writers the prewriting stage is disorderly and difficult. Though prewriting may be chaotic to experience and may seem uncontrolled to an observer, most writers report that it is a time of intense creative work as the mind shifts and sorts and rearranges the various components of writing until finally—sometimes suddenly—things begin to "fall into place" and a composition begins to take shape.

Tapping your experience is a good way to begin prewriting. Here are some possibilities.

Memory   Look back over past experiences; search through your life for incidents, events, people, places, and things to write about. Your memory is a vast repository of data concerning all your experiences. And you can go searching in this repository, forcing yourself to remember and bring back, in surprising detail, your past life.

Observation   Examine the world around you; watch the events of your daily life. You may include in this the viewing of television and films and the reading of books, magazines, and newspapers. With modern communications systems, anyone can have a wealth of material to observe, think about, and write about.

Participation   Your daily experiences—talking with friends, going on dates, participating in sports—may not be extraordinary (few are), but they are all grist for the writer's mill. You may include in this vicarious experiences, such as the intense involvement that is possible with great literature and, occasionally, good films. The entire inner world of subjective responses—emotions, sensations, feelings—can become the source of your writing.

Imagination   Project yourself into situations and even into others' minds and bodies. This is the major technique of the fiction writer, but the nonfiction writer too may speculate and hypothesize. You may invent (speculate on), for instance, a crisis in which China and the U.S.S.R. confront each other along the Sino-Soviet border, in order to imagine (hypothesize) what course of action the United States might take in such an event. Even if you are going to attempt to describe an object, you will discover how much imagination can aid observation if you project yourself into the object and imagine how the object must appear to someone not familiar with it.

Research   Conduct experiments, seek out answers and data, use the library, interview sources. Using the skills of researching, you can become very knowledgeable quickly about practically anything. And this is one of the major prewriting techniques for academic or learned writing.

These and other possibilities you may discover for yourself will quickly reveal that there is always a great deal for you to write about. During prewriting, you must search for subject matter, which means not just finding "something" to write about but exploring, becoming thoroughly familiar with and even knowledgeable about the subject. You must come to know the subject matter at least better than your reader knows it if there is to be anything new or effective in what you write.

During this prewriting stage, you may take notes—formal notes as well as scribbles and jottings. You may or may not make an outline, formal or informal. At the prewriting stage, you collect, sort, and attempt to arrange material into a coherent organization. At some point in prewriting, you will attempt a first draft. You may plunge in almost immediately with a very rough draft. You may wait until you have a fairly good concept of the composition on paper or in your head. Or you may work in fits and starts, with false drafts—those crumpled sheets of paper that some writers make on their way to a first draft.

Prewriting does not necessarily stop at any given point in the writing process. As long as you still have questions to answer, as long as the composition is still in the shaping and discovery *process,* prewriting is ongoing. Thus, the first draft and perhaps the second may be part of the prewriting stage. There have been cases in which writers have "finished" their work and then discovered what it was they were trying to say.

WRITING: THE MIDDLE STAGE

If you are very sure of the answers to all the questions about purpose, self, experience, audience, and code, the writing stage can commence rapidly. (Writers sometimes speak of a composition "writing itself.") Very careful and well-disciplined writers who have spent a great deal of time in prewriting, searching for material, and drawing up working outlines can sometimes just sit down and write easily. Many writers, however, struggle back and forth between prewriting and rewriting so that there is no distinct writing stage by itself.

REWRITING: THE THIRD STAGE

A useful bit of advice for new writers is, *don't* write and edit at the same time. Laboring away over every word and sentence, crossing out and rewriting, and later returning for further changes all add up to a very discouraging and laborious procedure. A far better procedure is to work out the design and the substance of your composition in prewriting but leave the polishing for rewriting. The crumpled-paper syndrome is evidence of an author stuck at some point and unable to go on. It is far better to skip over the sticking point; force yourself to go on and return later to the problem spot rather than spend hours laboring over a sentence or paragraph of the composition that won't "write." Unfortunately, sometimes a problem spot means the design of the composition is faulty and in that case you need to return to prewriting. In either case, it is wisest to resist rewriting until you get to the end of your first draft. (Otherwise you may not *get* to the end.)

Writing by rewriting is the most typical procedure. Few authors are satisfied with a first draft.

For me it's [writing] mostly a question of rewriting. It's part of a constant attempt on my part to make the finished version smooth, to make it seem effortless. A story I've been working on—"The Train on Track Six," it's called—was rewritten fifteen complete times. There must have been close to 240,000 words in all the manuscripts put together, and I must have spent two thousand hours working at it. Yet the finished version can't be more than twenty thousand words.
JAMES THURBER, *Writers at Work*, Malcolm Cowley, ed.

It is no exaggeration to say that *rewriting* demands your real skill as a writer. It is in the rewriting that you become the reader's advocate, looking at the composition from the reader's point of view. At the rewriting stage, ask these questions. Considering the purpose of the composition, are these the most effective words? Do each of these sentences carry the information and maintain the reader's interest? Are the paragraphs well constructed? Does the composition begin well? Does it end effectively? Does the composition achieve its purpose?

Never permit yourself to turn in a first draft, no matter how good you think it is. Considering all the variables that are involved in writing, the odds are against any first draft's being as good as a second or third draft, even from a professional writer. Think of the first draft as a way to capture the design and content of the composition. The second draft should be used for revision, not for polishing. In the second draft, you should be highly critical. Two trouble spots will automatically appear—the beginning and the ending of the composition. These two very important sections of the composition are worth all the effort you can put into them. Furthermore, the body of the composition will benefit from a highly critical examination and revision. Do the paragraphs progress in a pattern leading to the end? Would the composition improve if you rearranged the paragraphs, added to them, or subtracted from them? The chances are great that major revisions in the second draft will better aim the composition at its purpose. One of the chief problems with many papers by beginning writers is that there is not enough information. Since the first draft has a tendency to be too skimpy, the second draft needs to come up with additional data, more examples, additional illustrations and details.

In the third draft you need to think of a critical reader who will respond not only to the information in your paper but to your style of writing as well. This is the place to cut excess verbiage, prune clichés and jargon, and in general clean up the English. In the third draft you need to look at your sentences and paragraphs the way a critic would. Can they be made more accurate? Can they be made more readable? By combining some and deleting others you can improve the style and tone and efficiency of your writing.

I believe a story can be wrecked by a faulty rhythm in a sentence—especially if it occurs toward the end—or a mistake in paragraphing, even punctuation. Henry James is the maestro of the semi-colon. Hemingway is a first-rate paragrapher. From the point of view of ear, Virginia Woolf never wrote a bad sentence. I don't mean to imply that I successfully practice what I preach. I try, that's all.
TRUMAN CAPOTE, *Writers at Work*, Malcolm Cowley, ed.

It is in the third draft that you must use the real skill of an artisan. This means seeing that a word you've used is not exactly right. It means seeing that changing the punctuation of a sentence changes the emphasis and gives new meaning to the sentence. Far from being merely finishing work, this final draft is the one most writers say is the draft that counts, and the one you should give your maximum effort to.

I rewrote the ending to *Farewell to Arms*, the last page of it, thirty-nine times before I was satisfied [. . .] Getting the words right.
ERNEST HEMINGWAY, *Writers at Work*, George Plimpton, ed.

PROOFREADING: THE FINAL STAGE

Rewriting is not the same as proofreading. In rewriting we are talking about *changing* the composition: revising. Proofreading is the last step, and it involves finding errors in the finished composition. The purpose of proofreading is to make sure that the composition says what you think it says. Check spelling, punctuation, grammar, and other things that tend to go wrong of their own accord. Proofreading means examining the finished copy that is to be handed in to a teacher or editor and finding and fixing errors. Errors must be neatly painted out with correction fluid, and then the pages must go back into the typewriter, if that is possible, or the correction penned in. You may cross out neatly with a pen and write the corrections above the errors, provided there aren't too many of them.

Writing activity

1 *Prewriting*   Select a topic that interests you and begin to investigate its possibilities. Jot down ideas, details, possible purposes and audiences, and so on. Then, after letting the ideas generated by your notes percolate for a time, decide what your purpose and audience will be.

2 *Writing*   Write a first draft of the paper. In your mind, choose a few words to describe the self you've chosen to implement your purpose for your audience. What special considerations of code will you use to harmonize with this self? After a day or two, look at your first draft. Enrich it with details from your notes and from your reconsiderations. Then write a second draft.

3 *Rewriting*   After letting your second draft sit for at least a few hours, write a final draft. Read it carefully to make sure you've accomplished what you want concerning purpose, audience, self, experience, and code.

4 *Proofreading*   Proofread and polish the final draft.

It is enough if I please myself
with writing; I am sure then
of an audience.

HENRY D. THOREAU, *Journal*

THE WRITER'S VIEW OF REALITY

Personal writing emphasizes *self*. How do *I* see the world? What does *my* life mean? Some of this writing can be private, such as a secret diary, but most of it is written to share personal views with others. The audience is largely the author, but with a personal invitation to others to join the author. The familiar essay, the memoir, the personal-experience story, sometimes even fiction can be seen as an author's personal view of reality.

Personal writing is concerned with the details of everyday life and usually includes the author's reactions to people and events. The common theme of such writing is that the life of a single individual counts for something. Instead of focusing on extraordinary people and unusual events, this writing reveals the virtues of the commonplace: strength, humor, sorrow, the vitality of human life. For example:

"Knock it off, you guys," Jeanette ordered firmly.

"Okay, go ahead and kiss her, we won't watch," Rick added giggling. It was when he said this that I first realized what was going on. It was a sleep-out, and there were three little peeping Toms: Rick, Kelley, and Rick's friend. I felt like they were Jaws, and I was waiting to be eaten.

This was ridiculous. I couldn't even be alone with my girlfriend at her doorstep. "This is a reunion," I said in disgust.

"I can't help it. Do you think I like an audience?" she retorted. We just stood there shaking our heads and looking separate directions into the night.

"Don't let us bother you," came Rick's giggling voice.

"Oh ———," I whispered.

"Blane, are you shy?" Kelley asked.

"Anything you guys wanna know, just ask," I sarcastically put in.

BLANE ROCKEFELLOW

From the beginning I had trouble getting into the helmet. The procedure was to stick the thumbs into the helmet's earholes and stretch the helmet out as it came down over the head, a matter of lateral pull, easy enough if you practiced isometrics, but I never had the strength to get my ears quite clear, so they were bent double inside the helmet once it was on. I would work a finger up inside to get the ears upright again, a painful procedure and noisy, the sounds sharp in the confines of the hard shell of the helmet as I twisted and murmured, until it was done, the ears ringing softly, quiet then in the helmet, secure as being in a turret. Then I would look out beyond the bars of the nose guard—the "cage" the players call it—to see what was going on outside, my eyes still watering slightly. It was more difficult to get the helmet off.

GEORGE PLIMPTON, *Paper Lion*

These examples of personal writing succeed to the degree that we *identify* with the author. We may not have actually experienced the same thing before, but if the author has written convincingly we can share in the experience through the words on the page; to a degree we can step into the author's shoes. The writer has extended a bridge to us; for a moment we can share in the life of another human being.

In personal writing the author illustrates and exemplifies, rather than proves, our common humanity. It's the difference between going to a lecture and going to a play. The one tells you the facts; the other shows them in operation. For example, have you ever had a blind date?

We went up to the house and were let in. Three girls sat in the living room. They had long dresses on for the concert. I instantly picked out the least attractive one and was pleasantly surprised to find her rather good looking. I smiled and looked into her eyes. She smiled back. We were introduced. I was Dave and she was Dawn's sister. Dawn was in the bedroom still getting ready. Shortly she came out. She was not good. This girl was the kind you have to practice looking at. I looked at John and laughed.

DAVID HINSKE

Have you ever seen people starving?

A special class of beggars consists of those who beg after nine o'clock at night. You stand at your window, and suddenly see new faces, beggars you haven't seen all day. They walk out right into the middle of the street, begging for bread. Most of them are children. In the surrounding silence of night, the cries of the hungry beggar children are terribly insistent, and, however hard your heart, eventually you have to throw a piece of bread down to them—or else leave the house. These beggars are completely unconcerned about curfews, and you can hear their voices late at night, at eleven and even at twelve. They are afraid of nothing and no one. There has been no case of the night patrol shooting at these beggars, although they move around the streets after curfew passes. It's a common thing for beggar children like these to die on the sidewalk at night. I was told about one such horrible scene that took place in front of 24 Muranowska Street where a six-year-old beggar boy lay gasping all night, too weak to roll over to the piece of bread that had been thrown down to him from the balcony.

EMMANUEL RINGLEBLUM, *Notes from the Warsaw Ghetto*

Have you ever had an accident?

I walked up to the bar and gave it a couple of hard pushes. Then while it was swinging, I ran back about ten feet from the set and began to run towards the bar. Back and forth it went. I watched it as I picked up my speed. The bar was just on a downward swoop when I caught it. I flew up into the sky. The roof was under my feet. Then I went higher. The kitchen was in my eyesight. All I could see was the ground coming up at me. I put my hands out to stop my fall. I hit the ground and pain came. I couldn't breathe. I rolled over onto my back, experiencing a momentary panic as I fought for air. I wanted to catch my breath and scream at the same time. After what seemed like five minutes, I got my breath and yelled. Unfortunately this did nothing to relieve the pain. My brothers had seen the terrific swing and came running. The first thing I heard was, "Look at Nan's arm!" I knew something was really wrong. When I looked at my arm, even I could tell that it was broken.

NANCY MYERS

Ever had a confrontation?

My real confrontation with Fred came on another day when I'd been working at the plant about a week and a half. I was bent down under the conveyor trying to clean off some hardened plastic that was preventing the machine from moving freely. Fred, in the meantime, had been playing with the electric motor that ran the conveyor. He suddenly turned it on, almost running a five-hundred-pound mold off the end of the conveyor and onto my head. Luckily I was able to shove the thing back before it clobbered me. At this point, Fred told me to "watch what the hell you're doing!" I calmly told him to watch what the hell *he* was doing, that is, if he and his teeth wanted to stay in the same general area.

DOUG BELL

Ever lived somewhere you disliked?

The room I lived in was heavy ceilinged, perfectly square, with walls the color of chipped dry blood. Jules Weissman, a Jewish boy, had got the room for me. It's a room to sleep in, he said, or maybe to die in but God knows it wasn't meant to live in. Perhaps because the room was so hideous it had a fantastic array of light fixtures: one on the ceiling, one on the left wall, two on the right wall, and a lamp on the table beside my bed. My bed was in front of the window through which nothing ever blew but dust. It was a furnished room and they'd thrown enough stuff in it to furnish three rooms its size. Two easy chairs and a desk, the bed, the table, a straight-backed chair, a bookcase, a cardboard wardrobe; and my books and my suitcase, both unpacked; and my dirty clothes flung in a corner. It was the kind of room that defeated you. It had a fireplace, too, and a heavy marble mantelpiece, and a great gray mirror above the mantelpiece. It was hard to see anything in the mirror very clearly—which was perhaps just as well—and it would have been worth your life to have started a fire in the fireplace.

JAMES BALDWIN, "Previous Condition"

Have you ever had an operation?

After the nurse left I went back to counting lights but was interrupted once again, this time by another nurse. She told me to bare my chest, and as I did I noticed her taking a straight razor out of a little package. She rubbed a little bit of soapy water on my chest and then began to hack away. She shaved the left side of my chest from the shoulder down to below my breast. When she was done, my left side was beet red and full of sting and irritation. I was glad this chick wouldn't be the one using the scalpel. I noticed she also had with her what looked like a woman's plastic bathing cap, and she ordered me to put it on. I hesitated for a moment, but as I looked around the room I saw that all the other patients were wearing them, so I complied.

THOM HELLER

The incidents created by these writers are all different. The thread that unites them is their humanity.

FREE WRITING

When confronted with a writing task, many beginning writers say, "I just can't write. My mind goes blank. I can't think of anything to say." They are surprised to hear that this feeling of hopelessness is common among experienced writers too. But experienced writers know this fear is only a writer's hang-up, not a sign that they can't write. Getting started is often the hardest part of writing, and experienced writers have discovered that one solution to the problem is to force themselves to begin writing immediately.

If you allow your mind to go blank each time you sit down to write, you may develop a kind of writer's paralysis, in which you are permanently conditioned to freeze up when you have to write. To overcome this fear of the blank page, practice *free writing*—sitting down and writing anything at all, without interruption. Free writing is "free" in the sense that there are no rules to follow. Spelling, punctuation, and grammar are unimportant; you don't even need an idea or plan. The only thing that is important is not stopping. Let the words pour forth spontaneously. Let the stream of your consciousness flow onto the paper.

Free writing is designed to sharpen a writer's talent for thinking on paper. You may believe that professional writers carefully think out in great detail what they are going to say, make an outline, and then just sit down and dash off the finished work. Very few writers can do that. Most writers say that their works begin to take shape *after* they have struggled with their ideas *on paper*. You need to learn to think with a pencil or pen in your hand. Instead of first thinking and then writing, you need to learn to think and write at the same time.

Here is the free writing of a writer whose mind is blocked. He is convinced that he has nothing to say until he forgets that he is writing and begins to think on paper:

CARL WINSLOW

Nothing, nothing, nothing, nothing, nothing, nothing, nothing, nothing, nothing, I have nothing to say, nothing, blah blah sounds like a duck blah blah, quack quak what is this anyhow? what a nut nothing. I thought this was suppose to be college? Free writing, free writing FREE WRITING. How can I write if I dint have nothing to say? Let your hand do the writing the man says — let your fingers do the walking just like in the *yellow pages, everybody is doing it, write, write, write. The guy next to me is drawing doodles—like this ꙮꙮꙮꙮꙮꙮ wonderful. I paid a fortune for this? or my dad did anyway. Why? This is how I get to be an engineer, sitting here trying to unfreeze my mind. My minds set in cement, maybe that's the point—too much mind cement, a mind set. Don't let the ink dry. Isn't ten minutes up yet, forgot my watch. Something, something, something*

Writing activity

Try a ten-minute free writing. Start writing as fast as you can. Instead of thinking about what you are saying, let your hand copy whatever is going on in your head—words, pictures, emotions, physical sensations, anything at all. Don't censor your mind: let it range freely. If your mind truly is blank, just write "nothing" or "blank" over and over again. Remember, don't stop; don't let the ink dry before you write the next word. Keep practicing free writing until you have proved to yourself that you have conquered your fear of the blank page.

When you are confident that you can write freely, you'll discover that there is little difference between thinking and writing. When you reach the point where your hand automatically records what your mind is thinking, you can set your mind in any direction you like and produce free writing on specific subjects. For example, here is another example of free writing. The writer isn't controlling his mind consciously nor watching over his writing. But he has directed his mind to think about running.

MATT HARDY

My legs ached like crazy, I had just run past the four mile mark of a ten mile race. In my mind kept running the workouts that I have had before and now this distance seemed so difficult to reach. Sweat started to break all over my body especially on my forehead where it would run down into my eyes. The sweat contained salt which would make my eyes hurt. I reached the 5 mile mark. Where in hell am I? There are cornfields all around me, I hope I can make the whole distance because it is so embarrassing if I didn't. Oh no another runner passed me. I keeping telling my body to relax do not tighten up on me. It is important for a runner to keep all his muscles loose so they do not tighten up on you. My heart is pounding against my chest so hard I think it just might pop out. All this for a lousy breakfast run which I haven't even trained for. Ugh there is the drink truck if I drink anything now I think it might come up as fast as it went down. Oh who cares boy does that taste good. Splish-splash I can feel the water bouncing around in my intestines. 3 more miles to go and I can rest. I never dreamed 3 miles could be so long. My legs are taking smaller and smaller steps. There is the coach and here I am the last of the 22 runners in the annual breakfast run. Maybe I will have better luck next year.

Writing activity

Try a directed free writing. Set your mind to thinking about some subject that interests you. Write about the person who sits next to you, the weather, your goals, problems—anything at all. If you begin to daydream or wander from the subject, let it happen. If your mind doesn't want to stick with the subject you have chosen for it, find out what your mind does want to think about, and write about that.

JOURNALS

If you decided to become a ballet dancer, an artist, a pianist, a tennis or racquetball player, you would spend a great deal of time —some enjoyable, some tedious—practicing these skills. You could not become proficient by practicing only once a week. Like any other worthwhile skill, writing also takes practice.

Most good writers write almost daily; Hemingway set aside the morning hours to do his daily quota of writing. All writers know that there is nothing easier than *not* writing: television looks interesting, visitors drop by, a headache starts. There are dozens of excellent reasons for postponing writing, and you have to resist each one. The difference between a writer and everyone else isn't just that a writer *can* write; a writer is someone who can and *does* write.

To get regular practice in writing, try this aid: the journal. Keeping a journal is not only a good way to get daily practice in writing, it also gives you the chance to practice specific writing skills. The journal allows you to describe objects, people, events from different perspectives, to practice noting details, to *focus*. Sitting down to write in your journal can give you a break from your daily responsibilities and problems. These minutes can be a time for reflection, introspection, self-examination, a time for remembering. The journal can also be a notebook of your ideas— a soapbox where you can expound on life, politics, philosophy, the latest fashions—and a source for essays and stories you might want to write later. See, for example, what these three journal writers have done:

VERONICA SARGE

This is not the first time I have kept a journal. My high-school English teacher, Rita Emeriz (now Rita Schutz), introduced my senior class to journal keeping. She said we'd have to do it in college, and though I doubted it, I dutifully obeyed. After all, who was I to disagree with authority. But in spite of all the moaning and groaning that came from the rest of the class, I wanted to keep a journal. We didn't have to write in it every day, and it could include everything we wanted. My first one ended up looking like a scrapbook. It's full of fragments of poems, songs, books, magazines, etc. We had to do two journals during our senior year. My second one came much easier, and was more meaning-ful to me than my first one. It had reached puberty I guess. The first journal was a mere babe in arms.

I can remember all the kids who were frantic the last week before it was due, trying to put a semester's worth of meaning into one week of work. They ended up being rather hastily-put-together scrapbooks, without much insight into the author.

I remember I carried my journals with me daily. I didn't neces-sarily make an entry each day, but it was there. And at night it rested next to my bed like an attentive teddy bear. It eventually got to the point where I couldn't get to sleep unless I wrote in my journal. It was an intellectual and emotional release. It was like my best friend, someone to talk to before calling it a day. Being the only girl in the family, and being at an age when "parents just don't understand," there really was no one to talk to at those late-night hours, when my head would spin with its adolescent cravings and questions.

Although we were only required to keep two journals during the school years, I kept writing furiously, trying to untangle all the thoughts that raced through my head. Eventually my journal became introspective, so that even if I were required to hand it in, I couldn't have. But to me it was a great way to record things in a personal, meaningful way. I managed to keep about five journals in two years' time. As I reread them from time to time, I appreciate them more. I can step back and begin to understand myself more.

But as time passes, I realize that too much introspection can be dangerous and confusing. So, hopefully, this journal will be more animated, more light-hearted, more external. Perhaps too, more useful. Something I am not afraid to share, something that people can relate to.

ANNE MOODY,
*Coming of Age
in Mississippi*

I worked for Linda Jean throughout my seventh grade year. But that spring and summer Raymond tried farming again, and I was only able to help her on weekends. When I entered eighth grade the following fall we were poorer than ever. Raymond had worse luck with the farm than the year before, so we weren't able to buy any new clothes. I had added so much meat to my bones that I could squeeze into only two of my old school dresses. They were so tight I was embarrassed to put them on. I had gotten new jeans for the field that summer, so I started wearing them to school two and three days a week. But I continued to fill out so fast that even my jeans got too tight. I got so many wolf whistles from the boys in class that the faster girls started wearing jeans that were even tighter than mine. When the high school boys started talking about how fine those eighth grade girls were, the high school girls started wearing tight jeans too. I had started a blue jeans fad.

HENRY DAVID
THOREAU, "April 16,
1852," *Journal*

His tail was also brown, though not very dark, rat-tail like, with loose hairs standing out on all sides like a caterpillar brush. He had a rather mild look. I spoke to him kindly. I reached checkerberry leaves to his mouth. I stretched my hands over him, though he turned up his head and still gritted a little. I laid my hand on him, but immediately took it off again, instinct not being wholly overcome. If I had had a few fresh bean leaves, thus in advance of the season, I am sure I should have tamed him completely. It was a frizzly tail. His is a humble, terrestrial color like the partridge's, well concealed where dead wiry grass rises above darker brown or chestnut dead leaves—a modest color. If I had had some food, I should have ended with stroking him at my leisure. Could easily have wrapped him in my handkerchief. He was not fat nor particularly lean. I finally had to leave him without seeing him move from the place. A large, clumsy, burrowing squirrel. *Arctomys,* bear-mouse. I respect him as one of the natives. He lies there, by his color and habits so naturalized amid the dry leaves, withered grass, and the bushes. A sound nap, too, he has enjoyed in his native fields, the past winter. I think I might learn some wisdom of him. His ancestors have lived here longer than mine, he is more thoroughly acclimated and naturalized than I. Bean leaves the red man raised for him, but he can do without them.

HOW TO WRITE A JOURNAL

How you handle your journal is your decision, but the following hints may help you get started:

1 Write every day. Regular, specified periods of writing are better than fewer and longer sessions. Don't try to cram a week's worth of writing into one night; you'd get the same effect as if you tried to cram a week's worth of jogging into a single session.

2 Try to write in the same place at the same time each day. Don't let anything interfere with your schedule.

3 Write at least a page a day, even on the days when you'd rather not. (Especially then.)

4 Write anything you want, any way you want, but remember that a journal is not a private, intimate document for your eyes alone. An effective journal is a record of your thoughts that others should be able to read. Your instructor may want to check your journal to see your growth as a writer.

5 Do not treat your journal as if it were merely a record of your activities:

Got up early. Studied for test. Went bowling in the afternoon. Nothing much happened today.

Entries like this are a waste of time because the writer is *avoiding* his thoughts and recording only actions. Instead, the writer might have written about why he studied for the test. Was he worried about failing? Is he chasing grades? If so, why? Did he enjoy the bowling? What is the significance of "Nothing much happened today"? Is he bored? Disappointed? A journal, then, should be a record of what your *mind* is doing.

Writing activity

Keep a journal for two weeks. Write in it at least once a day for the fourteen days. If you can find the time, write in it more than once a day. On days when you can't think of anything to write, you may want to start your reflective writing with a topic from the following list:

The present . . . today, this week, this year

The past . . . high-school days, home life, friends

The future . . . yours, the country's, the world's

The ideal . . . life, day, place to live, car, form of government, partner

An open letter to . . . a politician, minister, civic leader, bigot, old friend, the world at large

Advice . . . to anyone about anything

Please repeat! . . . places and people you'd like to see again, things you'd like to do again

Never again! . . . things to avoid, places not to visit

Pet peeves . . . letters of complaint

People . . . what they look like, think about, their interactions with you

Moods . . . feeling sad, lonely, happy, silly, coping with moods

Problems . . . money, health, sex, fears, studies, appearances, drugs, smoking, too fat, too thin, too short, too tall

Philosophy . . . what life is all about, God, good and evil, personal identity

Discussion activity

Select one of the journal entries that follows and discuss its strengths and virtues. Is the person who wrote the journal entry getting anything out of journal writing? What can you tell about the journal writer as a person?

JEANNE PARRISH

Thurs. Sitting on my table are two roosters. Ceramic. They rest on top of a set of hot pads (maple with cork bottoms, oval in shape), and on either side of a small yellow lamp. All of these sit together on top of a table. It is old and painted with several coats of paint, the last of which is grey for the table top, and white and yellow for the legs. It's a heavy table and I have added clear modern casters to help make it easy to move. It's a pretty table. I know because I like the way it looks and there is a spot of chipped paint which reveals a lovely oak under. I will refinish the table one day, but it is so heavy and lumbersome to move that I will have to start *very* early in a day. I wouldn't want to move it out and in more than once. There is a split in the table top, and I shall have to get another person to help reglue it. Perhaps Graydon will help. Even when the piece isn't his, there is a satisfaction in the repair and refinishing of a piece for him. The maple pads need refinishing too. As you unstack them to use, one can see how the sun has faded them, beating at them thru the window where they sat on a table. Not this table—another of Grandma's. They sat just as now—three-stacked and a lamp (small) centered, and the roosters, one each side of the lamp.

The roosters are unusual looking. They look like a regular ceramic rooster except the tail; each feather is separately curled. The roosters are salt and pepper shakers.

Each time we were at Grandma's I would touch them and look at them. The tails made them fascinating.

When Grandma died in May, Mother and Dad, and all their children except one were at the funeral. (Lon lives too far to have come.) Since all were there and Grandma's possessions had to be taken care of, each chose special things. I was sure each one would want the roosters, but no one did. Grandma's roosters came home with me, and the hot pads, and the table. There were other things, too, not mentioned here.

They sit in my living room now, arranged so. For a couple of months, after bringing them here, I didn't like to look at them. Looking at them made me cry. I cried a lot. I've stopped crying now, but I still miss you, Grandma.

TERRY KUNST

Your wrist is bent almost at 90° angle as you open all the way. The tachometer is climbing rapidly. Your left hand is gripping the other side of the handle bars. The vibration from the machine is hitting your body from many different positions. Your fingers and hands have a numb, tingling feeling in them as the tach needle reaches the red line. Your left hand automatically reaches forward, grabs the handle in front of it, and pulls; simultaneously your right hand rolls the throttle back, and your foot hits the gear lever. Your foot's back, lever forward, and throttle open again. Thundering down the hill. The trees flashing by so fast that it is a constant blur on either side of you. Your eyes fixed upon the trail ahead. The wind hitting your face with the impact of a tornado. Blinking eyelids, trying to keep the airborne debris from the main part of seeing.

There's a small knoll up ahead. Taking a tighter grip on the handle bars, until you feel the increased vibrations running through your body, you raise slightly off the seat, let the machine take most of the shock. You hit the knoll, the front wheel leaves the ground, the back tire struggles to carry the entire load itself. Throwing large parts of grass and dirt into the air. Just at the top of the knoll you are standing straight up on the machine, the front wheel off the ground as high as you can handle. Gravity starts to do its thing with the front wheel. The front hits hard. The shocks bottom out and the rest of the shock is absorbed through your body. Your head snaps forward. You struggle to keep your eyes on the trail ahead. What trail? All you see in front of you is a big oak tree. Its limbs reaching out to gather you in. Right hand rolls off the throttle, left hand pulling the lever, right foot and right hand pushing the two levers. Right foot pushing so hard that it becomes numb. The tree is closing in for the kill. Decisions and ideas race through your mind. The bike slows down, a little. The back tire is plowing up the earth as it seeks to find a good hold on the earth. Rear tire is not turning at all, front wheel's turning some, but the bike is still going faster than both tires together.

Leaning to the left, the bike is at a 10° angle as your left foot makes contact with the ground. Before you realize it you are hitting the ground with your whole body as the bike slides on its side toward the tree. You look up. The bike is on its side, engine is running wide open and back tire is spinning. You jump up and run to your bike with a limp. Reaching down you struggle to pick up four hundred pounds of dead weight. Looking it over with a trained eye, you are satisfied. Everything seems to be all right. Hopping back on, you again take the controls in hand. Once again you are free. Nothing out here but you and mother nature.

TRACY ROOT

Waves
Dark, Rough
Rolling, Churning, Beckoning
Frothy, Stingy, Quieting, Drowsy
Settling, dieing, Resting
quiet, peaceful
calm

JAN MAY

Oh, God, what am I going to do! This is ridiculous! My mind is shot all to hell. For the past couple of days now I've shut myself in my room and studied from the time I got home to way late at night. From about 6:00 to after 12:00! All I can do is cry! It's all so frustrating. That chemistry is especially frustrating. I work that long and I never finish all my work. Damn it! I'm trying so hard to understand it and I've even been in for special help. But there it sits and tears drip down my face and onto the page. I have a headache and I must have a cramp in every part of my body. I don't know how much longer I can take this. I'll probably end up on a nut farm. My damn mind! Let it alone! I want to see my friends! Last night I lay here slaving away, I heard the band playing in the distance and I wanted to be there so bad. I want to feel the contentment I so often feel when I'm with my friends. I want to touch them! I'm tired of being alone here. I need help! Maybe I'll die tonight while I'm sleeping (if I ever get to bed). Well, now I feel at least a little better after writing this.

September 6, 1977

When I found out the news, all I could feel was shock. I feel bad now for at the time I couldn't cry, shout out or anything. All I could do was stand with my mouth agape, like a piece of rock. I just couldn't believe it could happen. It seemed like I was walking in a fantasy world and it remained as such for the next week.

It all started on Sunday night or really Monday morning at twenty to one. I remember because I was just coming home from the Hall and Oates Concert and was undressing for bed. The phone rang and I felt a sensation of dread as if something terrible had happened. As I picked up the phone the dread turned out to be real. The voice was a familiar one, the son of my parents' good friends and the brother of my very closest girlfriend. When he talked, it was a very quiet, well-controlled voice which came over the receiver. My stomach was churning with anticipation, as Bob asked to speak to my father. My brain was racing with ideas as to what could be wrong. I walked to my parents' room in a trance and shook my father awake without speaking, for something was freezing my mouth. My movements were that of a mechanical robot, hearing what my father said into the receiver but not comprehending. When my father hung up the phone my face had gone quite pale and before I could get my wits back together, he was rushing to his room. I followed automatically without realizing it. My father was talking rapidly now and I heard what he said from a fuzzy distance. What was happening, what I was hearing couldn't possibly be true. Terri was in a car accident and severely hurt, she had been taken to the hospital, but how? What happened? When I floated back to some sort of sanity, my parents were rushing out the door. For the next five hours I lived in a state of dreamlike chaos. I couldn't sleep so I walked. The night air was soothing against my hot cheeks but it could not help the turmoil that was passing through my brain. My mind was spinning, never touching down on one coherent thought. When I walked into the house my body could have dropped from pure exhaustion but my brain kept racing on. The phone was ringing and I walked to it with a steady calm which was surprising. It was my mother who was at the other end, saying words I couldn't bear to hear, didn't want to bear them. Terri was dead. A one-car accident with her boyfriend at the wheel, stone drunk, she was sound asleep. The car skidded and slipped. Terri was thrown out and cracked her skull. She was killed instantly. All was over, all was quiet.

The realization of everything that happened that night is finally beginning to sink in. It was a time of total bewilderment. I still to this day can't remember everything that happened after my mother's phone call. My mind was numb, devoid of emotion. In a way I think I knew what had happened when Bob had called, but I couldn't accept it until it had been confirmed. Even then I don't think I fully comprehended the full extent of what had happened. Terri Lynn, my best friend, dead at the age of eighteen, just four days after we graduated. I didn't even cry for days afterward, I couldn't, it seemed as though something held me back. I did cry though and tears still prick my eyes when I think about the first two weeks of June. The days when a beautiful girl's death shook the hearts of many and whose laughter will remain in the memory of those who loved her.

VOICE IN PERSONAL WRITING

Free writing and journal writing help you learn to "think on paper"; soon your writing should begin to "sound like" you. If you look back at the examples in this chapter, you will see that each one sounds slightly different; each one shows you a distinctive self.

When you become completely at ease with your writing, the *voice* on the paper—the "sound" of the self you've chosen—will sound like you. Most good writing sounds like someone talking. Of course, we can never be sure whether the voice on the paper is really the author's own unless we know the author personally. Fiction writers very often adopt the voices of their characters or adopt the role of a narrator who is very different from the writer. Such literary voices are called *personas*. They are like masks the author is using for the purposes of a story. But in nonfiction writing, most readers assume the voice they hear represents the author's real self.

Composition books sometimes say to "try to sound natural; sound like yourself." This is good advice to follow, but there is a trap in it. As we pointed out in Chapter 1, you have several selves; thus you have several voices. Which voice you use depends on your purpose. When you talk to your family, you use your family voice. And you have more than one of those too, depending on whom you are talking to and why: there's the voice you use when you want the family car or some other favor, the voice you use when you are explaining why you didn't take out the garbage or something else you should or shouldn't have done, and several others. Then there is the voice you use with friends—different voices for different friends and different situations. And there is the voice you use with strangers and strange situations: the one for the officer who is writing you a traffic ticket, the one for a personnel director during a job interview, and so on.

The problem in college composition becomes, Which voice should you use? There is no such thing as a "nonvoice." Your writing will have a voice even if you are deliberately trying to be bland, objective, and toneless. So you must choose: which of your many voices is the right one for college? The voice in your free writing and journal entries comes close to it. In that writing the self you know best shows through. Your free writing may be a little too free though, and your journal writing may be a little too focused on personal matters. You can write more formally in this "natural" voice simply by avoiding things that distract readers who are anticipating a certain degree of formality. If you have been too slangy, or perhaps just not entirely clear, you can change these things to make them a little more polished. The end product should still sound like you, minus some of the things that you would allow in your free writing. In short, your writing voice should be your natural voice modified by your purpose. If you are telling a story, street slang may be appropriate. If you are explaining a problem in conservation of forests, street slang wouldn't be appropriate, but the writing should still sound like you, writing naturally but modifying the language to fit the situation.

You may think your writing should sound learned and very formal. That assumption usually leads to very difficult writing and forces the reader to pay more attention to *how* you are writing than to *what* you are saying. For example, here is a paragraph about a student's first impressions of college. The writer has made some assumptions about what the composition teacher expects, and this causes some problems. Why is the student writing this way? Is this a good way to write? What would you tell this student to do in order to improve the writing?

Being that I am a freshman at this university, which I just enrolled at, I feel I have some authority for the assertions which I am about to elucidate. This institution is one of higher learning, and one could suppose that its intentions were of the highest academic merit. But this is not the case in actuality. In fact the conditions are such that just exactly the reverse is true. The average freshman here, of which I count myself as one, soon discovers that instead of serious contemplation of scholastic matters, a rather casual attitude is prevalent concerning the acquisition of progressive knowledge. The real function of this university is as to promote the social development of the individual, which is essentially a high-school orientation of education.

The student has used a dollar's worth of language to convey a dime's worth of information: she is unhappy because she finds college too much like high school. Because she is criticizing the college, she feels that she must adopt the voice of someone intelligent and well educated. (We know this is an adopted voice because no human being *talks* like this naturally.) The student assumes her subject is very important and she assumes the professor will enjoy a display of big words. The true motive behind such writing is to impress the reader with the writer's intelligence. But the outcome sounds unnatural and pretentious, and most readers come away with a negative reaction to the writing and the writer.

DIALOGUE

One way to focus on *voice* in writing is to practice writing dialogues. Dialogues enliven writing, make it seem more realistic, more immediate. They let the readers hear exactly what went on and participate as if they were there. Dialogues also let the writer practice "sounding like" different people, using different voices. A short episode with dialogue follows. The writer is trying to sound like himself and a police officer. Does he succeed? Does the writing sound "natural"?

DAN NIELSEN

"Stop that bike and hop your fanny off 'afore I pull it off, boy!" the police officer hollered brazenly through the open window of his police cruiser.

"Whaa?" I turned my head and sure enough, my ears hadn't failed. I was staring eyeball to eyeball with one of the thickest-skinned rhinos on the force.

After wrestling my bike over to the loose gravel shoulder and calming down a certain female passenger who was alternately screaming and scolding me for the minor confusion I'd created, I climbed off, immediately putting on my give-me-a-break face. I actually didn't even know what I had done.

"Do you know you're riding that bike with an out-of-date license?" the cop hollered while climbing out of his vehicle.

I managed to glance at the man before reaching for my wallet. He would have made a good-sized refrigerator freezer. I pulled out my driver's license and gave him probably one of the most confused looks he has ever gotten.

"It says here it's good until 1981."

"No, you smart-assed kid, not *driver's* license, license *tags*, boy, the metal things you get from the state every year to put on the back of your bike."

I felt like a real dummy as I walked around to the back of the bike and looked at the muddy, bent-up, year-old license plate. Then I remembered, "Oh yeah, those, well you see sir, this is my brother's bike and, uh, he didn't have current registration or something, but he's got all the papers that say he's legal."

"Well, where's he keep all these so-called documents, boy?"

"In his boot."

"And where's his boot?"

"Well, to tell you the truth, he's wearing them, but he said it was okay to ride his bike."

"He did, did he? Well that's real nice o' yo' brother, boy, but I'm afraid he didn't ask the police department if it was okay. Why don't you go sit in my police car, son."

So, giving my girlfriend a please-excuse-me-for-a-moment look, I waddled over and sat in his car while the cop got a real important-looking notebook out and wrote a bunch of stuff in it. Then he came over to his car.

"Okay, so this bike belongs to your brother, huh? What's your brother's name?"

"Dave, David Nielsen." The cop picked up his microphone and called it in. "Car nineteen to dispatch."

"Dispatch, go ahead."

"Registration for South Carolina motorcycle tag, M–Y–1–0–2."

After a pause, the dispatcher came back on: "Bike registered to Robert Marion."

"Oh my lord," I whispered.

"Sixty-seven West Fourth Street."

My brother had forgotten to change registration.

"Virginia Beach, Virginia."

I was in heap-big trouble. The cop, misunderstanding the whole problem, glared at me a minute with eyes that would knock Dracula cold, and then, very quietly, spoke: "You stole that bike, dinja, boy?"

"No sir, you can take me home and ask . . . ."

"Ain't takin' you nowhere, 'cept the police station."

Here are some things to think about and avoid in dialogues:

Bravelys Try to let the words of the dialogue show your readers what the speakers are feeling. "Bravely," "kindly," "hopefully," and "cheerfully" are descriptive overkill in this example:

"I'm all right, doctor," she said bravely.

"Of course you are, my dear," he said kindly.

"I know I'll walk again," she said hopefully.

"Without a doubt," he said cheerfully.

Stilted English Try to capture the sound of real people talking about real things. No one really talks this way:

"Good evening, Mother dear; I am home for dinner!"
"How nice to see you, Lester; we are having pot roast!"

Too Many Speech Tags "I said," "she retorted," and so on, keep
your reader constantly aware that a writer is present:
"Hi," I said.
"Hi yourself," she retorted.
"What's new?" I inquired.
"What's new with you?" she countered.

In good dialogues, the writer fades into the background. Use
speech tags only to tell the reader things that aren't clear from
the words of the dialogue itself. Realism is the goal. In oral
English, people take liberties with language. They tend to use
contractions and informal English. And, if a dialogue is meant to
be read aloud, too many speech tags will overwhelm the speakers'
words.

Writing activity

**Try a dialogue or a story with dialogue. You can make it all up, but
it will be easier just to remember and write a real dialogue or one
close to it. Conflict situations usually make for easy dialogues, and
they have built-in tension. Without tension, dialogues tend to sound
like two people trying to talk to each other when they have nothing
to say. Try to recall a conflict between you and your parents, you
and a girl- or boyfriend, you and the police, you and a teacher, and
so on. Put yourself in the other person's role for a moment; try out
the other person's *voice*. (You can have three speakers, if you like.)**

Discussion activity

**Read the following dialogue. Does it sound realistic? Describe the
different voices you hear.**

GORDON PARKS,
Born Black

"Do all of you sleep on this one mattress?"
"That ain't nothing, brother. There's a poor fella livin' down the
hall what's got six children and their place ain't no bigger'n this. There
was eight of 'em till two of the young'uns got drafted in the army a
month or so ago."
"Where's your toilet and bathroom?"
"Take him down the hall and show him, Lil. Show him good." Lil,
his wife, nodded toward me and I followed her down a dark corridor,
where she opened a door and pointed in. There was an old bathtub
with most of the enamel broken off and a filthy toilet. The seat next
to it had rotted and fallen apart, lying in a heap of other decaying

boards and fallen plaster. The foul air was unbearable. "Would you wash your child in that mess?" she asked. I didn't answer. I knew she didn't expect me to. I just took a picture of it; and we went back to her husband and children.

"Well, how'd you like it? It's a dog, huh?" I nodded, and he went on, "Eight families use it, brother. See that baseball bat over there in the corner? Well, my boy there don't play ball with it. We kill rats with it."

PERSONAL-EXPERIENCE STORIES

Once you have conquered the blank page and have some control over your writer's voice, you are ready to move on to more unified kinds of writing. Personal-experience stories are a first step in learning to structure your writing to a specific end. Shaping your materials so that they come out the way you want them to is what "composition" means. Rather than start with something complex like an argumentative essay, you'll find it simpler to start with something you know very well: a personal experience.

Look at your own life to find something that had particular meaning. Your goal then becomes to show the reader what the experience meant. You may say, "But I've led a dull life; I've never done anything unusual or extraordinary to write about." Few of us have anything extraordinary to write about, but you can try to show the meaning of commonplace events. Indeed, great writers have already written about every aspect of human existence, over and over again. The only thing new in the world is each individual. *You* are new; your perceptions, your understandings, your own experiences are new, unique to you. Almost every human being has had a love affair, or will have sooner or later; yet writers never tire of writing about love, and people never tire of reading about love. Why? Because each story is slightly different; each writer gives the story an individual interpretation.

For example, here is a story about a very simple event—taking a canoe ride down a river. Is the writing good? What is there in the story that is new, that only *this* person could have known about and written? Would you say the writer is being honest about her experience? Can you tell that she is selecting details to include or leave out of this story, shaping her materials?

From that first moment we launched our canoe, I knew it would be disaster.

"Which end do you want?" I asked my partner, Merry, who had never touched a canoe in her life.

"Oh, I don't know, what's the difference?"

"Well, do you want to steer or just paddle?"

"I guess I'll steer," she said, heading towards the front of the canoe.

"If you want to steer, you go in back." I turned her around and headed her to the rear. Boy, listen to me, the voice of experience. I had only been canoeing twice, but in this case I guess I was the expert of the crew.

We launched it into the river and we both clambered in. Using the same side for leverage, we immediately leaned the canoe to its brink, spilling all its contents into the river.

We were both frantically reaching for our possessions—the sandwiches, lemonade, and bag of dry towels. Of course the canoe was whirling down the river and we lost our balance, practically tipping ourselves over, as our belongings went sailing along the river.

"Oh brother," I moaned. We were starting out well.

"Well, at least we didn't fall in," said Merry cheerfully. With that happy, reassuring note, we were off. Boy, were we off. The second we got caught up in the current, we were both hanging on for our lives. The canoe rocked and swayed precariously, and suddenly I realized it was time for some definite action: we were headed straight for a fallen log.

"Hey back there, steer this damn thing!" I screamed.

"But I don't know how!" she answered with rising hysteria. Great, I thought, just great.

"Just stick the oar in the water like we're going to pivot around it!"

"Okay," she said, but I didn't feel us veering in any other direction—just straight for that ominous log.

"Push the oar in farther!" I yelled.

"Okay . . . Oh! . . . Oh! . . . Oh, *help!*" she screamed. Definite hysteria. And the canoe came to a halt, the water rushing past us. We were docked.

"What the hell's going on?"

When I looked behind me, all I could see was Merry's rear conspicuously staring at me, as the rest of her was standing, leaning over our vessel and hanging onto the oar, now stuck in three feet of muck.

"I can't get it out!" Merry's pitiful wail.

"Well don't let it go, for heaven's sake, that paddle cost us six dollars!" Boy, would good old Jerolim's Canoe Rental make a haul on our venture.

"What do I do?"

I was just asking myself that same question, actually. I thought about telling her to jump out, grab the oar and then swim like hell back to the canoe. Unfortunately, the river is a bit faster than Merry. I also thought of telling her to jump out and wait, perched up on the oar, for the Coast Guard to show up. Man, I'd do anything for six bucks.

"Need some help?" a friendly voice called. That was quite the understatement.

"Yah, we sure could use some of that," I said.

A young man and his dog, paddling down the river, came to our rescue. Skillfully pushing alongside our canoe, he gave the paddle a swift yank, washed off the mud, and handed it to Merry, all the while keeping our canoes side by side.

"Thanks a lot!" we yelled, relieved and thankful. With a smile he was off, his dog riding along contentedly. Thank heavens for heroes!

Well, we were a little bit more warmed up by this time. We sort of made our way down the river, crashing and rebounding from bank to bank. After about an hour of bumper-canoe, we decided we needed a little rest.

The next problem was how we were going to pull over. We decided our best bet was to just let ourselves glide over to the bank, then stop and get out. But of course that was our worst possible choice.

I didn't see it until we were right up on it. We had both stopped paddling and were just floating along peacefully when I saw it—it was a giant underwater rock, with the current dancing deceptively over it. I swear to God it was the size of a buried volcano. Man, we were dead.

"Oh, my God! Oh, my God! Hang on, Merry!" I screamed. We both clung to the sides like we were glued to them, but to no avail. We hit it full force—sending the canoe over on its side and finally completely turning it over, dumping us into the ice-cold river.

"Why didn't you steer, you stupid moron?" I came up sputtering at Merry.

"Me? Why didn't you warn me it was there? You're in front!" she said, teeth chattering. We stood in the middle of the river, dripping, shivering, and bickering until I suddenly spun around. Oh man, we were in trouble!

"The canoe!"

We both started running after it, while it just went along its merry little way—upside down and all. We were like two clumsy buffaloes—running, slipping, and crashing heavily through the water. We finally managed to catch up with it, after it had conveniently gotten tied up in some branches. We both staggered up to it and leaned on it, breathless.

"God, we lost the paddles," I moaned despairingly.

"No, we didn't. I managed to grab them when we were running up here," said Merry, smiling.

"Wow, Merry, you life-saver!"

"How do you like that? And to think only a minute ago I was a stupid moron!" We looked at each other, and then at our beat-up, dented-in canoe, filled with water, and we burst into laughter. We plopped right down onto the dirty, muddy bank and stayed for a long while—two freezing, wet, dripping girls with stringy, tangled hair and faces covered with mud; two cold, bruised, tired bodies—and we laughed until we cried.

Laurie tells her story with humor and enough details to allow the reader to participate. Notice her use of dialogue. It is the dialogue that gives the reader a you-are-there kind of participation.

Laurie's story illustrates an important principle in personal-experience writing. You can't just *tell* the reader what happened— you must *show* the reader. The idea is to re-create, dramatize the event so that the reader will see, hear, and feel your experience.

You can avoid many problems with personal-experience stories if you will remember to *limit your story to one specific incident*. Pick a moment in time, an hour or less of your life that had some meaning for you. Then tell what happened in that moment, in detail. If you try to write about something that took longer to experience, you will find yourself summarizing, just hitting the highlights, being general when you should be specific. If you try to write "My Trip across the Country" or "My Day at the Grand Canyon," the reader will fall asleep long before you get to the important part of your story. So will you.

See if you can determine the time limit of the following story. What would you say this writer is doing right in his personal-experience writing? How is this story different from the preceding one?

FRECKLES

RON KRAMER

It was just about 7:30 when the sun started to touch the treetops of a distant woods, and already I could feel the dampness in the April air. My brother, Jim, had left only ten minutes ago, leaving half of the twelve-acre field yet to be dragged. He was going to a dance and left early to make sure he had plenty of time to get ready. Quick thoughts passed through my mind of my first contact with girls and I hoped that Jim would have the nerve to ask that favorite girl to dance. I remember the time I mustered the guts and asked Suzie Schmidt; boy did I love her freckles, took me three whole days before I could touch ground again.

The vision of the tiny girl with freckles vanished and I noticed I'd better pay attention to my work. Looking back I saw a line of newly turned soil in the shape of a tall S. Murmuring a simple "———," I steered the tractor back into a corrected straight line and continued, checking the drag for a collection of corn stalks.

The C-shaped teeth usually collect the stalks like a strainer, packing them tight as hell. To my surprise, there were none, and wondering why, I remembered a disc that had sat near the field's opening and figured that someone must have disked over the corn stubble from the previous year. A lucky break, for now I wouldn't have to stop every ten minutes and pull my arm out of joint to clear the damn drag. The sooner I got done tonight, the better. A full moon was starting to yellow in a clear sky, there would probably be frost tonight.

I huddled up on the tractor seat as the dampness in the light breeze hit me. A red, hooded sweatshirt was not keeping me warm enough, and blasts of warm exhaust from the tractor felt good on my face when sent in that direction. The left brake ground as I turned the tractor around again. I flicked the light switch and lit a dim path ahead.

The noisy *putt-putt* of the old tractor took me back a few years, for it was as old as I was. I remembered the time we had just finished baling hay and it started to pour. My dad immediately hooked two wagon loads of hay together and took off wildly for the barn. Up the lane we came with both wagons swaying from side to side; I thought for sure both the hay and me were goners. In my fear I swore at Dad and told him to "slow down, dammit," which he didn't appreciate at all. I probably would have gotten whipped, but I was getting too big to lay over Daddy's knee.

A big stone hit the front tires, causing the wheel to jerk, waking me up. Fortunately, during this last daydream I had stayed on course and was just starting up a small hill. Toward the top, hard clusters of dried clay made for a bumpy ride and were almost impossible to break the first time over. Dragging them a second time would have to wait until morning though, for my feet and hands were getting numb.

Once in a while the wind would carry dust from behind, forward past the tractor. I could smell the dirt as it rose up and made my skin and nostrils feel dry and tight. It was good to know I only had to put up with these conditions for one more round. As I finished I sang songs, making up the words I didn't know. The tractor was terribly loud, but was my only means of accompaniment. They were the same songs I had sung when I plowed, picked corn, did chores and a host of other farm jobs that required little mental effort. And now, just like always, they helped pass the time and made it more enjoyable. At last the job was done and it was time to unhook the drag and head for home. Maybe if I got home in time I could give Jim a few pointers for the dance. As long as I got stuck with his job, he'd better enjoy himself . . . boy, did that Suzie have cute freckles.

Ron's story is basically about how routine and even dull it is to plow a field. That is, he is telling us about a very commonplace event. But his thoughts and reactions during that event are his own, and we get a unique look at *him.* Notice that through the use of details and especially by appealing to the senses, he re-creates for the reader, dramatizes the scene so that we feel that we are there with him. Look back through his story to see how many of the five senses he mentions. Can you hear Ron's voice? What kind of person does he strike you as? Where are the clues to his personality?

Writing activity

Write a two- or three-page personal-experience story of your own. Pick a moment in time that meant something to you. For your first try at personal-experience stories, you would do well to pick an *instant* (one second) of time. If you are writing about a car wreck, condense all the preliminaries into a single introductory paragraph: why you had the car, where you were going, the road conditions, and so on. Spend most of the paper describing—re-creating—in great detail the actual instant of the crash. Use all your senses: what did you see, hear, feel, smell, taste? What thoughts went through your mind? Finally, when you get to the end of the story, stop. Don't tack on a moral: "I've learned never to take Deadman's Curve at fifty miles an hour again." The reader should be able to learn the moral, if there is one, just as you learned it, by experiencing the wreck with you. If you have to tell the reader what it meant, there is something missing from your story. For your first story, a good rule to follow is, the more details the better, even though you know it is possible to have too many details in a story.

DISCUSSING PERSONAL EXPERIENCES

A good story needs to be told. Ordinarily only the instructor gets to read student papers, but there are a number of ways to share your story with your classmates. One way is to form groups of five or six and take turns reading the stories out loud. The point of the group is not to criticize or find fault with each other's writing but to select from the group one story that you think the whole class should hear. Here are some noncritical, nonthreatening things you can say or ask about a personal-experience story:

1 Good use of details. They let the readers (listeners) feel they are right there with you.

2 Good words. Sounds like the author really knows what he or she is talking about. The author didn't settle for just common or general terms but picked just the right words for the paper.

3 Nicely put together. Doesn't waste too much time on preliminaries. Ends where it should, doesn't tack on an unnecessary ending.

4 I had a similar experience; I know just what you mean and how you felt.

5 Why do you suppose things like this happen? Did you feel it was all your fault?

6 Your voice comes through good and strong, sounds very realistic and natural, shows your personality.

7 Good title, fits the paper well, interesting and lively.

8 Had anything like this ever happened to you before, or to anyone else you know? Was it different this time? Were you surprised?

9 What happened afterward? How did your parents, friends, relatives feel, react?

10 The best part of your paper was . . . . It really makes the point stand out, shows how you felt, makes me see what you meant.

11 How did you prewrite this? How did you get your idea, start your paper?

12 Was it hard to write? Did you have any difficulties, or did it write itself?

Discussion activity

In groups or as a class, use the list above as a guide to help you find positive things to say about the following story.

STEALING
APPLES—
NO FUN,
NO PROFIT

BILL PILCHAK

"And don't anyone holler about a dog unless it's chewing on your leg!"

Wow! I had been drifting along in a daydream until the words brought me back. And there we were again, once my head focused: five guys, a girl, and a dog—a puppy—all crammed into one tiny Fiat humming along M–20 to a well-known local apple orchard. It was three o'clock into the Saturday morning; an apple feast would end the night's activities.

"Did someone say something about a dog up there?" I finally asked. I'd hoped they were part of my daydream.

"Yeah," Lucci turned to face me from the crowded front seat. "Every time we go to this place, we hear dogs. Eric thinks he has seen bloodhounds around, but we think they have some kind of record with a timer. So don't yell unless you get bitten." Lucci turned around and squeezed back between the shoulders beside him.

"Don't worry, if I get bitten, I'll yell. These farmers get pretty serious about this, eh?"

"Bill, we're really stealing apples." He emphasized "stealing." The way it sounded it was every man for himself. The trick was to get into the orchard, pick two grocery bags of apples, and then scram. If you get caught—tough. I was worried, but it wasn't nearly as dangerous as I then believed. Bloodhounds? If someone said that they had bloodhounds today, I'd say they were nuts. There probably aren't two bloodhounds in the whole state. But on that Saturday night, I would have believed that the whole Russian army was lurking behind those trees.

Irony, I pondered, was hitting home. Wasn't it I who supported this idea in the first place? Weren't Pendergrass and I the only ones who really wanted to go? Yeah, I thought with remorse, and now everyone is so dead-set that my only alternative was to get out and pay my respects to that raccoon that John just ran over, and wait until they got back, if ever. After a while, I just settled into the seat and became absorbed in the music.

When the tapedeck was turned down below the audio-destruct level, I knew something was up. "There's the farmer's house," Eric said to everyone, although I was the only one who didn't know.

"Hey, all the lights are on. Every single one." A spark of panic had been ignited. Voices started coming all at once.

"Man, that's not cool."

"What do you suppose it means?"

"They're probably catching apple-snatchers out there right and left."

"Sure, on a Saturday night with all the stars and no moon."

"Would you guys shut up!" It was Lucci again. He was staying cool, keeping organized. "That farmer always parties his brains out on Saturday nights, and besides, the trees that we hit are a mile from his house." Lucci really knew how to steal apples.

In another minute we were turning off the highway onto a gravel road. John cut the lights and at the same time yanked the small car into a tight circle until it again faced the pavement. The whole maneuver seemed pretty snazzy to me.

The six of us started tumbling out of the car while at the same time stuffing shopping bags under our arms. John made it out first, then Pendergrass, and finally me. As soon as I got out, I walked to the back of the car and noticed how quiet the night was, and how dark. The sky was covered with stars, but there was no moon; it was very much three o'clock in the morning. And then suddenly, although I could see nothing, there came a definite rustle from a distance in the grass. "Pendergrass, your dog's loose. You'll never see him again," I warned.

"Ziggy is still in the car."

Oh, I thought, then said, "Well there's someone out here besides us then," very calmly.

"Come on now, who can be out here at three o'clock in the morning? Quit being paranoid."

That's right, I thought. And I had recently alluded to being a definite paranoid anyway. Sure, there was no one out there. I believed that for about two seconds, until I heard a second rustle in the grass.

"I heard it again." I was running the risk of becoming monotonous.

"Right," was all I got.

Seeing John run down into the small valley separating the orchard from the road, I decided to be second from last in line. Safest spot, I thought. As he started up the other side, I was glad I had.

"Oops," John said; "Excuse me. What the hell?"

"Damn right 'oops,' I live here."

"Let's get out of here."

We must have resembled volunteer sardine fillets once we heard the farmer. When we were all finally back in, and Eric had jumped over the front seat into our laps, we all noticed one conspicuous absence: we had no driver. The farmer still had John.

"John's still out there," Lucci said. I could tell he was thinking heavily, making decisions. "To hell with him. I'll drive and we'll come back for him later, maybe Monday." But as he slid over and took the wheel, he found the keys were gone. They were in John's pocket. We all knew at once.

The car flooded with embarrassment and guilt. There was nothing we could say; no one even thought to turn off the overhead dome light so the farmer couldn't see us worrying. Someone finally broke the silence. "If anyone can talk us out of this, it's John."

Soon he returned and entered the car, his face a blank.

"He's gonna let us go, eh John?"

"Well," he began, "first off, that wasn't the farmer. That was his son. Turns out he hates his old man. He's taking us to the best apples." He turned and grinned, "He's gonna help us steal his own apples!"

The little car pitched and rocked with the convulsions of five guys laughing and carrying on. For a while we were completely satisfied with ourselves, until the reality of the situation hit us. In fact, we had been caught. As of now we were not stealing apples, merely taking them. The group was subdued. The farmer had won. Our simple victory rang only in the crunch of bitten apples and echoed in no one's ears.

GHOST WRITING

Many celebrities, among them former President Gerald Ford and too many film stars to name, who "write" their autobiographies actually hire ghost writers to do it for them. These books are usually written in the first person ("I"), often with no mention of the ghost writer.

For you, ghost writing, like dialogue, is a good technique for practicing other voices, especially because to be a ghost writer, you must completely assume someone else's voice for a time.

Read the ghost-written story that follows. How does the author achieve realism? Whose voice do you hear, the ghost writer's?

A NEW
ADVENTURE
AT ROSE

As told to

HEIDI JENKINS

"I *don't* want to do this! How did they ever talk us into going with them?"

"Well, we can just leave and make up some excuse later. Oh forget it, there they are," I said disgustedly.

"Let's tell them we changed our minds and have some other idea. Let's go bowling."

"Not with our bathing suits on. We might as well go and get it over with. They've done it before, so they should know what they're doing." Woody (her real name was Candy) sometimes thought of good ideas, but she didn't usually think of them soon enough. This time we were really stuck into going.

Kevin and Mac were wearing jean cut-offs and T-shirts with their bathing suits underneath. They looked brave and daring, so Woody and I tried to be the same. How could they have ever talked us into sneaking into Rose (the phys ed department!) to swim at night— crazy! It was a warm, clear summer evening, just right for a swim. I never dreamed I would do this just to go swimming.

So on over to Rose we headed. I spent most of my time talking to Kevin. I sort of had a crush on him. That's half the reason I was daring this great adventure. Kevin was tall, dark, and handsome. He had straight, shiny, brown hair, brown eyes, and a smile that would melt anyone's heart. He was getting a golden tan which made his muscular, hairy legs *so* sexy.

Even though Woody never admitted it, I knew she had her eye on Mac. They looked so cute together with the same color blonde hair and both wore glasses. Mac always reminded me of Robert Redford; what a hunk! Although Mac wasn't quite that "hunky," his build would do, especially in Woody's case. He had a medium build and she was a bit smaller, which made them a perfect couple (at least in my eyes).

Mac's and Kevin's usual matchbook trick worked and kept the door from being locked, so we crept into Rose very easily and sneaky-like. I felt like a rookie thief, scared to death wondering what to say if we were caught. My legs were shaking to death, and my whole body just didn't want to move. I was a total mess being dragged the whole way, feeling like somebody was going to pop out from around a corner at any time and arrest us.

My own shadow scared me, and I heard every noise possible to hear in that building. I felt like I had bionic ears. I kept turning around thinking that somebody was following us, but nobody ever appeared. Everybody was trying to calm me down, and I began feeling like a real jerk. I decided if we were caught, I would be the dumb, innocent-looking one, who really didn't know what was going on.

I thought we would never get to the pool, but after what seemed hours, we finally got there. The only way to get to the pool was through the boys' locker room. I had never been in a boys' locker room before, but it had the usual musty, sweaty smells, except worse than in a girls' locker room. Everything looked so different. The walls were a dull blue compared to the girls' plain white walls. I couldn't help staring at the stalls because they were so strange looking. The stalls reminded me of drinking fountains. I'll never drink out of *that* kind of drinking fountain again! The more I looked around, the more I began to realize it was just like the girls' locker room but backwards, except that the boys' locker room had a few extras.

When we finally made it in, I had one big sigh of relief. My heart felt ten pounds lighter, and my body was once again in one controllable piece.

We all quickly stripped down to our bathing suits and jumped into the water. The water felt so warm and refreshing, which helped me to recover. I was actually beginning to enjoy myself. We kept the curtains shut to keep away any unwanted viewers from the window and had the lights off, which made the swim even more enjoyable. The water glowed and looked so shiny and peaceful.

Everything echoed onto each wall. One little splash seemed to make such a full sound. We were trying to be so quiet, but it just wasn't working. The air was so crisp and invigorating and the water was so refreshing that soon all our worries, especially mine, seemed to disappear. We played games, dived and did dumb jumps off all the boards and just had a great time.

The time went by so fast. We didn't want to leave. I could have stayed forever. I felt like a new person but felt like a fool for acting like such a coward. The air just wasn't so nice as the water. I was too used to the water and wanted to stay in it longer. The water was as unique-looking as it was when I first saw it, with a peaceful glow that just wouldn't leave us. I completely forgot about anybody catching us and didn't care if they did. I felt so carefree and happy. The only consolation of leaving was going to get an ice-cream cone. My stomach was empty and when I thought about it, I was hungry. I knew that wasn't the last time I'd see the pool like that. All I talked about the rest of the night was to plan the next time we would have another adventuresome evening at Rose.

Heidi's story is so well written that we are inclined to forget that it isn't her story but her classmate's. It sounds exactly like a personal-experience story, and indeed it is, but not Heidi's. She has been successful in getting details from her classmate, and she has been successful in projecting a voice or personality that we can believe belongs to the narrator. There may be some feeling of letdown in a reader because the story seems to be building to a different ending—one in which they are all caught, the thing the narrator fears throughout the story. If this were fiction, we might ask Heidi to change that ending. But it isn't fiction; it is a true story, and as true stories go—as life goes for most of us—the ending sometimes falls short of expectations. You do not need a story with a socko surprise ending, but you must try, as Heidi has, to write the ending so that it fits the story. In this case, we have to understand that the girl in the story lost her fear in a thoroughly enjoyable romp in the pool. *Perhaps* we need a few more details to carry that point, but overall this is quite good. Notice what Heidi has done with language. The many short sentences and simple language echo the oral language of the interview between Heidi and her classmate. Note especially the use of dialogue at the beginning of the story.

Writing activity

Try a ghost-writing assignment. Team up with a partner and exchange stories. Then write up your partner's story in the first person. Make the voice in the story your partner's. Your objective is not just to tell your partner's story but to tell it in your partner's voice. As with your own personal-experience stories, it's a good idea to use a very limited incident—a moment in time—for this ghost writing.

Choosing, defining, creating harmony, bringing that clarity and shape that is rest and light out of disorder and confusion—the work that I do at my desk is not unlike arranging flowers. Only it is much harder to get started on writing something!

MAY SARTON, *Plant Dreaming Deep*

Now that you've gained some confidence and fluency from personal writing, it is time to move on to strategies for more structured writing. You will keep on using the skills you learned in personal writing, but you will learn to use them in new ways. A reporter may write a first-person account of a crime (I saw the body), but the news article should have a sense of objectivity rather than emotionalism, and it should conform to certain procedures and principles of exposition. In exposition, or explanatory writing, there is a very definite sense of composition, the author shaping the materials to his or her purpose. Ultimately, we can say that the writing is not about the reporter but about the crime.

Here, for example, are two excerpts from the same issue of *Newsweek*, a news magazine aimed at the general public:

There is something irredeemably patronizing about much of the wowed response to Rosalynn Carter's trip—"Would you just look at that little lady, standing right up there talking about *arms control . . .* I mean, *did you ever?*" Let's knock it off.
MEG GREENFIELD, "Mrs. President," *Newsweek*, 20 June 1977

They figured it was more than a match for Jimmy Ray—a hard-case con who, in half a lifetime squandered in various prisons, had tried so often to break out that fellow inmates long ago dubbed him "The Mole."
PETER GOLDMAN, et al., "Ray's Escape," *Newsweek*, 20 June 1977

The first of these is a columnist interpreting the news. The second is a straight news report. Though the second is written in the third person, both excerpts share certain characteristics. Each has, for example, a good deal of informal language, even slang. Yet the

55

writing is fairly sophisticated; some of the words ("irredeemably patronizing," "squandered," "dubbed") require at least a high-school education, and the sentences are rather long and complex. One of the characteristics of this writing, then, is the *mix* of formal and informal language. And further, even though the language may sound personal, the subject matter is not the author's life nor even the author's reactions to his or her life. The subject is Mrs. Carter in the first excerpt and James Earl Ray in the second.

As you move from purely personal writing, you must deal with two facts. One is that the less the subject has to do with yourself, the more you will have to hunt for information outside yourself. The other is that when you deal with impersonal subjects, you will need to find effective ways to organize your information; but there are many interesting and effective ways to do this, as you will learn in this chapter.

INVENTION

In Chapter 2, you used free writing and journal writing to help you generate subject matter for your personal narratives. And you probably relied mainly on your memory to provide details for your stories. But in writing more formal nonfiction, you will find that memory won't always provide you with enough details. You will need more systematic methods of invention. Invention is derived from the Latin word *invenire*, "to find," and it means finding the material and the strategies you'll need in order to convince your readers of the attractiveness or persuasiveness of your ideas.

PARTICLE-WAVE-FIELD ANALYSIS

A systematic method of generating subject matter, particle-wave-field analysis works on the principle that you can explore anything from three points of view. Taken together, these three perspectives will generate the maximum amount of information about any object or topic in your experience.

Particle   Anything—a physical object, an event, a topic—can be thought about in terms of its smallest units, or particles. For the purposes of analysis, you can take something apart to examine each piece or section of it, as if these pieces were the building blocks from which the object was created. Obviously, many things are not created in this building-block fashion. Tearing the petals off a rose will provide you with a handful of petals you can look at, but the petals themselves will not tell you how the rose was created, and you will destroy the rose in the process. Nevertheless, if you want to investigate something, one of the ways you can think about it is as a collection of parts or components. Imagine looking at a coffee mug sitting before you. You can see that it is composed of an open cylinder and a handle, and these are composed of china or glazed clay. The glaze itself is a component, and on the surface of the mug, let us say, there is a painted scene of a Chinese garden. You could give the details of this painted garden too. But the point is that you can identify the separate components that are involved in the makeup of the coffee mug. If you are trying to find something to write about, you can begin with this kind of particle analysis of a film you saw, a book you read, an organism you studied in biology.

An interesting feature of this kind of analysis is that you can shift the perspective up or down to get different sets of components. If you look at your coffee mug you can identify components such as shape, color, the cylinder, and the handle—all of which have to do with the external appearance of the mug. But you can find smaller particles, such as the clay and glaze, that make up these external parts; and if you had a microscope you could find even finer particles that underlie these.

Wave   Still, particle analysis is not sufficient to tell you everything you need to know about a new object or topic. A list of all the components of a coffee mug is not very enlightening data. How these components fit together into patterns of organization is also important information. The particles join together into waves, the second perspective in this kind of analysis. The coffee mug really does not look like a collection of separate components; it looks like one object. The separate particles have all fused together, melted into each other so that they are no longer distinctly separate. Even the handle of the cup flows smoothly into the cylinder without any clear division between them. These joinings or fusings of the particles are the waves of the object. Whereas each particle is static and separable, the waves are composed of dynamic relationships between the particles. The handle and the cylinder of the mug join together so that each gives definition to the other and neither is clearly distinct from the other anymore. The clay and glaze and paint have all fused together to form both the substance and the appearance of the mug, and from this perspective it is no longer possible to isolate the particles as such. You have restored an important aspect of the object: some of its oneness, its wholeness, the sense that it is one object.

Field   Finally, there is field perspective, in which the waves fuse together and produce the entire object. When form (appearance) and substance (components) fuse together, the coffee mug takes on familiar characteristics, the overall appearance of one object separate from the surrounding environment. But the coffee mug also has a relationship with other kinds of mugs and drinking vessels. The coffee mug is part of a larger system in which drinking is involved. Indeed, you may think of the coffee mug itself as a system: it has components and relationships among those components; it has design and function; it exists in time and space. When looking at the whole coffee mug in relation to other things like it or as part of a larger system, there is an interesting set of questions that can themselves be used for further analysis.

Contrast   If you view anything as an isolated unit—as a single thing that you are analyzing—how does it contrast with other things more or less like it? What are its contrastive features? A coffee mug is obviously somewhat different from a coffee cup or teacup. It is also different from a glass or bowl, both of which could be made to hold coffee. And even machine-made coffee mugs have minute differences: no two of them are exactly identical. Differences exist at all three levels—particle, wave, and field—and the thinking you do about the contrastive features may well give you an idea you want to write about.

Variation   You can also look at your coffee mug as just one kind, one example of an object that may have many variations. A coffee mug, coffee cup, and teacup are all variations of the same idea. And though the one you are looking at may have a painted blue Chinese garden on it, you would allow any and all variations of the color and design on it. All these variations are acceptable as different versions of the object. The question becomes, How much variation can you allow before the object becomes something else, before it loses its identity? For example, is the handle a necessary component, or can you accept a handleless variation of your coffee mug? Can a coffee mug be glass or tin instead of clay, or does it then become a beer glass or tin cup? Can you accept a much smaller version, such as a demitasse cup, or is size a necessary component? Can you envision a square cup, a spherical cup, or is the cylindrical shape mandatory? Just how far can you vary a coffee mug before it becomes something else? Again, an idea for a paper may emerge from your thinking about likeness and variation.

Distribution If you are going to try to classify your coffee mug, place it in some kind of system of time or place or function, how does it distribute? What is its appropriate classification? No doubt, you would class it with cups and glasses and bowls and other sorts of vessels to drink from, and all these you would classify with plates and crockery and silverware—other things to eat and drink with—and so on, until you were satisfied that you had correctly located the coffee mug in a classification scheme of things it belongs with.

If you choose to, you can see the entire mug not as an object but as an event. It is a constructed object, the embodiment of the forces and tensions that went into its making, and it is held together by the dynamic interaction of those forces and its parts. At this level it obviously contrasts with other constructed objects. You can accept a good deal of variation at this level too—no matter how old it gets, it remains a coffee mug. Events are occurrences in time, and in the course of time a coffee mug may become stained, chipped, discolored, and repaired. And it distributes with other things that interact with human beings to assist them in various ways, such as tools, instruments, and so on. The mug may be kept on a shelf, hung from a nail, moved with other household belongings and so on. As a phenomenon in time and space, the mug can be viewed as something that has a beginning and an ending (it can break); it changes with time.

Furthermore, and finally, the coffee mug can be viewed in the abstract as a part of a larger system. It is an expression of civilized behavior and ritual in which people care about not only the objects but the etiquette of eating and drinking. These aspects of "coffee-mugness" can only be known by study of the culture; you cannot tell by looking at the coffee mug that we accept blowing bubbles in it from children but not adults, or that using two hands to hold it is acceptable behavior in some cases but not in others. In short, there is contrast, variation, and distribution even at this abstract level in which we view the coffee mug less as an object and more as a concept, a cultural phenomenon. Thus the coffee mug has been explored from its reality as grains of clay to its reality as an object in a specific culture. How many ideas for papers have been triggered in your mind?

You can see that this kind of systematic analysis reveals a great deal of information. If you use it on something more complex than a coffee mug, you may be overwhelmed by the amount of data you'll produce. So when you try particle-wave-field analysis to generate ideas, don't get bogged down in your reflections. A systematic analysis will provide you with more information than you can use. It's *not* your objective to write the composition "Everything You Could Possibly Learn about a Coffee Mug." The point of the analysis is to help you find something new and interesting to say about your topic. Though the procedure is systematic, it is not at all mechanical. The outcome depends on your inner resources: imagination, intuition, self-discipline, curiosity, and so on. Out of all this information, finally restrict yourself to one, limited idea. Exactly how you work your data into a composition will depend on your overall purpose.

Writing activity

Select a topic that interests you and investigate it by means of a particle-wave-field analysis. Consider your subject's contrastive features, its range of variation, and its distribution. Write down the ideas generated by your analysis that you could turn into an interesting and imaginative paper. Which part of the analysis triggered the limited subject you like best?

Any object, event, or idea is suitable for investigation by means of particle-wave-field analysis. If you can't come up with one that interests you, you may want to use a topic from the following general subjects:

capital punishment
crime
disco dancing
dormitories
jewelry

pollution
poverty
small cars
sports equipment
women in the military

BRAINSTORMING

A less formal but very productive way to generate subject matter is brainstorming, a technique many writers use to probe a subject. Brainstorming involves selecting a subject like smoking and writing down everything that comes into your mind that is in any way related to smoking. To begin probing your subject, approaching it from every possible angle, write every thought that enters your mind. Write down each fact, opinion, statistic, or idea in a single word, a phrase, or even a complete sentence. As you keep working at your subject, you'll discover that one of two things will happen. You may realize that this subject is not for you; it may bore you or you may not know enough about it and don't care to find out. (This rarely happens.) What is more likely is that your mind will begin to generate a flood of information about the subject. Facts, opinions, counterarguments will begin to appear in chaotic fashion on the page. Your mind will probably run ahead of your hand.

Don't sift and analyze at this stage. Keep writing. If you think a fact or idea has doubtful relevance, write it down anyway; you can delete it later. Surprisingly, many seemingly irrelevant facts may prove to be useful later as you develop your paper.

Imagine that you've just seen a tobacco commercial or read an article on the tobacco industry and decide this might be an interesting topic to write on. Brainstorming the topic "The Tobacco Industry," you come up with the notes in Figure 3.1.

FIGURE 3.1

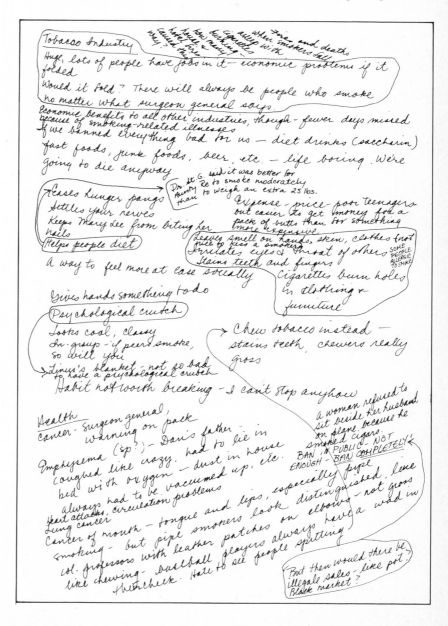

As you examine your brainstorming sheet, you can see that this probing of your experience has yielded a rich harvest. You have a great deal to say on this subject, but it all looks confusing and ill-organized.

Focusing   It is now time to *focus*, to zero in on your topic, to find out if you have a workable idea to develop into an interesting paper. As you think about the ideas you've accumulated, you begin to realize that the subject was too broad. What really interests you is the effects of smoking. And you have fairly strong feelings about this subject. You can even feel recommendations coming on!

At this stage it is useful to select only those words or phrases that are relevant to your new, more focused subject, "The Effects of Cigarette Smoking." It is obvious from your brainstorming sheet that most of your data either favor or attack cigarette smoking, so you decide to make two lists, each in no special order. (You'll find, though, that like things will tend to drift together. The mind instinctively tries to organize experience.) Figure 3.2 shows these lists, one headed *Con smoking* and the other *Pro smoking*.

FIGURE 3.2

CON SMOKING
Causes lung cancer
Should ban smoking
Ban smoking in public
Ruins teeth
Causes emphysema
Poor circulation
Heart trouble
Causes early death
  (males and females)
Nonsmokers nauseated
  by fumes
Cancer of lips & throat
Economic benefits — fewer
  days missed from work

PRO SMOKING
Constitutional right — smoke if you
want to
Economic disaster
Kids get started smoking to be cool
Settles your nerves
Stops hunger pangs (temporarily)
A way to communicate socially
A habit not worth effort of
  breaking
Can't stop
Life boring if we banned every-
  thing bad for us (saccharin,
  fast foods, beer). We die anyway

Expanding Within the Focus: The Journalistic Formula and the Pentad   This new list may make you feel a little uneasy. Moving from the more general subject "The Tobacco Industry" to the more focused "The Effects of Cigarette Smoking" caused you to discard many facts and ideas. You have a more manageable subject, but have you exhausted all the possibilities? Are there areas within this focused topic that you have not explored or discovered? At this stage in the process of invention, it's useful to examine the facts and ideas of your more focused subject in a structured way by using two complementary invention devices: the journalistic formula and the *pentad*.

The journalistic formula consists of asking: Who? What? When? Where? Why? How? News reporters are trained to use these six questions as they learn to produce news copy. If you use the questions creatively, you will discover many aspects of your subject that did not occur to you during the initial brainstorming. The *pentad* restates the journalistic formula in a more revealing way, one that stresses the possibilities for interaction between different elements in this scheme:

Action: What is happening?
Agent: Who is causing it to happen?
Agency: How is it being done?
Scene: Where and when is it being done?
Purpose: Why is it happening?

Although not all these questions will generate useful information for every paper, they are designed to cover most of the possibilities, especially if you use the basic questions in a variety of ways. Instead of simply asking the *Who?* or *Agent* question—Who smokes?—you can just as readily ask, Who does not smoke? One possible answer: people who suffer eye and throat irritation and/or infections. Isn't most of the statistical evidence that is cited to support a ban on cigarettes based on data from people who smoked cigarettes with a high tar and nicotine content? What if they had smoked cigarettes with low tar and nicotine content? A question like Who has a stake in the cigarette industry? might generate economic arguments against banning cigarettes. Why do people smoke? might generate a number of productive responses. What effect would a ban on cigarette smoking have on individuals? Would it result in diet problems or in nervous disorders? Why *do* people smoke? As you ask these questions while examining your pro and con lists, you might generate notes like the ones shown in Figure 3.3.

The *pentad* is especially useful when you begin investigating your topic in magazines and journals. If, for example, you were examining an article that was pro-tobacco industry (*Action*), it might prove useful to ask who wrote the article and check on the

*Irritates eyes and throats
of others
Cigarettes expensive – an
unnecessary luxury*

Psychological crutch

*** NEED STATISTICS ON
HEALTH HAZARD – CHECK
MAGAZINES

*But smokers seem unrelaxed
especially when they're
dying for a cigarette*

Nail biting

*Economic disaster for huge
tobacco industry – thousands
would be out of work*

*Psychological crutches may
be necessary – like Linus's
blanket
Social acceptance, especially
teen in-groups
Helps you relax (say smokers)*

FIGURE 3.3

author's background (*Agent*). Why does the writer favor the tobacco industry (*Purpose*)? You might be swayed by the statistics used in the article only to discover they were supplied by the cigarette industry, which solicited the article in the first place.

As you examine the latest version of your brainstorming sheet you will, of course, have further questions. Articles have to be read, statistics checked. But you will also be pretty confident. You have strong feelings toward your topic—"Ban cigarette smoking" —and you have facts and opinions to back this assertion. It is now time to begin writing the paper. During the writing of your first draft, don't hesitate over details. Formulate an overall plan of attack and implement that strategy. Rely on your *intuition* to guide you. Writers often refer to intuition as a mystical event. They struggle with a section of their writing, abandon it in frustration, and later inspiration strikes—a solution to their writing problem appears, seemingly from nowhere. Take advantage of such intuition "happenings"; they can prove to be the richest ideas in your paper.

Writing activity

Brainstorm a subject that interests you (you may want to choose one from the general subjects listed on page 60), and create a brainstorming sheet. Then focus on your evidence, using a combination of the journalistic formula and the pentad. Using this second brainstorming sheet, organize your paper and write a first draft. At the end of this first draft, write down what further steps you would need to take to develop a substantial and interesting paper on this topic.

THE THESIS AND SUPPORT PAPER

You have been learning to generate information from your experience, to focus on a topic, and to expand the focus for more information. Developing an overall plan or strategy for your papers comes next. In the rest of this chapter you'll learn about various strategies available to you as you write. Although you'll be practicing these strategies (thesis and support, comparison and contrast, classification, process, definition) separately, it is important to remember that much writing involves a combination of these techniques. For example, a comparison and contrast paper might use definition and classification as well as exemplification. Your paper's purpose will be the final determinant.

The basic strategy used in exposition is the thesis and support formula. The *thesis* is the key to nonfiction, and the word means simply "main idea," the point, the guiding concept your paper sets out to develop. What we are talking about in this section, then, is a paper that presents a main idea, a point, a guiding concept (the thesis) to the reader and then develops, explains, or substantiates it (support).

THE THESIS STATEMENT

If you look back at the writing you did in Chapter 2, you may find that you never actually stated a thesis. But each composition you wrote had a guiding *idea* behind it. As you write more formally, a useful strategy is to turn your thesis idea into an explicit thesis statement.

In the following informal introduction to a paper there is a very clear implication of what the thesis is, though the writer doesn't come right out and state it:

I was never much for pulling pranks, breaking minor laws, or being plain mischievous. But, the Halloween of my junior year I upset my straight life and went out with the gang, equipped with filled water balloons, two-week-old eggs, and red, ripe tomatoes.
LANA EMBERS

There can be little doubt in the reader's mind that we are about to hear the tale of pranks and so forth that occurred on that Halloween. Lana doesn't have to come right out and say that is what she is going to tell us; she has raised the *expectation* of a story in our minds and that is all a storyteller has to do. However, in the somewhat more structured paper that follows, the writer introduces an argument . . . and comes much closer to stating his thesis outright.

In these days of women's liberation, with women screaming about being oppressed in a man's world, I would like to bring to light that, at least in one situation, women are definitely favored over men. It particularly bewilders me because they are favored in an area in which, from six years of personal experience, I have found them to be hopelessly inferior to men: driving an automobile. (I can just hear the protests now.)
ED PLATO

Ed's thesis illustrates the chief quality of a formal thesis statement—it is a statement that someone could disagree with or take exception to. Ordinarily, the main idea of a story is not referred to as a thesis for this reason: no one is expected to agree or disagree with a story (which is not the same thing as liking or disliking the story). The true formal thesis, then, is an arguable proposition, and Ed has stated clearly in his first sentence that women are favored over men in one area. However, Ed is not writing a completely objective, formal paper. He is giving a personal opinion; and so his thesis is informally stated. The reader needs both Ed's first and second sentences to discover that Ed thinks women are favored over men in "the area" of driving. And at this point most readers would want to know exactly what he means. It takes the next paragraph of Ed's paper for the reader to discover that Ed thinks women get out of traffic tickets more easily than men do. At this point, the reader has a full, formal statement of Ed's thesis, although Ed scattered the information through two paragraphs of his personal-opinion paper. Though Ed's thesis is not stated as formally as it could be, it is more formal than Lana's, which is not stated at all.

The full, formal thesis statement, then, is a single sentence that contains an arguable proposition and clearly states the author's position on the issue. In the following example, the full statement of the thesis appears in one sentence. Which one?

I grew up with the problem, and I never got used to it. Too many meals were ruined when my dad puffed smoke into my face, for me to forget. I'm happy that I survived the smoke-filled cars and stuffy rooms. A problem? Yes, tobacco smoke bothers me and I resent having to breathe it. For the good of everyone, cigarette smoking should be outlawed.
PETER GRANTZ

In Peter's introductory paragraph the formal, arguable thesis statement is, "For the good of everyone, cigarette smoking should be outlawed." And Peter's argument is a real one; very few people are unaffected by the smoking problem. The "formality" of the thesis is somewhat reduced because Peter is starting with first-hand, personal information, but the rest of his paper relies on facts and figures he has found in his reading. "Formal" here means that the thesis is stated in a certain form, namely, a single sentence containing an arguable proposition. When we say a paper has a formal statement of thesis, we are saying only that there *is* a thesis statement and that it is complete, versus the implied thesis or the scattered thesis.

As in most writing, there are degrees of formality in thesis papers. They can be quite informal, such as the paper about women drivers, or they can be rigorously formal, such as a research report on a scientific experiment. The thesis statement itself can be implied, presented informally, or fully and formally expressed.

For most college writing, you should strive for the semiformal thesis paper, one that perhaps has a fully stated thesis (though that is optional) but that is not so completely formal as a government report. The reason for aiming at semiformality is that until you become very confident of your writing and have developed a mastery of your field of knowledge, it's hard to write totally formal papers without sacrificing interest level. In fact, it takes high art to write completely formal papers on complex subjects that are interesting and lively to read. Liveliness isn't just a matter of picking "lively" words and adding anecdotes to your writing. A mature and well-crafted style certainly helps; nothing good can come from a paper in which the writer can't make his or her sentences behave. But as you move away from the purely personal into more general subjects, the amount and quality of the information itself will carry much of the interest.

SUPPORTING THE THESIS

Once you have a fair notion of your thesis, you can begin trying to structure an essay for it. This doesn't mean starting in on a rough draft yet, though you can try that if you are very confident of your subject; instead, it means putting together notes or a working outline. Not every writer uses outlining, and even those who use the technique don't use it all the time. Very short and informal pieces probably don't need outlines, but as you work into longer and more formal writing, you may find that the outline—be it ever so rough and sketchy—is a very useful tool for getting over a hard problem: organizing your essay. Even if you are extremely confident that you have the whole essay in your head, it won't hurt to jot down a few key ideas; doing so may well show you some unexpected possibilities for your paper. A basic outline for the paper on smoking by Peter Grantz might look like this:

Outlaw Smoking
I. Smoking is harmful.
II. Smokers suffer coronaries and lung cancer.
III. Nonsmokers suffer from passive smoking.
IV. Everyone will benefit from a smoking ban.

But this looks pretty skimpy. This outline is more harmful than helpful because it seems to say everything Peter wants to say and leaves nothing for the essay. It represents the main *ideas* in his essay, but it doesn't offer much structure for the essay. Worse, it doesn't generate any new ideas or information for Peter to use in his essay. We have to ask, What do you mean? Where's your evidence? When Peter asks those questions himself, and begins to think in terms of the essay he is going to write—as a composition that has an introduction and that proceeds in a certain fashion to a conclusion—he explores each of these ideas and breaks them down into smaller components and produces a more detailed outline, one with more ideas in it, like this:

Outlaw Smoking
I. Introduction
    A. Personal connection with topic
    B. Thesis statement: outlaw smoking
II. Why smoke
    A. For pleasure and status
    B. Ignore dangers
III. Dangers real for smokers
    A. Medical evidence
        1. Coronaries
        2. Lung cancer
    B. Smokers' acknowledgement of danger
        1. Men
        2. Women
IV. Danger to nonsmokers
    A. Passive smoking
    B. Carbon-monoxide poisoning
V. No escape for smokers or nonsmokers
    A. Need for nonsmoking areas
    B. Total ban most effective solution

Peter is being very careful to follow the "rules" of outlining he learned in high school. He has a Roman numeral for each of his major points. He has both an *A* and a *B* for each of his points. When he is using a sentence outline, as he did the first time around, all the statements are full sentences. And when he is using a topic outline, as he did the second time, he is consistent there too. Of course, if you are just making a scratch outline for your own benefit, you needn't be so neat and tidy. The point is not to see how attractive you can make your outline but to see whether your outline can help you put your paper together.

In this case, Peter probably could have written his paper without an outline, either planning in his head or revising from a rough draft. But it is also clear, in this case, that the outlining procedure can serve as a way to *find* the components of a thesis. And it is through this rough- or working-outline stage that you can begin to see the shape and substance of your essay—a necessary step to discovering whether you have enough supportive material to write the essay your thesis requires. The well-known student procedure of outlining *after* a paper is written is mostly part of an academic tradition in which students were forced to write outlines whether they needed them or not. Even after the paper is written, the outline might show you what kind of order and material your paper does have and might suggest areas where you need to shore up the composition with additional material. (For a review of outlining, see "The Writing Process" in Chapter 1.)

THE THESIS ON TRIAL

The most common way to support a thesis is with examples. Nothing is quite so effective as concrete evidence; in fact, if you think of your thesis as being *on trial* and yourself as the prosecuting attorney, you will have a very good image of the situation a thesis paper requires. You say your roommate is a savage? Very well, present your evidence: "His personal habits are filthy! He has no sense of order or neatness!" In any court of law, the attorney for the defense would shout, "Objection! You are stating opinions, drawing conclusions!" The jury (your audience) needs to see the evidence on which these opinions are founded: "He never washes, shaves, or changes his clothes. He never makes his bed. He dumps books, clothing, trash at random on bed, table, floor." Now we are getting closer to concrete reality. If you continue in this manner, *you* won't have to convince the jury; the evidence will do it for you.

In less personalized subjects, you may have to rely on the testimony of others: "My friends who speak Spanish tell me . . ."; or rely on observation: "We all watched as Benny jumped on the window ledge shouting that he was Captain Marvel . . ."; or rely on research: "The Department of Health, Education, and Welfare found . . ." Wherever your information comes from, it is the concrete evidence the reader needs to see more than your generalizations, opinions, and conclusions. Concrete evidence is the one indispensable aspect of a thesis paper.

Read the following thesis paper. What is the thesis? Where is the thesis stated? Is there enough concrete detail to make the point? In other words, is the thesis adequately supported? What would you say this writer is doing right?

A MUSICAL
NAIL IN
OUR COFFIN?

MICHAEL KNAPP

A metallic hum, growing louder as it echoed off unseen walls, shattered the silence of my room. This hum was soon joined by the machinegunlike staccato of drums, and the effect was completed a moment later when a raspy voice wailed unintelligible words as if in pain. This senseless din was soon replaced by the sounds of car engines and tires squealing, accompanied by an obscenely husky voice and high-pitched cries of "Ooh-wah-oo" and "Sh-bop, sh-bop." This strange menagerie of sounds finally surrendered to the monotonous droning of violins and a long, sad moaning dripping with tears.

All of these, believe it or not, are examples of what is known to millions of Americans as rock and roll, or simply rock, which not only outsells every other kind of music, but has emerged "from a fifties teen subculture phenomenon to its present status as the dominant force in entertainment and the performing arts," according to John Burke in "A Look at 1973" (*American Libraries*, May 1974). This musical revolution has come to exert a powerful and far-reaching influence on the youth of today, an influence I fear is not as harmless as many seem to think; though the radical sixties are gone, rock has not yet released its all-encompassing hold on our society.

Surely one of the most obvious features of this influence is the tremendous amount of money generated by rock: over $2 billion was spent on pop music per year in the early 1970s, making this part of the recording industry quite lucrative. But the tremendous boost that this revenue gives to the economy is offset by other characteristics of a successful market: cutthroat competition and shady deals emerge in a trade that can supply a recording conglomerate with as much as a third of its total profits for a year. And an environment where such enormous profits are to be made inevitably attracts the criminally inclined, from the petty ripoff artist to organized crime, which controls an ever-increasing part of the scene.

Rock has also influenced quite strongly the way in which teens spend their money; rock music sells not only records and tapes, but also guitars and stereo equipment, and provides ample opportunities for the status seeker. Cars, the ultimate possession for a teen-ager, are being challenged by the complete stereo system and a massive record collection. Naturally, these stereo rigs, some of which would dwarf a computer in complexity, are providing many foreign companies the chance to saturate the market with their lower-priced components, giving them an edge on the homemade "Made in U.S.A." products.

Netting quite a sizable share of the action are the rock concerts, which, if the group is on tour, can gross as much as $9 million. These appearances give additional exposure to rock groups that otherwise would have to depend on the radio stations to sell their music; competition is fierce, and air play can make or break a song's chances for success. This risk is offset, however, by the possibilities of rapid stardom, with some performers attracting cults greater than those of Sinatra or Monroe in the forties and fifties. They are the new aristocracy of the entertainment world, and live much the way the Hollywood movie stars did, with real-estate investments and pension plans.

Because of the seemingly endless diversity of record styles, rock attracts many different kinds of listeners, and this has led, some critics argue, to a cheapness and theatricality that didn't exist before. Concerts have become mere light shows, with many groups dedicated more to out-sickening their opponents than to out-playing their music. With more and more performers bought and paid for, manipulation of them by the record companies has become common, resulting in "packaged" groups having no appeal other than that manufactured by promoters to "sell" the group to the public.

Rock brought more with it than mere commercialism, however. It gave a voice and the means for a whole new lifestyle to the dissatisfied antiwar generation. The key to understanding this movement, one author suggests, is in the music itself: the overamplified volume, electronic distortion and pulsing, driving beat create "passionate excitement" that carries the listener right into the music.

Rock also brought with it, through this total participation in the music, acceptance of drug use. Though there is the possibility of overdose, which can be fatal, the fear of this is lessened by the fact that both the musicians and one's companions are "high" so as to enjoy the experience more. One good thing about this is that there is relatively little trouble at rock concerts, as everyone is too doped up to care about anything around them other than the concert itself.

Musicians at these concerts increase the excitement by their antics on stage, and by their outlandish costumes. The nonconformist clothes and long hair signaled these people as the vanguard of the protest against society's standards. Also part of this protest was the notion of sexual freedom; words in songs mention love not between a man and woman, but a universal, brotherly love.

Rock, above all else, is a means of communication among today's younger generation. It unifies them and provides a means of relating not only to one's peers but to the world itself. As such, rock music has given teens a whole new culture of heroes to look up to, much different from those of their parents. Violence and money-grubbing pettiness are traits passed along by the modern supermen of the rock world. The subtleness of its influence is the most frightening aspect of rock, as it is seen to be desensitizing teens into adults bent on personal gratification above all else.

Rock music, because of its all-encompassing nature, poses not only mental issues, but physical ones. Because of its electronic aspects, rock music must be amplified many times, rock fans say, to be adequately appreciated. But continued exposure to these high-intensity sounds, according to research studies, causes irreversible hearing damage. A typical rock concert produces sound levels higher than those of a jet airliner on takeoff, and interestingly enough, it is not the electronically enhanced instruments themselves that pose the risk of ear damage, but the excessive sound pressure levels produced by the electronic systems. Rock concerts are not the only source of this damage, however; stereos blaring continually at top volume also produce similar pressure levels, which can eventually deafen the listener who gets used to high volumes.

This has proved to be a serious problem on college campuses where, in many places, rock obliterates "conversation, reason, and even genuine emotion," according to Russell Kirk in "Cacaphony" (*National Review*, 12 Nov. 1976). Students can't concentrate to study, an exception being the quiet-study dorms, reserved for the exceptional student. Loud rock is addictive; some students find they cannot study without a stereo drowning out all other sounds. After all, they can't help it if they were raised that way.

It is clear that though rock music is beneficial to our society in a number of ways, its all-powering presence and the changes it has brought with it are of doubtful merit. Whether or not the teens of today really are being adversely affected by this music is hard to say, but the evidence certainly would seem to indicate that society is being led astray by the recording industry, which is concerned only with how much it can take. Let us hope that rock is the art form it is hailed to be, rather than another means to our own demise.

Michael's paper raises an interesting question about rock music. His thesis statement is in the second paragraph: "This musical revolution has come to exert a powerful and far-reaching influence on the youth of today, an influence I fear is not as harmless as many seem to think . . . ." You may not agree with Michael, but that is one of the requirements of a good thesis; it should raise an issue about which reasonable people could disagree.

As soon as readers know what the thesis is, they expect to hear some evidence. On what grounds can rock be seen as harmful? Michael immediately begins to illustrate with examples: the involvement of organized crime, the exploitation of teen-aged consumers, the "packaging" and "selling" of performers by record companies, and other things, not the least of which is the possible physical impairment caused by the deafening volume of the music.

The paper ends with a concluding paragraph in which Michael reiterates the thesis and the compelling nature of the evidence. About his evidence we can say that some of it many readers would challenge but that on the whole the argument gains believability because Michael quotes from some of his reading; there is more evidence here than just personal opinion.

Note the introductory paragraph. Many readers prefer to have the thesis statement appear in the first paragraph of the paper. Others will enjoy Michael's "dramatic incident" as a means of capturing reader interest.

WRITING THE THESIS
AND SUPPORT PAPER

There are trivial and nontrivial ways to approach the thesis paper. Putting together a thesis on the basis of the available examples is usually a trivial approach. A writer who quickly comes up with three or four pet peeves and then creates a thesis like "I Have a Number of Pet Peeves" is making weary work for him- or herself and for the reader too. The best approach is to assume that you and your readers are taking part in a transaction of *reason*. To understand that statement, you should think about the motives behind thesis writing. What is the *purpose* for a reasoned approach to readers? Generally the thesis writer perceives some wrong, some deficiency, or some problem that affects not only the writer but the reader as well. The thesis can be worded in terms of a good or a benefit ("There Are Many Benefits to Be Gained from Going to Church"), but the implication is that people are not taking advantage of the good or not appreciating it enough. At the invention stage for a thesis and support paper, consciously set up a search procedure to find a subject you think your reader will benefit from.

The intention of the thesis paper, though we speak of "convincing" the reader, is to *explain* the problem. Your objective is to convince your reader that the problem is as you say it is; and the way to accomplish that is to explain without seeming either to argue with the reader or to bias the evidence. You should back up your examples with clear, concrete data so that your reader will not only understand the problem but will trust in your ability to present it objectively.

Writing activity

For your first thesis paper, think about wrongs, problems, faults, and so on, that need correcting. You may immediately think of starvation, health problems, energy shortages, or any of the other major problems in the world today, but these are all very big problems and require very big papers to deal with them satisfactorily. For a paper of three to six pages, restrict your thesis to something much less comprehensive than the whole energy crisis. The "size" of any thesis is determined by the amount of evidence needed to illustrate it. If you were in court, how much evidence would it take to convince the jury that international oil interests were manipulating the oil supply to create artificial shortages? The thesis is too big and too complex to attempt without a great deal of evidence. On the other hand, how much would it take to convince your readers that the price of gasoline has gone up at an extremely high rate of increase?

The key to this thesis and support paper is working out a clear thesis, one you can illustrate with a few examples in a short paper. You may want to choose a topic from the list that follows. Some of these topics can be used just as they are worded. Others can be further broken down to even more restricted statements. For example, "TV Commercials Create Distorted Views of Life" could be focused even further to "TV Commercials Create an Unnatural Concern about Body Odors."

College is Expensive
College Is Not Barrier-Free for Handicapped Students
Lawn Care Is Not Easy Work
Attack Dogs Do Not Make Good Pets
It Takes Know-How to Buy a Used Car
Co-ed Dormitories Do Not Promote Sex
TV Dramas Depend on Stereotypes
TV Commercials Use a Variety of Appeals to the Viewer
TV Commercials Create Distorted Views of Life
Film Violence Has Become Excessive
It Is Easy to Make a Bad Film
Dress Reveals Personality
Punk Rock Is Junk Rock

COMPARISON AND CONTRAST

A basic skill in both writing and thinking is the ability to compare one thing to another. To compare means to show both similarities and differences, and the purpose of comparison is discovery. Often we do not realize how much we value something until we compare it with something else. Sometimes we discover something surprising through comparison. Confronted with just one object, we can learn a lot through dissection. If you take a cuckoo clock apart, you will discover how that cuckoo clock works, and from this information you can generate other cuckoo clocks more or less like the first one. But if you compare a cuckoo clock with an electric clock, you may discover not only information about clocks but something about science and civilization as well.

There is no limit to the application of this skill. On the physical level, comparisons bring new insights to descriptive writing. On a higher level, the comparison of points of view, evidence, and arguments is fundamental to argumentative, philosophical, and research writing. We would not have advanced as far in technology as we have, without the ability to compare one thing to another, new information with old, one experiment with another.

Here is a writer attempting to be completely objective with a very simple subject, using comparison and contrast. What does he achieve? What does he learn about the subject through comparison and contrast?

TELEPHONE CHOICES

ROD MCGEORGE

The standard push-button desk model is the telephone that most people order today. It's the one the phone company supplies without additional cost. But the phone company also makes available, at a slight monthly charge, "decorator" telephones like the "cradle phone."

The standard model is all plastic, rather squat and compact in shape. Its modern aerodynamic shape makes it suitable for desk tops, where it will interfere very little with other objects. The handset is as nearly as possible integral with the base so that very little sticks out or rises up from the base. The handset is dumbbell shaped, and just fits neatly into the base.

The standard model is all one color, dark brown for example, to match desk tops. The cord is the same color. The clear plastic front-piece, or face plate, makes the dark brown under it appear gray. The effect of the coloring is to make the telephone unobtrusive, if not invisible.

The push buttons are arranged calculator fashion in the "face" of the phone: three rows across, four down. The numbers run from 1 to 9, with alphabet letters starting on number 2: ABC, DEF, GHI, JKL, MNO, PRS (no Q), TUV, WXY (no Z). The bottom row is marked asterisk (*), OPER (O), and number sign (#).

Thus the standard telephone is designed solely for its function; such attention to its appearance as there is has been devoted to making it appear unremarkable, or at best cleanly utilitarian. However, consider a telephone that seems to have been designed with exactly the opposite priorities, with maximum attention to eye appeal and far less attention to function: the Mediterranean-style cradle phone.

The cradle phone looks something like a French telephone in an old movie. The base is box shaped. The dial juts out from the top of this box (no push buttons). The "cradle" rises from the base on two posts about four inches high—like goal posts with a crossbar between them. The crossbar is like a two- or three-inch plaque or backstop; its function is for ornamentation and (possibly) stability of the posts. The posts terminate in two cradle arms, and on these arms rests the handset. It is shaped like the letter J. The earpiece is at the top of the J and the mouthpiece curves out and upward at the bottom of the J.

Not only does it not resemble the standard desk phone at all, the decorator cradle phone is attractive enough to be an art object (depending on taste). All the metal surfaces have the look of gleaming gold or brass: the dial, the posts, the cradle, and most of the handset have the golden-metal appearance. Furthermore, the handgrip, accent points on the ear and mouthpiece, the cradle posts, and the entire top of the base are done in shiny black plastic that looks like onyx or marble. The boxlike base appears to be carved, dark brown wood with a heavy hexagon design repeated all around the sides. The same dark wood appearance is repeated on the crosspiece between the posts; it has a curlicue design, vaguely Moorish.

Far from being unobtrusive, the cradle phone is striking enough to surprise people and draw compliments. No one comments on the standard phone. The cradle phone is quite heavy, a good deal heavier than the desk phone. The cradle phone was not meant to be moved about at the convenience of the user. Unlike the standard phone, the cradle phone does not fit well with other objects; the protruding ends of the handset can get in the way, and the whole telephone is considerably taller than the standard model, making it harder to reach over it. The cradle phone is slightly more troublesome to hang up. The handset has grooves for the cradle and won't hang up properly until the grooves are exactly over the arms of the cradle. The dial is slightly less or considerably less convenient than push buttons, depending on the individual. It is nearly impossible to hold the handset of a cradle phone between the shoulder and the ear without using the hands. If and when the phone company activates the two extra buttons (*) and (#) on the standard phone, the cradle phone will not be as useful, depending on what the extra buttons are for. And it must be remembered that the cradle phone costs two or three dollars a month more than the standard phone.

Thus the cradle phone appears to contrast somewhat negatively with the standard model on use and cost. But as a conversation piece or just something unusual to look at, the cradle phone is clearly superior. And many people find the differences in use and cost negligible.

Rod's comparison allows him to see the two telephones in relation to each other, and this view of them deepens his understanding of both of them. Notice that it is through the contrasts that the reader gets the best understanding of the two phones. The more two things are similar, the more important their differences become. (Try comparing any chair you can think of with an electric chair!) Rod's comparison is impersonal. He writes for an audience that is more interested in an objective treatment of a given topic than in him. He does not use "I" nor refer to himself at all.

In any comparison it is clear that *observation* is a very significant aspect of the process. To the casual observer, two chairs, two flowers, even two cats look very much alike; to the skilled writer, tiny differences may reveal a story or an idea. Notice in the following paper how observation brings out details and turns something as commonplace as a quilt into a study of contrasts.

SOMETHING
SPECIAL

TRACY ROOT

Neatly folded and tucked up into the top shelf of my closet lies my old quilt. Evenly spread out over my bed lies my colorful new quilt. Both are very beautiful but their uniqueness is quite different.

My new quilt is very colorful. Yellows and blues, greens and pinks are evenly printed over it in shapes of diamonds. Inside the diamonds are printed flowers and polka dots.

My old quilt is also colorful, but it isn't because of the printed colors on it. Little green bows peek out of it in certain spots. It's colorful because of the different patches of materials on it. There are checkered and plaid patches. Some of them have Raggedy Ann dolls printed on them. One of the green patches has a snag on it from my dog jumping off my bed. There's a faded pink stain on another part of it from the time I spilled my Kool-aid on it. I wasn't even supposed to be drinking it in my room!

On my old quilt, each patch on it was cut and stitched by hand, my mother's. I remember watching her take some of the clothes I had outgrown and carefully cut them apart in neat little squares. I wasn't very happy about it then, but now I think it was a very neat idea. I can lie down on it and study the different patches, remembering which dresses and skirts they came from.

My new quilt is stitched precisely in the right spots, but that is because it was done with a machine. It's very neat and all, but it doesn't hold the same personal value for me.

All of the stuffing inside my new quilt is evenly spread. There isn't a bump or a bulge anywhere on the entire quilt. It almost seems too perfect.

My old quilt is lumpy all over; the warm fluffy stuffing is very thick in some spots and very thin in others. It shows how much it has been used.

My old quilt is tucked up into my closet so that it won't get worn out. I want to be able to show my children one of the many things my mother has done for me. It makes me feel warm just thinking about it because I know it was put together by my mother with a lot of love and care. I really like my new quilt, but my old one will always be my favorite.

Tracy's paper is a good example of how close observation and attention to detail can lead to a discovery. The two quilts aren't *just* different. The old quilt, because it is handmade, has become an heirloom, an object with special family meaning, to be handed on from generation to generation. Furthermore, Tracy's paper amounts almost to an argument—that the old quilt is better than the new one. Looking at two sides of an issue is indeed the structure of an argument. You can see, then, why it is important to become skilled in comparing and contrasting: this is the beginning of the process that eventually becomes *affirming* and *denying*, or arguing and counterarguing, in formal writing. Here, for example, is a writer deliberately setting out to *argue* by means of comparison and contrast:

LIVING IN
TOWN . . .
NO THANKS!

JOHN SALATINO

If I had a choice of living in town or in the country, I'd pick the country, and I think you should too. Even though some people can't choose where they want to live, others do have the choice of picking one of these two areas to settle in, a very important question for those who are spending their life savings building that "dream house," or a newly wed couple who want the best possible environment for raising their children. This decision of where to live is one that will most likely affect us all at one time or another.

Living in town does have some advantages over living in the country. Kids can usually make friends within their own block. Mother can visit the neighborhood store for groceries whenever ·they are needed and also visit other wives daily for coffee. Of course, Dad too finds the relaxing atmosphere of the nearest bar a good place to escape from the noise and confusion of the home. Usually lots are small, and the work on lawns, gardens, and so on is minimal, leaving more free time available. Schools and public facilities, such as tennis courts, are quite near and can be reached easily, eliminating the need for parents to drive their children to Little League games or any type of extracurricular activities in which they may be involved.

The country has its share of advantages as well. By tradition, country life has been a simple life, and is basically that today—plenty of space, trees, and green grass. Nature is all the more present, and the change of seasons is spelled out by the surrounding countryside. The facts of life are learned more readily and naturally by children as they joyfully watch animals of forest and farm. Even though some people find the country life lonely and desolate, others find it relaxing and gain a sense of freedom from it. Even though there is more work involved with country life, it provides a good chance for a father to get his hands dirty and take pride in his house and lawn, rather than spending an hour at Joe's Bar. The children can pitch in, learning both to work and live together, rather than hanging around the malt shop all day. Mom too can use the time she might have spent having coffee at a friend's in caring for and helping her children. Then, when the time does come to visit a neighbor, this simple expression of friendship becomes a more meaningful gesture. The same is true for the kids: when a friend visits, it is a special occasion. The fact of living so far from town, and that the parents must drive their kids everywhere, only reemphasizes that the family must do more work in less time. To do this they must work as a unit, learning to get along with one another. After all, there is only one way to live, together . . . in the country.

WRITING THE COMPARISON
AND CONTRAST PAPER

Before you decide to sit down and write a comparison of your two friends, two cars you have owned, two places you have visited, think through the subject: what are the parts or points of comparison and contrast? What will be the outcome?

Some things are easier to work with than others. The bigger the subject is, the longer your paper must be to treat the subject adequately. Comparing Europe and America is doomed from the outset, no matter how well you know both places. You would do well to limit your first effort at comparison to physical objects: two chairs, two shoes, two hands, and so forth. Comparing the old with the new, as Tracy did in her paper on quilts, is a popular approach; compare your new car with your old one, your new home with the previous one, and so on.

There are three possible ways to organize a comparison and contrast paper: comparison of the wholes, comparison of the parts, and a combination of parts and wholes. Each of these is an acceptable method of organization; some subjects seem to lend themselves more to one method than the others. Comparison of the wholes means you first say everything you intend to say about one thing and then do the same for the other. This is the pattern John used to compare country and city life. First he described town life; then he described country life. Some readers find this an unsatisfactory plan because it requires them to remember too much at once. The other plan is to take up the parts of each subject at the same time, as Tracy has done. This is a more satisfactory plan for most readers and has a more sophisticated look to it. The last possibility is to combine patterns so that sometimes you compare parts and sometimes you compare wholes. This is probably the most sophisticated pattern of all. It demands the most deliberate planning on the writer's part, as for example in the following paper:

FREDDIE

RENEE CARSON

Stuffed animals make great companions for small children. When I was a little girl, accumulating them became my most recognized pastime. By the age of five, I had acquired ownership of a ferocious orange lion, an eight-foot-long scaly snake, a bright red puppy, a furry yellow kitten, and a lime green frog with orange eyes and pink cheeks. It didn't take long for him to become my favorite. No matter where I went, I would undoubtedly take Freddie with me. During long car rides he sat on my lap, or in bed he lay at the bottom of my pillow.

On my seventh birthday, my family went to Ohio on a vacation, and I lost Freddie. We had stayed in a hotel. I thought I had packed Freddie in my suitcase before we left. When I got home to unpack him, he wasn't there. I cried over his loss, as I would have for a true friend. To me he was more than a stuffed animal, he was a companion. My mother bought me another frog thinking it would replace Freddie, but it never did.

Freddie had orange fluorescent eyes the size of Ping-Pong balls, and bright pink cheeks the size of quarters that made him look as if he were continuously smiling. His face resembled the painted face of a circus clown. There's an unending smile that gives you a warm and cheerful feeling when you look at it.

Due to frequent handling, his fur was flattened and severely spotted. His face was chocolate covered, resulting from a candy bar being ground into his nose. My girlfriend thought she'd be friendly and try to share it with Freddie. His back was stained from red pop that had been dropped onto the floor, and which consequently splattered over Freddie. You could say that, overall, his whole body was dirt covered.

My new frog was larger and fuzzier. Its thick fur was dark green, and had black patches that nicely blended in. Its large eyes sparkled when the light hit them, reflecting the colors of the rainbow. It was constructed in such a way that it appeared to be ready to leap away at any given moment.

Freddie's body had been stuffed with soft, crushable foam, where my new one was filled with hard beans the size of small pellets. But the biggest difference was the smile. When I looked at my new frog, I didn't see a happy, friendly face as I had on Freddie; I saw a sparkly eyed normal frog. There was no warmth in its face, just a sober fixed expression.

On the other hand, they both had a wide, shiny ribbon tied around the neck. Somewhere I had heard that ribbons were a sign of good luck. And even though no one else seemed to believe it, I had my mind made up and no one could change it. I also thought the bigger the ribbon was, the better the luck would be. So directly after each frog had been purchased, I had my mother tie as wide a ribbon as could be found around their necks, and they were never to be removed.

Like many small children, when I cried I liked to cuddle against something that was soft and warm. This is where both Freddie and my new frog were useful. I would bury my tear stained face into its small body and weep.

They were both a source of security for me. Most small children have a blanket or a special doll that they like to take to bed with them. But I was attached to my frog, and I would faithfully take it along. They were the most devoted friends I had. If I had something to get off my chest, I would pour out my problem in great detail to them. I knew they couldn't hear, but just expressing my feelings always made me feel better.

It's strange how inanimate objects can have special meaning to certain people. Some people idolize money, while others idolize jewels. But to me, at the time, it was my frog.

You can see from Renee's paper the effect of a sophisticated arrangement pattern; it has so much variety that the pattern tends to fade away from the attention of the reader. As Renee moves from one thing to another, the reader simply follows along, unaware that Renee sometimes refers to the parts, sometimes to the wholes. Renee's paper demonstrates her considerable skill at observing—or at least remembering—details, but it also demonstrates her skill with sentences. She seems to be in complete control of her sentences, easily generating both long and short ones. The first sentence of her third paragraph is twenty-nine words long, full of colorful details, and it rolls along in a smooth, flowing rhythm. Notice the emphasis achieved by the shorter sentence that follows this one, expanding on the idea of Freddie's smile: "His face resembled the painted face of a circus clown."

Anything can be compared, even unrelated things, but you don't need to *strain* the comparison. (It would take a very nimble mind to make an easy comparison between dirty socks and a bottle of milk.) However, you may be surprised at what you can do with *analogy*—comparison of unlike things. An old man and an old car, for example, may produce interesting parallels. As long as two things have at least one major quality in common, you may be able to compare them meaningfully.

You might, for example, compare two points of view about the same subject:

CARSICKNESS

MARTHA GRAHAM

Until I met Dan I never appreciated the beauty of cars. To me, a car was a necessity for transportation and an unpleasant one at that, as I am extremely susceptible to car sickness. Dan, however, saw them as objects to be examined, criticized, admired, and appreciated. He looked at cars like a connoiseur looks at masterpieces in the Louvre.

Where I saw four round black tires, Dan saw wide ovals or slicks. What I called hubcaps he called mags or chrome reverses. As I would admire the color of a car, Dan would specify the paint job as being either pearled, candy appled, metal flaked, or factory. While I would cover my ears and cringe as a Corvette roared by, Dan would say, "Listen to the size of that engine!" or "It must have an over-sized cam." I detested the admiration and respect in his eyes as he watched it scream around a corner and disappear in a cloud of exhaust.

Little did I realize that there was more to an exhaust system than a muffler, until Dan bought some headers. I still don't understand their purpose, although they were patiently explained to me time and again.

I laughed when I saw a car with its rear jacked; I never saw anything look more ridiculous. I came to the conclusion that having a car tilted at a thirty-degree angle was the stylish thing to do. A lecture endowing me with the information of the purposes and functions of airlifts left me not only entirely bored but completely confused.

One thing that Dan and I both enjoyed about cars was speed. Only we both had different reasons for this enjoyment. I wanted to go fast so that the destination would be reached before I got sick. Dan drove for the pure thrill of power and control over a throbbing machine. I guess speed was our common denominator.

I dated Dan through a 1964 Chevy Supersport, a 1971 Nova, a GTO, and an MG Midget. As Dan's interest in cars increased, our relationship declined. Dan was sure he had educated me fully on the subject of cars. What can I say . . . I'm carsick.

Writing activity

Write a comparison and contrast paper of from three to six pages. Think about the points of comparison and/or contrast of the two things you choose for your topic. Think too about your thesis—the point of the comparison—whether or not you decide to state the thesis formally.

Topics for comparison are easy to think of, but you may wish to select one from the following list:

two short poems

two photographs

two roles for an actor

two cars

two attitudes toward truth

two paintings

two guns

two typewriters

two editorials

two rooms

two hats

two styles of skating

two personalities

two seasons

two teaching styles

two characters in a novel

two television commercials

two pets

two views of yourself

CLASSIFICATION

Classification is the means by which the mind groups experiences into types. The mind cannot handle very many unrelated ideas, objects, or events. It is necessary to find some pattern, some common property in order to catalog many separate things into a smaller number of *types* of things. For example, we can discuss singers because we can classify singers as sopranos, tenors, basses, and so forth, and also as classical, rock, country, and a number of other things. Thus, classification is really a basic skill of analysis. This may seem perfectly obvious as long as you are talking about familiar subjects (like singers), but suppose you were talking about nonhuman singers. The high-pitched squeals, whistles, grunts, and clicks of the humpback whale are called songs. If you were faced with the job of analyzing whale singers you would see immediately how important it is to be able to group, sort, divide, and catalog these apparently random noises:

When you go out to listen to a humpback sing, you may hear a whale soloist, or you may hear seeming duets, trios, or even choruses of dozens of interweaving voices. Each of these whales is singing the same song, yet none is actually in unison with the others—each is marching to its own drummer, so to speak.
ROGER PAYNE, "Humpbacks: Their Mysterious Songs," *National Geographic,* January 1979

There is nothing very obvious about the number of whales making noises, and it is no simple analysis to discover that each whale is singing the same song out of synchronization with the others. And there is nothing mechanical about the act of classifying. Classification is a creative analytical procedure. Consider the English alphabet we all learn as children. We usually divide the letters into consonants and vowels but make no other classifications. Yet linguists have discovered some intriguing classifications that look like this:

GROUP I	GROUP II	GROUP III
P, B, M	T, D, N	F, V

There are several other groups (for the other letters of the alphabet) derived from the same principle of classification. Most people say, at least at first, that they cannot see what the letters in each group have in common; the classification is not immediately obvious. With a little time to study the groups, people begin to see the basis for the grouping. For example, the letters in group I represent sounds made by bringing the upper and lower lips together (bilabial). The letters in group II represent sounds made by touching the tip of the tongue to the roof of the mouth near the teeth. And as you have probably guessed by now, the letters in group III also represent sounds made a certain way.* In short, linguists have discovered an important principle: we can classify the sounds of our language (and all languages) according to the way they are produced.

Ultimately, then, classification can be a powerful tool for *invention*. Classification is related to comparison and contrast: the close analysis of separate items may produce a concept that can govern them. The principle of classification we "find" (invent) is equivalent to an *idea* about the items. Thus you should think of classification not just as a pattern for organizing a paper but as an instrument or procedure by which you may be able to invent an idea for a paper. The *power* of classification to reduce extraordinary amounts of data to manageable categories is illustrated by a space-age event in 1977:

> . . . two extraordinary spacecraft called Voyager were launched to the stars. After what promises to be a detailed and thoroughly dramatic exploration of the outer solar system from Jupiter to Uranus between 1979 and 1986, these space vehicles will slowly leave the solar systems—emissaries of Earth to the realm of the stars. Affixed to each Voyager craft is a gold-coated copper phonograph record as a message to possible extraterrestrial civilizations that might encounter spacecraft in some distant space and time. Each record contains 118 photographs of our planet, ourselves, and our civilization; almost 90 minutes of the world's greatest music; an evolutionary audio-essay on "The Sounds of Earth"; and greetings in almost sixty human languages (and one whale language) . . . .
> CARL SAGAN et al., "Preface," *Murmurs of Earth*

The extraordinary *Voyager* recording will undoubtedly outlast the earth and all its civilization. Long before any alien race is likely to find the recording, earth will have been gone for eons. The message is just a fraction of the possible messages we might send out to the stars, just a few photographs out of all the archives of the world, a few fragments of music out of all that has ever been recorded. The selection of the pieces to be included—and

---

* The sounds are produced by placing the upper teeth on the lower lip.

excluded—was a monumental job of analysis and decision-making. If the task were yours, which pictures would you send, what music? Indeed, which languages would you select from the approximately 3,000 now known to exist? To answer this question, Carl Sagan and the others on the project had to derive some principles for selection, some system for classifying the great numbers of items they had to select from. For the full story of how the project was completed, you should read the book, *Murmurs of Earth;* all we can say here is that in the end, the *Voyager* record contained what was hoped would be a representative sampling of earth pictures and music and languages.

However, the *Voyager* project illustrates the primary function of classification: the analysis and sorting of large numbers of items into groups and types. It is by sorting into groups that we reduce large and unwieldy numbers to smaller and more readily manipulable sets. At any university, for example, there are likely to be too many students to allow us to make meaningful statements about "students." Fortunately we have a number of classifications we can take advantage of to reduce this large group to smaller subgroups: men and women students for example, or freshmen, sophomores, juniors, and seniors; or science, art, business, and education majors. The more discriminating our categories can become, the more accurate we can make our statements about them.

Which classification system we adopt depends entirely on our purpose and, in the case of composition, on the whole purpose-audience-experience-self-code complex of factors governing writing situations. Obviously we could invent trivial classifications: students with freckles, students with younger brothers, students with expensive cars . . . but it would take an unusual writing situation to justify such classifications. If you were asked to describe the types of students who could benefit from a course in modern poetry, the writing situation would have built-in constraints that would suggest the classes or types you should use. If you found yourself in a job that involved large numbers of items, which you had to sort by some criteria, the purpose of classifying would be built into the situation. For example, two scientists were once faced with the difficult problem of determining the population of elephants in an area of Africa, because in large numbers elephants will damage whole forests. The problem was how to keep track of elephant births and deaths. Its solution depended on being able to recognize elephants (who all tend to look very much alike, even to scientists):

Learning to remember an individual became like a geography lesson, in which the shape of a country's borders had to be memorized. Often an ear would be almost smooth, with only one or two small nicks, but the shape of the nick, whether it had straight or curved sides, its depth and position on the ear, provided useful material. Some nicks looked as if they had resulted from the ear catching on a thorn, others as if they had been deftly cut by a tailor's scissors in neat straight lines. Certain elephants had ears with as many holes along the edge as a Dutch coast line plastered with bomb craters along its dykes. The cause of these holes I never discovered, but I suppose it must be due to some internal physiological process, the result of which gave the ears a decaying appearance.

IAN and ORIA DOUGLAS-HAMILTON, *Among the Elephants*

The Douglas-Hamiltons solved their problem in part by learning to classify elephants by the configuration of ears. The scientists in this instance had a ready-made problem with its built-in purpose. They needed a classification system by which they could identify elephants. However, when you are not led into situations that imply certain specific classification systems, you will find that the analysis classification requires will provide you a new and deeper insight into subjects, even those you already know well. In short, classification is not simply an exercise you are asked to undertake to see whether you can do it. All the strategies of exposition are functions of the human mind, and all normal human beings can and do use them whenever the need arises.

We are not suggesting that you put together a classification paper as an exercise in orderly exposition. It is possible to write a paper in which you classify trees into two groups: those that lose their leaves annually and those that remain green all year. You could further subdivide each of these categories into several subtypes of each kind. But if we ask *why* trees should be classified in this manner, it becomes clear that the assignment is a mere exercise. What is missing here is some *purpose* for the classifying.

The actual process of analysis into types should precede the writing of the paper, even though there may be refinements and adjustments in the topic as you work on the paper. But thinking through the subject, *discovering* the principles on which to classify, should lead to new insight, new understanding of the subject. The classification paper, like any other, should make a point; the classification should lead somewhere. We all know that money can be divided into paper money and coins and that there are several varieties of each of these. So what? What is the point?

It is important to remember that people set up classification systems. The flowers and animals of nature exist in vast numbers and great variety because God made them so, but God did not invent the scheme by which we separate flowers from animals nor any of the other categories we use. (And just to emphasize the point, God has provided us with creatures who are ambiguously both plant and animal and not very easy to classify as one or the other.) No matter how logical or even obvious our categories seem, the act of creating the categories is specifically a creation of the human mind. There is no normal, natural, or necessary way to classify anything, and there should be nothing mechanical about the way you arrive at your categories of classification. A famous composer has illustrated this point:

We all listen to music according to our separate capacities. But, for the sake of analysis, the whole listening process may become clearer if we break it up into its component parts, so to speak. In a certain sense we all listen to music on three separate planes. For lack of a better terminology, one might name these: (1) the sensuous plane, (2) the expressive plane, (3) the sheerly musical plane. The only advantage to be gained from mechanically splitting up the listening process into these hypothetical planes is a clearer view to be had of the way in which we listen.
AARON COPLAND, *What to Listen for in Music*

What Copland achieves with this classification is not just a "clearer view" of listening but the conclusion, as he says later at the end of the section, that the reader should strive for "a more *active* kind of listening . . . not just listening, but . . . listening *for* something." Thus his classification has a point; it serves a purpose. It was probably not obvious to you nor to many others before Copland explained them that there *were* such planes of listening to music. They are his categories, invented to suit his purpose —to help the reader understand music better. The real question to ask is not just What classification can I make? but What point can I make that classification will help establish?

Read the following paper. How has the author derived her categories? What purpose does her classification serve?

WHO IS AN ALCOHOLIC?

PATTI DEWITT

Alcoholism isn't a very pretty subject to talk about. It makes some people uncomfortable and others angry. College students act like alcoholism is something that happens only to old people; some students refuse to talk about it. But some people want to know what the symptoms of alcoholism are or when do you "become" an alcoholic. There doesn't seem to be just one answer to this question; alcoholism seems to be very individualistic. From my work in the Crisis Center and from what I've observed with friends and relatives, I think there are too many individual variations to give a complete list, but if people can recognize the main types, they will be more able to tell whether a roommate or friend or relative is—or probably is—an alcoholic.

The first type is simply the heavy drinker. Most people agree that two or three drinks of any kind should be the limit at a party: two or three glasses of wine, two or three mixed drinks, two or three glasses or cans of beer are the maximum for most people. And even then we are talking about occasional drinkers who drink once or twice a week. The heavy drinker usually has much more than two or three drinks and is likely to have them several times a week.

There are basically two kinds of heavy drinkers: those who get very drunk and those who don't. We all know someone who can seemingly drink all night without becoming rowdy or unsteady or falling asleep. Sometimes these heavy drinkers appear sober even after they have enough to drink everybody else "under the table." Usually people admire this kind of alcoholic; they say things like "So-and-so can really hold his liquor." But So-and-so is usually the type who looks sober enough to drive, and he will fight anyone who tries to stop him. I would say that many college students are this type. The other type of heavy drinker is easy to recognize; he (or she) is the one who gets noisy and may even fall down or pass out. People usually say, "There goes So-and-so, drunk again." While the heavy drinker obviously drinks more than the light drinker, he or she resents any suggestion of alcoholism. And since they may not drink "too much" every time, many people will say those drinkers are not alcoholics but just "heavy drinkers," people who "really like their liquor." At a college bar, these drinkers are usually the ones who make fools of themselves or start fights.

A different kind of drinker is the "binge" drinker. This is someone who does not drink at all or who seems to be just a normal (light) drinker most of the time. But every now and then the binge drinker will "fall off the wagon" and drink very heavily for a night or a weekend or several days. Since binge drinkers can sometimes go for quite a while without a drink they are frequently thought to be nondrinkers. Or they may be thought to be not alcoholics because they can "stop" drinking. Sometimes the binge drinker can go on for surprisingly long periods without a drink, but sooner or later this kind of drinker goes off on a binge and usually drinks until he passes out. Often these drinkers are not thought of as having a drinking problem; instead they are said to be people who "shouldn't" drink because liquor "affects" them so badly. Often this kind of drinker is tolerated, depending on how often and how bad the binges are. "So-and-so is on a binge again" means the binge is a laughable thing because it will soon pass and then old So-and-so will be himself again. If the binges get very bad, the drinker may find himself in a crisis center or an alcoholic hospital. But since the binges wear themselves out, this kind of drinker is quickly "cured" and released. One thing that is common among binge drinkers is unexplained bumps and bruises. Drinkers who seem to have more than their share of black eyes and split lips may be binge drinkers, who usually do not stop drinking until they pass out. Almost all binge drinkers deny they are alcoholics and become very angry at the suggestion, because they only drink "now and then" and because "having a little too much to drink," they say, is something that can happen to anyone. Many binge drinkers, to avoid the charge of alcoholism, drink "only" beer and wine because they believe beer and wine are harmless social drinks and that "everybody" drinks beer and wine.

The most common type of alcoholic is the habitual drinker, someone who drinks every day. Some of these drinkers may be heavy drinkers; if more than two or three drinks is "heavy," then most of them are heavy drinkers. But they usually don't think of themselves as heavy drinkers, and they may not be seen as heavy drinkers by their friends (who are likely to be the same type of drinker). People who have a beer or cocktail for lunch and/or a couple of before-dinner drinks, and/or wine with dinner and/or one or two after-dinner drinks will usually "explain" that the alcohol is "absorbed" or "diluted" by food, and so they insist that their drinks are not the same as an equal number of drinks served without food. Or they will explain that two drinks before dinner and two drinks after dinner don't add up to four drinks because they are "separated" by food. The exact number of drinks isn't as important as the fact that drinking has become habitual. A man who has "only" two martinis for lunch and two before dinner several hours later, but *every* day, is an alcoholic, even though not very much alcohol is involved. Such drinkers will usually get upset if they have to miss one of their drinks. They will select restaurants, motels, and even their friends, based on whether or not they can get drinks. (I have a friend who won't go to a restaurant if it doesn't serve drinks.) Many drinkers of this type begin thinking about "happy hour" before it arrives, and as the drinking hour gets closer they become more and more "thirsty." Since many drinkers fall into this category, few people are concerned about this kind of alcoholic. But at the Crisis Center many alcoholics say the habit grows and gets worse. The drinking hour comes earlier and earlier, the drinking "hours" increase (morning eye-openers, midday pick-me-ups, after-dinner drinks, nightcaps). Potentially, the habitual drinker faces as severe a drinking problem as any other kind of alcoholic.

Finally there is the all-day drinker. There is sometimes a line between the habitual drinker who is drinking frequently during the day and the all-day drinker; at least, many habitual drinkers like to think so. If there is a line, it is crossed when there are no longer any periods between drinks. The all-day drinker is the one most people think about when you say "alcoholic." They are the ones shown in movies: housewives at home drinking all day, businessmen and laborers either secretly or openly drinking on the job, and skid row bums drinking out of paper bags. The all-day drinker starts drinking when he or she wakes up. The same way many people need several cups of coffee to start the day, these drinkers need several drinks. After this the drinks continue in about the same way that some people drink water or coffee all day. The all-day drinker is likely to be "tipsy" or "stoned" all day. A semisober state becomes their natural condition. People who don't know such drinkers are "high" get the impression that they are "strange" or "a little off balance." Oddly enough, these all-day drinkers can become so used to their alcoholic state that they are able to live and function for years in a semistupor without being very unusual looking to others. Of course, many of them end the day passing out in bed and many others end by ruining their lives. Even many of these obvious alcoholics will deny they are alcoholics since, according to them, their drinking doesn't interfere with their lives. Most parents would be shocked to find out how many college students are all-day drinkers. Every dormitory has at least one.

These four basic types—the heavy drinker, the binge drinker, the habitual drinker, and the all-day drinker—pretty well cover the alcoholics. Surprisingly few of them end up on skid row. Some of them don't even get "drunk" in the movie and television sense. We might conclude from this that practically anybody who drinks is an alcoholic, but this is not true. Those who are defensive about their drinking like to pretend that all nondrinkers or light drinkers are little old ladies who think anyone who has "a few beers" is an alcoholic. By this they mean it's natural and even "macho" or "sexy" to drink. But this classification of alcoholics doesn't mean everyone who drinks is an alcoholic. It only means those who regularly drink are alcoholics, those whose drinking falls into a recognizable pattern. One basic difference I have observed about the way alcoholics drink is how hard it is for them to change the pattern of their drinking. Heavy drinkers can't easily become light drinkers. Binge drinkers can't stop forever or break the routine of their binges. Habitual drinkers find it very hard to become occasional drinkers. If there is anything to be concluded from this classification it is probably just that once drinking becomes a habit, the habit takes over and becomes very difficult to change.

Patti's paper is a good example of insight through classification. By grouping drinkers into different categories based on how often they drink, Patti shows that the single group called "alcoholics" is actually four groups. You may disagree with Patti; there may be more groups or fewer according to your analysis. But Patti's analysis is interesting and it allows her to draw the conclusion that alcoholics are people whose drinking falls into a pattern *that they cannot easily change*. It is important to understand that Patti has *invented* this classification through analysis of her experiences (her data). Her paper is not just an exercise in organization. Instead, it is the outcome of some very purposeful thinking by Patti as a result of her attempts to classify alcoholics.

There is some overlap in Patti's categories: some habitual drinkers are also heavy drinkers. In the ideal sense, categories should not overlap. But in the real world, classification may not work out so neatly, especially when the subject is human beings or human affairs. In Patti's case the overlap does not invalidate her categories and therefore is not a serious problem.

Categories don't always fall into a pattern or plan of organization, but Patti has arranged her categories more or less in order of severity—beginning with the mildest (heavy drinking) and progressing to the most severe (all-day drinking). Notice that in some cases she has additional supportive paragraphs for subcategories: under heavy drinkers there are subcategories for those who do and don't become "drunk."

We can point out one other important fact about Patti's paper by contrasting it with a different paper on the same subject. Imagine a paper in which alcoholics are classified according to how much and what kind of drunken behavior they exhibit. The paper might begin with those who seem not to have any kind of abnormal behavior—people who seem not to get drunk at all—and progress all the way to those who are found raving in alcoholic wards. In between these extremes we would have all sorts of behavior, including laughter, staggering and falling, vomiting, and so on. By contrast, Patti's classifications seem much more significant. "Drunken behavior" is too individualistic for alcoholics and nonalcoholics alike. A single individual in a single evening may progress from soberness through various stages of drunkenness to final collapse. Thus Patti's classification not only divides and types alcoholics, it offers *significant* classifications (even if some people might disagree with them) that help us understand something about the subject.

Patti's purpose in this paper is to convince us that alcoholics aren't just those drinkers who are entirely out of control. Although she draws on her own experience, her paper is appropriate for a general audience. Each reader must decide how effectively Patti conveys her message, but it is clear that Patti has come up with some thought-provoking insights into a very serious subject.

WRITING THE CLASSIFICATION PAPER

You must keep in mind that the purpose of classification is to find (invent) an idea. A quick and obvious classification (there are three sorts of people: tall, short, and medium) merely demonstrates what we already know. You must try various groupings and classifications, looking for one that will give you a new insight. Ask yourself So what? about each classification: people are fat, skinny, and medium . . . so what?

Try to invent mutually exclusive categories; avoid overlapping as much as possible. There is some overlapping in Patti's paper because she classifies alcoholics on *two* criteria: how *much* and how *often* they drink. If you classify people on how smart they are and how self-disciplined they are, you can see that there will be some cross-over between categories.

It seems obvious, but it's worth saying that you should not think of the categories first and then see how well you can apply them to the subject. For example, you know you can classify people as young, old, and middle-aged; can you work this into a classification paper? This is a poor idea. For one thing it is unoriginal. For another, it *forces* the classification: the subject is being made to fit a preconceived idea. It is a much better idea to analyze the subject, and then prewrite by trying to see what categories you can find *in* the subject (versus imposing one *on* the subject).

Writing activity

For this assignment, you need a subject concerning groups of things or things that come in large numbers. You can start thinking about very elementary things or very sophisticated ones. Pursue the subject until it yields a concept suitable for a relatively short paper (three to six pages). To help you get started we have provided the following list of unrefined subjects. (By "unrefined" we mean that the subjects can be broken down further. You might do a paper about athletes, but you might also do one about ballplayers, joggers, swimmers, and so on.)

ambitions	dates	insults	police officers
animals	doctors	jobs	preachers
athletes	dreams	lies	restaurants
cars	emotions	love	roads

clothes	excuses	motives	salespeople
coaches	fads	music	sports
colors	guns	painters	students
courage	horses	parents	symbols
dancers	hunters	personalities	teachers

THE PROCESS PAPER

The writer's explanation of a process—a method of doing something—cannot rely on assumptions of knowledge or familiarity on
the reader's part. Yet many recipes, directions, and instruction
booklets today are written as if readers really know most of the
process already and only need directions to remind them of the
order of the steps. But many people today would not know what
is meant by "dredge chicken parts before frying" or "prime
engine" or a number of other explanations that in fact do not explain. As a general rule, a writer should assume that readers do
not know even the most basic or routine information. Here, for
example, is a rather standard description of how to change a flat
tire, which relies on a considerable amount of assumed information
on the reader's part.

Set brakes and block wheels so that the car will not roll. Remove jack
and spare tire from trunk of car. Place jack under bumper and raise
car until flat tire clears the ground. Remove hubcap and lug nuts
with jack handle. Remove flat, place spare on wheel, and replace lug
nuts. Tighten lug nuts securely, using alternating pattern of opposing
nuts so that tire will fit evenly on wheel. Replace hubcap. Return
tire and jack to trunk.

With minor variations, most people would agree that's about
right—that is how to change a flat. It is basically just a matter of
getting the flat off and the spare on (assuming you have a spare in
working order; otherwise call the auto club). But this description
is only a summary of the process; it is aimed at people who already
know how to do it, or at least have a basic understanding of the
problems involved. However, in the following version of how to
change a flat, we get a considerably different view of the matter.

HOW TO
CHANGE
A FLAT

SYLVIA MORGAN

It makes little difference where or how the flat occurs; you may be
driving or the car may be at rest, but sooner or later you will be faced
with a decision to make. Changing a tire *can* be accomplished by nonmechanical mortals, and the garage mechanic *will* charge you ten

dollars to come out with his wrecker and do it for you. So you have a choice to make—should you try to change it yourself or call AAA? The following explanation of what is involved may help you make up your mind.

First, you probably should "block" the wheels so that the car will not roll—it is nearly suicidal to try to change a tire on a hill or even a slight incline—but there is almost never anything available to block with, so just set the brake and hope for the best.

The first problem is getting the jack and spare out. In many big and medium-sized cars, the spare is far back in the trunk, and the only way to reach it is to climb into the trunk—which is dirty. The jack has been cleverly concealed *under* the spare, which has been bolted down by a local garage jock with a machismo problem. If you are very strong you may succeed in freeing the spare from its bolt. The spare too is dirty, it is also heavy and bulky and therefore almost impossible to wrestle out of the trunk without getting fairly covered with dirt.

The modern jack comes in four or five pieces—one of which usually manages to be somewhere else (somewhere in the garage, basement, or down under the rear seat of the car) when you need it. The jack will not work unless all the pieces are present and assembled according to the diagram that came with it. If—as is probable—you no longer have the diagram, you will just have to experiment with different arrangements until you get one that will do what a jack is supposed to do. *Warning:* when the jack is *properly* set up, you will find a very small lip of metal that just barely fits under the car, even in cars that have a little square cut out of the bumper especially for the jack to fit into, causing the jack to be set rather gingerly like a spring catapult. Jacks have a tendency to spring out at you with enough force to break bones. Never trust the jack; once you start lifting the car, proceed very slowly and carefully and be prepared to jump for safety. The idea is to lift the car, not the bumper. If the bumper starts to groan and twist upward while the car remains on the ground, you have the jack in the wrong place. Look under the car until you can see the heavy metal frame the whole car rests on; get your jack under that to lift the car.

If you do get the jack to work properly, don't lift the flat off the ground until after you have loosened the lug nuts: struggles with the nuts may spring the jack. First remove the hubcap. The procedure is to pry it off with the chiseled end of the jack handle, also called the tire wrench. Since the chiseled end is not sharp enough to really fit under the edge of the hubcap very well, it will take some effort to get the hubcap off—another reason for keeping the wheel on the ground. Once off, you can start on the nuts. The other end of the jack handle has a socket on it just shaped to fit the nuts. Theoretically this socket cannot damage the nuts (which if "chewed" up by a loose wrench must be removed by a different kind of wrench—which you haven't got), but unless you hold it firmly and flatly on the nut, it will "chew" the edges off the nut until the wrench just slides uselessly around the smoothed (chewed) nuts. And you will find that the nuts have rusted to the bolts so that it will take tremendous leverage to move them—if they can be moved at all—which is why some of them have already been chewed somewhat. All nuts in America unscrew counterclockwise, but usually you just try it one way, and if that doesn't work you try it the other. It will usually take considerable force to loosen the nuts. You will of course not have any solvent or other helpful stuff to unfreeze a "frozen" nut.

If you get them loosened (not off yet), go back to the jack and carefully raise the car until the flat is clear of the ground. If you're lucky the nuts will give you no further trouble and you can remove them. Place the nuts inside the removed hubcap and move the cap with nuts out of the working area. Setting the nuts carefully on the ground, in your pocket, or anywhere else is a mistake. They will some- how roll under the car, where it will quite literally be worth your life to retrieve them. Inside the hubcap they will rattle and alert you if you accidentally kick them, and your chances of finding them again are infinitely greater if you remember to take this simple precaution.

Removing the flat is a little difficult. It is very dirty and heavy and *resting* on the bolts. If you are strong enough you can just squat down and lift it *up* and off the bolts; otherwise the best position is kneeling or sitting on the ground, from which you can lift and *pull* the tire toward you—you will get quite dirty this way. Be extra careful of the jack at this point, because without the wheel the car is as lethal as a guillotine and will operate like one with the slightest provocation.

With the flat off, you can now put the spare on. Make sure it has air in it first. Not only will it not work without air, but you will be very unhappy to discover it too is flat *after* you have gone through the labor of putting it on. A fully inflated tire will bounce and will solidly resist even your hardest kick—so test it first.

You will probably find that while the car is high enough to get the flat off, it is not high enough to get the spare on. Since the car is already quite high in the air and putting maximum tension on the jack, which is probably near its maximum elevation now, raising the car still higher has about the same risk as trying to defuse a bomb—extreme caution is advised.

The spare is even heavier than the flat—the air in it is not weight- less—and the holes for the bolts usually refuse to line up properly so that it will take some grunting and maneuvering to get the tire on. Replace the nuts in an alternating pattern: after the twelve o'clock nut, replace the six o'clock; after the three o'clock, the nine o'clock, and so on. This is so that you won't clamp down one side of the wheel, causing it to wobble and shimmy when it turns. Most people say that you should tighten all the nuts firmly while the car is in the air but leave the final turn for when the car is on the ground. This is so the force of the last turn won't shake the jack loose and also so the wheel can "settle" on the bolts.

Lowering the car is dangerous. The jack has a trigger on it that must be released to reverse the lifting action. You do not reverse *your* actions to lower the car. With the trigger released, the jack will automatically go backwards as you continue to pump as if lifting the car.

Once the car is on the ground, you can put the final leverage on the nuts. You need a good firm twist on them, but it is not necessary to rupture yourself over it. The wheel will not come off even without the final twist. Replace the hubcap if you can. It is a size smaller than the ridge it is supposed to fit over but will stretch slightly with sufficient pressure. In a garage, the hubcap is hammered on with a rubber mallet—anything else will simply dent it. Some people can put the cap on by hitting it a karate shot with the palm of the hand. Kicking it will not work. It is the least necessary component, so if the cap gives you very much trouble, just throw it into the trunk along with the jack and the flat tire. There is no point to being neat about putting things away; the flat will have to come out again soon to be repaired. You of course need a shower and a new outfit and three fingers of Scotch by now. One last warning—never accept helpers or kibitzers. They do not help, and the presence of a critic during an already difficult job will unsettle you enough to make you unable to function—unless of course they are going to take over and do the job for you . . . accept all such offers instantly and then wander off "to look for help" while the flat gets changed.

Sylvia's explanation of the process includes everything the manufacturer's brochure does not. It includes what *not* to do as well as what to do, and it points out problems and troubles that are likely to occur and what to do about them. Rather than make the process seem stupidly simple ("any child can do it") Sylvia gives us a fairly realistic view of the process.

Sylvia's paper is a composite of experiences—what usually happens when you change a tire. It could also have been written as a narrative of a single incident—what *happened* last Saturday. And it is possible to write a combination of both what happened and what happens: "I barked my knuckles on the lug nuts when the wrench slipped—as it usually does when you wrestle with a stubborn nut." In any case you need the skills you have already been using in your writing. If you write in the first person, especially if you write about a specific incident, your paper will come out sounding like a personal experience. If you write in the third person about a composite of experiences, you will be "generalizing" about your experiences and will produce a less personalized paper.

The people who wrote the papers below are trying to explain how to do something. Do they succeed? Do they tell you what you need to know as well as what to avoid? What are they doing right?

QUICK AM-
PUTATIONS:
HOW TO
AVOID THEM

ZACH HUMMEL

Most people believe that operating a chain saw is a simple and easy task, requiring little experience or knowledge, except maybe how to start one. They assume that with one pull of the cord they will be instant lumberjacks—slicing through trees, logs, fence posts, and so on, quickly and easily. However, they seem to ignore the fact that it will cut through toes, fingers, arms, legs, and even torsos just as quickly. A chain saw must be handled knowledgeably and with a great deal of respect if one cares to keep his bodily symmetry intact. Remembering how to ready the saw for cutting, how to start it safely, what not to do with the saw, and precautions to take against accidents will give you a safer cutting spree, and lower medical expenses. Operating a chain saw is not as easy as it sounds; common sense, caution, and a little knowledge are required for safe usage.

One of the most important things in cutting with a chain saw is to have a saw that is ready to cut. If the saw is not prepared properly it will not cut well and may be damaged as a result. Obviously, it should have a full tank of gas. You should be sure to check the owner's manual for any special requirements, such as oil mixed in. This can sometimes be found on the saw itself, also. The oil in the saw itself should be checked and kept full at all times. The chain should also be tight. The blade on a chain saw consists of two parts—the bar and the chain. The chain, which is the real cutting edge, runs along the bar, the long flat piece of metal sticking out front. If the chain is too loose it will jam during the cutting, and this can cause it to break—which can be nasty if the pieces fly in your face. If the chain is too tight, it will not move and may ruin the saw. You also won't get much cutting done. Here, also, the owner's manual should be checked for how to adjust the tension on your particular saw. Now you are ready to begin cutting—if, that is, you can get it started.

On face value, starting a chain saw is easy; however, if you have used one before, you know better—much better. The first, and one of the most important parts of starting the saw, is addressing it properly. This does not mean remembering to include the zip code or its proper title (Mr., Mrs., Your Excellency, and so on) but the way you position yourself in relation to the saw—much as addressing a golf ball on the tee. The saw should be placed on a solid object below waist level (the ground, a stump, whatever) so that it has a sturdy base. Place one hand on the brace, flick on the starter switch, give a sharp pull on the starter cord, and give it a little gas with the throttle as it sputters to life, and your chain saw is now started.

It would be nice if the world were as bright and perfect as owners' manuals would have you believe. It is not, however, that simple. All saws have their eccentricities; some you have to use the choke on, others you can't or they will flood, and still others have to have a combination. Take my saw, for example. It has its own particular ritual that must be performed before it will start. First, it must be dropped on the ground from knee level; then I have to turn on the starter switch and pull on the starting cord a few times. It will not start, so I pull out the choke and yank on the cord some more—it still will not start. I then pause and utter a few choice words and threaten it with dirty oil next oil change. If, after a few more pulls, it refuses to start, I bang it up against my victim (a dead tree or whatever) hoping it will incur the saw's wrath so the saw will start just to cut it down. Now, after a few more pulls, it should start. If all this fails, I just tell my father I can't work because the saw won't start. He comes out, and it starts first pull. This *never* fails and can be applied to almost any situation— kids and parents, husband and wife, man and mother-in-law, whatever. As soon as you tell someone that you can't work because it won't start— it will start the next time it is pulled. Once the saw is running, the throttle will control the engine and, therefore, the blade speed. You are now read to cut.

The actual cutting is the easiest, and therefore the most dangerous part of using a chain saw. The minute the saw is started it is deadly. The ease with which it cuts is very deceiving. You should not be lulled into forgetting the power and destruction potential that the saw has. All that is required is to place the bottom of the blade on whatever you are cutting and apply light pressure. Always make sure your legs are not in the saw's path. Do not place any part of your body in the path of the blade. It is possible to slip off, especially when starting the cut, and to end up cutting what you had not intended to. Do not use the tip of the blade to gouge into an object. The saw will kick back hard, and if you aren't ready it could have disastrous results. Be very careful cutting with the top of the blade. It should only be done when absolutely necessary. You should position your body so that any kick-back will not have a chance to throw the saw into you. If you remember these simple and obvious cautions, you will have a much safer time cutting.

I can best give a few tips on cutting down standing trees (the trickiest part of chain saw use) by telling how I found them out. Our house is heated by a wood furnace—not oil or electricity, but wood. This means that in winter we must have wood or no heat, and that means frozen water pipes, frozen feet, frozen hands—just plain frozen everything. I, being the oldest, was given the task of keeping the wood supply from running out. We live on a cherry farm and there is an old, dying orchard right out the back door. Convenient, huh? It would be except that all the dead ones are at the back of the orchard (you've heard of elephants going to their secret graveyard to die; well, it's much the same with cherry trees—they migrate to the back of the orchard to die), and in between are two hills that make the Matterhorn look puny.

So I slogged my way through the waist-high drifts of snow pulling my trusty toboggan (I pull all the wood I cut back in with it) and my chain saw. Just after I had scaled the first hill I spotted a small dead elm—considered the prime timber because it is much easier to cut and transport than cherry—and decided to cut that first. Amazingly the saw started first try (the first such happening since the fall of 1970), and soon I was slicing into the trunk of the tree. About ten seconds later the chain jammed; I couldn't pull the saw out and it quit. The tree had leaned back toward where I was cutting from, and there I was with my saw stuck and no way to get it out. This illustrates two things: one, no matter how much the tree looks like it's leaning away from where you are cutting, it will most likely tilt back and trap your saw—so always cut a notch on the opposite side just below where you are cutting. This will cause the tree to fall in that direction. Two, always carry an axe, just in case. It will get you, and your saw, out of many a jam. So I waded back through the drifts, got my axe, and started off once more into the frozen North.

So now you see that operating a chain saw is not as easy as it seems. You must have some knowledge as to what the saw will do, precautions to take, and even preparations that are necessary in order to operate it safely and effectively. If you follow these basic rules you can get all the wood you want yourself—and it won't cost you (either way) an arm and a leg.

Zach's paper uses a combination of what happens and what happened to show the reader how to operate a chain saw. Thus the paper differs from the preceding one in degree of personalization; Zach primarily uses third person, but he switches to first when he brings in his own experiences as examples. Note that Zach has organized the paper so that he first presents the ideal (as stated in the owner's manual) operation and then the real, thus allowing him to set up a nice contrast in the paper between the way things are "supposed" to go and the way they "really" go. There are many complimentary things you could say about all these papers, but one very important thing to say is that the authors know what they are talking about, and this fact alone allows them considerable freedom and flexibility of expression, enough so that the authors evidently have fun writing the papers.

Have you ever driven down old country roads and seen bushes just packed full of luscious ripe raspberries that made your mouth water? You probably got out and picked all you could eat and there were still berries left for the next guy. Well, last summer I found such a road. As I stuffed my mouth full, I thought how nice it would be to eat berries all winter long. Then I realized that homemade jelly would be the next best thing. Jelly has always been a favorite thing of mine, but one that is becoming more expensive to enjoy. That night I got out my trusty cookbook and read all about grocery stores and pricing ingredients; I was even more convinced that making jelly was the right thing to do.

The first step of course is to pick the raspberries. The cookbook doesn't include any instructions on berry picking but what could be easier? The day I chose was a nice hot summer day, a perfect day for a suntan. I put on my shorts and halter top and proceeded out to my berry patch. It didn't take me long to realize why the book provided no instructions. If it had, you would've been discouraged before you started. Don't ever wear shorts and a sleeveless top, because it'll take you approximately ten minutes before you are so scratched up that a box of bandaids couldn't cover the scratches. Since everyone that drives down the road stops to pick them, by the time I got there all the berries in the front were gone. I had to reach through and around the bushes. Thoughts of jelly made me forget about the scratches and I kept picking diligently away. Soon the flies and mosquitoes found me and I did as much slapping as picking. But still I kept picking on and on and on. I never realized just how many berries it took to fill my Shedd's peanut butter bucket. Well, it took about four hours of picking and eating and slapping to finally convince me that my pail was full enough. I headed home with the hardest part over with, or so I thought.

The next step is turning those nice plump raspberries into juice. This consists mainly of adding some water and cooking them until they're all smashed and gushy, a very easy step. My confidence returns! Since nobody likes those little seeds that get caught in your teeth while eating, you need to strain your juice through a jelly bag. A jelly bag is two squares of cheesecloth sewed together like a sack. You pour a small amount of juice into the bag, squeeze with all your might and presto (!) red hands and a little bit of raspberry juice. The red hands are an added attraction that you get to wear around for a couple of days. After you have squeezed through a couple of bags, the cuts in your hands start to sting from all the acid present in the berries. They continue to sting until it's all you can do to keep squeezing. But after a few more bags you have your juice and you're ready to get on with your jelly making. Your whole bucket of berries makes about three cups of juice. By now you have to think very hard about your jelly because you've just spent four hours picking and two hours smashing and squeezing and you haven't even started cooking! But you continue; all this work has made you determined to have that jelly.

101

Now you can take a break from the berries to prepare your jars and melt your paraffin. The paraffin part is easy but there are a couple of things to remember. Paraffin is very flammable so the melting should never be done over direct heat but in the top of a double boiler. A coffee can, bent to form a spout, placed in a pan of water does just as well and doesn't destroy a good pan. The paraffin should also be kept just at the point of liquefaction for the best sealing results. After you have the paraffin started, you can turn your attention to preparing the jars and glasses. These are washed in hot soapy water and then sterilized in boiling water. They are left in the pan until ready for use. The hot soapy water helps get some of the red off your hands but your scratches don't enjoy it much.

Finally, with all the preparations out of the way you can get down to what you started out to do, make jelly. The only ingredients required are fruit juice, pectin, and sugar. The recipe tells you exactly how much you need. You bring the juice and pectin to a rapid boil, stirring constantly, add the sugar and continue cooking for three minutes or until the sugar completely dissolves. This is easy enough and raises your spirits since you are now in the homestretch. However, don't forget that while the jelly is cooking you must remove your jars from the boiling water. Be careful not to contaminate them. Place them on a level counter next to your jelly pot. You have all of five minutes in which to do this, not neglecting to stir your jelly at the same time. Good luck! Finally it's time to pour your jelly into the jars and finish this project that you have begun to have doubts about. This involves several precautions if you want your jelly to be sealed properly. Fill the jars about one half inch from the top, being extremely careful not to drip jelly on the rims. A funnel will work best. Also watch out for air bubbles; these can easily be skimmed off the top with a spoon.

Your jars are full and ready to be sealed. Pour the paraffin into the jars immediately and only one-eighth-inch thick. To ensure a good seal, paraffin must touch the side of the glass and be even. Prick any bubbles that appear on the paraffin, as they may allow spoilage. When the paraffin is hard, check the seal. Cover the jars with metal or paper lids. Store in a dark, dry place.

At last your jelly is done! Well at least almost done; it must cool and jell before you can eat it. This doesn't bother you much though, because after a whole day of berry picking and cooking you'd just as soon it was in a dark place out of your sight for a while. Having to clean up your mess doesn't improve your attitude much. Afterwards you may ask yourself if it was worthwhile, and though it may not seem like it at that time, it certainly was. This really becomes evident every time you open the cupboard door and reach for a jar of that sparkling, homemade jelly that tastes five times better than any you ever bought in the store and costs about one-fourth the price. The very best is when you can tell people, "I made it myself," and they look at you and think, "Oh, wow!" Of course when they ask you if it was hard to make, you casually reply, "Not at all." Let them find out for themselves!

Susan has divided her process into clearly recognizable steps or stages, and thus her paper has a very formal order, although the language in it is still somewhat informal. The wealth of physical description in this paper helps to turn an otherwise ordinary process into a colorful experience. Note that the writers of each of these three papers prefer the less formal "you" to "one" when referring to the reader.

WRITING THE PROCESS PAPER

When you describe a process remember your audience. People who already know part or all of the process don't need directions. In writing for the uninformed you cannot *assume* anything, not even names of standard tools and components such as crescent wrench, rotor, bobbin, and so on. (Ask a child if you are not sure what the audience may know.)

Break the process into its component stages. If there are preparatory stages or a necessary order to the steps, be sure to present them in the order they are needed. Readers may not read all the directions first—even if you tell them to. It may be too late after several directions about salting and flouring the inside of a chicken to mention the fact, "You should be sure to wash out the body cavity with boiling water *first*." You must also anticipate every conceivable problem and tell the reader what *not* to do *before* the reader is likely to do it.

Writing activity

Write a three- to six-page paper in which you describe a process. Keep two things in mind. First, choose a process that you understand thoroughly so that your description will be accurate and complete. Second, stay aware of your reader. A step-by-step description need not be boring, as you can tell from the process papers in this section.

You may want to choose a process to describe from the following list:

How to fry, bake, roast, or otherwise cook a chicken or other food
How to clean a rifle, carburetor, typewriter, or other machine
How to make a dress, shirt, other clothing
How to tie a fly
How to clean (for cooking) a fish, rabbit, deer, other game
How to embalm a body
How to fill out the income-tax long form
How to conduct an interview
How to wax skis
How to cut down a large tree

How to use the subway
How to present yourself in traffic court
How to shop in a second-hand store
How to put on makeup
How to impress a date
How to behave at a tea party
How to bathe a dog, cat, other pet
How to conduct yourself in a job interview

DEFINITION

A considerable amount of modern knowledge is devoted simply to *identifying* reality. We are constantly defining and redefining ideas, terms, objects, situations, and so on, not out of curiosity or as an intellectual exercise but because we are aware that we react to reality according to the way we define it—even if the definitions are wrong! Thus the definition of "Negro" or "woman" has become the reality that blacks and females have had to fight against. A definition is more than a label; it is a mind-set.

Most people do not bother themselves about the definitions of things. Their concepts are unexamined; they take things for granted. They assume the world is whatever it was when they were children—when most words are learned. But a writer cannot afford to operate with unexamined or naive concepts. In fact, it is chiefly the writer's duty—specifically—to explore concepts and thus to reexplore and redefine reality. The dictionary, unfortunately, is not very helpful. Dictionary definitions are invented by the dictionary makers, who must give in the least possible space, with the fewest possible words, the most general, overall definitions. The dictionary is a good place to start if you are trying to define a word, but as a writer you then go on from this general definition to say, or try to say, what the word means specifically, in a given context.

Here, for example, is a writer's attempt to define a word:

SENIORITIS

CONNIE TRUJILLO

Ever since my freshman year in high school I had heard many references to people having had cases of a thing called "senioritis," but I had never seen a definition of the word. I just knew the seniors used the word to explain why they were doing things that they weren't supposed to; and when teachers used it, it provoked sighs, exasperation, and sometimes mildly indulgent smiles. Perhaps the word is relatively new? Maybe someone recently invented it? I don't know, but "senioritis" is real, as I discovered in my senior year.

Senioritis is a frame of mind particular to high-school seniors. Most seniors experience their first tinges of this feeling after the class ahead of them graduates. It is then that seniors find themselves at the top of all the other grade levels, for they represent the class with the greatest number of years of education. This advanced status and the few but well-deserved privileges that are traditionally extended to seniors lead to a feeling of superiority over the underclassmen—the proverbial "swelled head."

Senioritis's particular state of mind carries with it rather odd and sometimes whimsical actions on the part of seniors. For instance, a senior may decide to sing in the library for the sheer intention of remaining impervious to the librarian's scornful stare. I found myself caught up in the spirit of senioritis one afternoon one week, when I raced two of my best friends across the grass to the cafeteria for lunch —and our lunches were not that good! I have seen several of my fellow seniors caught up in such frenzies of whimsy that they develop "skip-school-or-die" complexes, and despite rigid penalties, many mysterious absences subsequently occur. Thus seniors' actions, while under the influence of senioritis, are not logical or subject to reason.

However, senioritis is not a mere desire to create total havoc or mischief. Although havoc and mischief frequently result, they are merely byproducts of the affected senior's mind. Also, senioritis can not be encompassed by the word "pride," for pride is only one of many elements that affect the senior's ego. However, the special treatment given seniors does lead to the formation of a class pride, which is responsible for a large portion of the senioritis symptoms. Senioritis is not quite a tradition either, for although it occurs in each subsequent class year, it is not really handed down and passed on. It seems to be more of an annually recurring phenomenon.

Thus, senioritis is a way of thinking, feeling, and acting that is not logical and is frequently impervious to social codes. It is an odd and whimsical state of being that can only be truly experienced by a high-school senior.

You can see from Connie's paper that she hasn't set herself a linguistic problem—it isn't just a *word* she wants to define, but an idea or concept. She doesn't rush to the dictionary for help; in this case there wouldn't be any help, but if she had found the word in the dictionary, the definition would have been something like "The peculiar restlessness of high-school seniors." This is only a generalization and leaves the reader with a big question—*What* peculiar restlessness? And it is that question that Connie tries to answer by giving specific concrete examples. Connie also goes on to distinguish "senioritis" from a closely related term like "self-pride" because the reader needs to be able to see what the thing is *not* as well as what it is, especially when there are similar but not quite the same terms for it (like the difference between love and affection). You can try this same kind of defining with other "itis" words: freshmanitis, examinationitis, and so on.

Surprisingly, there are any number of concepts for which we do not have words; we either just ignore the concepts, or use some inexact term for them, or invent a new word:

NON-MECHANICAL

BILL YEKESTITCH

Some people are "nonmechanical"—not just that they don't do well at mechanical tasks; it's much worse than that. There is something very hostile or negative about their interactions with mechanical things. They are people for whom doorknobs come off in their hands, people who cannot assemble the components of a coffeepot no matter how simple the components or how obvious the assembly, people who break or have accidents with mechanical objects. They are people like my girl Alice, whose approach to mechanical things is so *unmechanical* that I can't stand to watch her do it. It isn't that machines and such intimidate her or cause her problems—they don't. Alice is blithely unconcerned for the *logic* of a machine, for the *mechanics* of anything mechanical. Thus if a picture pulls loose from the wall, she will grab a hammer and a three-inch nail, and before I can stop her, hammer two fist-sized holes and a foot-long crack into the frail plaster. If the Mixmaster jams, she will thump and pound it and twist at the metal beaters until the machine expires and then dump it in the trash as "broke." Her attitude is that mechanical things are there to serve her and they had better not fool around, because if there is going to be any intimidating, it is the machine that is in trouble!

Bill shows us that "nonmechanical" is the closest thing that we have to define the concept, but "nonmechanical" is hardly an accurate term for what is involved. He is looking for a term like "antimechanical" or something similar, to describe a much more actively hostile attitude than the milder "unmechanical." Distinguishing between closely related terms is one good technique for defining, as in the following:

EMBARRASS-MENT AND HUMILIATION

YOLANDA SHERWOOD

I have a friend who is forever saying that everything is so *humiliating* —it's so *humiliating* to have to live in a dorm, it's so *humiliating* to go to a lecture, it's so *humiliating* to sweat, and so on. She uses the word to cover everything from mild embarrassment to simple annoyance but almost never uses it in connection with true humiliation. I'd say the difference between embarrassment and humiliation is the difference between an accident—a *faux pas*—and an insult. The one you cause yourself, but the other has to be done to you.

For example, I was taking a survey on Ecology in a men's dormitory. Being female I didn't mind at all, although I was a little uneasy at the prospect of interviewing so many men in such a short time.

Two of the things that made my rounds so hazardous were the fact that I was unannounced and that it was at about ten o'clock at night, a time when many of the men don't expect female visitors.

The first few rooms weren't very active. When I got to the sixth room, though, things really began to roll.

I knocked on the door, expecting someone to open it. Instead one of the occupants answered my knock with a gruff "Come in." Being a little apprehensive at what I might find, I knocked again, this time receiving a loud, powerful chorus of slightly irritated "Come ins." I still didn't think that I should enter without an okay, so I knocked a third time, and what a response! I heard a thunderous, bellowing roar of "God-dammit-to-hell!" The door was suddenly flung open so hard I thought the door would rip off its hinges for sure. It was almost as if a hurricane had attacked it.

There just inside the door stood the biggest hunk of man that I had ever seen! He was a six-foot, five-inch giant with curly black hair almost completely covering his very muscular chest and legs. His huge hands were still grasping the door, making the tremendous muscles of his arms stand out. He stood there in his skivvies in absolute shock. As for myself, I was shaking so much that I thought my legs were going to buckle for sure. I could feel my face turning from white to red to darker red and then white again. All of this happened in about four devastating seconds: *this* is embarrassment.

It didn't take him long to revive. Within another second he had slammed the door in my face and retreated inside, accompanied by the laughter of his roommates. But before I could move a muscle, the door opened again and he was back, leaning smugly against the door jamb. With his arms folded across his chest and a nasty sneer on his face he said, "Well, now that you've seen it all, little girl, what can I do for you?" I could feel my face doing a slow burn, staying red this time, but I recovered my mind almost instantly. "Now that I've seen it, you haven't got it, sonny," I said and stormed out of there in a huff. We had both been embarrassed by the sudden confrontation, but when he tried to recover his poise by putting me down, that was humiliation, and I hope I gave him a little lesson in it myself.

Yolanda's paper is a good example of distinguishing between two related terms, which is very similar to distinguishing between different degrees of the same term, as in the following:

EARL TORRENTO

There is drunk and then there is *drunk*. In my experience, there are at least three or four stages of drunkenness, ranging from a pleasant glow of tipsiness all the way to the roaring blind staggers. My mother immediately accuses my father of being "drunk" after the first sip of beer, and thereafter dismisses anything he says as "drunken ravings." Obviously she does not understand the term or the condition. This paper will graph the various degrees of drunkenness and its characteristic behaviors and symptoms.

One other technique in defining is to distinguish the real from the ideal. We have myths, stereotypes, common ideas (cant), legends, and any number of other "variations" of reality. Advertising in particular is very good at giving us a view of reality that sounds too good to be true. In the following excerpt, for example, the writer distinguishes between the ideal and the real automobile much as if he were writing a comparison and contrast paper:

HAL REED

Sleek, powerful, gleaming with luster and shine, a high performance, efficient dream machine crouches lovingly at the curb. Sex symbol par excellence! Swiftly, silently, it will sweep you away in one long, smooth, sweepingly luxurious flight away, away, away from where you are to where you would rather be. Magic! Transportation Unlimited. Forward, forward, forward unhindered, couched and cradled in beauty, comfort, and love. Imagine being in it! Imagine owning it! Imagine DRIVING it! The is the a-u-t-o-m-o-b-i-l-e! *Car,* the ad man hurls at us.

Would this wonder cause you a problem? Could anything associated with it not be beautiful? Is it possible that the automobile is anything less than God's final and most perfect creation? Well, have you looked at your crate lately?

Hal's paper goes on to dissect the myth of the car by contrasting what the car is "supposed to be" according to car makers with what it turns out to be—an unromantic machine that frequently doesn't work.

In all these definitions, the *concrete example* or illustration is the important element. After that, the comparison or distinction between one term and another, between different degrees of the same term, or between different interpretations of reality (the real and the ideal) helps to make the definitions precise.

Read the following paper. Is the term well defined? What method of definition does the student use?

FRUSTRATION

LINDA BLACK

From the time you unsuccessfully attempt your first steps until the time you unsuccessfully attempt to lift yourself out of your rocking chair, you will have undoubtedly felt the feeling known as frustration. While there are varying degrees of frustration, results ranging from mild irritation to acute rage, the main problem with frustration is that it breeds on not knowing how to handle frustration itself. Therefore, defining frustration might be useful in learning to cope with it.

Frustration is experienced when you must overcome some obstacle to reach your goal. The only problem is that the obstacle is usually insurmountable, and the goal unreachable. This can occur in a number of situations. One example of mild frustration would be your reaction to telephoning a friend for a ride home for the weekend and finding that his phone is busy. You might react with a simple sigh. If, after two hours of calling every five minutes, his line was still busy, frustration could develop into a more advanced stage, and your response might be one of verbal distaste. If after four hours, and missing two classes and the bus home, your friend finally answers and informs you that he's not going home for the weekend, frustration could become uncontrollable and your response could be one of resorting to physical violence, such as ripping the phone off the wall.

So, frustrations can vary as to the degree of responses they bring out. Everyday frustrations, while very annoying, probably cause the least amount of response since you must cope with these types on a daily basis. Some situations that can cause everyday frustrations are as follows: when you are playing Euchre and your partner trumps your ace, when you really *are* eighteen and the bar still won't accept your I.D., when you wake up at 10:15 and you had an 8:00 class, or when you stay up until 4:00 A.M. to study for an exam and then find out that the professor was called out of town and the exam is postponed for a week. Since these kinds of frustrations can occur on a daily basis, you learn to respond to them in socially acceptable ways, such as gritting your teeth, counting slowly to ten, or swearing silently to yourself or to your roommate.

The number of frustrating experiences that occur on a given day is also directly related to the degree of response. Since responses to frustrations are almost always negative, the more frustrations that occur, the more negative the responses will become. Suppose, for example, that you wake up on an average Tuesday morning to find that the only clothes you own are either dirty or are presently being worn by your roommates. Without getting too upset, you attempt to do your laundry, and discover that your dorms provide two washers and one dryer for approximately eighty-five females, and just about thirty of these females do their laundry on Tuesday morning. At this point, you might be able to detect your face growing a little hot, fists clenching and unclenching, but gradually you calm down, accept the circumstances, put on the cleanest pair of dirty jeans you have, and go to class. Once in class, you learn that the professor has prepared a pop quiz for you. Feeling pretty much at ease, since you have been studying hard for this class, you take one look at the quiz and discover that it is written in Urdu, or some other equally unintelligible language, and your mind, now totally blank, refuses to function. The first reaction might be one of panic, gradually dissolving to a "what's-the-use" attitude, and finally to an extreme dislike for the professor. But at this point, you would probably only mumble something under your breath.

This frustrating Tuesday continues with such occurrences as forgetting your key and getting locked out of your room and losing your food card, each time the responses becoming more and more openly negative, and leaning more and more towards uncontrolled violence. Finally in an effort to unwind and relieve some of the tension brought about by the day's frustrations, you go to the bar for the ten-cent draft-beer special. As you are standing in line with your two dimes, actually starting to feel human again, the bartender rings a bell and announces "Special's over!" Something in your brain snaps as you feel the blood rushing towards your face and your hands rushing towards the bartender's neck, but something holds you back. Perhaps it is the last thread of self-control.

Wanting only to go home, take a shower, go to bed, and end this dreadful day, you walk back to your room, undress, and step into the warm, steamy shower. Suddenly, as you are standing in the shower in your altogether, you hear the bathroom door fly open and several loud, mirth-filled chuckles from your roommates as they grab your clothes, and all the towels in the bathroom and run down the hall with them. This is frustration. Perhaps under normal circumstances this little pimp * would not have bothered you too much, but as the frustrations of the day slowly piled up, your response could be explosive. You then have the choice of killing your roommates, beating your head against the shower stall, or having a nervous breakdown.

Because one requirement of frustration is not having any control over the situation, maybe there really is nothing you can do about the negative responses that result from it. And that's frustrating.

* *Pimp:* to play a trick on; obscure midwestern college term.

WRITING THE DEFINITION PAPER

Expand, illustrate, give examples to demonstrate the meaning of the word; contrast the word with others close in meaning; show varying degrees of meaning. Compare the old meaning with newer meanings, or contrast the ideal meaning with the real. In every case, offer the reader concrete details with which to understand the word.

Writing activity

For your first attempt at defining, write a two- to four-page definition. Avoid large and difficult abstractions like *honor, philosophy, love,* and so on. You will have the most success with words for physical objects or physical behavior, such as the following:

dancing	mania
dating	nonathletic
freshmen	poverty
hassles	rip-off
helpful people	sarcasm
hustling	tension
insults	vitality
kleptomania	winter

W

here there is much
desire to learn, there
of necessity will be much arguing, much writing,
many opinions; for opinion in good men is but
knowledge in the making.

JOHN MILTON, *Aereopagitica*

One of the advantages of writing over speaking is the depth and precision of reasoning that writing permits. With the written word you can construct longer and more complex arguments. And since you can edit and revise the written word, you can achieve greater accuracy of both thought and expression. It is no wonder, then, that people have such high regard for the writing that presents human thought: opinions, arguments, judgments, and persuasion.

It is not enough to collect data, sort it, and file it away. Computers are better at such work than we are. It takes a human mind to challenge the data, to argue the merits of an idea, to upset settled notions and arrive at new insights, new concepts. For the writer, the real challenge is not in recording facts, but in questioning them: ultimately, writing is *thinking*.

How we convince each other of the truth is at the heart of democracy. It is built into our legislatures and our judicial system: evidence is introduced; reasons are given; conclusions are drawn. We argue for our convictions. Learning how to create a carefully developed, reasonable argument represents a significant step in the development of a writer.

CRITICAL WRITING

Critical writing, in the sense in which we are using that term, is writing that evaluates, that judges the worth of something. Very often such writing seems negative rather than constructive because critics feel the need to warn us against inferior works. But obviously a critique or critical review could be largely positive or constructive.

In order to criticize something either positively or negatively (or both), the critic must be thoroughly knowledgeable not only about the specific work being judged but also about the principles and techniques of the art represented by the work. You will have more to say about any particular car if you know a lot about cars in general: engineering, design, and performance. If you are writing about art, literature, films, television, and so on, you need to tell the reader both *what* happened, in a play, for example, and *how* it was performed, what techniques were used. And then of course you must *judge* the performance. Was it good, bad, mediocre? Were the techniques effective? Was the message worthwhile?

To make such judgments, you must have a sense of what is good—from your own experience, from study, from cultural tradition, and so on. To be a critic you must care about quality. You must have a strong sense of how things *should* be done, even if human effort is not capable of perfection.

For example, read the following critique of a recent film:

THE DEEP

LINDA LENAHAN

The Deep is a chilling underwater adventure based on the book of the same title by Peter Benchley. *The Deep* has mostly the same elements as *Jaws*, Benchley's first financial blockbuster: the ocean, danger, adventure, and death. It is a typical good-guys-versus-bad-guys plot.

The movie is about a young couple, played by Nick Nolte and Jacqueline Bisset, who are vacationing at a Bermuda resort. While diving one day, the two find a shipwreck which contains thousands of ampules of morphine. Under the World War II wreck, there is another old Spanish ship with royal eighteenth-century gold and jewels buried in it. A Haitian drug dealer chases the couple throughout the movie to get access to the morphine so he can sell it as heroin to dealers in New York City. The couple is more interested in the royal treasure, though. They hire a boat captain, played by Robert Shaw, who is also a courageous treasure hunter and expert diver, to help prove the authenticity of the royal treasure.

The movie is full of adventure, and parts of the show may be too violent for a young viewer to see. There are scenes of voodoo, the sound of someone's neck breaking, the sight of a turning propeller on an outboard motor held close to someone's face, a deadly moray eel attacking a man in one of the sunken ships, and an outdoor elevator falling and killing a man.

At times the movie got quite boring. This is a problem for all underwater movies, though. The basic problem is that when people swim under water, it seems like it is done in slow motion. This makes the movie seem more stretched out and boring. The writers of *The Deep* were clever enough, in some cases, to distract us from the problem of underwater slowness by piling up devices such as the moray eel, the beautiful reefs, the sunken ship, sharks, and great underwater photography.

The acting in the movie was pretty good. Of the three stars, though, Robert Shaw outdid Bisset and Nolte with his performance. Nick Nolte, who's supposed to be a prime contender for Robert Redford's spot as number one sex symbol, didn't really add too much to the role he played. Ms. Bisset just proved how nice she could look under water in her much publicized T-shirt.

It's really hard to judge acting in an underwater movie. Everyone has a mask on, and no one can talk, so it's really hard to judge a person's acting ability. It would be easier to judge their swimming ability.

My last gripe about the movie is that it makes the bad guys (who all happen to be black) look like sex fiends. In one scene they force Ms. Bisset to strip in front of them, even though they know she could not possibly hide the large medallion that they are searching for. Later, the Haitians invade her room dressed in voodoo outfits, smear her body with blood, and they seem to do something rather queer with a chicken claw that they carry around for their ritual.

Although there are many bad points to the film, there are good ones too. The photography was just terrific. Even if you don't enjoy watching underwater films, the photographs of the activities are so exceptional, you'd surely admire the photographer. Overall, it was a good movie, but it was overpublicized by the media. After seeing all of the publicity, a person would be led to believe that *The Deep* was the biggest hit next to *Gone with the Wind*, and it really can't stand up to that sort of competition.

Linda is a very convincing critic. We can believe she thoroughly remembers the film. Notice the kinds of things she recalls: names of actors, key incidents of the plot, and even specific details. Furthermore, she makes comparisons between this film and another based on a novel by the same author and between this film and other adventure films in general. We can believe Linda understands the work she is evaluating.

There are many elements one might judge in a film review: plot, acting, directing, dialogue, pacing, setting, photography, and so on. The more you know about how films are made, the more confident you will feel in your critiques of them. The same is true of television shows, sports events, and any other performance or work. The more you know about the art, the more you can analyze it critically. Linda has selected several of the key elements in film-making to use in her critique, those that seem most relevant to *The Deep:* the plot, pacing, acting, social commentary or point of view (which Linda feels is racist), photography, and even the publicity campaign, which seemed to promise more than the film could deliver.

And Linda attempts to be fair. She cites problems in the film —such as pacing—but shows that she understands this as inherent in films of this kind. She does point out good qualities of the film.

WRITING THE CRITICAL PAPER

One of the critic's jobs is to give the reader a reasoned evaluation of a work so that the reader can judge whether to experience that work for him- or herself. Another is to help establish or maintain standards of excellence by which to evaluate similar works. As a critic, your basic function is to report what you observed and what you thought about what you observed. Therefore, one good way to start a review is to describe for the reader what the performance was like; you can't assume the reader also saw the concert or read the book or listened to the album.

Of course, there are different criteria for evaluating such diverse kinds of works as films, television shows, graphic arts, writing, music, and even food. As you explore any of these fields, you will learn about both the specifics to be judged and the standards of excellence by which other people judge works in the field. But you can be a critic without being an expert, because the general principle for criticism is to experience and judge simultaneously, and then to convince the reader of the reasonableness of your judgment.

Merely describing the plot of a film, for example, isn't enough. Is the plot believable, even if it concerns Superman or Frankenstein's monster? (Does the audience forget about the improbable and get caught up in the story?) Do you *care* about the story and the characters? Does the story have moral, social, psychological, or some other kind of value? In the same way, just describing the lines and colors of a painting isn't enough. Is the idea behind the painting clear, even if the painting is a yellow square painted on a white background? What reaction does looking at the painting create in you? What causes the reaction: the idea, colors, lines, subject? Is there any value to the painting? In all cases, what do *you* think? How do *you* rate what you've seen, heard, felt, touched, tasted?

In giving your criticisms, there are two things to remember. Critics gain influence to the degree that the public perceives them as reasonable and accurate. Critics who seem to be biased or merely personal in their criticisms will appeal only to those who share their biases. So try to give a balanced criticism; state both strengths *and* weaknesses if you can. Second, back up what you say by citing examples. Note in the following papers how often the writers give examples to illustrate their criticism. Using supportive evidence goes a long way toward establishing the critic's believability. In effect it says, "Don't take my word for it; judge for yourself. Here is the evidence!"

Assume the following three papers are the winners in a contest to select the new critic for the school newspaper. Which would you select? Ask yourself these questions: Is the writer factual? Is the writer interesting? Does the paper appeal to the general reader? What has the writer done to convince the reader?

THE TELEVISION MOVIE *SYBIL*

ANNE BASSETT

Sybil is a book by Flora Rita Schreiber about a woman who was so torn apart psychologically that she could cope with life only by dissolving into sixteen separate personalities.

Several years after the book (which is an actual case history) was released, Sybil's story was depicted in a television movie, which starred Sally Field as Sybil and Joanne Woodward as her doctor. This review will concentrate on the movie.

Although most movies that are based on a book tend to be disappointing, *Sybil* paid honest attention to the facts and was exceptionally good for a television movie.

The movie did omit quite a bit of material, but this was because of the time factor and because some of the scenes in the book—for example, the grotesque punishments Sybil's mother inflicted on her—would have been too graphic to portray on television. Some of these punishments—hanging Sybil upside down from a light-cord, giving her icy enemas, and stuffing her in a wheat bin—were shown, but they were done in good taste.

I had doubts that the most fascinating aspect of Sybil's story—that of her fall into mental illness and the complexity of maintaining her sixteen personalities—could be portrayed well, but I was surprised. Although the complete puzzle of Sybil's inner makeup could obviously not be shown in a three-hour movie, the producers of this show did an unusual thing for television: instead of attempting to show the complete puzzle and inevitably leaving pieces out, they simply made a smaller, whole puzzle. Therefore, although some information was left out, the movie remained unified, and no real harm was done to the story.

The performances by Joanne Woodward and Sally Field were superb; I think Sally Field did an exceptional job, since she was, in a sense, taking an assignment meant for sixteen people. Both of these actresses managed to make the characters they portrayed real and convincing.

In short, I think the movie version of *Sybil* was a well-organized, factual, and thought-inducing show.

THE
ENFORCER

DON JOHNSON

Clint Eastwood movies always seem to remind me of the most violent occurrences in the world, and *The Enforcer* was no exception. Good old Clint single-handedly knocks off about half of San Francisco in this flick.

Inspector Harry Calihan (Eastwood) is the blueprint of the tough city cop. He handles life-or-death situations with the coolness that only he possesses.

The movie is about a revolutionary group that steals some of the army's most dangerous weapons and leaves a trail of blood wherever it goes. Harry's partner is killed by one of these terrorists and he and his .44 Magnum vow to put them behind bars or in their graves. The first woman detective on the force is assigned as Calihan's new partner and his only reply to this move is a sarcastic "marvelous." She proves to be an asset to him, however, as she ends up saving his skull twice. The second time is fatal to her as she takes two bullets in the breast just to save Harry. Harry becomes rather irate and blows up the remaining member of the group with a small bazooka.

The Enforcer is basically a second-rate movie with its ups and downs. Unfortunately, the downs outnumber the ups. When there is action it is exciting. They say violence isn't good in the movies, but I love it and I think everyone else does too. The only thing better is sex.

The bloody scenes that stand out are truly thrilling. A man comes walking out of a house with a couple of bottles of beer. The killer stands waiting with his double-barreled shotgun. He blasts the man, making sure to hit the bottles. The white shirt suddenly turns crimson red.

Another part showed Harry's partner putting a slug through a nun's head. The nun was just going to shoot Harry. You just can't trust anyone.

The movie would be better if better dialogue and plot were used. Eastwood's wisecracks are funny, but they just don't seem to fit the situation. Here is an example. The mayor of 'Frisco has just been kidnapped, and the captain comes to Calihan for some information, just after suspending him. The captain questions him, and Harry asks if he can tell him something personal. "Your mouthwash just ain't making it," says Harry.

The plot jumps from part to part and never seems to stay consistent. One minute they're fighting bad guys and the next they're at a baseball game.

Clint Eastwood is one of my favorite actors because he is the baddest good guy I know. I get a kick out of seeing him blow somebody's head off. *The Enforcer* is not an award winner, but it is a movie where you can sit back and watch some good, clean violence.

SO MUCH FOR ROCK-JAZZ

SUE MACMANAWAY

Last evening was the long-awaited performance of Jean-Luc Ponty at Warriner Auditorium. Anticipation was very high among ticket buyers and in the crowd awaiting entrance before the concert. This was going to be good. Jean-Luc Ponty in person—jazz-rock would never be better.

Or so I thought. Anticipation was first replaced with thoughts of survival. When the doors opened, the crush of people for choice seats literally pushed you in ahead of them. But the ticket takers were just as quick at grabbing as people were at pushing. Next thing I knew, I lost my stub right after getting shoved into a squeeze play between two competing fans. Concert crowds are always predictably pushy and rowdy, especially for any musician who plays anything but serious music. The younger the crowd, the more pushing and grabbing there seems to be; crowd control is no control.

Back to Ponty. Promptly at 8:05 P.M. the warm-up came on. Usually, I expect the warm-up to be a bit dull and just a stall tactic so the main man won't have to play so long. Jim Amend, pianist, entered stage left and gave us all a surprise. He was good. A one-man concert that could stand on its own without leading Jean-Luc Ponty. Jim was swift to enter stage and begin playing, an unusual aspect of concerts. A late start of fifteen to twenty minutes is common, and general goofing around by the artist before he begins playing is the norm also.

Jim, with his kinky, long hair and red jump suit looked like a leftover from 1970. I awaited something brash to come out of his piano. What I got was a masterful piece of art which was a joy to hear and to watch being played. No new music experiments with finger-pluncked keys or excessively repeated strains. The style was serious, almost classical in origin. Interesting runs and chords punctuated his original melodies and themes. Between themes he would give us a sometimes humorous recital of a theme familiar to us all. Something from Looney Tunes cartoons or a horror movie. Other times he used familiar passages from the classics of Beethoven and Bach.

Two of the selections he played contained short sections of verse, mostly original, about love and loneliness. At a couple of points he borrowed verses from a popular song called "Motherless Child" and an old English song, "Wild Mountain Theme." At the conclusion of each piece, all of which were lengthy, the audience gave Jim a sound ovation. Acceptance of his music and style was complete. We were entertained thoroughly. One would almost have thought he would have been called back for an encore except that it was 9:00 P.M. and we wanted Jean-Luc Ponty.

The stage crew had it very much together and rearranged equipment quickly and with no problem. Concert crowds appreciate swiftness. The stage was set to go, but no Jean-Luc Ponty graced the stage until ten minutes later; at least he did not make it twenty minutes. Clapping was commencing and angry crowds please no one.

The band entered and then Ponty came on with violin bows in hand. We were ready. The band warmed up swiftly and they went right into "Tarantula." It was good. The sound equipment was excellent. Mixing and lighting were just as well done. Ponty's violin bow danced across the strings quickly, slowly, hopped, raced, and sent shivers down your spine. The succeeding songs, "Garden of Babylon" and "Fantastic Voyage," proved his excellence in playing violin.

One problem ruined the entire experience. The P.A. was too loud. Ponty's mix of jazz and rock is effective and beautiful, but not at 120 decibels. My ears hurt and my head ached to the point of just wanting to get up and leave. My favorite jazz violinist was driving me away. Such an excellent concert should never be ruined by such a simply corrected problem. At least the P.A. had no distortion to ruin the beauty of Ponty's music. Two encores proved that.

Writing activity

Select a recent film, television show, book, concert, athletic event, or some other happening or work to review in a three- to six-page paper. Use as your guide only that what you choose to write about should be something you really do have a reaction to, and something you remember well enough to treat with detail and specificity. You will be surprised to discover that with a little effort you can remember names, dialogue, and other useful details. Pick a single work—a specific performance or a specific book—to evaluate. If you try to do a composite (what *All in the Family* is usually like, instead of what last week's episode was like), you may find the job is too big to handle in a short paper, and too hard to remember accurately.

REASONING AND REASONABLENESS

The foundation of much formal writing is logical thinking, or more broadly, reasoning. In informal situations, especially emotional ones (such as a fight), logic may not be very effective, because once the emotions have been aroused, most people insist on settling matters at *that* level. It is a cliché, but true, that it takes cool heads for reason to prevail. Nevertheless, it has been the hope of educated people throughout history that, at least in formal situations, especially in formal writing, the prevailing strategy would be logic, reasonableness.

Though the full development of a logical system can be complex, the basic machinery of logic is relatively simple. Logic is a system for making statements without error and as such has three components that any writer should learn: a method for making clear statements, a method for testing statements, and a list of typical errors to watch for.

CLEAR STATEMENTS

It is sometimes said that most of our arguments would disappear if we would just define our terms. That may not be completely true, but it is a good idea to define the terms of an argument as precisely as possible. Before you test any statement, you should reduce it to its *standard form:* the simplest statement of subject and predicate.

SUBJECT

The thing being discussed, the name of someone or some other designator of a person (usually).

PREDICATE

A statement about the subject, some characteristic or quality of the subject we can argue about.

EXAMPLE

   (*subject*)   (*predicate*)
The government / is corrupt.

If you choose to argue about this statement, you will soon find yourself relying on statements about how a corrupt government differs from other governments.

             (*subject*)   (*predicate*)
Any government that uses tax money to support vice / is corrupt.

And this is the key to all logical statements—the distinctions made between and among *all, some,* and *none.* In order to test the truth of any specific statement, you need to know the possibility of truth in general. Before you can argue about any particular government, you must know what you believe about governments in general. *If* you believe that all governments are corrupt, you can assume that any given government is corrupt. If you believe that all philosophers are brilliant, you can assume that any specific philosopher is brilliant.

One small complication of the standard forms is caused by negation. The double negative, among other forms of negation, is often condemned because it creates a positive: "No philosopher is not brilliant" means the same thing as "Every philosopher is brilliant." It is not necessary to condemn the negative for its power to create the positive, but you must be alert to the possibility of confusion with negatives. A useful rule to follow is to convert negatives into standard forms. A little analyzing will convert any statement into standard form, but you may want to memorize a conversion table to get you started.

CONVERSION
TABLE

STANDARD FORM *(Concerning All the Cases)*	EQUIVALENT FORM *(Concerning Negatives)*
1 Every S is P **Every preacher is a teacher.**	Every nonP is nonS **Every nonteacher is a non-preacher.**
	No S is nonP **No preacher is a nonteacher.**
2 No S is P **No preacher is a teacher.**	No P is S **No teacher is a preacher.**
	Every S is nonP **Every preacher is no teacher.**
(Concerning Some of the Cases)	
3 Some S is P **Some preachers are teachers.**	Some P is S **Some teachers are preachers.**
4 Some S is not P **Some preachers are not teachers.**	Some nonP is not nonS **Some nonteachers are not non-preachers.**
	Not every S is P **Not every preacher is a teacher.**

The object is to make sure that you do not fool or confuse yourself. An argument can quickly become too complicated to understand, let alone solve, if you do not insist on converting to standard forms. For example, if you argue that every professor is old, you have a statement concerning all the cases: every S is P. But suppose you introduce into this same argument the term "not young." That looks very much like an equivalent form for the second statement: every S is nonP. Rather than allow this confusion, it is better not to introduce synonyms and antonyms into the argument. Once you decide that the predicate is to be "old" it is better to keep that term and its negative, "not old," instead of confusing yourself about which standard form you are using and also raising additional arguments about whether "not young" in fact means *old* (versus middle-aged, and so on).

Not Every   Some speakers of English insist that "not" can join with "every" even when one of these words is in the subject and the other is in the predicate. Thus, "Everyone isn't born lucky" means "Some are born lucky and some aren't." But the statement looks like it means every *S* is non*P*, when in fact it is a variation of not every *S* is *P*. As long as it is clear to both parties in an argument that these "not every" statements are equivalent to a statement concerning *some* of the cases and not to a statement concerning *all* the cases, there should be no confusion. But you need to decide exactly what any statement does mean before you allow yourself to get involved in an argument about it.

Tautologies   Watch out for statements that repeat some form of the subject in the predicate: "Every male is a man." If you accept this statement, you will have trouble with its negative, "No male is not a man" (boys are male). The trouble lies in the tautology of the statement: "man" and "male" are synonymous in one sense. If the point of the argument is to discover whether a "real man" can be effeminate or whether chromosomes identify sex, the question needs to be stated in some unambiguous way to avoid tautologies. You will be less confused if you make a general practice of stating the subject as a noun and the predicate as a quality or characteristic; thus "Every flower is beautiful" instead of the more cumbersome "Every beautiful thing is a flower." The two statements are incompatible. The first only identifies a quality that, you assume for the sake of argument, all flowers have and does not exclude other things from having the quality. The second statement ascribes the quality to flowers only and excludes everything else: people, butterflies, works of art, and so on.

Informal Interpretations   Informal interpretations of language can cause considerable ambiguity. For example, "No Greek is an American" is equivalent to "No American is a Greek," yet people frequently have difficulty accepting the equivalence because of some ambiguity in the terms "Greek" and "American." If the terms mean "one who lives in Greece or America," it is possible that while no Greek may live in America, some American could be living in Greece. If the terms mean "those who have Greek or

American ancestry," it is possible that no Greek has American ancestry while some Americans have Greek ancestors. It is important to define the terms. Perhaps you mean that no one who holds Greek citizenship can also hold American citizenship, and therefore, no American citizen is also a Greek citizen. You would do well to state at the outset just what you do mean. If you propose that no Greek lives in America, the equivalent statement may be no one who lives in America is Greek, and you may be able to accept that. But if, after all, it turns out that you mean only that anyone who is now *in* Greece is not now *in* America, the argument is tautological and to be avoided altogether. (Rather than argue whether God can make a stone so heavy that even He can't lift it, it is advisable to dismiss the argument as tautological, equivalent to, "Can God do something that God can't do?")

Practice

Are the following statements equivalent?

1 **Every lizard is a reptile : No lizard is not a reptile.**
2 **No writer is stupid : No one who is stupid is a writer.**
3 **Some Greeks are not poets : Some poets are not Greeks.**
4 **Every orator is a logician : Every nonlogician is not an orator.**
5 **Every six-year-old is a kid : Every kid is a six-year-old.**
6 **Some athletes are clever : Some athletes are not clever.**
7 **No teacher is tired : Every tired person is not a teacher.**
8 **Some books are hard : Not every book is hard.**
9 **Some bats are rabid : Some rabid creatures are bats.**
10 **No astronomer is lazy : Every astronomer is not lazy.**

Obviously it is important to define statements as precisely as possible before getting too far into the reasoning process. But sooner or later the argument must shift from considerations of the *language* of arguments to considerations of the *substance* of arguments. In writing, this means you must first find the facts and then group them so that you discover, as suggested earlier, whether you are talking about some or all of the cases. (Smoking is hazardous to *some* or *all?*) Try to keep clear the difference between facts and statements *about* facts, or the difference between facts and *inferences*. Facts can be verified, usually, by physical tests—you can count the number of people in a room, for example. An inference, on the other hand, is an unverified deduction or conclusion you come to in any of several ways, including guessing. If you can't see the people in the room, you might guess (infer) that some of them are male and some are female from the sounds of the voices. Or if you can see them through a window but can't hear them, you might infer that they were listening to a lecture from their seating arrangement and manner. Both these *inferences* can be verified, of course, if you enter the room. They are therefore low-level inferences—not very far removed from physical observation—but inferences nevertheless. (Voices do not invariably identify sex of speakers; people sitting attentively in rows are not necessarily listening to a lecture.)

Unfortunately there is no upward limit to inferences. Suppose you happen to know the people are listening to a political speech. Can you infer (deduce, conclude, surmise, judge, gather, *guess*) that they will vote for the speaker in an upcoming election? It would be very useful to be able to make such high-level inferences, because there aren't satisfactory physical tests for verifying the facts in every situation. Even direct questioning is not always a reliable procedure for obtaining accurate information. If it were easy to predict election results or stock-market trends or even horse-race results, ours would be a different world. Beyond predictions of events lie abstract philosophical and legal questions that seem (so far) entirely divorced from physical tests. How shall we conduct the affairs of the nation? (Shall we have a strong President or a strong Congress?) Since these abstract questions eventually involve physical behaviors, it is important for us to be able to anticipate what is likely to result from any action we take—or fail to take—before we do it. No one can avoid logic. As long as we deal with facts and inferences our choices are only between good logic and bad.

INDUCTION AND DEDUCTION

If we could make logic fit our world perfectly, we would work out a list of generalizations or general "laws" to cover everything. If we could know, for example, that everyone who listens to a political speech will vote for the speaker, even if we could know just that sixty percent would and forty percent would not vote for the speaker, we would very much simplify life. And, as far as possible, that is what science and education have been attempting to do. We have two sets of principles, or two methods of handling data, to help us in this work.

Induction   The primary tool of science, induction holds that specific observations lead to general truths. (If you see enough redheads with freckles, you may conclude that, in general, redheads have freckles.) That redheads have freckles (generally) is one of our *premises,* one of the basic truths accepted by most people who have thought about the matter. Our premises are not always correct; sometimes they apply far less often than we think. But it is the business of science to keep observing and testing one incident after another, so that we become more and more confident of our premises or discard them for better ones. The term "induction" refers to the process by which specific observations "lead to" general laws or premises.

Deduction   The method of classical reasoning, deduction holds that general laws *predict* specific instances. (Once you know that redheads generally have freckles, you can predict that the next redhead you meet will probably have freckles. If your general truth is universal enough, your prediction will be true.) This is the kind of reasoning we use most often, though we usually don't realize we are doing it. When you look at the sky and conclude that it may rain, your conclusion is based on a general "truth" that a dark and cloudy sky generally means rain is coming. And you can understand why this was the preferred method of reasoning among the ancients: how much more elegant to determine truth with your mind than to trudge about observing things! Unfortunately such an attitude often led the ancients into error. Today a reasonable person would use induction to determine those things that can be observed and use deduction in those matters where induction won't help. Deduction, then, means "drawing out" the specific cases from the general law or premise.

TESTING STATEMENTS

The syllogism is the basic formula of deductive reasoning. It is based on the assumption that whatever is true of a group of things must be true of any member of the group. The standard form of the syllogism is as follows:

MAJOR PREMISE
A universal truth acknowledged by all reasonable people, usually, but not necessarily, arrived at through induction.

MINOR PREMISE
A specific instance within the general statement. If you make a general statement about *all* dogs, then any specific dog is an instance within the category of dogs.

CONCLUSION
An "inescapable" result based on the formula that what is true for the group must be true for the members of the group; thus whatever is true for all dogs ought to be true for any given dog.

EXAMPLE

Major premise: All dogs bark.
Minor premise: Fido is a dog.
Conclusion: Fido barks.

If it is true that all dogs bark, then it *must* be true that any given dog you can find will bark. However, it so happens that some dogs do *not* bark (basenjies, for example). You can see that the syllogism would be perfectly good *if* the major premise were true. That is, the syllogism is constructed properly. You have a major premise about all dogs and a minor premise identifying a specific dog; thus the minor premise is contained in the major premise. You could introduce a different kind of error: all dogs bark, some squirrels bark; thus some squirrels are dogs. Here the problem is that the syllogism isn't properly constructed. The minor premise does not identify a member in the major premise but instead introduces a new group entirely (squirrels).

To account for the different kinds of errors, you need different concepts. For "truth" we mean coinciding with reality. (In reality some dogs do not bark.) For properly drawn conclusions in properly constructed syllogisms, we will use the concept "valid," regardless of the "truth" of the premises. Thus a conclusion can be valid but not true. In fact, you can have these possibilities:

VALID AND TRUE
All men are mortal.
Socrates is a man.
Socrates is mortal.

VALID BUT NOT TRUE
All men have wings.
Socrates is a man.
Socrates has wings.

NOT VALID BUT TRUE
All logicians tell lies.
Socrates tells lies.
Socrates is a logician.

NOT VALID AND NOT TRUE
All women tell lies.
Socrates tells lies.
Socrates is a woman.

The error in the "Not Valid" syllogisms is called "affirming the predicate." In the standard syllogism, validity is achieved by affirming the subject, not the predicate. For example, in "Not Valid but True," the fact that logicians tell lies does not preclude the possibility that others do too; the major premise does not say that *only* logicians tell lies.

Diagrams can help you to understand syllogisms. Figure 4.1 illustrates the "Valid and True" syllogism. Socrates is "contained" within the inner *Men* circle, and the *Men* circle is itself contained within the outer *All mortals* circle. Thus, whatever is true of the whole group of men must also be true of Socrates. Notice, though, that the diagram leaves room for mortals who are not men.

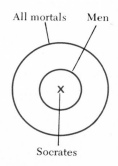

FIGURE 4.1

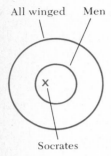

All winged   Men

Socrates

FIGURE 4.2

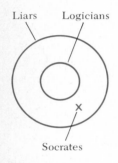

Liars   Logicians

Socrates

FIGURE 4.3

A similar diagram (Figure 4.2) will work for "Valid but not True." The circles show that all men are inside the *Winged* circle. You know this is not "true," but you may imagine such a thing anyway. And Socrates is again one of the men, so he too must be inside the *Winged* circle.

"Not Valid but True" presents a problem, though, as seen in Figure 4.3 It is clear enough that the logicians are all inside the *Liars* circle, and Socrates is inside the *Liars* circle too, because the minor premise puts him there. But there is nothing in the premises to tell you to put Socrates inside the *Logicians* circle; that is, there is no *necessity* for putting him there. The premises only tell us that he is inside the *Liars* circle . . . somewhere. Thus the conclusion is *not warranted,* and in fact, according to the diagram, is false—or at least not valid.

The same thing is true of the last syllogism (Figure 4.4). You can get all the women into the *Liars* circle, and you can get Socrates in there too, but the premises do not direct you to put Socrates into the *Women* circle, and therefore the conclusion is unwarranted.

Note the difference if you change the premise to "*Only* logicians lie" (Figure 4.5). In that case the *Logicians* circle and the *Liars* circle would be the same. If then you affirm the predicate ("Socrates is a liar"), Socrates will have to become a logician, since only they lie.

Practice

Are the following syllogisms valid?

1 All logicians tell the truth.
   Plato tells the truth.
   Plato is a logician.

2 All logicians tell the truth.
   Plato is a logician.
   Plato tells the truth.

3 All rhetoricians smell bad.
   Aristotle is a rhetorician.
   Aristotle smells bad.

4 All students love logic.
   Professor Stout loves logic.
   Professor Stout is a student.

5 All Athenians hate war.
   The President hates war.
   The President is an Athenian.

6 All thinkers are clowns.
   Bozo is a clown.
   Bozo is a thinker.

7 All Greeks love beauty.
   Socrates loves beauty.
   Socrates is a Greek.

8 Descartes is a philosopher.
   All philosophers eat meat.
   Descartes eats meat.

9 All women have beautiful minds.
   Muhammad Ali has a beautiful mind.
   Muhammad Ali is a woman.

10 All women have beautiful minds.
    Raquel Welch has a beautiful mind.
    Raquel Welch is a woman.

People seldom realize they are using syllogisms. They take short cuts and leave out one of the premises, and they don't state things in syllogistic form. For example:

Don't lend Bill money; you'll never get it back!

The implied (unspoken) syllogism is something like this:

People who don't pay me back won't pay you back.
Bill didn't pay me the $5 I loaned him.
Bill won't pay you back.

Liars   Women

Socrates

FIGURE 4.4

If you dig the syllogism out of its linguistic hiding place, you can determine its truth or validity. In this case, you would say that the reasoning is valid, but you'd question the major premise, which seems a hasty generalization. (Bill may very will pay you back even if he hasn't paid others.) It is this same kind of questionable logic based on debatable assumptions that causes insurance companies and credit bureaus to brand customers "risky."

Logicians
and liars

Socrates

FIGURE 4.5

Practice

Find the syllogisms in the following statements. You may be able to come up with more than one syllogism for a given statement.
1 She reads communist books; she must be a commie.
2 You should take Professor Occam's course; it's got lots of logic in it.
3 Socrates was a fool; he killed himself to prove a point.
4 If you like peanut butter, you'll love Skippy.
5 People who live in glass houses shouldn't throw bricks.

UNIVERSAL NEGATIVES

Negative syllogisms are slightly more complex to work with. As with affirmative syllogisms, the negatives can be valid without being "true." For example:

VALID AND TRUE
No dogs have wings.
Snoopy is a dog.
Snoopy has no wings.

VALID BUT NOT TRUE
No students like logic.
Plato is a student.
Plato doesn't like logic.

But notice:

NOT VALID
No good lawyer loses cases.
Katherine Hill doesn't lose cases.
Katherine Hill is a good lawyer.

The problem with this syllogism is that there are too many negatives in it. It would be clearer to say that good lawyers *win* cases. (So do bad ones, occasionally.) If we were to diagram this syllogism, we'd get three separate and unrelated circles: a circle for good lawyers, a separate circle for those who lose cases (containing no good lawyers), and a third circle for Katherine Hill, who also is not in the losers' circle. But there is nothing in either the major or the minor premises that allows or requires us to put Katherine Hill in the lawyers' circle. Therefore the conclusion is not warranted; it is not valid.

Practice

Are the following syllogisms valid?

1 **No rhetorician speaks ill.**
   Phaedrus speaks ill.
   Phaedrus is no rhetorician.

2 **Some detectives are not smart.**
   Sam Spade is not smart.
   Sam Spade is no detective.

3 **No student knows Greek.**
   Isocrates is a student.
   Isocrates does not know Greek.

4 **No angel is alive.**
   The President is not dead.
   The President is an angel.

5 **No thinking man makes errors.**
   Gorgias is a thinking man.
   Gorgias makes no errors.

6 **No Greek hates logic.**
   Aristotle is a Greek.
   Aristotle hates logic.

7 **No person is not happy.**
   Aristotle is not happy.
   Aristotle is no person.

8 **No young woman needs makeup.**
   Athena needs makeup.
   Athena is no young woman.

9 **No girl hates what is good for her.**
   Andrea hates what is good for her.
   Andrea is not a girl.

10 **No clown is a philosopher.**
   Bozo is no philosopher.
   Bozo is a clown.

Review

Determine the validity of the following syllogisms.

1 **All orators are speakers.**
   A rhetorician is an orator.
   A rhetorician is a speaker.

2 **Every student is a scholar.**
   Some students are not young.
   Some scholars are not young.

3 **Every book is to be read.**
   Every poem is to be read.
   Every poem is a book.

4 **No lawyer is a magician.**
   Bailey is a lawyer.
   Bailey is no magician.

5 **Every writer is a reader.**
   Some poets are not readers.
   Some poets are not writers.

6 **Every graduate is literate.**
   Some graduates are musicians.
   Some musicians are literate.

7 **Every rhetorician is a teacher.**
   No corpse is a teacher.
   No corpse is a rhetorician.

8 **No person is a fool.**
   Every philosopher is a person.
   No philosopher is a fool.

9 No animal is a stone.
   Some unicorn is an animal.
   Some unicorn is not an animal.

10 Every gourd is a melon.
   Some squash is a gourd.
   Every squash is a melon.

11 Every death is a tragedy.
   Some deaths are a mercy.
   Some tragedy is a mercy.

12 No daughter is a son.
   Some girl is a daughter.
   Some girl is not a son.

13 Every house is a castle.
   A cabin is a house.
   A cabin is a castle.

14 No Athenian is a Roman.
   Plato is an Athenian.
   Plato is not a Roman.

15 Every tree is a plant.
   Some pine is a plant.
   Some pine is a tree.

16 No dog is a cat.
   Benjy is not a cat.
   Benjy is a dog.

17 Every oration is a speech.
   Every sermon is an oration.
   Every sermon is a speech.

18 Every human is mortal.
   Some people are human.
   Some people are mortal.

LOGICAL FALLACIES: ERRORS TO AVOID

The logical fallacies discussed in this section occur often in conversation and in writing. You must avoid them when you are trying to build a reasonable case in your writing.

Logical fallacies fall into several categories: fallacies based on insufficient evidence; fallacies based on irrelevant information; fallacies based on ambiguity; and fallacies based on faulty logic. As you read the following section, it's more important to understand the kinds of flawed reasoning inherent in insufficient evidence, irrelevancies, ambiguities, and faulty logic than to memorize the names of the logical fallacies. (But it's fun to be able to say, "That's an *ad verecundiam* fallacy" when you see a football star attesting to the merits of a car-rental agency.)

FALLACIES BASED ON INSUFFICIENT EVIDENCE

Ad Ignorantium   Appeal to ignorance, arguing on the basis of what is not known. If you can't prove something is false, must it be true? "You can't prove there *isn't* a monster in Loch Ness, so there must be one!" "Anyone who takes the Fifth Amendment [refuses to deny the charges] must be guilty!" The same fallacy is involved whether you insist on the validity of anything not proved false or insist on the falseness of anything not proved true.

Card Stacking   Concealing, withholding, or ignoring the evidence; *selecting* only evidence favorable to your side. "Richard Nixon is tall, good-looking, a family man, an experienced politician, a world leader. Let's get this man back into politics!"

Hasty Generalization   Drawing conclusions from too little evidence. (This is the chief error in reasoning.) "I know several jolly fat people; therefore I conclude that all fat people are jolly!" It is unlikely that we could know enough people to draw many accurate generalizations about them. *Many* generalizations turn out to be inaccurate because they are based on insufficient evidence. In argumentation, you must learn to *back up* your generalizations with specific evidence.

Post Hoc Ergo Propter Hoc   Literally, "after this; therefore because of this." Events that follow each other chronologically are falsely assumed to have a *cause* and *effect* relationship. "His grades started to fall after Harold met Cindy; she must have been a bad influence!"

FALLACIES BASED ON IRRELEVANT INFORMATION

Ad Baculum   Appeal to force. "If you insult Smith's wife, you'll get a black eye!" "If you investigate Gassone Motors, they will expose your sex life!" "There are three hundred voters in my precinct; you'd better listen to me!" Force doesn't have to be physical; it can be psychological.

Ad Hominem   Literally, "to the person." *Ad hominem* attacks the person who is arguing and ignores the argument. The idea is that the person is too contemptible to have valid ideas. "What you say may be true, but aren't you a member of the Communist party?"

Ad Misericordiam   Appeal to pity. "Here's poor William's paper; the unfortunate lad's been having trouble lately. Perhaps I can cheer him with a good grade!" "There is no more pathetic sight than handicapped children; we must all give to the March of Dimes!" "Governor Wallace would have made a good President, even though an assassin's bullet left him confined to a wheelchair!" Appeals to pity are not always wrong, but most readers object to them when they seem to obscure the real question.

Ad Populum   Appeal to popular prejudices and slogans. "Down with big government!" "Down with invasion of privacy!" "Down with federal intervention!" "Vote for law and order!" "America for Americans!" A populist is someone running for office on the basis of these traditional ideas, campaigning against social change or against "newer" attitudes. Essentially populism is an appeal to return to the good old days. (What *are* the popular ideas in America?)

Ad Verecundiam   Inappropriate authority. "O. J. Simpson says rent from Hertz, and he should know!" "What do you mean Sugar Lolly can't act? Senator Fogburn likes Sugar Lolly!" "Professor Snore has just finished his great work on Shakespeare; perhaps we should invite him to speak at the Children's Literature Festival!" When a celebrity or authority is dragged into an argument as expert witness, you have every right to challenge his or her expertise.

Bandwagon   Appeal to peer pressure, group identity. "Join the winning side!" "All the really important people smoke Torchos, you should too!" Bandwagon is sometimes called "snob appeal"; its opposite is "plain folks": "You can trust me folks, I'm just a simple, unpretentious soul like you!" "Beware of pointy-headed intellectuals!"

Common Sense   Appeal to common knowledge, practical truths. "She may be a brilliant intellectual, but she can't chew gum and walk at the same time!" "Anyone should know that it takes money to make money!" "You shouldn't insult people who control your oil supply; that's only common sense." "The world cannot be round like a ball, otherwise the people on the bottom would fall off!" Appeals to common sense are not always wrong, but often they are used to simplify difficult issues or to assert the virtues of the commonplace over intellectual or esoteric values. Common sense is not helpful in matters requiring *uncommon* sense. Besides, common sense isn't that common!

Fallacy of Opposition   Anything the opposition approves must be bad; an attack on the ideas on the grounds that those who support them are incapable of right thinking. Fallacy of opposition is different from *ad hominem* only to the degree that the idea itself is made unacceptable because of its supporters. "Sure, you favor welfare, social security, government insurance, and all the rest. But did you know that these are socialistic ideas and communistic as well?" The attack is on the ideas *because of* those who support them.

Genetic Fallacy   The source of an idea influences its worth. Similar to fallacy of opposition, but different in that the idea is attacked, regardless of who supports it, on the grounds that where the idea came from makes the argument bad. "The new tax law is ridiculous! It was written at Montezuma State College and everyone knows that's Mickey Mouse U.!"

Guilt by Association   You are known by the company you keep. "Birds of a feather flock together!" "Don't invite Renford to the party; his roommate was caught cheating on an exam." "Why are you defending the rights of criminals; do you have a criminal record?"

Red Herring   Arguing beside the point; *switching* to some side issue or entirely new issue to distract from the main argument, a favorite device of politicians when asked hard questions: "Perhaps you're right about integration and busing, but has anyone considered the *safety* of those buses?" Also favored by some students on exams: "In order to understand the causes of the Civil War, we must look at the warlike nature of human beings. The history of Europe is full of wars . . . ."

Tu Quoque   You did it too; the accusation is invalid because the accuser is guilty of the same "sin." "Anyone in prison obviously cannot pass judgment on criminal matters!" "The senator accuses his opponent of campaign irregularities, but has anyone examined the senator's campaign practices?" "So what if I cheat on my taxes? So do you!"

FALLACIES BASED ON AMBIGUITY

Amphiboly   Language ambiguity, deliberately misusing *implications*. "Three out of four doctors recommend this type of pain relief!" The implied assertion here is that three out of four means seventy-five percent of *all* doctors and also that what is true of a *type* of pain reliever is true of *this* one.

Begging the Question   Tautology, circular reasoning; the conclusion is merely a restatement of one of the premises. "The President is such a good man . . . because he is so moral!" "Murderers should be executed . . . because they are killers!" "You can see that God exists . . . because of all the things He made!"

Equivocation   Arguing over the meaning of a word; using the connotations of a word to disprove or distort an argument. Equivocation always involves the *meaning* of words—deliberate or accidental misuse that confuses argumentation. "Senator Gonzo claims to be a *conservative,* yet he lives lavishly!" (Two meanings for "conservative" are involved here.) "How can you claim to be *pious?* You never go to church!" "No, we are not retreating; we have moved into the Vietnamization phase of the war!"

False Metaphor or False Analogy The metaphor or analogy used has more dissimilarities than similarities. "The President has seen us through a crisis of state; he has kept late hours in lonely vigil; he has brought us soothing relief; he has wasted his strength to revive our faltering nation. Let us reward him now with our gratitude!" The metaphor or analogy of the President as doctor tending a sick nation is false, however poetic it may be.

FALLACIES BASED ON FAULTY LOGIC

Complex Question Loaded questions that are simply not safe to answer. "When did you stop beating your wife?" "Do you favor our current policies of fiscal irresponsibility?" "If elected will you put an end to frivolous welfare programs?" The complex question need not be put in the form of a question; it can be worded as a complex issue: "Let us examine whether the President's aggressive foreign posture is weakening our bargaining power!" It is necessary to determine first whether the President's "posture" is aggressive before we can examine its influence on our bargaining power.

False Dilemma Either/or thinking; presents only two options, both (usually) unattractive. "Either we must support private charities or we must increase welfare taxation!" "If you don't quit smoking, you'll die of lung cancer!" In almost all situations there are more than two options.

Non Sequitur Literally, "it does not follow"; this general term is often applied to any fallacy in which the argument cannot be followed. A non sequitur argument is one in which the conclusion does not follow from the major premise. "Inflation has made our money worth less, so we might as well spend it and enjoy life."

Rationalization Making excuses; choosing the least threatening (or most self-serving) explanations. "I'm flunking calculus; that instructor hates me!" "Of course I hit the mailbox; you've got the stupid thing where it's impossible to miss!"

Reductio ad Absurdum   Literally, "reduce to an absurdity"; disproof of an argument by showing some absurdity to which it leads if carried to its logical end. This is not always an error. It is an error if the user is merely being sarcastic, ridiculing the opposition, or erroneously leading (via hasty generalization, either/or, and so on) to an absurdity that doesn't necessarily follow. "So you would give the government the power to tax, would you? The next thing you know they'll use that power to take away your home and property, and finally your life. We will then have the amusing consequence of the government taxing its citizens out of existence—and finally the government itself must fall with no citizens and no new taxes to support it!"

Slippery Slope   One evil leads to another. "If you eat desserts you'll end up weighing three hundred pounds!" Of course it is possible that one evil *may* lead to another, but it is obviously not true that one evil *must* lead to another.

Practice

Identify the fallacy in the following; in some cases you may feel that more than one fallacy is involved.

1 Did you see the way those Indians made it rain? Just as soon as they stopped dancing it really poured!

2 All Germans are warlike and belligerent!

3 Everybody's going to the rally to listen to protest songs; you better come along too!

4 God never lies. The Bible is the word of God, and the Bible clearly teaches that God exists. Therefore, God must exist, because of course He never lies!

5 Pay your taxes or go to jail; it's just that simple!

6 The great capitalist free-enterprise system must struggle against the godless, enslaving communist conspiracy!

7 Consider joining the American Nazi Party. It is a small, fraternal group permitting individual participation. It is active, vibrant, alive. Its objectives are clear and comprehensible!

8 Ustislav Keldysh's ideas and designs for space flight cannot be considered here: the man is a communist.

9 About a month ago, Stultus failed to sacrifice to Vulcan, and he was killed when Vesuvius erupted. Impiety is always avenged by the gods!

10 Are nuclear plants safe? There are so many complex aspects of this issue; consider for example what abundant cheap energy will mean to our economy!

11 Love is truth. I love all people, and therefore have all truth in my heart. Why then should I read books, which can add no truth to that absolute truth which is mine?

12 The university is greatly alarmed that the students may be becoming alcoholics!

13 I will be happy to argue tax evasion with my opponent, but why will he not deny the suspicion in everyone's mind that he defends tax evasion out of self-interest?

14 Better dead than red!

15 It is very depressing to see the young behaving so promiscuously; such license will surely lead to unwanted pregnancies and abortion.

16 We'd like to believe in the President's morality campaign, but the truth is that several members of his administration are known to be having marital troubles.

17 Like a skillful conductor, a good administrator orchestrates the many activities of the university into one harmonious whole.

18 I will hear no more of my opponent's "patriotism"; she does not go to war; she does not applaud those who do; she finds virtue in other nations; and now she will not sign a loyalty oath! Is this patriotism?

19 Do you use illegal drugs very often?

20 Sure, life is full of opportunities for you; you're tall, blonde, and good looking. I'm short, fat, and ugly. No wonder you won a fellowship for a year in London!

21 Most of the women interviewed on this campus said they prefer athletes!

22 Charity benefits the less fortunate; it is immoral not to give to charity!

23 The great promise of America is that if you work hard, save your money, and mind your own business, you will prosper and succeed; if you don't make it, you have no one but yourself to blame!

24 It would be better if your virtuous workers, scientists, and artists remain poor; for if they become wealthy they will surely lose the incentive to work hard, and you will see that by rewarding virtue you will encourage sloth!

25 Unable to reach any official spokesman this morning, reporters cornered a Senate page, who said that as far as she could tell negotiations were proceeding smoothly.

26 Today the United States has sent the Sixth Fleet to another world trouble spot to make our presence felt.

27 Several interesting educational innovations have come, unfortunately, from sources outside the educational establishment and cannot be given serious consideration.

28 That's just the kind of reasoning we'd expect from someone with your ancestry!

29 What do you mean, my clothes look terrible? You've got the same thing on!

30 Either you are a liar or you aren't; there are no degrees of honesty.

31 It is a good thing that it is so cold out in the winter; otherwise, the heat in our homes would serve little purpose!

32 Find out why Drivel is the number one ice cream; twenty million Americans can't be wrong!

33 Historically, the leaders in every field—art, science, business, medicine, and so on—have been predominantly *men,* and therefore it is difficult to understand why women should now be treated as *equal* to men.

34 You can say what you want about the good work of unions, but I think the whole idea is communistic.

35 All politicians are crooks.

36 Despite endless efforts, no one has been able to prove that God exists; we may as well stop trying and accept the truth: there is no God.

37 Alicia started gaining more weight than ever when she started taking Slimdown; the stuff must be fattening.

38 Sure, Arbuckle argues for conservatism; he's a paid establishment flunky!

39 My worthy opponent accuses me of owning shares in Devilish Corporation; yet he himself is a major stockholder in Awful Products Incorporated!

40 It isn't fair to ruin students' lives with poor grades; let us give only good grades!

41 A day's work for a day's wages; no more gold-bricking!

42 For that chic, *au courant* look, wear Slick, the elegant skin cream of celebrities and beautiful people everywhere.

43 If you don't study, you won't pass.

44 The rattlesnake is a beautiful creature, attractively colored, clean, and has an intriguing rattle with which to catch your attention; excellent mouser and house pet!

45 Men don't make passes at girls who wear glasses.

46 Dr. Hessel, well-known physicist, has taken a stand against our policy toward African nations on the grounds that our racial policies are hypocritical.

47 Clearly the Democrats are the true defenders of democracy, else why would they be called "democrats"?

48 This critic would suggest that the new treatise in philosophy before her is a new adventure in confusion, were its author not the head of the philosophy department at one of our greatest schools, Maxima Ivy League University!

49 There's no use in entering the contest; they've probably got it rigged so only insiders can win.

50 Half the class failed when the school introduced a new standardized test; it just shows how worthless those tests are.

PERSUASION

The twentieth century has become so science oriented that we are all unconsciously skeptical. We are accustomed to thinking in terms of evidence, counterevidence, proofs. Even advertising today has taken to pseudoscience: nine out of ten doctors approve Mopex; three out of four people prefer Schnitz; Ammeloy works twenty percent faster . . . . Yet there is very little in life that we can solve with this approach. In most human affairs—politics, religion, romance, and so on—science can offer information, but usually not answers to our questions. Who should be our next President? Should everyone go to college? Is television harmful? Is the press too powerful? Should teenagers get married?

The time-honored solution to these problems is to argue about them and, perhaps, eventually take a vote on them. Without an overt display of power it is very difficult to *make* people do anything. You can *prove* that cigarette smoking causes cancer, but that fact won't make people quit smoking. In fact "proving" things in human affairs seems almost irrelevant. And so the arguing goes on, sometimes for decades.

If facts and figures and sometimes even aggression won't move people, what will? Obviously something *does* operate on people or we would never get anything done. Advertisers try to get us to buy products—and succeed, by and large—teachers try to get students to learn, politicians try to get other politicians to pass bills. People are often successful at getting others to do what they want. Even in the home, family members "work their wiles" on each other. How does a teenager get the family car, avoid chores, and so on?

Persuasion is the high art of getting others to agree with you. In almost any human activity we rely on our ability to persuade each other: something is or isn't good, should or shouldn't be done. Guns, bombs, armies, and other means of force may make people do certain things temporarily, but they do not persuade people. Force begets force and resistance, and though you may beat up and tie up your opponents and temporarily triumph over them, as soon as they get loose they will come after you again, this time with friends. To persuade means more than just winning an argument; it means changing the opponent's mind so that he or she agrees with you *in fact*. Persuasion means to urge, to coax, to influence, to encourage—it is much more related to psychology than to debate. In a debate, you can present facts and figures, brilliant reasoning, counterarguments, and so forth, and make your opponent look foolish, and this will win the debate; but after the debate the opponent may blacken your eye. To *persuade* the opponent requires that he or she stop arguing and say something like, "I guess you're right; I never thought of it that way."

The persuasion paper focuses on the audience. If you are going to try to persuade certain people to change behavior, to see the world differently, to feel differently about an issue, to act differently, you must analyze these people with care. You must get to know your audience. What do they know about this issue? How do they feel about it? Why don't they already agree with the position you are advocating? Are there any ideas or feelings they have that you can agree with so that you can establish a bridge of understanding between you both? Your biggest challenge will be getting your audience to listen, to pay attention to what you have to say. That is why you must begin by trying to get into their shoes, to feel as they feel, to view the issue from *their* perspective. Only then will you know what evidence will be likely to change their views.

The point to remember is that if you want to *persuade,* you must avoid starting a *fight*. And there is no quicker way to start a fight than to accuse someone of being emotional (that is, not rational) or irrational (again, not rational). The heavy reliance on rationality has always been our means of warding off superstition and ignorance. Thus, to be irrational carries a very negative connotation. To accuse opponents of being irrational (emotional) amounts to accusing them of being superstitious, ignorant, primitive, and a host of other uncomplimentary things. It is the verbal equivalent of a slap in the face:

An Incredibly Short Lesson . . . in Persuasion?

HE: Which sweater should I wear, the red one or the yellow one?

SHE: Oh, I don't know . . . the yellow one looks okay.

HE: What's the matter with the red one?

SHE: Nothing. Wear the red one.

HE: My mother gave me that red sweater.

SHE: The red one is fine.

HE: You hate my mother.

SHE: Wait a minute. I didn't say that.

HE: Why do you hate my mother?

SHE: Hey . . . you're getting emotional! Let's be rational about this.
HE: Rational! I'll show you rational. You can just go to the show alone!

Persuasion, therefore, relies on some very basic human inter-actions, all of which can be summarized by the word *reasonable-ness*. If you would persuade others, *you* must be reasonable. The study of persuasion is fascinating and complex, but at this point you can do a great deal with just three principles: fight a worthy opponent; fight fair; accept compromise.

THE WORTHY OPPONENT

No one knows everything and no one knows nothing. You cannot be entirely right, nor can your opponent be entirely wrong. Each of you has *part* of the truth. Thus you must show that you respect the opponent. There is no point in arguing with those who do not respect you, and there is no point in arguing with those you do not respect. Any word or tone or hint that the opponent is less intelligent, less well informed, less honorable, or even less *right* than you are will set off hostile vibrations that can only lead to a fight. You should enter into an argument with the idea that *both* you and the opponent have misunderstood something, and you will both help each other to understand better. The opponent is *not* wrong. (You would not be involved in an argument with someone less honorable than yourself, so it is inconceivable that the opponent would be a liar, a fool, and so on.)

FIGHT FAIR

Do unto others as you would have them do unto you. Sarcasm, name calling, insults and any other obvious attacks on the op-ponent violate the worthy-opponent rule. But even something as hard to define as an air of superiority will set off hostile vibrations. Lying, distorting, falsifying evidence or just using *unsupported generalizations* ("Everyone knows that aspirin causes bleeding!") all put the opponent on the defensive and have no place in *reasoning* between reasonable people. Basically you must remember that the opponent is *not* wrong, and therefore you must not introduce anything *negative* into the argument. The pessimist says the bottle is half empty, the optimist says the bottle is half full. Who is right? They are both right, but they see the truth from different perspectives. If they talked reasonably to each other for a while they might discover that they have no argument. But most people enter an argument "spoiling for a fight." The chances for reason to prevail, then, are slim at best, and they will immediately evaporate if either party is unfair.

ACCEPT COMPROMISE

Democracy cannot survive without compromise. Our culture is highly competitive and most of us are conditioned to *win*, but you must be willing to accept less than total victory if persuasion is your goal. If the opponent is partially right and you are partially right, then both of you must accept *partial* victory. Some issues seem so loaded with emotion, so obviously one sided, that only one solution is possible. Rape of a child is so horrible that nothing but the death penalty will do; bigotry and prejudice are so repugnant that there can be no good in a racist, and so on. Yet when you explore, examine, investigate these one-sided questions, they often turn out to be complex, many sided, and confusing. To enter an argument at all is to acknowledge that the issue is arguable, that there are two sides to the question—two valid sides. Moral outrage accomplishes little and violates the fair-fighting rule. Democracy is slow; we argue back and forth and eventually come up with answers that do not completely satisfy anyone. Yet no one has found a better way. A *considered* opinion is precisely one that has been examined, argued, analyzed, and finally has arrived as the best answer that can be had at the moment . . . all things considered.

You do not go into a persuasive argument to prove the opponent wrong or to prove yourself right. Through an exchange of ideas you *advance the argument*, not your own idea of the truth. If, after all, you succeed in getting a watered-down gun law passed, you are closer to your objective than you were. The gun-law argument has moved off dead center. The opponent who wanted no gun law whatsoever must accept partial change, and so must you, who wanted the strongest possible law. It is a maddeningly slow way to proceed—you may die before the argument ends—but the only other alternative so far is violence. In a nuclear world, violence is too dangerous, no matter what good we imagine it might produce.

In the following paper, the writer tries to convince us that hunting is a worthwhile sport, an emotional issue with some people who feel that hunters are senseless killers destroying wildlife. Should hunting be outlawed? Is the student being reasonable? Is he also being persuasive?

As a hunter, I have probably heard all of the arguments against hunting and hunters; and although most can be countered effectively, there is one that I agree with wholeheartedly: there are too many dangerous, thoughtless, and inconsiderate hunters. While these kinds of people go hunting for different types of game, and in all seasons, deer season is the biggest attraction for most hunters, therefore the time when the greatest number of these pseudohunters is in the woods. I call them pseudohunters because any true hunter and sportsman sees them as a sham, a mockery of the real thing. I will give some examples to illustrate exactly the types to which I am referring.

On the second Saturday of deer season this year, I went back in the woods for some morning hunting on my dad's enclosed land. I walked quietly back to a spot that I had chosen, hoping that I could be quiet enough to catch one by surprise, but no such luck. After I had stood in my spot for perhaps two hours, I decided to go back to the house to warm up, and maybe go back out in the afternoon. It was while walking back to the house that I discovered it—an abandoned deer. It was a small doe lying on its side, bloated and misshapen, its eyes open and glazed. It looked as if it might have been dead for several days, and one hindquarter was partially torn away, probably by some kind of wild animal. The doe was shot through the neck and abdomen. Several questions arise in a situation like this—questions of who, where, and why. Who was the person who shot it? Did he shoot it right there where it was, or had it wandered onto our property after it was wounded? Last, why did he shoot it? Did he think it was a buck?

When all factors are considered, just about any set of answers one could give to these questions would be damning. For instance, even if the hunter was one who had permission to hunt wherever he was when he shot the deer, even if he wasn't trespassing on private property, the question of why he shot the deer is still unanswered. Does he have poor eyesight? Is he the excitable kind who shoots first and looks for antlers after he has made his kill? Did his gun go off by accident? Was he shooting at a nearby buck and hit the doe instead? Not likely with two bullet holes in the body. Did he realize all along that it was a doe, and intend to take the meat, or did he just shoot it to be shooting something? If he had taken the meat, it wouldn't have been nearly so bad, because, even though it was killed illegally it wouldn't have been wasted. Of course, he might have been afraid of being caught and punished. He should have thought of that first. If it ran after he shot it, was he too lazy to track it? Any of these alternatives raises serious doubts about his competency as a hunter.

Later that same day I went over to hunt with my girlfriend's father, who lives in Flint, but has a trailer and a lot bordering on state land near Beaverton. Joe wasn't there when I arrived, so I was going to go out in the woods anyway, thinking I'd probably find him. When

I started out along the trail, I saw three "hunters" walking ahead of me. One of them I knew as Joe's acquaintance who owned a lot near Joe's and had a camper set up on it. The other two I didn't know, but one thing became very clear to me, walking along behind them—all three were staggering drunk. They passed a pint bottle of liquor around two or three times, and I saw one of them stumble and fall. The other two weren't walking much better. Watching them staggering along, their gun barrels swinging crazily, I suddenly felt very sick, and not at all certain that I wanted to be in the woods with those fools. If there is anything more stupid than carrying a gun, hunting, while drunk, I can't think of it. No wonder people are killed in accidents.

I think there are some measures which should be taken to reduce the number of pseudohunters in the woods. These would include vision and marksmanship tests administered when the individual applies for a license, and stricter fines and punishments for trespassers. This would mean that the only licensing agencies would be Department of Natural Resources headquarters, since most of the sporting-goods stores, and so on, that now distribute hunting licenses wouldn't have the facilities for such tests. This may help to cut down the number of people hunting. Also I think it might be a good idea to require prospective hunters to pass a complete physical examination before receiving their permits. This would help assure that they are at least physically able to undergo the rigors of tracking a wounded deer, and also cut down the number of hunters who die of heart attacks in the woods. All these things considered, there would probably need to be an increase in the cost of a hunting license, but this too might be advantageous, in cutting down the number of hunters.

The problem of drunken hunters can't really be solved on this level, but I believe that if such measures were taken, as I have suggested, there would probably be fewer people inclined to be drunk while hunting. I think that we would have mainly true sportsmen and hunters in the woods. We would certainly have fewer hunters, a fact which would in effect make the drunks less dangerous.

Ken starts his paper by agreeing with the opposition; there *are* some hunters who are dangerous and thoughtless. And this isn't just an agreement for effect; Ken wholeheartedly agrees and goes on to *illustrate* the point. He thoroughly condemns the thoughtless hunter and the drunken hunter. It isn't necessary for him to point out where he disagrees with the opponent or where the opponents (those who condemn all hunters) are in error. By concentrating on the positive, on those aspects where he and the opponents *agree,* Ken has turned an argument into a problem, for which he has a solution. Antihunters may not like Ken's solution, but they must be impressed with his reasonableness. He acknowledges there *is* a problem; and therefore he invites the opposition to acknowledge that he may have a solution.

CONVINCING THE READER

The more evidence you have, the more convincing you will be. It is not enough to say that the vegetables are overcooked to show that the cafeteria food is not good. If the vegetables are overcooked, the meat is tasteless and tough, and the potatoes are either lumpy or runny, the evidence is convincing. If you eat most of your meals in the cafeteria (versus just Wednesday night) the case is better yet. If your friends have the same opinion and you also observe that others return their trays with half-eaten meals, the case is highly convincing.

The quality of the evidence can also be convincing. Showing that the food is tasteless and inedible is only one kind of evidence, no matter how many examples you have. Suppose however that the food also *looks* bad (shapeless, mud-colored blobs of apple pie; beef slices covered with congealed white ooze). Suppose too it *smells* bad (rank asparagus emitting fumes of decay). If the food actually makes people ill too, you then have different kinds of evidence—all supporting the same argument—that the cafeteria food is bad.

However, there is a point of diminishing returns with evidence. At some point most people feel they have heard enough; to go on piling up evidence after this point can turn the tables so that *you* become the villain and your victim becomes the unfortunate underdog. It can seem that the case is so heavily loaded against your opponent that your reader begins to suspect you of bias, of unfairness.

Unfairness is a fatal mistake in persuasive writing. The heart of law and morality is *justice*—another word for fairness. An eye for an eye is fair, but to take both eyes, an arm, and a leg is unfair. The concept of fair play is so powerful that it *alone* can carry more weight than all your evidence. Thus it is a mistake to manufacture and/or distort the evidence. (Exaggerating or lying about the cafeteria will backfire on you.) It is also a mistake to insult the opponent. (Calling the cook a sadistic moron won't help.)

Why is it that most reasonable people have such a bad reaction to unfairness? Unfairness is a form of dishonesty (distortion of or outright violation of the truth), and those who would use it to convince us that they have the *correct* view of the argument are caught in a contradiction: you cannot convince us that you have the correct opinion when in fact your evidence is dishonest (unfair). Most reasonable people know that there are two sides (at least) to any question—two good sides, not one good one and one bad.

To be fair means to *weigh* the evidence; that is why the statue of *Justice* is represented as blindfolded and carrying a set of scales. If you wish to convince the reader that you are fairly presenting your opinion, it will be necessary to give both sides of the case. Then, if you have presented both sides well, the reader will be able to see which side has the better evidence. Thus to convince the reader it is not necessary—nor advisable—to *force* the reader to agree with you (by biasing the evidence). Instead, you only have to show the reader which of two sides to a question is better; if you have been fair—your readers will convince themselves that you are right.

Read the following paper. What is the author trying to do? Does she have enough evidence? Is she fair? Does she convince you?

MY
OPINION ON
TALLAHASSEE
POLICEMEN

ELLEN SLATER

Maybe if my brother had never gotten a beach buggy in the first place, I wouldn't feel so hostile towards Tallahassee policemen, but he did, and the one year he had it was long enough to prove to me that our local police force is indeed prejudiced against unconventional cars.

At first glance, any policeman might think that the buggy was a hazard. It was homemade, unpainted, and appeared to be held together by baling wire. The fact that it lacked doors, a roof, a trunk, and fenders would tempt any officer to reach for his ticket pad. In addition to this, the appearance of my brother was enough to make anyone stop and stare. Dressed in a bright red sweater, green gardening gloves, and a pair of welder's goggles, he could easily blow any cop's mind from two blocks away. Policemen just seemed forced to believe that this car and driver had to be illegal.

As a matter of fact, the buggy had passed inspection for highway driving. All equipment required was in working order—brakes, headlights, taillights, and so forth. But this fact did not stop policemen in their search for violations. On one occasion, the officer began to lecture us on the penalties and other consequences of not having a car inspected, and even when my brother pointed out the safety sticker on the dashboard, the officer would not concede. He proceeded to write out a ticket for not having a windshield. Later, in court, this charge was dismissed. Another incident that supported my observation of such malicious attitudes in our policemen was the night we were stopped by an off-duty cop in a silver Corvette. The Corvette had pulled up to us at two red lights. My brother raced his engine only to a small level (mainly because it would probably have stalled out if he really raced it), and then the other guy raced his. The light turned green and away we sped at the amazing speed of twenty-five or thirty miles per hour. At the next red light he pulled up and flashed a very challenging grin. At this, we chuckled and repeated our performance of such speed. As we rounded a corner and began to slow up for the next light, the Corvette rumbled up and the policeman let us see his badge, which he had beside him. He pulled us over and charged my brother with reckless driving. This charge was later dismissed in court when my brother explained it all to the judge.

It is true that policemen do have the responsibility of checking suspicious-looking cars. Many beach buggies are not even licensed to be driven on the roads—only beaches. Also many teen-age boys are very risky drivers and have conditioned the police to be extra watchful of them. Therefore, it is understandable that officers would pay this special attention to my brother and his car. But the extent of this search for culprits must also be considered. In our case, the officers went "beyond the call of duty" in enforcing the law. They not only were extra bitter in their language, but actually gave illegal citations. It is because of this that I believe that many policemen prejudge beach buggies and are unfair to their young drivers.

WRITING THE PERSUASION PAPER

How Much Evidence?   There is no simple answer to this question. The bigger the subject, the more evidence you will need. If you are trying to show that capital punishment does or does not deter violent crime, you will need a great deal of evidence; the subject is so big and controversial now that there may not *be* enough evidence to convince people one way or the other. For a short composition (say, two or three pages), you need to limit your subject so that you can be sufficiently persuasive without having to bring in a great deal of evidence. (For a three-page paper, two or three examples are the absolute minimum.) If your evidence is high quality—reliable, authoritative, and fair—you will not need so much as if your examples are questionable or subjective.

Being Fair   Remember to state the other side of the question. Is the cafeteria understaffed? Are the students hard to please? Is the food budget limited? These circumstances don't excuse inedible food, but they help us to understand it, and they help us to believe that *you* understand both sides of the question. If the reasons are good enough, we may not feel so angry at the cafeteria, even though we agree with you. You must be accurate. If you try to make the food seem worse or the reasons less good than they are, the reader will wonder why you are maligning the cafeteria. And it is not fair to toss in the other side *after* you have made the cafeteria seem awful—"Of course there are reasons for this terrible food." To be fair give the opposing side *first*. Doing so will establish that you respect the opponent, and it will give you something to argue *against:* "Despite these problems, a public cafeteria ought to maintain minimum standards for edible food."

Organizing the Paper   The simplest plan of organization is often the best. For example:

Cafeteria Food

I. Introduction: The food is terrible (some say).
II. The opposing side: There are many factors to consider in a public cafeteria.
III. Your side: Despite all the problems, cafeterias must provide edible food.
IV. Conclusion: We can sympathize with the cafeteria managers, but they must improve the food.

Read the following paper. Is the writer fair? Does he convince you?

STUCK IN
THE MIDDLE
SCOTT HATINGER

On Wednesday, October 10, Jane Fonda spoke in front of a student-filled auditorium on a diversity of subjects, including corporate business. Fonda was paid by the Association for Women Students, who thought that Jane would comment on the plight of women—what can and could be done. As the A.S.W. soon found out, however, Fonda was intent on vocalizing her own beliefs about the free enterprise system and about big business, citing many times for examples the Dow Chemical Company, a Midland-based firm. Immediately after the speech, a series of events enacted by Dow U.S.A., resulted in the cancellation of *all* Dow aid to the university. Upset by Fonda's doubting of corporate competency, including Dow U.S.A., the company felt that Fonda expressed communistic belief and that she was and is intent on the destruction of corporate control of Americans. Dow feels that the university should scrutinize anyone they invite to speak on campus and what they should speak about. Arbitrarily, the battle ground for the Dow-Fonda contest is the university, which is being used by both parties for personal grievances in the freedom-of-rights issue. Ironically, both parties are trying to manipulate the university and enforce their opposing beliefs on it.

The A.S.W. supposed that Fonda would talk about women's liberation issues and were quite unprepared for Jane's opposition to big business and freedom of rights in general. Fonda, a member of Californians for Economic Democracy, eventually stated that she is "against corporate irresponsibility and greed," and that corporations are a new group of tyrants and rulers who control Americans and their lives. As an example of corporate domination, Fonda cited the Dow Company and said that big business has the power to control the freedom of Americans, and they exercise this power many times. When Dow retaliated by cancelling grants to the university, Fonda stressed the fact of domination by big business and used Dow's retaliation as an example of "corporate blackmail." Fonda then agreed to come back to the university in defense of freedom of speech. In doing so, Fonda would get more attention in her fight and therefore abuse the university in accordance with her own personal needs and goals. In essence, what Fonda is doing is exercising her prestige and fame in the betterment of her own situation, and trying to impose her view of freedom upon the campus.

My roommate is a double major in microbiology and chemistry and was chosen by the university (along with about twelve others) to represent them in science programs at the Midland Dow Company (twenty miles from campus). The university has many such programs at Dow, including student co-op (working for credits), and they feel that this is an important asset in training for future jobs. What my roomie will work as is a medical/inorganic lab technician; that is, if he gets the job. You see, along with cancelling all university funds, Dow also shut down three science programs, involving many students. The head executives at Dow feel that Fonda is a threat to freedom and to their own well being, that she is spreading "her venom against free enterprise." Dow also felt that their funds should not be used to support people who are intent on the destruction of freedom, such as Fonda, and that the university should screen speakers who wish to overthrow the free enterprise system in the United States. What Dow is implying is that if the university wishes to continue getting aid, they (Dow) have the right to oversee who speaks at the university, and what they speak about. Dow attempted to persuade the public by calling Fonda "an avowed communist sympathizer"; yet Ms. Fonda seems to have exercised a very *democratic* belief: freedom of speech.

It doesn't matter to me if Dow and Fonda have a debate. I really don't care who is right or wrong, for it's a matter of manipulation. The university is caught in the middle, and is being used as a stepping stone to further public recognition by one side (Fonda), and as a scapegoat by the other side (Dow). The university invited Fonda to voice her opinion on certain topics and is therefore exercising the subject of this heated debate: freedom of speech. The university cannot *make* Fonda say what they want; they just try to get various speakers to talk about diverse and sometimes controversial subjects, which, in essence is what Dow is punishing the university for. Subsequently, the university cannot be used and manipulated by Fonda, who is trying to benefit in this situation. If the university allows a debate between Fonda and Dow, Fonda will get all the press coverage she wants. Neither side is suggesting an aura of *freedom,* the subject that they are disputing, for they are far more concerned with reputations and personal achievement, at the expense of the university.

Scott's paper is interesting because it involves *three* sides. If you think Scott was right to condemn both Fonda and Dow, what evidence in his paper would you cite? If you think he has not argued well, what would you cite as needing improvement in his paper?

Whatever you think of Scott's ability to persuade, you should take a look at his language. There are some personal references in his paper, but by and large he sticks to the issue, and so his paper has a much less personalized air to it than most of those in the personal-writing section. And most of Scott's sentences are fairly sophisticated. His third sentence "As the A.S.W. soon found out . . ." is thirty-seven words long; but Scott has used sentence combining (the subject of Chapter 6) to blend his thoughts skillfully into a unified whole so that the sentence can be read easily. One characteristic of modern writing is that the farther you move from personal writing, the fewer short sentences you will write. This is partly what gives writing a formal "sound." Scott has been very careful to see that he doesn't write long sentences just for the sake of length. He uses long sentences to show the major and minor points he wants to make.

Writing activity

Write a persuasion paper three to six pages long. Keep your subject simple. You need a subject you have first-hand evidence on, something you have personally experienced. And the length of the paper rules out most of the big, controversial subjects like inflation control and energy problems.

Select an audience you know well, and carefully examine their views on the topic you select. What evidence will persuade them to change their beliefs? What views do you have in common? How can you establish a bridge between you and your audience? How will your audience react to the evidence you have accumulated? What emotional and rational appeals might persuade them to alter their position?

You may want to choose a topic from the following list:

1 My dormitory room isn't fit for studying.

2 Excessive violence in hockey should be banned.

3 Freshmen should be allowed to have cars on campus.

4 The telephone company is a ripoff.

5 Insurance companies discriminate against males under twenty-five.

6 We ought to change TV . . . (advertising, entertainment, news, sports, and so on).

7 Manufacturers should give better warranties on . . . (cars, TV sets, and so on).

8 High-school football should be abolished.

9 Females/males should change their dating techniques.

10 Off-campus housing should be abolished.

11 (Smoking, drinking, eating, nudity, and so on) is good for you and should be mandatory.

12 There ought to be a law against discrimination against . . . (fat people, ugly people, young people, old people, short people, people with big noses, and so on).

13 Professors should give fewer assignments.

14 Salespeople should treat customers with respect.

15 Christmas has become too commercialized.

16 Smoking in restaurants should be abolished.

17 Horror movies should be abolished.

18 Celebrity sports events should be abolished.

19 Amateur talent shows should be abolished.

20 Sentimental love stories, "tough detective" stories, or other popular fiction should be abolished.

The folly of mistaking a paradox for a discovery, a metaphor for a proof, a torrent of verbiage for a spring of capital truths, and oneself for an oracle, is inborn in us.

PAUL VALÉRY, *The Method of Leonardo da Vinci*

Writing with sources—research writing—is usually the most formal, and often the most challenging, kind of writing you will undertake for now. Such writing requires the greatest attention to the procedures and "rules" of writing—there is more need for agreed-upon forms. Research writing, therefore, is more orderly and predictable than any natural language. Many of the variations of English, for example, which we accept as perfectly natural and acceptable elsewhere, are disallowed in academic kinds of writing. But just because formal writing *is* more orderly and predictable, there is a real danger of its becoming stuffy and boring. Your task is to control both style and content; the challenge is to remain lively and interesting while writing with sources. For an example of effective research writing, read the following paragraph from a respected scientific journal, reporting an experiment in which students pretended to be insane:

The pseudopatient, very much as a true psychiatric patient, entered a hospital with no foreknowledge of when he would be discharged. Each was told that he would have to get out by his own devices, essentially by convincing the staff that he was sane. The psychological stresses associated with hospitalization were considerable, and all but one of the pseudopatients desired to be discharged almost immediately after being admitted. They were, therefore, motivated not only to behave sanely, but to be paragons of cooperation. That their behavior was in no way disruptive is confirmed by nursing reports, which have been obtained on most of the patients. These reports uniformly indicate that the patients were "friendly," "cooperative," and "exhibited no abnormal indications."

D. L. ROSENHAN, "On Being Sane in Insane Places," *Science*, 19 Jan. 1973.

The author of "On Being Sane in Insane Places" is a professor of psychology and law, and he is writing for psychologists and lawyers. In the experiment, no doctor ever discovered that the "pseudopatients" were only faking insanity, and this fact has serious implications for both psychology and law! The article represents very formal writing. It deals with academic subject matter, and there is little or no attempt on the author's part to "express self." The writing is clear and informative and objective. Later in the article, Rosenhan writes in the first person: "I do not, even now, understand the problem well enough to perceive solutions." But this is done to avoid what many think is an awkward research point of view: "This researcher does not now understand the problem . . . ." Even with an occasional first person reference, Rosenhan's article remains objective research writing aimed at a very special audience, and it is therefore quite formal in tone and language.

For most research writing in college, something less than extreme formality is desired. You should aim for language suitable for educated audiences; that is, you should write on the formal side but not at the extreme end of the writing continuum, where only the most specialized audiences will be able to read your work. For example, here is the beginning of a research paper written with about the right degree of formality:

THE NAVY'S
DOOMSDAY
MACHINE:
PROJECT
SEAFARER

MARK STARBUCK

The discovery of power from the atom had once accompanied a dream of a world moving on to bigger and better achievements. Atomic energy could be harnessed to do a number of things. It was soon to be discovered, however, that the power from the atom was capable of great destruction. With nations growing and becoming more powerful, with science and technology at their fingertips, the threat of a nuclear attack by an aggressive nation has been a major concern of the government's defense planners for as long as such a threat existed. The navy came up with what it believed to be the answer—a communications system capable of communicating with submerged American submarines armed with nuclear-tipped missiles.

"The logic on which the U.S. retaliatory nuclear weapons system is based rests on strategies of mutual deterrence in a world where the superpowers depend upon weapons of extreme technological sophistication in order to keep their fears of each other manageable."[1] Consider a hypothetical day in 19—. Scores of nuclear missiles advancing toward the United States suddenly show up on radar screens, early warning systems, and nearly all detection devices. The nightmares we have lived with since Hiroshima and Nagasaki begin to take place as nuclear warheads explode on their targets. There can be no doubt, our country is under a massive attack by an aggressor nation with first-strike capability.[2] To prevent such a disaster, one need possess such a strong retaliatory force to make any aggressor think twice before launching such an attack. The United States Navy has spent over seventeen years researching and developing a communications system with a proposed potential for retaliation called Project Seafarer (originally known as Project Sanguine). So far, the system has cost over $100 million.[3]

The construction and development of Seafarer in Michigan has, to date, been stopped. Political and social forces have brought the controversial communications system to a halt. Nevertheless, it is still believed by the navy that Seafarer is essential to the nation's security in the event of a nuclear war, but obviously this belief is in doubt. Is Seafarer truly what the navy has envisaged or has it been an expensive miscalculation?

Mark's paper hits just about the right tone. The language is formal, but not too formal. We are aware of the writer's personality, though his voice is pretty well submerged under the technical talk about Seafarer. If we had to identify the writer's self, we might say something like, "This sounds like an intelligent, well-educated, easygoing person. He knows what he is talking about, but he isn't being stuffy or showing off." Mark offers the reader a hypothetical attack on the United States to dramatize the importance of the Seafarer question. Mark knows he has an audience, an audience that will listen to him as long as he doesn't get too technical or dull. Other than that, Mark's writing here is not drastically changed from his other writing. The subject matter itself has forced him to be a little more technical, but that is unavoidable. Note that Mark's semiformal writing is very readable.

USING THE LIBRARY

Most research begins in the library, and as you learn more and more about research, you will soon discover just how much information a college library can provide you on almost any subject, especially the most recent, up-to-date information. Unfortunately, many students avoid the library or are simply confused and overwhelmed by it. They feel they can never find anything useful or that it takes hours and hours of frustrating search to come up with one or two items. It is true that the library is not quite so simple that any child can use it, but neither is it so complex that only the librarians can find anything. The single most useful thing that you can teach yourself while in college is how to use the library with speed and efficiency.

As confusing as it may appear, the library is not an arbitrary jumble of books but a highly systematized retrieval network. Many libraries use the Dewey Decimal classification system; others use the Library of Congress system; some use both or are in the process of changing from one to the other. If you know which system your library uses, you can quickly learn the overall scheme by which books have been sorted and shelved.

DEWEY DECIMAL

000–099 General Works (bibliographies, encyclopedias, periodicals)
100–199 Philosophy, Psychology, Ethics
200–299 Religion and Mythology
300–399 Sociology (civics, economics, education, vocations)
400–499 Philology (dictionaries, grammar, language)
500–599 Science (biology, botany, chemistry, mathematics, physics, zoology)
600–699 Useful Arts (agriculture, aviation, engineering, medicine, radio)
700–799 Fine Arts (music, painting, photography, recreation)
800–899 Literature (criticism, novels, plays, poetry)
900–999 History, Geography, Biography, Travel

LIBRARY OF CONGRESS

A General Works	L Education
B Philosophy-Religion	M Music
C History	N Fine Arts
D World History	P Languages and Literature
E U.S. History	Q Science
F Local History	R Medicine
G Geography, Anthropology	S Agriculture
H Social Sciences	T Technology
J Political Science	U Military Science
K Law	V Naval Science
	Z Library Science, Bibliography

College libraries often take up several floors of a building and sometimes spread to more than one building, so it is important, before you actually start looking for books and information, to get a good overall understanding of what is in the library and exactly where everything is. Also, many libraries have special collections or libraries within the main library that may be very useful to you; for example, the law library or medical library is likely to be housed as a special collection, away from the general periodicals and books. If you were doing a study of euthanasia, you would find important information in the law and medical libraries. Find out where all the special collections are and what is in them.

THE KEYS TO THE LIBRARY

Once you know the general classification scheme of your library, you can take advantage of the three major keys to information: the *card catalog,* the *indexes,* and the *general reference works.*

THE CARD CATALOG

The card catalog is the primary key to the library; it tells you where most of the material in the library is kept. Some libraries also have subsidiary catalogs for special areas of the library. Learn where the card catalogs are and how to use them.

What Is Cataloged   Most card catalogs list more than books. Does your library contain magazines and other periodicals, newspapers, maps, pictures, and other "nonbook" items? To find out, look in the card catalog.

Card Catalog Organization   Most of the items in the catalog are listed three different ways: by author, by title, and by subject. The subject cards are important because they provide a handy cross-reference to works related to each other.

Card Information   The catalog card supplies you not only with the call number of a book, but also with other useful information. For example, the subject card in Figure 5.1 tells you (A) the call number; (B) the title and author of a book under that subject; (C) information about the library's copy of that book; (D) the place of publication; (E) the publisher; (F) the year of publication; (G) the number of preface pages; (H) the number of pages in the book; (I) the size of the book in centimeters (1 centimeter = 0.4 inch); (J) publishing information about the book; (K) the

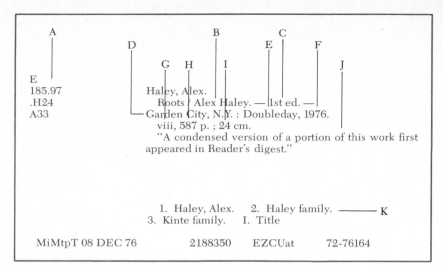

```
        A                          B       C
                    D                  E       F
                         G   H      I                   J
    E
    185.97
    .H24              Haley, Alex.
    A33               Roots / Alex Haley. — 1st ed. —
                   └─ Garden City, N.Y. : Doubleday, 1976.
                      viii, 587 p. ; 24 cm.
                      "A condensed version of a portion of this work first
                      appeared in Reader's digest."



                      1. Haley, Alex.    2. Haley family. ──────── K
                   3.  Kinte family.    I.  Title

      MiMtpT 08 DEC 76            2188350    EZCUat      72-76164
```

FIGURE 5.1

number and headings of cards for this book in the catalog. The librarian uses the information at the bottom of the card to order the book or a new catalog card.

Suppose you were doing a report on Alex Haley. You know you should read his novel *Roots,* so you look it up in the catalog, write down the call number, and go hunting for it on the shelves. But, you discover, the book is out. Now you must go back to the catalog to see what else you can find for your report. And perhaps in the meantime you lose the scrap of paper on which you have written the call number for *Roots.* The library, you may decide, is more work than you care for. But this is because of the faulty procedure you used with the card catalog. A better procedure is to break your search into steps, so that when you go into the library you go in with the idea that you are first going to see how much information you can get out of the card catalog. Instead of scribbling down call numbers for a book or two, spend thirty minutes to an hour constructing a bibliography of items listed in the card catalog. List the call number, and the *full* bibliographic reference you will need if you use the book in your paper:

E
185.97
.H24
A33 Haley, Alex. <u>Roots</u>, Garden City, New York: Doubleday, 1976

Then, when you go to the stacks or turn in your call for books, you will be armed with everything you need from the card catalog, and you will also have all the information you will need for your bibliography when you write your paper. And, having the call number means you can keep after the book until it turns up, without having to go back to the catalog again and again. In other words, you can greatly cut down on the time and the frustration level of research if you establish and follow a routine for gathering information. Running back and forth to the catalog and redoing steps you have done before can be eliminated. If you have ever traced the references in a dictionary, looking up the words under the first word you find, and then looking up the words under those words, and so on, you will get some idea of what you can do with the card catalog. Set yourself the task of constructing a working bibliography (book list) first, and you will find that the library and the librarians are more helpful. Librarians will cheerfully direct you to books if you know the call number; they may be less cheerful about helping people who haven't yet made use of the card catalog. Further, if—as often happens—the book you want is not available, you can order it through the library's own search and recall procedure, or place it on order for when it comes back, or send away for it through interlibrary loan.

THE INDEXES

In addition to books, the library also holds popular magazines, scholarly journals, and newspapers—all of which contain potentially useful information. To find a book about drug abuse is relatively simple with the card catalog, but how do you find a magazine article or a newspaper report? The great indexes are comprehensive catalogs of articles, essays, reports, and other information not published as books. The most generalized index is the *Reader's Guide to Periodical Literature*, which covers many popular magazines, starting with the year 1900. In the index you will find articles listed by title, by author, and by subject matter— and also extensively cross-indexed under many different descriptors, so that even if you have only the fuzziest notion of where to start, the indexes will quickly put you on the trail of a wealth of information.

Just as with the card catalog, there are routines to follow with the indexes. Unless you make yourself sit down and work on your bibliography first, you will soon find yourself running back and forth between the indexes and the bound volumes of periodicals.

Since the indexes are bound chronologically, and many of them go back several decades in time, you will discover that a broad subject like "drugs" will produce hundreds of articles spread out through the years—far too many for you to read. Thus, you will save yourself even more time if you carefully narrow your subject down to some smaller and more manageable aspect of the overall topic. Suppose you were interested in just the psychological profile of marijuana smokers; you could ignore many of the articles in the indexes. Even so, you will still find many articles. How should you proceed? Unless you are doing a historical study (marijuana in the 1920s), there is a general rule that all research starts where you are. That is, you start with the most recent research and work your way backward in time. You might, for example, limit yourself to research done in the last ten years or the last fifty years. But research is never *random,* and it does not make much sense to jump into the research at a random point in time. Furthermore, the tradition that recent research is based on previous research means you can quickly uncover the bibliographic material you want by finding the most recent research, which should summarize and list earlier research. (If the most recent source does not, go backward to the most recent research that does.)

In addition to the *Reader's Guide,* there are many specialized indexes, listing information not generally found in popular magazines, that may be very useful to you. For example:

Applied Science and Technology Index, 1913–
Art Index, 1929–
Bibliographic Index, 1938–
Biography Index, 1947–
Book Review Index, 1965–
Business Periodicals Index, 1958–
Cumulative Book Index, 1898–
Dramatic Index, 1909–1949
Education Index, 1929–
International Index, 1907–1965
   RENAMED *Social Sciences and Humanities Index,* 1965–1974
   DIVIDED   *Humanities Index,* 1974–
              Social Sciences Index, 1974–
London Times Official Index, 1906–
Monthly Catalog of the United States Government Publications, 1895–
Music Index, 1949–
New York Times Index, 1913–
Poole's Index to Periodical Literature, 1802–1907

Find out as much as you can about your library's indexes: which ones the library has, where they are, how to use them. With a little time and effort, the indexes will yield dozens of articles on practically any subject—which is one good reason for limiting yourself to the smallest possible aspect of any subject. The broader the subject, the more books and articles you are likely to find that you have to read and assimilate into your study.

THE GENERAL REFERENCE WORKS

The card catalogs and the indexes are the best guides to books and articles, but the library also holds a number of reference works that fall under the broad heading of encyclopedias and dictionaries, many of which can be useful to you. In addition to the general information encyclopedias such as the *Britannica* and the *Americana,* there are other works, such as the following:

Dictionary of National Biography
Encyclopedia of American History
Encyclopedia of Educational Research
Encyclopedia of Religion and Ethics
Encyclopedia of World Art
International Encyclopedia of Chemical Sciences
The Oxford Dictionary of Quotations
The Oxford English Dictionary
Reference Books: How to Select and Use Them
Webster's Third New International Dictionary of the English Language
Who's Who in America
World Almanac and Book of Facts

Begin your research with these reference works because they provide excellent summaries of large areas of research. They constitute what is known, in general, about an area, and your research probably should begin where the encyclopedias end. There is no point in "discovering" what is already in the encyclopedias; the information there can be considered common knowledge, or basic information available to anyone. You, the researcher, are expected to offer something new, something not in the encyclopedias; therefore, it may be a good idea to read and get the overview, the background material, in the encyclopedias before you begin your research.

There is some bias against quoting the encyclopedia or listing it as a source. Many researchers assume that you have read the encyclopedia entry (or entries) on your subject, but that the information is too general and probably outdated by more recent research. Furthermore, although encyclopedias are generally reliable, it is not safe to assume that they are *absolutely* reliable and *completely* accurate. However, many encyclopedia articles contain bibliographies and source material you can include in your research. Avoid encyclopedias designed especially for children, and if you list any encyclopedia as a source, be sure you have other sources to back up what you say. The best use you can make of an encyclopedia is to read it for background and the overall area of which your study is a part.

EXPLORING THE LIBRARY

There is no substitute for actually going to the library and exploring it first hand. Many libraries offer tours and provide special handouts of information about where things are; you need to assimilate as much of this information as possible right at the outset. To help you get the most out of your early library visits and avoid wandering around aimlessly, you need to have specific goals in mind, specific information you are after.

Library activity

When you have answered the following questions about your library, you will have made a very good beginning to learning how to use the library. Don't ask the librarians for help until after you have made a thorough search on your own.

1 Which classification system does your library use: Dewey Decimal or Library of Congress?

2 Exactly where in the library is the card catalog?

3 What, if anything, does the card catalog list besides books?

4 Does the card catalog list a book titled *A Grammar of Motives?* Who is the author of this book? What is the call number of this book? Where is the call number given on the catalog card?

5 Some reference works are not kept on the shelves; they are kept at the reference desk. List one or two useful reference works that are kept at the reference desk.

6 *Webster's International Dictionary* has gone through several editions. What is the most recent edition of this dictionary in your library?

7 Where is the *Oxford English Dictionary?* How is this work different from other dictionaries? Look up the word "have" in the *OED;* how long is the *OED*'s explanation of this word?

8 Where are the general encyclopedias found? Does any encyclopedia have an article on the Library of Congress (the great library in Washington, D.C.)? List two or three facts about the Library of Congress. Which encyclopedia has these facts?

9 Does your library have any special or technical encyclopedias? Give the titles of two or three specialized encyclopedias in your library.

10 Suppose you need a book your library does not have. Could you get the book from some other library through your library? What is the procedure?

11 Many years ago, J. D. Salinger's book *The Catcher in the Rye* was printed in a paperback edition. Is the paperback version still in print? Where is this information? Where could you find out whether a *casebound* (hard-cover) book is still in print?

12 Suppose you have an assignment to find out everything the Bible says about love. What reference book could you use? Where can you find this book?

13 Under what subject headings in the *Reader's Guide to Periodical Literature* will you find data for a paper on job prospects for college graduates?

14 Use the *Reader's Guide* to find out how many pages are in Merrill Shiels's article, "Why Johnny Can't Write" (*Newsweek*, 8 Dec. 1975).

15 The *English Journal* is usually not listed in the *Reader's Guide*. Why not? Where should it be listed?

16 Where are books of quotations kept? Who is the author of the following quote: "Learning is but an adjunct to ourself"?

17 What is the title of the index for government publications? If you found a pamphlet listed in this index, where might it be kept in your library? If your library doesn't have a government publication you need, how could you get it?

18 Where is the *New York Times Index*? Exactly how do you use it? What was the headline of the *New York Times* on the day that you were born?

19 Suppose you wanted to read newspaper articles in some local newspapers, which your library has on file, but which aren't indexed. How could you go about finding articles?

20 An article you need has been ripped out of its periodical. How can you get that article?

21 A celebrity you are researching made an important speech at your school some years ago. Could you hear that speech on tape?

22 Where does your library keep pamphlets, brochures, leaflets, and other unindexed materials?

23 You need a large map of Florida to check some details for a paper you are writing. Where can you find it?

24 What is in the *Britannica Yearbooks*?

25 Does your library contain any special collections or specialty libraries within it? What are they? Where are they?

26 Where are doctoral dissertations listed? What is the title of former Secretary of State Henry Kissinger's dissertation? How could you get a copy of this dissertation to read?

27 Does your library have Master's theses written by former students? Where are theses kept?

28 Where are the *current* issues of newspapers and magazines kept?

29 Suppose your instructor has placed a book "on reserve" for your class. Where will it be? What is the procedure for finding it?

30 You need facts and figures of a statistical nature to back up your research paper on modern marriages. What references might contain such information?

31 Where is the *Book Review Digest?* What's in it? How might it be useful to a researcher?

32 You are writing a paper about something that happened one hundred years ago (such as the Civil War). Could you find magazine articles that old in the *Reader's Guide?* Where are old magazines indexed? If you did find a reference to an old magazine article, how could you get a copy of the magazine to read?

33 Where is ERIC? What is it? How do you use it?

34 Suppose you need background information on a living American (such as the senior senator from your state). What reference work might give you some biographical information?

35 Suppose you were doing a paper on product reliability. What publication might give you facts and figures about new cars?

The more you find out about your library, the more you will come to understand what higher education is all about. Becoming a skilled, independent researcher is one of the rewards of a college education—a highly useful skill you can take with you when you leave college. You need to develop the habit of spending time in the library, especially during those "off" hours when the library is relatively empty. Poking around in corners, learning how to use the library, should be your first priority—your first step to becoming a researcher.

THE OBJECTIVE SUMMARY

A good place to start your work with source material is the objective summary. As you get more and more experience with formal writing, and especially research writing, you will discover how useful the summary can be. Few people can remember verbatim everything they read; we all summarize and condense information. And one of the important tasks of any researcher is to summarize research studies. As a researcher yourself, you will discover that a good summary is often as useful as—occasionally more useful than—a full article from a magazine or journal. You can tell from a good summary whether an article or book might be useful for your research. For example, you can tell from the following summary whether "frisbee golf" will fit into a paper on new developments in recreation:

THE
ST. ANDREWS
OF FRISBEE
GOLF [1]

JOAN LEONE

The Los Angeles County Department of Parks and Recreation has a new type of recreational facility—the Frisbee golf course. The course, which was opened in the summer of 1975, has become extremely popular with the public and has captured the media with enthusiasm.

Ed Headrick, founder of the International Frisbee Association, originated the proposal for developing a formal permanent Frisbee golf course. Oak Grove County Park is a fifty-three-acre natural oak grove, which is where it all began.

An eighteen-hole course was built at the park for the relatively small investment of $2,000. The sport requires no fees, scoreboard, other materials, or activities requiring personnel; there are no operating costs. In addition, it promotes casual, less competitive play and attracts many families visiting Oak Park Grove.

The course itself is relatively simple. The basic rules and diagrams of the course layout are posted at the first tee. At the start of each hole, tee-offs are ten-foot circles delineated by quartered redwood logs. Safety hazards, information on out-of-bounds, direction of the hole, and the distance involved are provided at each tee.

Target posts, presently standing four feet high, must be hit by the Frisbee. Players begin throwing one Frisbee in the tee-off area, and take their next shot with their foot on the spot where the Frisbee landed. The score is determined by the number of throws it takes to hit the target. Similar to golf, the player with the lowest score at the end of the round is the winner.

The ideal Frisbee golf course must have trees to block wind, and hilly terrain makes it all the more enjoyable. Being laid out in the hilly, densely wooded areas, the course is not confronted with other traditional activities, such as baseball.

The participation of Frisbee fans has grown, from an average of two hundred, to one thousand persons using the course on weekend days. After-school use has also become so popular that the high school located near Oak Grove Park has begun Frisbee classes! Frisbee golf has much to offer to all age groups, including men and women and the physically handicapped.

[1] Seymour Greben, "The St. Andrews of Frisbee Golf," *Parks & Recreation*, Oct. 1976, pp. 22–23.

You can see at once from Joan's summary that the article is mostly a description of how to play a new game with a Frisbee. Except for the fact that the game is popular and offers recreation to everyone, the article does not say anything about trends or developments in recreation. You might mention Frisbee golf in your

165

research paper, but you probably wouldn't need any more information about it than Joan has provided in her summary. Her summary is a research tool—a condensation of the information in a longer article, given in enough detail that the reader gets a good idea of what is in the article.

As a general rule, any summary should reduce the amount of reading by at least fifty percent, and most summaries reduce by even more than half. The guide on length of summary depends on the purpose of the summary. If you were looking for articles related only to women in sports, a one-sentence summary of the Frisbee article would be sufficient to tell you the article doesn't fit what you're looking for.

WRITING THE OBJECTIVE SUMMARY

It often happens that you write objective summaries for the benefit of someone else, such as an instructor, with only the general direction to "summarize all articles on new sports." The general rule—reduce by at least fifty percent—applies, as do the following guidelines:

1 Get the main ideas. You can usually find the topic sentences and key words in each paragraph. How much supportive material you include depends on how important you think that material is; but the main points are the heart of the article, and leaving any of them out will distort the summary.

2 Use your own words. You can condense greatly by combining ideas from the original into new sentences of your own. Avoid copying the original language as much as possible, and put quotes around any that you do borrow. Especially if you are summarizing for someone else, it is important to distinguish between words that are yours and words that are in the original. Among other things, summarizing is a good way to learn, to assimilate material, but the process doesn't work very well unless you translate the original into your own language.

3 Follow the organization of the original. Your summary should begin where the original begins and proceed in the same order as the original. You should try to give a true but condensed picture of the article, including the way it is organized.

4 In an objective summary, you record only the information contained in the article, and nothing else. Keep your opinions to yourself. Do not add commentary, interpretation, or anything else not in the original. An *objective* summary means that you are conveying just the information and nothing else. When you write an objective summary, you are processing information, as accurately and economically as possible, rather than evaluating, disputing, or agreeing with that information. The reader wants to believe that you are an impartial researcher and that your summary is a reliable condensation of the article.

5 Always give the source of your material in a footnote. Nothing is quite as frustrating as good information without a source; the un-

fortunate researcher must trudge back to the library to find the article again—if it can be found. Notice in the summary by Joan Leone that she has used a footnote number after the title of her paper. Since there is only one footnote, you do not really need to number it, but if you do use a number (superscript), put it after the title.

Basically, summarizing is a simple but useful skill. The most frequent problems beginning writers may encounter in summarizing are either that they are too summary or that they are not summary enough. A little practice should produce summaries of the proper length, but one thing to watch out for is the article that is too short to summarize. To produce a one- or two-page summary of a magazine or newspaper article, you need an article that is at least twice the length of your summary. A single column of print or a little half-page article may already be too condensed or too skimpy to summarize. Select an article that *can* be summarized.

Writing activity

Write a one-page summary of a magazine article or a newspaper article. Select a recent article, one published within the past year. Assume that you are summarizing for a researcher who has hired you to condense the material.

THE CRITICAL SUMMARY

The library will provide you with dozens of articles on any subject, but are they all equally good? You have to decide which ones to use. Researchers must learn to evaluate their sources, to be critical of the articles they find. Because something has been published does not automatically mean that it is good; and in any case, the quality of any article depends a great deal on your reasons for reading it. Here, for example is a writer's critical summary of an article read for "general information":

**THE KING AS-
SASSINATION
REVISITED** [1]

KARL WITBOLD

A sniper's shot killed Martin Luther King on April 4, 1968. *Time* magazine traces the flight from justice of convicted assassin James Earl Ray. The article covers his steps from escaping Missouri State Prison on April 23, 1967, to plastic surgery in Los Angeles and finally his arrest at Heathrow Airport in England. *Time* attempts to answer questions that still linger after eight years, using information accumulated by George McMillen, the author of a book about the crime to be published this fall. A few questions raised are, Did Ray kill King?

Why did he kill him? Did he act alone? How did Ray acquire false identification and establish four credible aliases without help?

Time presents Ray as a small time, butter-fingered burglar, nazi sympathizer, and devoted racist. McMillen and *Time* seem to agree that "Ray's anti-black sentiments turned into intense hatred for King."

Circumstances around Ray's conviction are also questionable. No one saw Ray fire the shot; the bullet that killed King could not be traced. Was the one state witness against Ray reliable?

The article, though quite interesting, was not very informative, asking more questions than it could hope to answer. *Time* seemed to be more interested in plugging the McMillen book and causing controversy than seriously discussing Martin Luther King's assassination.

[1] "The King Assassination Revisited," *Time*, 26 Jan. 1976, pp. 16–17.

Karl's summary is in fact a critique of the article in *Time* magazine. It has three important components: (1) a summary of what the article contains; (2) clues throughout that Karl is talking about a magazine article (note how many times Karl refers to the magazine by name); and (3) Karl's opinion of the article. He criticizes *what* was said in the article ("interesting" but "not very informative") as well as *how* it was said ("It asked more questions than it could hope to answer").

CRITICIZING CONTENT

Content is subject matter: *what* is said, as opposed to *how* it is said. In an article on alternative energy sources, for example, the content is what the author has to say about alternative energy sources, and you can discuss the author's knowledge and handling of this subject. The listed criteria can help you to evaluate content.

1 Is the author accurate? Does the author distort, exaggerate, or diminish the facts? Does the author *seem* to have the facts straight?

2 Has the author supplied the reader with new facts, new information, or new interpretation of the facts? How newsworthy is this subject?

3 Is the subject interesting? Does the material raise your curiosity about the subject? Does it hold your interest? Is it interesting only to you personally, or do you think it is likely to appeal to the general reader?

4 Is there enough information? Is this a thorough treatment, a summary, or a sketchy overview? Is the author treating the subject with

sufficient depth? Has the author supplied the reader with enough facts or enough details to achieve his or her overall purpose?

5 Is the material worthwhile? Does it treat a subject that most readers would agree is worth treating? If the material seems trivial or "light," did the author intend it to be that way?

6 Is the author fair? Is the overall interpretation biased, subjective, slanted, objective? Does the author present material to justify his or her stance? Does the author try to look at both sides of the issue? Do you trust this author? Does the author violate any of the rules of logical writing?

7 Did you feel satisfied or disappointed or puzzled by the article? If the author started out to prove something, did he or she fulfill your expectation? If the author started out to analyze something, did you feel he or she lived up to the commitment? Did you come away feeling the author knew the subject and did a good job of presenting it to the reader?

CRITICIZING STYLE

Style is the author's manner of writing: how the material is written as opposed to what it says. Evaluating a piece of writing with the following criteria can help you to criticize style.

1 Is the author readable? Are there too many big words, too many long sentences, too many abstract concepts not explained in concrete terms? Is the writing aimed at the right audience? Can the educated general reader handle this material without difficulty?

2 Has the author chosen vocabulary that is accurate, colorful, effective? Is the author expressing a lively point of view, or does he or she sound bored? Are the language and the attitude boring? Is the author being matter of fact, disinterested, objective, ironic, or something else?

3 Is the language appropriate? Does the author treat dignified subjects with dignity and humorous subjects light-heartedly? Or is the author showing off, being sarcastic, or smart-alecky? Are there any surprises in language? An unusually good word? An especially adept phrase? A well-turned sentence? Can a careful reader find variety in the sentences? Or is there evidence that the writer was having a hard time writing: labored sentences, fuzzy language, humdrum words?

4 What is the author's attitude toward the subject? Does the author like the subject? Does the author think the subject is important? More important than you do?

5 What is the author's attitude toward the reader? Is the author friendly? Indifferent? Sarcastic? Patronizing? Too technical? Who does the author think the reader is: a little child, God, an educated adult?

6 Who does the author think he or she is? Very Important Person? Poor-little-old-me? Is the author's view of self (the author's voice) one you can relate to?

7 Did you enjoy the piece of writing? Did you feel pleased by the way it was written? Did it occur to you that the material was especially well written? Did you finish the article thinking, "This was a good piece of work"? Would you recommend the article to others?

When you talk about *how* something is written, you must discuss style and organization, just as you do in your composition class. Everyone's favorite comment on a piece of writing is "interesting and informative," but having said that, you should go on to explain *why* you say it. Is the reasoning acceptable? Does the author avoid slanting, bias, exaggerations, obvious faults in reasonable writing? Do you need a Ph.D. to understand the article, or is it aimed at elementary-school children? Is the tone light, heavy, dull, and so forth? Very often some one feature of an article will stand out as the chief virtue or overriding fault—such as an overreliance on technical vocabulary. It may be a good idea to deal with that feature as the primary aspect of your critique, but then relate others to it. Why, do you think, does the author use such language? Is it justified, appropriate, and so on?

Note that Karl *quotes* the article where it is appropriate to use the original words. Read the following critique. Explain how the writer has followed the advice above. What are the writer's strengths?

HONK, HONK, IF YOU LOVE MARY HARTMAN, MARY HARTMAN [1]

JOAN LEONE

Don't be surprised if you find Mary Hartman washing lettuce with detergent. In her television parody of a soap opera, she is portrayed as being a "copeless" housewife beset by assorted calamities in Fernwood, Ohio. *Reader's Digest* brings out the reality of *Mary Hartman* by stating: "It's the news about American life—complete with issues like impotence, alienation, homosexuality and adultery, and references to Vietnam, Richard Nixon, Watergate and Howard Hughes." The article compares the show to the news by pointing out that *Mary Hartman* is the news and TV news tells us almost nothing about people's lives.

The show has been analyzed and interpreted by many viewers. Donald Freed, novelist and coordinator of an extension course at the University of California, believes that Mary's uneasy feeling that things should be different is a form of existential awareness.

The article has a relaxing and honest air to it. This casual style makes it easy to read and interpret. *Reader's Digest* justly recognizes that there are two sides to the story. "It's not all applause for *Mary Hartman,* of course. A station in Richmond, Va., cancelled the show."

Mary Hartman lives the life of a mother, a lover, rejector, and rejectee. How can she be them all? Easy, she's the star of the show. *Reader's Digest* portrays the character of Mary Hartman as a symbolic figure in today's society. Should we be laughing at her or is she capturing the true reality of our own lives?

Like a tattered housewife we search for love and understanding.

What qualities make this show a success? Television critic, novelist, and teacher, Peter Sourian, sees the producer, Norman Lear, as a "Marxist who is chronicling the decline of a capitalist society."

The satire soap opera *Mary Hartman* is more than it is apt to project. *Reader's Digest* covers the article with humor and signifies the symbolic aspects that relate to our daily lives. Through the somewhat far-fetched half-hour episodes *Mary Hartman* reveals the real you. That is why it is a uniquely American show. It could only happen here.

Although viewers have trouble clearly defining the show, *Reader's Digest* has handled *Mary Hartman* with frankness and perspicuity.

[1] Ted Morgan, "Honk, Honk, If You Love Mary Hartman, Mary Hartman," *Reader's Digest*, Feb. 1977, pp. 57–65.

Writing activity

Write a two- or three-page critical summary of a recent article from a magazine or newspaper. Your criticism of the article is an important part of the assignment; do not devote more than one-half page to the summary.

Read and analyze the article carefully, using the guides to criticism on pages 168–169. It is a good idea to jot down the points you want to make and the examples you want to use. You need not make a formal outline, but some prewriting notes to yourself will be very useful.

COMPARING SOURCES

One of the most enlightening aspects of research is to compare the work of two different authors on the same subject. It is simply not safe to assume that any given author should be relied upon for either the facts or the interpretation of the facts in a given case. Writers have different styles, they write for different audiences, and they write from different motives—even when they claim to be writing objectively (without personal bias). It is important for you, in research writing, to be able to evaluate your sources, to see the differences between authors, and to appreciate the influence the writer has on his or her materials. Author *X* says Adolf Hitler was a deranged maniac; author *Y* says he was a dynamic leader. You cannot decide who has the more tenable position until you understand your sources. What would lead two supposedly intelligent writers to draw such different conclusions about the same subject?

Here is a writer comparing two magazine articles about the boxer George Foreman. Can you tell from what the writer says that the two articles are in fact different? How does the writer bring out the differences?

FOREMAN'S
FIGHT

GORDON WYMORE

Far from the flag-toting days of Olympic boxing are the problems of the heavyweight boxer. George Foreman, remembered by many Americans for waving the American flag after winning the Olympic gold medal, has encountered many problems since the heavyweight title was taken from him by the flamboyant Muhammad Ali. His problems are outlined by magazine articles in *Sports Illustrated* and *Newsweek*.

Peter Bonventre is the author of the article in *Newsweek* magazine. Bonventre states, "The defeat shattered his image of himself, pulled him apart from old friends and advisors, and made him question why he had ever laced on a pair of boxing gloves."[1] Foreman fired his trainer and hired one of the best in the business—Gil Clancy. Bonventre claims Clancy has built Foreman's confidence up and changed his style of fighting. According to the author, Foreman is ready for a shot at the heavyweight championship of the world.

The *Sports Illustrated* article is written by George Foreman with Edwin Shrake assisting. This article is mainly concerned with making excuses about his loss to Muhammad Ali for the heavyweight championship. Foreman states, "First, let me tell you some truths. Let's go back to the ring at Zaire . . . ."[2] Foreman tries to lay the blame for the loss on his ex-trainer, Dick Sadler. Foreman says that Sadler trained him wrong, used the wrong strategy for the fight, and told him to stay down on the canvas, a move that lost the fight. He then goes on to defend his controversial exhibition in Toronto, where he fought and beat five challengers on the same night. Finally, Foreman concludes all his problems are behind him, and he deserves another "shot at the crown."

The two authors' approaches to Foreman's problems vary greatly. Bonventre writes his article on Foreman from a third-person point of view, while the *Sports Illustrated* article is written by Foreman himself. Foreman's facts are distorted, and he only brings out the facts that will enhance his image in the reader's mind. Meanwhile, Bonventre deals in what he considers to be the truth; however, it is enlivened by his own comments.

The grammar used by both writers also varies. Foreman's article is full of "street talk," slang, and clichés. He overuses the word "man": "Man, I really got messed over there."[3] "Man, I was back in the ring . . . ."[4] Repeated use of street talk distracts from the overall impression of the article. Bonventre's essay had more vivid details than Foreman's, but the words are such that most people can comprehend them.

The former heavyweight champion of the world clambered into the ring, and his features froze into a glare as frightening as any of the punches that he exploded against his sparring partner. He even looked dangerously trimmer, and each blow was punctuated by a harsh grunt that echoed through the gym . . . .[5]

Bonventre's nice transitions between paragraphs make the article a pleasure to read. In contrast, Foreman's article has no pattern of arrangement. It is as if it was written down as the thoughts occurred to him. Foreman's writing could be condensed into a shorter essay, without losing the meaning, by cutting out useless material: "Maybe you didn't even read about the fight. I mean, there was no TV, and papers didn't fall all over themselves to cover it." [6] Phrases like this could be eliminated throughout the article. Bonventre's review is presented so that he puts forward the facts and draws a conclusion in one smooth-reading paper.

In conclusion, Bonventre's article is clearly superior to Foreman's if the basis for quality is grammar. Bonventre writes with a polished touch while Foreman writes at the level of his ninth-grade education. However, Foreman's article includes an inside view of boxing—a view readers rarely see. Bonventre's essay has the experienced writer's touch but lacks the "personality" of Foreman's article. Overall, the two articles are both good, but for different reasons.

[1] Peter Bonventre, "Tiger, Burning Bright," *Newsweek,* 26 Jan. 1976, p. 38.

[2] George Foreman, "Man, Big George is Back," *Sports Illustrated,* 15 Dec., 1975, p. 82.

[3] Foreman, p. 84.

[4] Foreman, p. 86.

[5] Bonventre, p. 38.

[6] Foreman, p. 86.

Gordon's analysis of the two articles is fair and insightful. He begins by summarizing the content of the two articles. After an introduction that lets the reader see that he is going to discuss two magazine articles, Gordon describes the *Newsweek* article objectively. He summarizes without evaluating. In his next paragraph, Gordon summarizes the *Sports Illustrated* article, again objectively. These two paragraphs are important for the reader; it would be difficult for us to appreciate the critical comments if we did not have some notion of what is being criticized.

In his fourth paragraph, after a transitional sentence, Gordon begins his critique of the two articles. In this paragraph Gordon presents an overview of his reactions to *what* the authors say and *how* they say it.

In the next two paragraphs, Gordon focuses on the style and organization of the two articles, because it is here that he finds the greatest differences between them.

Finally, in his concluding paragraph, Gordon gives his overall view of the two articles and concludes that whereas Bonventre's article is better written, Foreman's has a view of boxing that most people don't get to see, and therefore they are both good articles. Gordon has managed to be both critical and fair, and the reader comes away with a very good notion of what is in the two articles.

WRITING THE COMPARISON OF SOURCES

The comparison of sources is based on two articles on the same subject. In some cases the two articles may treat different aspects of the same subject, as when one article discusses the President's foreign policy and another discusses his relations with Congress or his family life. These different views or different aspects of the subject will work very well for your purposes. In fact, you should expect to find more differences than similarities in your sources, unless your authors have been borrowing from each other. In theory, two newspapers covering the same national or international story should come up with the same information, but *in fact,* they usually do not, unless they are both relying on one or more of the news wire services for their information; and even then surprising variations can occur.

In the first paragraph of a comparison of sources you must make clear to the reader that you are discussing two articles. Mention them by title, or refer to the magazines or the authors or all of these, so that there can be no mistake about your sources. If there is a common thread through the articles (the President's woes increase both at home and abroad), you should say so. If the two articles are very different, you need only point out this difference (two views of the President: national leader and family man).

As Gordon did in his paper on Foreman, spend two paragraphs describing what is in each of the articles. Even a one-paragraph summary can give the reader a fair notion of what is in each of the articles.

After considering the articles separately, it is a good idea, as Gordon did in his fourth paragraph, to consider them together.

Analyze the overall approaches to the articles. You should be concerned with both *what* was said and *how* it was said. Do both authors have the facts? Who—or what—is the source of information? What is the point of view: objective reporter, news analyst (interpreter), human-interest reporter (entertainer), or something else? Analyzing an author's *approach* to his or her materials can tell you a great deal about how to judge what is being said. Is the author accurate, fair, comprehensive, informed, and so on?

When considering the writers' styles, you may want to distinguish between the actual words and sentences they use as opposed to the way they have set up or organized their articles. It is important *throughout* your paper to back up what you say by quoting from the articles, but especially here, where you are talking about *how* the articles are written, it is important to quote from the sources. Not only does quoting help back up what you say, but it gives the reader some of the flavor and texture of the sources. Nothing is quite so revealing about sources as examples in their own words.

Finally, in your conclusion you must give your opinion of the articles. Are they good journalism, good research, good writing? You need to be fair here: point out strengths as well as weaknesses. It is possible to conclude, as Gordon does, that the articles are effective on different grounds, for different purposes. You must try to avoid fence sitting and hedging too much. If one is truly superior in your eyes, you must say so and explain why. Try to avoid the all-purpose evaluation: "Interesting and informative." Anything well written is likely to be interesting and informative. As critic it is your job to try to explain why. On what grounds have you evaluated something as interesting and informative? You may want to review the guides to criticism on pages 168–169.

Footnotes   Even if you have identified the articles in your paper, it is a good idea to give a full footnote for each of them at least once. Since there are only the two articles involved, it is not strictly necessary to use a new footnote reference every time you quote from one of the articles. But if you are going to footnote each of your direct quotes, it is a good idea to do it as Gordon has, with a shortened form of the first reference instead of with *ibid*.

Writing activity

Find two articles on the same subject, and write a three- to six-page comparison of them. It should be relatively easy to find two articles that interest you using the *Reader's Guide to Periodical Literature*, but you might also want to try two newspaper articles or one news-

paper and one magazine article on the same subject: two articles on the President, two articles on the Olympics, two articles on a sensational crime, and so on.

THE RESEARCH PAPER

There is a kind of intellectual excitement and satisfaction in pursuing information; each researcher hopes to find one new fact, one new idea to add to the world's great store of knowledge. Thus, researching is a bit like detective work—first finding the facts, and then understanding them, especially understanding them. Charles Darwin's work as a researcher, finding and cataloging lifeforms, led finally to his understanding of a great principle of nature; his book *On the Origin of Species* was the outcome.

If you know how to use a modern library and understand the rules of evidence and the procedures for writing research papers, you will be able to explore for yourself the ideas and areas of research that interest you. You will also have a solid basis for any work in your chosen profession. Some curious fact, some unexplained puzzle, some problem that won't go away has been the start of many an investigation, leading to important discoveries in every field of study.

In large part, finding the right research question to ask is the key to finding useful answers. Researchers can start with only the vaguest general notion, but they must continue to research and refine their notion until they discover a precise research question. In general, the procedure has these steps:

1 Select a general topic or area (based on personal interest).
2 Begin the preliminary reading.
3 Refine the research question (based on reading).
4 Start the research; make further refinements in the research question.
5 Finish the research; write a report on the research.

The second and third steps are most important. The preliminary reading accomplishes two things: it lets you know whether your topic is researchable, whether there is information available on it. And it lets the research itself tell you how to shape the research question. Beginning researchers sometimes make the mistake of deciding in advance, before looking at any of the materials, exactly what to research; worse, sometimes they agonize over the research question for days, unable to reach a decision, without looking at any of the materials on the subject. This makes hard work of research, and more serious, it introduces a research bias into the process. If you set out to prove a preconceived idea or you set out determined to find an answer to a preconceived question, you have adopted a mind set that will prevent you from viewing your research objectively and that may eventually cause you to distort your findings.

FINDING A THESIS

Naturally, we would all like to be the one who discovers some important new fact; we would all like to be able to write a profoundly significant research work. For these reasons some researchers start out with enormous questions of great significance: Is there a God? What will the future be like? How can the political structure of the world be changed? It might be rewarding to be able to answer questions like these, but they are just *too* big for any researcher. A skillful researcher with endless energy, time, and financial backing must still settle for quite a small research question. For example, medical science has been looking for a cure for cancer for decades, but each researcher has a much smaller problem to work on, which may or may not lead to the answer to the overall question. Some researchers are in chemotherapy, others are in radiology, and still others are in immunology (the study of the body's own defense mechanisms against disease). Researching is patient, painstaking, detailed work, and it often takes years and years of such patient work from many researchers before the right answers are discerned. Once in a while, a researcher may get a lucky break and accidentally stumble onto an answer quickly, but generally speaking, the bigger the question, the longer the research will take.

In a college classroom, then, with no more than a semester or quarter to work in, you cannot tackle a big question. You must find for yourself the smallest possible question to work on. Sexism was a popular subject throughout the 1960s and the early 1970s. Many students attempted to write research papers about it (Are men and women equal? Are girls and boys taught stereotyped sex roles? Do women have legal recourse against discrimination?). None of these questions could be researched very well in a short time because the questions were one sided and involved areas of research that had not been examined in depth by science or jurisprudence. To answer such questions (Are girls and boys taught stereotyped sex roles?) requires *primary* research—experiments, laboratory investigations, field work. Few beginning researchers are ready for such work. For your first research paper, you should rely on research you can do in the library.

Mostly, the library contains what other researchers have *said* about various subjects, and it is well suited, then, to *secondary* research. Suppose we change some of those sexism questions so that they could be answered with secondary research, in the library: Do scientists believe that men and women are physically equal? Does the public believe that women should be paid the same wages as men for doing the same work? Have there been any court cases arguing against the denial of opportunity based on sex? You can see that these questions could indeed be answered through library research. The basic question for secondary research is, *Who said what?* The *words* that have been written on nearly anything are what is in the library, and any question involving who said what or how many people said what or what kind of people said what starts research off in the right direction: looking for things the library actually does contain. In short, the answer to the question, Does sexism exist in America? probably cannot be found in the library. What can be found is what people have said about this question, what judges, lawyers, doctors, and others have said. And this leaves the *conclusion,* the answer to the question, up to you, as it should in worthwhile research.

For example, a growing concern in this country is developing over euthanasia (mercy killing) and the right to die. One day you may have to vote on this issue. After reading everything you can find about this issue, how do you as a researcher think you would reach your conclusion? The question involves morals and also law, medicine, and several other profound dimensions of human life. Imagine being the judge listening to all the evidence on both sides of the case. Research usually does not *prove* anything, in the sense of providing a single, indisputable answer; you will not discover a Dead Sea scroll that says at what point life-support measures should be discontinued. Instead, you will find evidence, pieces of information. You must weigh the evidence. And then you must *decide* what the answer is. The researcher must decide what the evidence means and then formulate conclusions from what the evidence shows. It is not surprising, then, that many researchers decide that the evidence is inconclusive, that there is not enough evidence or that the evidence is not good enough to allow a single, final conclusion to be drawn. Such research is perfectly valid; far better to know that you are not yet ready to give an informed answer to the question than to deceive yourself, or draw an inappropriate conclusion.

Coming up with a good topic for research is always the hardest job. Even after preliminary reading and thinking about your subjects, you may still start off with a subject that is just too big or that has some other built-in problem. You must keep reminding yourself that no matter how small the subject is, you are likely to find large amounts of research materials you will have to read, so the smaller the better. Four guidelines—specific, limited, worthwhile, researchable—can help you decide upon your thesis.

Specific Is the wording of the thesis specific enough? Is the object of investigation clear? A researcher who sets out to investigate "morality" will quickly discover that there is no single interpretation of that term, and even that what people do with regard to that concept differs widely. To investigate today's morality might involve things like numbers of robberies, incidents of cheating, church attendance, any number of *subtopics* within morality. Perhaps one of the subtopics is what you should investigate.

Limited "Trucks," "labor unions," "World War II" all seem specific enough; at least it is likely to be clear to most people what you are talking about. But even "trucks" is quite a large subject. To test the size of any subject, see how many questions you can ask about it. The more questions, the bigger the subject. (How did the truck develop? How many kinds of trucks are there? How are they made? How does a truck work? What are the political issues involving trucks? And so on.) The smallest question you can ask about anything is likely to be one that can be answered *yes* or *no*, and that is an excellent place for you to begin your research. Do trucks pay sufficient taxes to pay for the damage they do to highways? (Yes or no?) Do trucks cause more pollution than cars? (Yes or no?) Are truck drivers the safest drivers on the road? (Yes or no?) You may discover through your research that these questions really cannot be answered with a yes or no; the issues may be far more complex than they seemed at the outset (they almost always are). But if you frame your question in this highly limited yes/no formula, your chances of having a workable research thesis will be much improved. If the answer then comes out to be maybe or sometimes yes and sometimes no, so much the better; your conclusion will show the reader how to make sense out of the question, which is the point of research in the first place. Furthermore, stating your question in a *two-sided* manner like this avoids the problem of what to do with contrary evidence. If you start out determined to prove that trucks cause more pollution than cars, you may have to ignore evidence that contradicts your thesis.

Worthwhile   Is the question worthwhile? Does it provide information that most people would care to hear about? This is the hardest aspect of a research question. What seems relevant and important to the researcher may not strike the public or the funding agency as worthwhile. A researcher who wants to study a rare sea creature off the shores of California will have to show why the research is worthwhile. Since almost anything will interest someone, it shouldn't be too hard to show that even very rare and unusual subjects have their value. But if you follow the formula that the more specialized and limited in interest your subject is, the fewer readers you will have, it would seem that, as a general rule, you should not select subjects with a very highly specialized audience. Still, this is no easy decision to make. If the subject is worthwhile, even to a limited audience, perhaps it should be pursued. If you are truly interested in and excited about a subject, you should be able to show your audience why it is interesting, why it is worthwhile, why it should be researched. In college, though you can assume that you have an educated audience, your classmates all have different interests and areas of specialization; even your professor is likely to have interests different from yours, so you cannot assume an elite audience of enthusiasts.

Researchable   It is difficult to imagine many subjects not available in a good college library; but if for some reason the library does not have much on your subject, you need a new thesis. It is not a good idea to attempt to research primarily, or even largely, through interlibrary loan. If you cannot readily get your hands on a sufficient quantity of material, the task of collecting material will quickly overshadow everything else. Highly technical or abstruse knowledge may not be available even through interlibrary loan. And there is always the possibility that some subjects simply have not been well researched, meaning that there is little information anywhere. Eventually, researchers may have to reconcile themselves to traveling to libraries and research centers all over the world to find information, and to undertaking field studies to fill in where research is missing. But in your first year at college, when you are still learning how to research, you would do better to stick with subjects you can research easily.

Thesis exercise

Using the criteria specific, limited, worthwhile, *and* researchable, *try to decide which, if any, of these suggested topics could be turned into a workable research thesis. Which ones seem to you the most promis-*

ing for research? Can you explain why you would vote against the others? The topics are given here just as they were proposed by students; some of them we decided could be worked into good research questions; others we decided were not so good. What do you think?

1 *Honor* Is there any honor left in America? What is honor today? I plan to show how honor has declined in many aspects of America.

2 *Hobbies* Many people have fascinating hobbies. Some surprising people have hobbies that you wouldn't think of. My paper will discuss the different kinds of hobbies different people have.

3 *Arabian horses* Why are these horses so much loved by everyone? What makes them wanted by kings and movie stars? I want to tell why I think the Arabian is the most beautiful horse in the world.

4 *Campus sex* Who is doing what on campus? I want to do a survey by interviewing students. I'll ask them about their sex lives and write up the results as a research paper.

5 *Republicans* What does it mean to be a Republican? I want to tell about my work as a Young Republican, what we stand for, what we are trying to do.

6 *Witchcraft* Are there any witches today? There have been lots of books and magazines about modern witches. I want to write about modern witchcraft.

7 *Lincoln* I think he was our greatest President, and I think more people should know about his real life. I want to tell about Lincoln's life.

8 *Euthanasia* Do we have a right to end a life? I'd like to show both sides of this issue.

9 *Motorcycles* The motorcycle is a fantastic device. There is more to it than most people think.

10 *Childless marriage* Children are no longer thought of as necessary to modern marriages. The attitude about having children has changed.

11 *Ecology* We have got to stop polluting our atmosphere. We will all die of suffocation if the factories don't stop.

12 *Horror movies* What is it about horror movies that fascinates people? Why are people drawn to terror and horrible stuff?

EVIDENCE: DATA AND DOCUMENTATION

TAKING NOTES

With the advent of copying machines, some students have developed the habit of simply photocopying entire articles or chapters in books, even without reading the articles beforehand. This practice merely delays the actual work of note taking and is generally a poor way to go about research. Occasionally, you may find an article of such importance that you would like to have a copy of it, but most of what you find in the library can and should be handled in a simpler fashion.

Read Much, Write Little   Copying volumes of notes, even with the aid of the nearest copy machine, is a waste of time. You must still read, understand, and *extract* from this material only the information you need. Copying without understanding can lead to problems, as when later paragraphs contradict the one paragraph that seems to support your thesis.

Take Notes   Most of your notes should be notes, messages to yourself about the source: "Smith agrees with findings of Stennis Committee." Unless you intend to quote it, you need not copy the sentence in which Smith says he agrees with Stennis.

Copy Exactly   If you are going to copy, copy exactly. *Never* paraphrase while you copy. You can paraphrase later, when you write the paper, but at the outset it is important to keep clear which are your words and which are in the source. If you develop the habit of copying exactly what you find, you need never be confused later over who said what.

USING STATISTICS

Researching any subject today is likely to involve the use of statistics. Statistics can mean anything from simple numbers, such as the number of students at a concert, to complex mathematical computations and figures. Figures can be used as incidental data, or they can be the whole body of research. Here, for example, is a paragraph from a student paper lamenting the fact that insurance companies favor young women over young men:

At first you might say that I'm exaggerating, but here are a few facts. I own a 1969 Chevy, while my sister owns a 1972 Plymouth. I pay $330 compared to her rates of $120 yearly. She is only one year older than I am, but she has had a total of four accidents, while I have never had one. How in the world can this be?
PAUL SCHLEUTER

The power of numbers is such that they carry more weight than other kinds of data. If Paul had said only that he had paid more for insurance but his sister had had more accidents, the statements would have been less convincing. The numbers constitute facts; statements about "more" and "less" are generalizations about the facts. Virtually all readers will prefer the facts to the generalizations. Thus, the primary rule about numbers is to prefer numbers over quantitative generalizations. There is nothing to be gained and much to be lost by statements that allude only vaguely to quantities, such as "the incidence of cancer is on the rise," especially if you have the actual figures on hand.

Look at the two versions of the following paragraph concerning Hank Aaron's record-breaking home run. Why is the second version better?

A On a night in the early seventies, Hank Aaron of the Atlanta Braves stepped into the batter's box early in the game against the Los Angeles Dodgers. The seats in Braves' Stadium were filled in anticipation of witnessing a big event in baseball history: Aaron's next home run would break Babe Ruth's career record for home runs.

B On the night of April 8, 1974, Hank Aaron of the Atlanta Braves stepped into the batter's box in the first inning of the season opener against the Los Angeles Dodgers. All 55,000 seats in Braves' Stadium were filled in anticipation of witnessing the biggest single event in baseball history: Aaron's next home run, which would give him 715, and break Babe Ruth's career record of 714.
BRAD SOLBERG

Brad's version (B) immediately gains specificity and accuracy because Brad supplies us with all the missing data, especially the key statistics: Ruth's home runs and Aaron's. But it also gains power and significance: because Brad knows exactly when the event occurred, exactly how many seats are in the stadium, and exactly how many home runs are involved, the reader *trusts* Brad. Here is someone who has investigated and found convincing numerical evidence. Here is someone who really knows what he is talking about. Here is someone the reader can believe! Why is this important? The paragraph is the introduction to a paper in which Brad attempts to compare the two ballplayers. Since the times and conditions under which the two men played were considerably different, and since baseball fans can be fairly emotional about this question, Brad is being careful to be fair and accurate. That is the power of statistics: they help the reader to believe in the knowledgeability and the fairness of the writer.

Since statistics are widely available today and have so much persuasive force, you should know a few cautions about their use. First of all, you must carefully consider your audience. Today everyone has calculators, and everyone has had at least some math in high school. Still, a surprising number of people are confused by numbers. You must try to estimate what sorts of figures your audience can handle. For example, the following statement appears in a composition arguing for a higher drinking age: "Right now, 32.4 percent of children from ages twelve to seventeen use alcohol, as compared to 15 percent in 1971." Many readers will have no difficulty with the statement. But there may be some who will misread it since the figures identify a percentage of a *group* of children (not all children) and compare it with comparable figures from an earlier time. There is a severe limit on the complexity of figures the general reader can handle with ease; few readers can handle much more than simple arithmetic. Only a very limited audience, for example, will understand statistical concepts such as the following: "With a *t* value of 8.4 and 99 degrees of freedom, we find from Table F that the mean difference is significant beyond the 0.01 level" (Popham and Sirotnik, *Educational Statistics*).

Another problem arises when writers use too many statistics. Though numbers are powerful data, they can quickly overload the reader's ability to deal with them. Except for those who are particularly talented in mathematics, most readers soon grow weary of numbers. There is no easy rule about how much is too much. For example, read this sentence from a paper on the advertising industry: "These media, along with their respective percentages of the number of advertising dollars spent, are as follows: thirty percent for newspapers, twenty percent for television, fourteen percent for direct mail, seven percent for radio, five percent for magazines, and the remaining twenty-four percent for samples, posters, and other promotional materials." Perhaps this is not too much for most readers. But this is only one sentence. If there are going to be many such passages, the reader may soon begin to nod off. Most people have a surprisingly limited ability to process numbers. If your research must make use of many statistics, consider presenting them in charts.

Finally, we have all learned to be suspicious of statistical generalizations. Numbers are useful and important in research, but they don't automatically solve things. Writers cannot afford to be naive about numbers. Suppose we find the statement, "Fifty percent of the students in any class are likely to be wearing blue jeans." What would you be willing to conclude from this? A careful look at the statement itself will reveal that it actually only says half the students may (or may not?) be wearing blue jeans.

Beyond that, you need to know who the students are, where the school is, and even what time of day and what season of the year the observation was made before you can draw any strong conclusions. People have also learned to be suspicious about the sampling techniques of much modern research. Therefore, it is important to be cautious about using figures to prove things (see "Amphiboly" in Chapter 4). Certainly you should be on guard against the sweeping statistical generalization, such as the one in the following excerpt:

It [*Saturday Night Fever*] spoke to the condition of millions of well-dressed, physically beautiful boys and girls who have everything—and nothing. Who have made love and taken drugs and lorded it over their little worlds like princes and princesses to the manner born. Modern youth are still lonely, but they're not seeking love. They have found it—in their own reflections.
ALBERT GOLDMAN, "The Delirium of Disco," *Life,* Nov. 1978

Goldman may be right, of course, but we cannot tell from his statement. "Millions" is a very large number . . . millions who are all well dressed and physically beautiful? All of modern youth? Every writer—every researcher—must be alert to the fact that while numbers greatly add to the persuasiveness of research, careless or inappropriate use of statistical data will have just the opposite effect.

USING SOURCES

Since most of what is in the library is secondary sources, some complications arise concerning the nature and quality of evidence. Most of these problems arise out of the fact that you must rely on what someone tells you about your subject; some authority stands between you and the thing you wish to investigate. Suppose you were interested in the question of whether apes can talk. You probably do not have the means to experiment or even to observe apes directly. Instead, you must rely on the work of others who have worked directly with apes—their work with the apes is *primary* research; the books and articles they have written about it constitute *secondary* research material for you. Because a great deal of research relies on secondary sources, and almost all research makes at least some use of secondary material, it is important to understand and appreciate some of the problems associated with its use.

For one thing, it is important for the researcher to realize what he or she is doing. As a college student, you probably cannot investigate the question of whether apes can talk. That is, you must frame your question in such a way that it accounts for *secondary* rather than *primary* research. If you ask instead what is *known* about the question of whether apes can talk, or what is the state of knowledge of the research on this question, it is clear that you have in mind a library project, one that will require you to read and report what others have said on this subject. The distinction is crucial. The primary research question (Can apes talk?) is a matter of fact, to be answered with evidence from observation and experimentation—the methods of science. The secondary question (What do researchers say about whether apes can talk?) is a matter of *opinion,* based as far as possible on fact, to be solved with library search procedures and the rules for handling expert testimony. In short, the rules for answering the primary question are the rules of the laboratory; the rules for the secondary question are the rules of the courtroom.

CONVINCING WITH EVIDENCE

It is a television cliché that in a court of law, expert witnesses are contradicted by other experts. Psychiatrists for the defense agree that the defendant is insane, or was at the time of the crime; psychiatrists for the prosecution are equally certain that the defendant is now and was at the time of the crime quite sane. What is the jury to believe? Your position is somewhat similar in the library. Expert X says that apes can talk. Expert Y says they cannot. What do you say? Research is partly science, partly art. There is no sure-fire formula for determining the answers to research questions; usually, the best you can do is give reasonable answers based on the currently available knowledge—knowing full well that later researchers may find reason for discarding your present answers. In general, three "rules" are useful as you approach the evidence.

Consider the Weight of Evidence   The more evidence there is for one side of a question, the more believable that side is likely to be. If ten psychiatrists find the defendant sane and two find him insane, the jury is likely to believe the ten. But the weight of research is not the only consideration. *All* the researchers could in fact be wrong, or all partly right. Or, as has happened in the past, the majority opinion could be the wrong one. In fact, it happens quite frequently that the majority, established opinion is later overthrown by new research. A hundred experts swearing that apes cannot talk can be rebutted by a single talking chimpanzee; so the question is not automatically solved by discovering the distribution of evidence. It is important, however, to discover what the experts think. Do most say that apes can talk? Cannot talk? Is the break about even, half saying one thing, half saying the other?

Consider the Authorities   Usually in a dispute over evidence, we find a war of credentials. The defense would like to claim that its experts are *better* (more expert) than those of the prosecution, and the other way around too. This is a useful step to take only if some of the "experts" are in fact not authorities at all. If the defense has brought in five world-renowned psychiatrists and the prosecution has brought in nurses, orderlies, and administrators from an unknown psychiatric clinic, the jury is likely to think the defense has *better* experts. But, unless the prosecutor is very naive, the experts on *both* sides will be respected authorities. In that case there is little to be gained from splitting hairs over who has the most degrees, the most publications, the wealthiest clientele, and so on. The jury is not likely to find such a war of experts worthwhile. At best, you as a researcher should be alert to witnesses who have a vested interest in research. Some groups, for example, have an interest in the energy question—they are not "impartial" witnesses. We could suppose that relatively few people would not have an impartial ("scientific") interest in the question of whether apes can talk, but it is not safe to ignore the possibility. (Research grants, professional reputations, and other intangibles may be involved in many so-called impartial investigations.) Besides, an authority may be wrong no matter how important his or her credentials. And, an authority may be right no matter how humble his or her credentials. So the credentials game is only of limited use, something you should look into, but no shortcut for finding the answer to your question.

Consider the Evidence Itself   Assuming the authorities are all more or less respectable, your only recourse is to examine the evidence they offer. What kind of evidence is being offered? What conclusions are being based upon it? If the prosecutor's psychiatrists, as it sometimes happens, have made only a brief examination of the defendant, the defense may successfully argue that its psychiatrists, who have had an opportunity to do an in-depth study, have more persuasive evidence. If the prosecutor can then show that the defense's evidence was gathered under suspicious circumstances (the defendant's family has donated a large grant to the investigating institution), the jury will be presented with the kind of argument it can handle—namely, disputes over evidence.

EVALUATING THE DATA: A TEST CASE

The following "evidence" represents the source material you might find if you researched the question of whether apes can talk.

1 . . . nothing is more human than the speech of an individual or of a folk. Human speech, unlike the cry of an animal, does not occur as a mere element in a larger response. Only the human animal can communicate abstract ideas and converse about conditions that are contrary to fact.

CLYDE KLUCKHOHN, *Mirror for Man*, 1949

2 Thus the basic feature of linguistic fluency is its creativity . . . . Suppose we are testing someone to determine whether or not he has gained fluency in a foreign language. Obviously, we do not credit him with mastery of the foreign language if he is only able to understand or produce those sentences whose meaning he has been previously taught. Analogously, we do not credit animals with fluency in language if they merely respond appropriately to verbal commands in which they have been extensively drilled. Rather, the criterion to determine if someone has acquired fluency is whether or not he can understand any sentence of the foreign language that he has not before encountered (and that a speaker of the foreign language would be able to understand). The theoretical significance of the ability to produce and understand novel sentences is then—that is the real test of fluency.

JERROLD J. KATZ, *The Philosophy of Language*, 1966

3 The large apes are our nearest relatives. This means that our genetic inheritance has developed from the same stock that produced the large apes. In our chapter on the evolution of the apes, we saw that man's common ancestor with the large apes was living, in all probability, in the Oligocene period, and that the gibbon line had already diverged from the main ape stock by the middle of the Oligocene; we saw too that the hominid line is not directly related to the monkey line, which was also distinct in the Oligocene. The hominid line must have become distinct toward the late Oligocene or very early Miocene, at much the same time as the forerunners of chimpanzees and gorillas were differentiating too.

VERNON REYNOLDS, *The Apes*, 1967

4 Communication among chimpanzees in the wild consists chiefly of "talking with facial expressions and with the hands." Holding up the hand, that official gesture of the policeman means exactly the same thing: "Stop!" These apes likewise signal "Come here" or "Walk quickly past me," with gestures that are amazingly human. The hand outstretched in a begging gesture . . . signifies a greeting, a plea, or a recommendation to a fellow chimp to calm down. The reciprocal greeting or the gesture of accord consists in holding out the hand reversed, that is with the palm down. In such a gesture the fingertips of the two animals may touch. But the gesture can also be well understood at a distance.

VITUS B. DROSCHER, *The Friendly Beast,* 1970

5 The two chimpanzees that are learning "language" have done so by different systems, which are intended to reveal rather different aspects of language. Premack (1970) taught a young female chimpanzee named Sarah to place variously shaped pieces of plastic on a magnetized board. Each plastic chip represented a word, whereas a string of chips was a phrase . . . .

Within these limits, Sarah clearly used symbols. She had about forty words: "same" and "different"; "yes" and "no"; "on," "under," and "insert"; and a number of nouns and adjectives. As Premack said, he was not concerned in ascertaining the possible size of a chimpanzee's vocabulary, but its possible grammatical complexity. He tested Sarah to see if she was really using the words as symbols by asking "Apple same as . . . ?" and then offering a number of choices: red or green, round or square, and so forth. Sarah's "word" for apple was a blue triangle, but she described it as red and round, as with a stem, and as less desirable than grapes.

ALISON JOLLY, *The Evolution of Primate Behavior,* 1972

6 Washoe, on the other hand, learned a far more open system, which raises all the ambiguities and questions that surround language-learning by human children. The Gardners taught Washoe the American Sign Language for the Deaf (ASL) . . . . ASL is not finger spelling. Each position of the hands corresponds to a separate word. The Gardners call her words "signs," which would be confusing in the present context; so, except in direct quotes, I shall call them words. ASL, as the Gardners say, "is a language by the most widely used criterion we have: that it is used as such by a community of people."

JOLLY, *The Evolution of Primate Behavior,* 1972

7 The Institute for Primate Studies now has about a dozen chimps with varying degrees of skill in using Ameslan. Fouts has now begun to extend and fill out the original work done with Washoe. One would like to think that criticisms of Washoe would provide some points of departure for his work, that the critics would have used Washoe to focus attention on some kernel linguistic ability that Fouts might

then seek to explore. Unfortunately, the critics have focused their attention on the deep anxieties summoned by the idea that a chimpanzee might be capable of language. And so, essentially, Fouts has had to start afresh, using Washoe as the bedrock on which to construct a new view of language, rather than using her to modify old views.

EUGENE LINDEN, *Apes, Men, and Language*, 1974

8 When conversing with Roger in Ameslan, Lucy would look at him with intense concentration; however, her movements in making signs were not intense, but leisurely, as though communicating by using Ameslan was the most natural thing in the world for a chimp to do. She seemed to understand spoken English. It was eerie to be talking with Roger about Lucy's mirror or doll and then have her run over and pick it up. Roger noted that earlier that week he had lost Lucy's doll. He glossed his error by replacing the doll with a sightly different one, which he handed Lucy the next day. Lucy was very suspicious of this new doll, and the day after this surreptitious exchange she went over to her toy chest and signed to Roger "out baby." She wanted to see where this strange doll had come from.

LINDEN, *Apes, Men, and Language*, 1974

9 For instance, if a chimp signs *come-gimme tickle* as frequently as he signs *tickle come-gimme*, it may simply be cranking out the signs appropriate for the incentive of being tickled, which is not the same as generating a sentence. And, Brown argued, since word order is "as natural to a child as nut gathering is to a squirrel," unless one had frequency data for appropriate and inappropriate word order, Washoe's "semantic intentions" would remain a matter of guesswork.

STUART BAUR, "First Message from the Planet of the Apes," *New York Magazine*, 1975

Now you've read the evidence. What conclusions should you come to? You have to evaluate all the evidence before you can begin to answer, even for yourself, the question of whether apes can talk. As you go over the evidence, you should ask yourself questions about each item. Is it relevant? Is it valid? Is it significant? For example, read the following analysis of the evidence on apes and language.

Item 1 It would be convenient if all the experts were to agree on your research question, but they probably won't. Kluckhohn's statement that *only* the human animal can communicate abstract ideas seems to contradict the idea that apes can talk. What can you do with Kluckhohn's statement? A researcher *must* account for contradictory data. You cannot simply discard Kluckhohn's statement or forget that you read it.

Do not undertake research to *prove* a preconceived idea. The *one* piece of data that does not fit may be more important than all the others. It would be a mistake to start out to prove that apes *can* talk. If you phrase your research question so that *either* answer is appropriate, you will not have to ignore contradictory information. The question should be worded, Can apes talk?—suggesting an investigation into research on *both* sides of this question. With that qualification, Kluckhohn's work is no longer contradictory; he is simply one of those who may think apes cannot talk.

Note the date of Kluckhohn's book. It would not be wise to draw any strong conclusion from Kluckhohn's statement; later research may have made his work irrelevant. Kluckhohn himself may have changed his mind since this book was published.

Kluckhohn does not directly address the matter of whether apes can talk; perhaps his ideas aren't even relevant. What is the significance of Kluckhohn's thinking that human speech is "unlike the cry of an animal"? You cannot determine the importance of Kluckhohn's statement until you know the significance of your own question: can apes talk? Is this a significant or merely an interesting question? After all, research is difficult and time consuming and can be expensive. (We have already said that all research should be worthwhile.) Perhaps you cannot see the immediate importance of a given study, but at least there should be some theoretical reason for the study. While Kluckhohn's book does not seem to address itself to the practical side of the question (data on apes), does it offer anything on the theoretical side (significance of the study)? See the Linden note (item 7) about "deep anxieties summoned by the idea that a chimpanzee might be capable of language"; there may be more to Kluckhohn's study than you at first imagined.

Item 2 As you might guess from their books, Kluckhohn is an anthropologist; Katz is a linguist: neither one of them seems to be talking specifically about *apes*. Other than the theoretical implications in either of them, are their statements relevant to the question? You will find that no matter what you think or intend when you start your research, the evidence *itself* will begin to direct your investigation. In other words, research is not so simple that you can merely draw up your outline and then start filling it in by copying from books in the library. Kluckhohn and Katz are suggesting that there is a very important *qualification* to the question: namely, it depends on what you mean by "language," what you are willing to accept as "talk." It will do you no good to say that everyone knows what talking or using a language means; nor will it do you any good to look up "language" in the dictionary. Two scholars in the field you are investigating suggest that you must define your terms before you can answer your question.

Kluckhohn suggests that talking involves communicating "abstract ideas" and conversing about "conditions that are contrary to fact," and Katz suggests that talking is the ability to "produce and understand novel sentences." And on these "tests" of language, both of them seem to doubt that any animal can "talk." Therefore, the previously simple question Can apes talk? has now suddenly become complex, and there is no way to get around the complication. Your report will have to examine carefully what is meant by "talking" or "communicating" when anyone suggests that apes can talk.

Item 3   The Reynolds quote is interesting because it seems not to be at all relevant. In your note taking, you will sometimes find something that seems useful at the time, but that later you will have trouble fitting into your report. Since it is painful to discard anything once you have gone through the process of finding and copying, the temptation will be strong to find a way to use it. Perhaps the Reynolds quote can be worked into the introduction of the paper, as background or into the conclusion, as you speculate on the relationship of human beings to their ancestral brethren. Both of these are poor ideas, requiring you to distort the data or to distort your study. Matters are complex enough without squeezing in peripheral elements. In the *present* study, the evolution of the hominids is not relevant and the Reynolds quote should be discarded.

Item 4   Droscher's book seems to be the first one to concern itself clearly and directly with the question of whether apes can "talk"; but it is not at all clear what we can conclude from this. He tells us that apes do communicate *with each other* by means of gesture and facial expressions. Does this fit the question? Maybe, but you will further have to qualify your definition of "talking" to include sign language and nonverbal communication. If you do so, you will raise an important question—are you getting so far removed from the normal definition of "language" that no one will be able to agree with you? Will other researchers say, "Well, of course, if you mean something like nonverbal *signs,* even my dog can 'talk.' He barks when he wants to go out, looks quizzical when I talk to him, and so forth. But that is *not* the same thing as human use of language." Certainly Kluckhohn and Katz would say that kind of behavior does not fit *their* definitions for human communication. So you must think carefully about Droscher's contribution. At least, it is safe to conclude, certain *kinds* of communication seem within the apes' capability. Droscher seems to be saying something important, but you should examine the rest of your data before deciding exactly what his contribution is.

Items 5 and 6   Jolly's contributions get to the heart of the matter; she describes the "languages" being taught to apes, one an abstract symbol system, the other a sign language. Now you can see better the relevance of all the previous research; the "tests" of language suggested by Katz and Kluckhohn can be applied against these "languages." And now, for the first time there is evidence that, indeed, apes can talk; certainly Sarah and Washoe seem to be using language within the normal definition of the word. Droscher's statements about sign languages in the wild now seem to relate to the experiments with Washoe, who was taught American Sign Language. You could conclude that although *speech* is not natural to animals, *sign language* is; and therefore it is not at all surprising to discover that animals can "talk" when provided with a language suitable to them. But a little additional thought may raise a troublesome notion: the very fact that sign language *is* natural for apes could mean that Washoe and the others have simply been coached to make appropriate signs (like the trained dogs and seals in the circus) on command. So the issue *is not settled*, even though Jolly's data are interesting and compelling.

Items 7 and 8   Linden seems to be backing up Jolly, but here it is important to understand your source material, especially to know who your authorities are. Alison Jolly is a scientist interested in animal behavior; specifically, she is interested here in the parallels between humans and the other primates. For some of her data, Jolly relies on *other research:* she cites Premack and the Gardners. Linden is a freelance writer, who also relies on *other research:* Fouts and Premack and the Gardners. Both Jolly and Linden are respected writers, but although they seem to be backing each other up, they are in fact relying on the same information in some cases. They are both drawing conclusions based on primary research done by someone else. Thus, instead of *two* authorities, Jolly and Linden, you really have only two views of the same information. This does not diminish the contributions of Jolly or Linden; it merely suggests that before you draw any hard conclusions from their data, you probably should look at the work they cite—Fouts, Gardner, Premack—listed in their footnotes. (Here you have firsthand evidence of the importance of footnotes and bibliographies: serious researchers will not only allow but will help us to find the material we need to evaluate their contributions.)

Item 9 You could, of course, content yourself with Jolly and Linden. They are both respected researchers and, you may think, far more knowledgeable than yourself. (Who am I to challenge professionals in their own area of expertise!) But one of the virtues of research is its total democracy; *even* a beginning researcher can make important discoveries if he or she is careful and thorough. Furthermore, time marches on, and with time may come new discoveries. Although Linden's book is dated 1974, the research he relies on is considerably older than that. Baur reports more recent research in his 1975 article. Here, it would seem, an important criticism is being raised about sign language. Perhaps those who claim that apes can talk are wrong after all. How important do you think Brown's argument is? Do you need to see Brown's work or are you content with Baur's description of that work?

Summing up the Evidence It may seem to you that there is no end to this question, that each new piece of research just raises new questions and that perhaps you never will be able to answer the original question. You are right, to a degree. To be a researcher means to give up your old way of thinking. Very little in life can be answered in the simple yes/no, right/wrong terms used with children. Even seemingly elementary and obvious questions often turn out on examination to be quite complicated, and it is not at all surprising that the more you research, the more questions you will raise or find raised in your path. Don't expect to find simple answers to complex questions.

Because of the indeterminate nature of most research and the inconclusiveness of most data, researchers are very careful about the kinds of *conclusions* they are willing to draw. Good research usually does not lead to answers but to reasonable *conclusions*.

If the question were, What does the research show about the question of whether apes can talk? and this were all the research you had to rely on, it would not be safe to conclude that apes *can* talk. You could say that there is some evidence suggesting that apes *may be able* to talk, depending on how terms are defined, but the question is still open to debate. Some researchers are not entirely satisfied with the definitions of language being used. Moreover, Sarah and Washoe may be freaks—most researchers would hesitate to answer the question based on what two chimpanzees can do, or are *reported* to be able to do. (Can these results be duplicated by other researchers using other chimpanzees?)

On the other hand, if you assume Jolly and Linden are correct, or are at least not incorrect, the evidence on Sarah and Washoe will not simply go away. It is too easy to say the case is not proved and so should be dismissed. That is, it would not be fair to conclude that apes *cannot* talk from the data. Have you made any progress on this question at all? Yes, you have. The present research, while inconclusive, demonstrates at least that this is a serious research question. Whereas you may once have been able simply to laugh the question away, it appears now that serious doubts have been raised on *both* sides of the question. And researchers are beginning to see what directions to go, in order to answer the question satisfactorily. Thus, it is appropriate to say that further research is needed, and Baur's article makes specific suggestions about the nature of future research.

DOCUMENTATION: BACKING UP
WHAT YOU SAY

The purpose of documentation is to back up what you say. It is not enough to say that current research shows that gasoline-alcohol mixtures are safe fuel for cars; you must show the reader *who* says so and *where*. Other researchers will wish to check and verify your findings; the more thorough and accurate documentation you offer your readers, the more reliable your research becomes. Faulty documentation is a violation of the basic concept of research.

STYLESHEETS

There is no one set of rules about the style of your documentation, the style of your footnotes and bibliography. There are several different stylesheets used by modern researchers in different fields. The chief "rule" about documentation is to be logical and consistent in the way you write your notes; therefore it might be a good idea to buy one or another of the available stylesheets and then follow it carefully. The style in this chapter is based on the *MLA Handbook for Writers of Research Papers, Theses, and Dissertations* (New York: Modern Language Association, 1977), a standard stylesheet for work in English and the humanities. On page 204 there is an example from another widely used stylesheet, the *Publication Manual* of the American Psychological Association (the APA).

DOCUMENTATION NOTES

Documentation notes were, by convention, placed at the foot of the page (hence, "footnotes"), but modern practice increasingly moves them to the back of the research paper, preceding the bibliography, on a page or pages marked "References" or "Footnotes" or "Endnotes." For most college writing, notes numbered consecutively throughout and listed at the end of the paper will be the most efficient procedure.

Note that if you use APA, there are no notes. Instead, there are short references in the text to sources fully identified in the bibliography:

```
The long-term effects of gasohol in unmodified gasoline engines may include
"carburetor clogging, exhaust-system deterioration, and internal engine
damage that hasn't yet shown up" (Trent, 1978, p. 89).
```

SUBSTANTIVE NOTES

Most of your notes will be references to books and articles. But occasionally you may wish to give a *substantive* note, an actual note from you to the reader in which you give additional information relevant to your research but not entirely necessary to what you are saying at that point in the paper. There is mixed feeling about these substantive notes; many researchers feel that any *relevant* information ought to be included in the main text and that irrelevant information should be omitted entirely. But, since other researchers do use substantive notes, the best advice is to use substantive notes only when you cannot get the information into your text otherwise.

WHAT TO DOCUMENT

DIRECT QUOTATIONS

Any words you copy from a source should be placed in quotes, followed by a note number. The note number is a superscript, a number raised a half space above the line of text. No period follows the superscript:

Even Holden's brutal encounters with reality are quickly transformed into fantasy: "About halfway to the bathroom, I sort of started pretending I had a bullet in my guts. Old Maurice had plugged me."[1]

IDEAS AND WORDS FROM A SOURCE

Words and concepts that you take from a source and incorporate into your own sentences should be documented:

Never at a loss for words, Holden manufactures adjectives from nouns and verbs to describe "vomity" taxicabs and "hoodlumy-looking" street people.[2]

Be especially aware of the obligation to acknowledge ideas, interpretations, analyses, and concepts that represent someone else's thinking on your topic. It can be easy, sometimes, to incorporate ideas from your sources into your paper as though they are your own. To do so is dishonest scholarship, and it is to be avoided rigorously. You may have been warned about *plagiarism* before now; people often describe plagiarism as copying words from a source and passing them off as your own in a composition. But you are plagiarizing too if you pass off someone else's ideas as your own in a composition. You can document someone else's thinking the same way you do their words:

Holden can be thought of as a model of lost and confused adolescence,[3] but he is a prototype for a very small, privileged class of modern people.

[3] See Sarah Birkfeld, "A Jungian Look at Catcher in the Rye," Psychology Today, May 1975, pp. 72-77, for the interpretation of Holden Caulfield as an archetype.

PARAPHRASES AND RESTATEMENTS

When you change a source's phrases or ideas into your own words, document them:

Jefferson's notion in the Declaration of Independence that everyone is born with the same rights and privileges as everyone else[4] simply ignores the privileges of wealth.

ALLUSIONS AND INCOMPLETE REFERENCES TO SOURCES

Regardless of whether you quote or paraphrase from them, document all allusions and incomplete references:

For a full discussion of footnote style, the reader is referred to the <u>MLA</u> <u>Handbook</u>.[5]

REFERENCES IN THE TEXT

Unless you give *full* documentation in the text itself, containing all the information normally found in a note (and in many cases it is cumbersome to do so), use a note in addition to the text reference:

S. I. Hayakawa in <u>Language in Thought and Action</u> (Harcourt, 1964)[6] warns

that we confuse both language and thought when we forget that words are not

the same as the things they stand for.

MAJOR SOURCE

If you make many references to the same source—for example, if you are writing *about* a book, poem, play, or other source—you need not keep documenting it:

[7] Leo Tolstóy, <u>Anna Karenina</u>, trans. David Magarshack (New York: Signet

Classics, 1961), p. 98. All further references to this work appear in the

text.

Later references in the text need only the page number:

Kitty's love affair with Christianity began with her acquaintance with Madame

Stahl (p. 233).

SOURCE WITHIN A SOURCE

You may discover one author quoting another in such a way that you will want to quote the second author yourself. If it is at all possible, you should find the *original* source and quote from that, instead of quoting from the second-hand source (for accuracy's sake, if nothing else). Suppose you were doing a paper on the relevance of grammar to composition, and you were reading Virginia Allen's article "Teaching Standard English as a Second Dialect." In it you would find the following:

Martin Joos, who has made a special study of people's attitudes toward language, says:

> Long before any teacher began to correct his English, the child has learned all he needs to know, at his age, about people and their places; he has developed considerable skill in judging adults by their speech . . .[2]

The note number refers to Martin Joos' article, "Language and the School Child." If you want to use the Joos quote, you should find the article it comes from and quote that, instead of quoting from Virginia Allen's article:

8 Martin Joos, "Language and the School Child," Word Study, 11, No. 2

(1964), 95.

However, sometimes the original source is not available, or for some other reason the researcher must rely on the second-hand source (and you must be very certain that there *is* a good reason for so doing). In that case, you need a rather complicated note:

8 Martin Joos, "Language and the School Child," Word Study, 11, No. 2

(1964), 95, as quoted in Virginia F. Allen, "Teaching Standard English as a

Second Dialect," Teachers College Record, 68 (Feb. 1967), 358.

You can see that the business of quoting second-hand sources can easily get out of hand. Your job is to tell the reader where you found your information; if, for example, you found the Allen article not in its original journal but in an anthology of journal articles, to be perfectly accurate you would need the following:

8 Martin Joos, "Language and the School Child," Word Study, 11, No. 2

(1964), 95, as quoted in Virginia F. Allen, "Teaching Standard English as a

Second Dialect," Teachers College Record, 68 (Feb. 1967), 358, in Teaching

High School Composition, eds. Gary Tate and Edward P. J. Corbett (New York:

Oxford Univ. Press, 1970), pp. 359-60.

Not only is such a note ungainly, but you rely upon Tate and Corbett to quote Allen accurately, not to mention the additional reliance on Allen to quote Joos accurately. Since these are all respected scholars there is reason to assume the quotes are accurate, but there is always the possibility of error. There is the further danger that in quoting Joos out of context (without reading the rest of his article) you may distort his intention or misapply his meaning.

WHAT NOT TO QUOTE

Common knowledge need not be documented. There is no certain test for common knowledge, but in general you can consider knowledge to be "common" if it is widely known by educated people, if it is readily available in most general reference works such as encyclopedias or almanacs, or if it is available through the popular communications media—television, newspapers, and popular magazines. There is no need to document, for example, who the President is or where the White House is or that Shakespeare is the author of *Hamlet*.

Uncontested knowledge need not be documented, even if it is not common knowledge. Dates of historical events, for example, may or may not be considered common knowledge, but unless the precise date is relevant to the case you are arguing or unless the dates are a matter of dispute in the research, they can be considered uncontested information. A handy rule to follow is this: anything that would damage your case if it were removed from your paper or proved to be wrong should be documented.

To a degree, documenting is part of a researcher's style, part of his or her view of self. Some researchers are very careful to document everything in their work. Others take a more relaxed attitude. To avoid the suspicion of plagiarism, beginning researchers should be very careful to document everything taken from sources.

HOW TO DOCUMENT

The following examples give first the bibliographic entry and then an example note entry for each item.

BOOK, ONE AUTHOR

Murray, K. M. Elisabeth. <u>Caught in the Web of Words: James A. H. Murray &</u>
  <u>the Oxford English Dictionary</u>. New Haven: Yale Univ. Press, 1977.

[1] K. M. Elisabeth Murray, <u>Caught in the Web of Words</u> (New Haven: Yale
Univ. Press, 1977), pp. 87–100.

BOOK, TWO AUTHORS

Burdick, Eugene, and Harvey Wheeler. <u>Fail Safe</u>. New York: McGraw-Hill,
  1962.

[2] Eugene Burdick and Harvey Wheeler, <u>Fail Safe</u> (New York: McGraw-Hill,
1962), p. 159.

BOOK, MORE THAN TWO AUTHORS

Braddock, Richard, et al. <u>Research in Written Composition</u>. Champaign,

Illinois: NCTE, 1963.

³ Richard Braddock et al., <u>Research in Written Composition</u> (Champaign,

Illinois: NCTE, 1963), pp. 52-53.

BOOK WITH AN EDITOR

Tate, Gary, ed. <u>Teaching Composition: 10 Bibliographic Essays</u>. Fort Worth:

Texas Christian Univ. Press, 1976.

⁴ Gary Tate, ed., <u>Teaching Composition: 10 Bibliographic Essays</u> (Fort

Worth: Texas Christian Univ. Press, 1976), p. vii.

CHAPTER IN AN EDITED WORK

Young, Richard. "Invention: A Topographical Survey." In <u>Teaching Composi-</u>

<u>tion: 10 Bibliographic Essays</u>. Ed. Gary Tate. Fort Worth: Texas

Christian Univ. Press, 1976, pp. 1-43.

⁵ Richard Young, "Invention: A Topographical Survey," in <u>Teaching</u>

<u>Composition: 10 Bibliographic Essays</u>, ed. Gary Tate (Fort Worth: Texas

Christian Univ. Press, 1976), pp. 1-43.

BOOK, COMMITTEE OR GROUP AUTHOR

Commission on Obscenity and Pornography. <u>The Report of the Commission on</u>

<u>Obscenity and Pornography</u>. Toronto: Bantam Books, 1970.

⁶ Commission on Obscenity and Pornography, <u>The Report of the Commission</u>

<u>on Obscenity and Pornography</u> (Toronto: Bantam Books, 1970), p. 228.

BOOK, TRANSLATION

Garnett, Constance, trans. <u>Crime and Punishment</u>. By Fyodor Dostoyevsky.

New York: The Modern Library, 1950.

⁷ Fyodor Dostoyevsky, <u>Crime and Punishment</u>, trans. Constance Garnett

(New York: The Modern Library, 1950), p. 224.

MAGAZINE ARTICLE, AUTHOR NAMED

Hughes, Robert. "Night and Silence, Who Is There?" _Time_, 12 Dec. 1977,

   pp. 59-60.

[8] Robert Hughes, "Night and Silence, Who Is There?" _Time_, 12 Dec. 1977,

p. 59.

MAGAZINE ARTICLE, NO AUTHOR GIVEN

"Byrd of West Virginia: Fiddler in the Senate." _Time_, 23 Jan. 1978, pp. 12-16.

[9] "Byrd of West Virginia: Fiddler in the Senate," _Time_, 23 Jan. 1978,

p. 13.

NEWSPAPER ARTICLE

Talbert, Bob. "Why Are We in Such a Downer?" _Detroit Free Press_, 10 Jan.

   1978, Sec. A, p. 9, cols. 3-4.

[10] Bob Talbert, "Why Are We in Such a Downer?" _Detroit Free Press_,

10 Jan. 1978, Sec. A, p. 9, col. 3.

PROFESSIONAL JOURNAL, EACH ISSUE STARTS WITH PAGE 1

Rubin, David M. "Remember Swine Flu?" _Columbia Journalism Review_, 16, No. 2

   (1977), 42-46.

[11] David M. Rubin, "Remember Swine Flu?" _Columbia Journalism Review_, 16,

No. 2 (1977), 45.

PROFESSIONAL JOURNAL, PAGES NUMBERED BY VOLUME

Haswell, Richard H. "Eight Concepts of Poetry for College Freshman."

   College English, 39 (1977), 294-306.

[12] Richard H. Haswell, "Eight Concepts of Poetry for College Freshman,"

College English, 39 (1977), 299.

DISSERTATION (UNPUBLISHED)

Blank, William Earl. "The Effectiveness of Creative Dramatics in Developing

   Voice, Vocabulary, and Personality in the Primary Grades." Diss. Univ.

   of Denver 1953.

[13] William Earl Blank, "The Effectiveness of Creative Dramatics in

Developing Voice, Vocabulary, and Personality in the Primary Grades," Diss.

Univ. of Denver, 1953, p. 12.

HANDOUT, MIMEOGRAPH, AND SO ON

Olson, John L. "Chronology of Renaissance Events." Handout for Class in

    European History. Central Michigan University, 1979.

    [14] John L. Olson, "Chronology of Renaissance Events," Handout, Central

Michigan University, 1979.

LECTURE OR SPEECH

Haworth, Lorna H. "Figuratively Speaking." Annual Meeting, National Council

    of Teachers of English, New York. 25 Nov. 1977.

    [15] Lorna H. Haworth, "Figuratively Speaking," Annual Meeting, National

Council of Teachers of English, New York, 25 Nov. 1977.

FILM

Ashby, Hal, dir. _Coming Home_. With Jane Fonda, Jon Voight, and Bruce Dern.

    United Artists, 1978.

    [16] Hal Ashby, dir., _Coming Home_, with Jane Fonda, Jon Voight, and Bruce

Dern, United Artists, 1978.

PLAY

Lindsay-Hoagg, Michael, dir. _Whose Life Is It Anyway_? By Brian Clark. With

    Tom Conti and Jean Marsh. Trafalgar Theater, New York. 19 April 1979.

    [17] Michael Lindsay-Hoagg, dir., _Whose Life Is It Anyway_? by Brian Clark,

with Tom Conti and Jean Marsh, Trafalgar Theater, New York, 19 April 1979.

MUSICAL PERFORMANCE

Levine, James, cond. _Parsifal_. With Jon Vickers and Christa Ludwig. The

    Metropolitan Opera Company of New York. Metropolitan Opera House, New

    York. 16 April 1979.

    [18] James Levine, cond., _Parsifal_, with Jon Vickers and Christa Ludwig,

The Metropolitan Opera Company of New York, Metropolitan Opera House, New

York, 16 April 1979.

RADIO OR TELEVISION PROGRAM

"TV or Not TV." Comment. Bill Moyers. _Bill Moyers' Journal_. PBS, 23 April

    1979.

    [19] "TV or Not TV," comment. Bill Moyers, _Bill Moyers' Journal_, PBS,

23 April 1979.

RECORD ALBUM OR TAPE

Taylor, Kate. <u>Sister Kate</u>. Cotillion Records, SD 9045, 1971.

[20] Kate Taylor, <u>Sister Kate</u>, Cotillion Records, SD 9045, 1971.

PERSONAL LETTER

Easterly, K. T. Letter to author. 6 Dec. 1979.

[21] Letter received from K. T. Easterly, 6 Dec. 1979.

PERSONAL INTERVIEW

Fonda, Jane. Personal interview. 10 Oct. 1978.

[22] Personal interview with Jane Fonda, 10 Oct. 1978.

APA STYLE, BOOK

See page 196 for a brief explanation of APA reference style.

Murray, K. M. Elisabeth. <u>Caught in the web of words: James A. H. Murray &</u>

<u>the Oxford English dictionary</u>. New Haven: Yale University Press, 1977.

APA STYLE, ARTICLE

Sekuler, R., & Levinson, E. The perception of moving targets. <u>Scientific</u>

<u>American</u>, 1977, <u>236</u> (1), 60-73.

ABBREVIATIONS AND BIBLIOGRAPHIC TERMS

In general, we recommend that you avoid using abbreviations.
The space they save can cost much in terms of possible misreading. However, as a researcher you will encounter some common
abbreviations and bibliographic terms used in writing and publishing and in college reading in general. You should become
familiar with the following:

A.D.	*Anno Domini,* in the year of our Lord
anon.	anonymous; the author's name is unknown (Never appropriate for an article which is merely *unsigned* as in a magazine or news-paper.)
ante	before
attrib.	attributed; authorship is not positive
B.C.	before Christ

b.	born
bib.	biblical
bibliog.	bibliography
©	copyright; date of publication
ca. or c.	*circa*, about; date is approximate
cap.	capital; capitalized
cf.	*confer*, compare
ch. (chs., *plural*)	chapter(s)
col. (cols., *plural*)	column(s)
d.	died
diss.	dissertation
ed. (eds., *plural*)	editor; edited by; edition; editors
e.g.	*exempli gratia*, for example
esp.	especially
est.	estimated, estimation
et al.	*et alii*, and others
etc.	*et cetera*, and so forth
f. (ff., *plural*)	and the following page(s)
fn.	footnote
fr.	from
ibid.	*ibidem*, in the same place; cited immediately above
id.	*idem*, the same person
i.e.	*id est*, that is
l. (ll., *plural*)	line(s)
loc. cit.	*loco citato*, in the place cited; in the same place mentioned earlier
MS (MSS, *plural*)	manuscript(s)
n.	note
N.B.	*nota bene*, note well; take notice
n.d.	no date of publication
n.n.	no name of publisher
no. (nos., *plural*)	number(s)
n.p.	no place of publication
obs.	obsolete
op. cit.	*opere citato*, in the work cited recently
p. (pp., *plural*)	page(s)
passim	here and there; at intervals
pl. (pls., *plural*)	plate, plural; plates
pseud.	pseudonym
pt. (pts., *plural*)	part(s)
q.v.	*quod vide*, which see
rev.	revised; revision; review; reviewer
rpt.	reprint; reprinted

sec. (secs., *plural*)	section(s)
ser.	series
sic	thus it is; mistake in the original
var.	variant
v.	*vide*, see
viz.	*videlicet*, namely
vol. (vols., *plural*)	volume(s)
vs., v.	*versus*, against

WRITING THE RESEARCH PAPER

After you have read all your research, have come to *know* the subject thoroughly, and have given yourself time to assimilate the information, you are ready to begin trying to make your outline. Since the research paper is usually longer and more formal than most of your other writing, it is almost impossible to write one without making some kind of outline. You may keep refining the outline as you work on the paper, but you will avoid headaches for yourself if you work from at least a simple version of your outline. The outline itself need not be very elaborate, just detailed enough to give you (and anyone else) a clear picture of the points you are going to try to cover.

The overall plan of your paper, and thus of your outline, should follow these principles:

I INTRODUCTION

In highly scientific writing (reports and so on not meant for publication), researchers sometimes dispense with the formal introduction. But published research usually needs an introduction for the same reason everything else does—to catch reader interest, to help the reader "get into" the paper. Somewhere in the introduction you must ask your thesis question. The thesis *question* is preferable to the thesis statement, because it does not give away at the outset what position you intend to take. Some instructors prefer to see the thesis question as the first sentence of the introduction, but it also makes very good sense to have it as the *last* sentence of the introduction, to finish the introduction and make a good transition to the rest of the paper. An introduction is ordinarily a single paragraph, but you may write an introduction of more than one paragraph if doing so doesn't give the impression that the introduction is running on too long and holding up the paper unnecessarily.

II THE OPPOSING VIEW

Since you are presenting yourself as a disinterested researcher, you have to deal with a small problem: there is some bias involved in the *order* in which you present information. The best choice is to present the opposing view first. If your research has convinced you that cigarette smoking causes cancer, you must first present the other side, the side of those who feel that cigarette smoking does not cause cancer. Presenting the other side first, and presenting it well, will help to convince the reader that you understand the issues well, that you are a fair and unbiased researcher. It also has the advantage of providing you with something to argue *against*. You must lay out the reasons and the evidence that the opposition would use; make the case for the opposition as strong as it can be made. Do not offer any counterevidence or argue against the opposing view here. In this section you are trying to present the opposing side as well as possible. Instead of finding fault, you should end this section by showing which of the opposition arguments are the strongest. Point out to the reader what a reasonable person should concede in the opposing argument. (It is necessary to concede, for example, that some people have smoked all their lives without contracting cancer.) The more positively you can treat the opposing side, the stronger you can make the opposing side look, the fairer you will seem—and of course the more imposing your own side will seem. Anyone can win an argument against a weak opponent; but it takes a skillful debater to win against a *strong opponent*. It is conceivable that you could concede *all* of the opposing view (the opponent is not "wrong") and still demonstrate the superiority of the other side—which may simply have newer information to offer in the argument. You must keep in mind that you do not have to *prove* anything in a limited research paper; your job is only to examine both sides of the question for the reader's benefit. In the *conclusion* to the paper you can tell the reader what a reasonable person should conclude from the data in your paper.

III THE BETTER VIEW

Usually, a researcher-writer will decide that one side of the case is in fact better than the other side. If your research leads you to conclude that both sides are equally strong or equally weak (for lack of data, for example), then you must arbitrarily pick one side or the other to present first; but in such a case you must also take extra precautions not to bias the arguments in favor of one side or the other.

However, if there is a "better view," this section can be started with counterarguments, if you have some to offer. If you have discovered, for example, errors in data or reasoning in the opposing view, this is the place to point them out. You must still try to remain the objective, dispassionate researcher; it would be well to offer contradictory evidence if you are going to find fault with the opposition. But you need not go looking for flaws in the opposing view. If you have a good research question, solidly two-sided, you will probably find that both sides have plausible data and authorities to back them up. You yourself may find abortion, euthanasia, or capital punishment abhorrent, but there is quite likely to be a valid point of view on the other side of the question. In a good research paper, it is to your advantage to present the opposing view in a fair and interesting way: otherwise, you will not have a worthy opponent to argue against. The better view will seem obvious and unimpressive.

In a counterargument, an effective strategy is to concede the more reasonable points of the opposing view, especially if they have some basis in fact or are founded on believable assumptions. The challenge is then to demonstrate the overall inadequacy of the opposing view or to show that your argument is more powerful, more persuasive, a more reasonable *interpretation* of the evidence.

With or without counterarguments, make the case for the better view—present examples, data, arguments. Especially if you have new arguments to offer—new, meaningful ideas that apparently have not occurred to the opposition—this is the place to present them.

IV CONCLUSION

The conclusion of a research paper should be the *climax* of the paper. There is still important work to do in the conclusion; so far, your paper has shown that there is a research question, that there are two opposing sides to the question. Now, you must *answer the thesis question*. It may be helpful to the reader if you start the conclusion with a brief summary of the arguments. But you must, finally, conclude with one of three positions: the opposing view is correct, the better view is correct, or there is not enough evidence available for any intelligent conclusion to be drawn. If you decide after all that the better view is indeed the correct view, you must help the reader understand why it is better: more substantive data, better authorities, more convincing and logical arguments, and so on. Perhaps the whole argument will hinge on some key point: "If the Heidegger study done three years ago is correct, as several authorities have indicated, the evidence is conclusive—five million case histories are difficult to dispute."

You should save something good for the conclusion. The conclusion isn't just the end of the paper—it is the *point* of the paper. If you use up your best material in the body of the paper, the conclusion will likely look weak by comparison. In addition to showing the reader the outcome of the argument, you must bring the paper to completion, give the reader a sense of "ending" (see Chapter 7 for advice on effective concluding paragraphs). An apt quote, some striking fact or statistic, a relevant personal note, or even just an especially well-worded final sentence will round off the ending and help the reader to "get out" of the paper (similar to the problem in the introduction of getting the reader into the paper). But you must avoid raising any new or irrelevant questions in the conclusion. If you have demonstrated to your satisfaction that cigarettes have been shown to cause lung cancer and heart attacks, you must resist the temptation to increase the charge ("and perhaps they will one day be linked to arthritis and insanity as well") or to extend the argument by easy analogy ("and if cigarettes are so bad, we must suppose that cigars and pipes and even chewing tobacco must be as bad or worse").

V REFERENCES

Different publishers require different formats for documentation notes and other references; some professors also have different requirements. Before handing in or submitting documented papers, you would do well to inquire first which format is preferred. In *general*, footnotes (at the bottom of the page) are going out of style. Preferred modern practice is to list endnotes, numbered in sequence, on a separate page (or pages) immediately preceding the bibliography. These endnotes are usually titled "References." Follow your stylesheet exactly.

VI BIBLIOGRAPHY

There are many different kinds of bibliographies; they serve different scholarly purposes. For example, an annotated bibliography gives the author's evaluations of the sources cited. However, a bibliography that is nothing more than a list of the same books and articles in your references is not the best idea. A bibliography should be a useful part of your paper by itself—a list of significant books and articles on the issue, not just those you have actually cited in your paper. The bibliography lets the reader see how recent your research is and also whether you are aware of important publications. It would seem strange for a researcher to miss a very important book, for example. Thus, the bibliography is indeed an aid to other researchers who may come after you.

A selected bibliography is a list of resources available, not just those you actually cite in your paper. You will undoubtedly *read* more than the works you cite. Ideally, you should read and assimilate everything available on a research question, but practically, there is likely to be too much available for such thoroughness in anything shorter than a doctoral dissertation. You can at least *skim* through a great deal of material to determine whether it would be useful for researchers on your topic. The idea is that research is cumulative, and as each new researcher adds to the existing bibliographies, an increasingly complete list of the works available will be compiled. You will soon get to know from a little reading which are the important works, which things you *must* read. You read as much of the available material as you have time for—aiming to have read and understood as much as it is possible to read in the time you have. Never put anything into your bibliography that you haven't actually seen. You will find many things listed in the indexes, for example, but you must not simply build your bibliography from the indexes without at least skimming through each item, to see that it is, in fact, related to the issue and likely to be useful to other researchers.

Read the following research paper. Does the topic seem to you to be specific, limited, worthwhile? Does this writer do a good job of research? That is, do you understand the evidence she presents? Is the evidence believable?

Sherryl Talbot, the
author of the
outline, research
paper, notes, and
bibliography re-
produced in the
following pages,
submitted these
materials with a
separate title page.
Your instructor
will probably tell
you how to submit
your papers. If not,
a heading format
is suggested inside
the back cover.

Outline

I. Introduction

    A. Quote

    B. Brief description of nuclear power plants in operation: their bene-

        fits and their hazards

    C. Thesis question: Are nuclear power plants' hazards greater than

        their benefits?

II. Arguments for nuclear power plants

    A. The arguments

        1. The great need for new sources of energy--nuclear power plants

            being the most feasible

        2. Argument that they are safe because of all the steps taken to

            make them free of hazards

        3. The good health and safety record of plant workers as compared

            to other industries

        4. The economics aspect--the building of these high-cost plants

            and their maintenance is job-producing and economically

            stimulating

    B. Evaluation of the arguments (the best argument is that we need

        alternative energy sources)

III. Arguments against nuclear power plants

    A. The counterarguments

        1. The high risk involved in the plants no matter how many pre-

            cautions are taken

            a. The Brown's Ferry incident

            b. The Detroit incident

        2. The opposing economic problems of the plants

            a. The insurance costs

            b. The continual layoffs resulting from defects

    B. Other evidence

        1. The chances of sabotage and nuclear theft

2. The effects on the environment

   a. Nuclear waste

   b. Nuclear pollution

   c. The problem of shipping wastes

3. The effects on the health of the people living near the plants

4. The risk of a natural disaster, such as a tornado, causing a nuclear disaster

C. Evaluation of the arguments

IV. Conclusion: Although it seems that nuclear power plants are a feasible solution to the energy crisis, there are too many risks involved. These risks outweigh the benefits we could obtain by using nuclear plants. Putting all the large technical problems of nuclear waste and sabotage aside, all it would take would be one accident--such as the one we came within seconds of having in Detroit--and the population of at least the state the plant was in would suffer terrible losses in lives and injuries. One of these accidents is only too likely to occur, as the past has pointed out. Under the current way of building and managing these plants, we simply place our population under tremendous risk--a risk they should not have to endure.

V. References

VI. Bibliography

The Power and Peril of Nuclear Energy

Introduction

An
interest-arousing
beginning

The average cost of electric power generated in oil, coal, and nuclear plants in 1975 as determined by an industry survey of electric utilities is as follows: oil, 3.36¢ per kilowatt-hour; coal, 1.75¢ per kilowatt-hour; nuclear, 1.23¢ per kilowatt-hour. The utilities surveyed reported total savings of more than $2 billion in 1975 from power produced in nuclear plants instead of their fossil-fueled alternatives.[1]

The United States, along with Europe and Japan, is facing a problem: we are almost totally dependent on foreign oil sources. This problem can only get worse unless we come up with a self-sufficient energy system. Nuclear power is a proposed alternative. There are already many nuclear plants in operation (we are most familiar with the Detroit and Palisades plants). These nuclear centers provide about 5 percent of our electrical energy at present. It is conceivable that they could supply well over 50 percent in the future. We could then rely on our huge coal supplies to make up the difference. We could be self-sufficient. We wouldn't have to worry about cartels and oil embargoes. There are many plusses to nuclear power besides the fact that it would help to make us self-sufficient. It is economical: once the initial investment is made in the building of the plant, there are only upkeep costs. Nuclear power plants provide jobs. They are relatively clean. But there is another side: what about nuclear theft? What about accidents? Are nuclear

The thesis question

power plants' hazards greater than their benefits?

Arguments for Nuclear Power Plants

What will you do when the lights go out? And they will go out if we keep our dependence on fossil fuels as strong as we have in the past. We use 35.4 million barrels of oil per day in the United States.[2] We use tremendous amounts of even scarcer natural gas. We must face facts; there is only a certain supply of these fuels. When they are gone, they are gone. Our supply of any kind of fuel is very limited, but what about the demand for fuel? The United States has an ever-increasing demand for energy. As our technology increases, so do our needs. Because we have such an inelastic demand for oil, we are the subject of oil embargoes and the strong fist of the Middle East cartel. They can keep demanding higher and higher prices and all we can weakly say is "Conserve." "The U.S. oil imports were $8 billion in 1973, they were $30 billion in 1975."[3] Not only are we supporting the cartel, we are lining the pockets of the fuel companies, such as Standard Oil of New Jersey and Exxon.

Notes are numbered consecutively throughout the paper. The numbers refer to the documentation entries on the Notes page at the end of the paper.

What can we do? We can conserve as much as possible. But facing facts, this is only a stopgap measure. However, there is also the prospect of alternative power, and nuclear energy is a feasible candidate. A nuclear power plant functions in much the same way a conventional plant does. Instead of having a furnace as a core, it has a reactor:

Note that the block-style quote is indented from the left. Indenting takes the place of opening and closing quotation marks. (Format guidelines for typed papers are given inside the back cover of *The Writer's Work.*)

> The reactor is simply a machine in which the atom is split [this is called fission] and useful heat is produced and controlled. The means for applying atomic heat to make steam from water may also be different from conventional boilers, but the turbines, generators, and other equipment are similar to those of other plants.[4]

A nuclear reactor uses uranium as its base. The United States has a rich supply of this element. Even if we did have a scarcity, the new fast-breeder reactors effectively reuse their energy source to make it last for thousands of years.

There are fifty-six operating plants in the United States today. In 1975 they supplied us with 5 percent of our energy. Would it really be cheaper if we built these plants on a large scale? Yes, it would. At present, oil power plants cost 3.36¢ per kilowatt-hour. This is compared with one of the already operational nuclear power plants' costs of 1.23¢ per kilowatt-hour.[5] It is

WRITING THE
RESEARCH PAPER

As an objective
researcher, the
writer presents the
case for the
opposition in the
best light, without
limiting or
diminishing the
facts.

already cheaper. And if you figure in the economy of size (the larger an industry is, the cheaper its marginal cost or relevant costs are), nuclear
plants really come out ahead. Add the fact that with a breeder reactor you
have only your initial investment in the building of the plant, except for
wages, upkeep, and insurance, and the plants compare well with other kinds of
energy centers. The original power source--uranium--is recycled. In short,
nuclear power plants are very economical.

Nuclear power plants appear to be economical, but are they safe? There
are so very many precautions taken with these plants because we have realized
what dangers there are. These plants are built away from highly populated
areas, and there is an area surrounding the plants that people may not enter
without authorization. There are evacuation plans. There are very tight
safeguards on the employees to make sure they aren't exposed to radiation
(they must wear radiation shields at all times in the plant). There are great
precautions taken against theft of uranium. The core containing the uranium
is isolated by a series of concrete and other physical barriers. There is a
cooling system for the core, with many automatic backup systems. There are
many automatic backup systems for every system in the plant itself. There are
automatic shutdown systems. Every conceivable precaution is taken. Everything that can be foreseen has a preventative.

Before a plant can be certified for operation, it must be thoroughly
checked by the following: the Nuclear Reactor Regulation Committee, the state
and local governments, the Atomic Safety and Licensing Board, and the Nuclear
Regulatory Commissioners, who issue a permit decision. To qualify for a permit, the plant must also meet environmental standards. All the operational
plants have a good safety record so far. There have been two near-accidents,
but none that resulted in injury.

What about the people living near a plant or working in a plant? What
about their safety and health? Inevitably there are going to be some people
living near or working in one of the plants. Since all plants must be

environmentally safe, there is no problem for the few people living near a
center, and the plants have excellent safety records for their personnel, too.
The number of days lost because of an occupational health problem is 480 days
(on an average) annually for nuclear power plant employees. This is compared
to 600 days for coal plants and over 1,000 days for both oil and natural gas
plants. The death rate is also substantially lower for nuclear plants. The
public health risk is also minimal. Nuclear power plants' air pollutants
rated a 20 on a relative hazard index. This is compared to a rating of 37,630
for coal and of 16,586 for oil. The accidental-death statistics rate radiation poisoning caused by nuclear power plants on the bottom of their lists,
with a zero.[6]

Nuclear power plants also have the ability to boost the economy by re-
ducing unemployment and providing a stimulant effect. At the beginning of the
nuclear research and plant building project, 185,000 jobs were initially
created. This number has well quadrupled since then.[7] Nuclear power plants
will very effectively help stop price inflation by making us self-sufficient
in energy. Some of the largest price-setting and inflationary industries are
the oil companies. These plants would reduce their power and lessen the
inflationary price spiral. Nuclear power plants have already provided jobs
for many people and could easily provide more. You must have planners,
builders, employees, and many more to get a plant on its feet. By providing
jobs, these plants stimulate the economy.

Such are the arguments for nuclear plants. They all seem valid. I feel
the strongest one is the argument that we need alternative sources of energy.
We can conserve all we want; we can require people to turn down their thermo-
stats and insulate their houses, but our need for energy is far greater than
our ability to conserve. This argument for nuclear power is the best. It
presents a feasible solution and then backs it up with what I consider the
other other excellent argument--the safety aspects of nuclear power. I have
been very concerned with this side of the question, and I still am, but I was

Transition from
presentation of
data to evaluation
of arguments. Note
that the writer
concedes there is
some validity to
all the arguments.
She estimates the
relative strength of
each argument.

not aware of the extent of the safety precautions in a nuclear plant.

The other two arguments are weaker. Because you are dealing with an essentially different type of plant than oil or gas, it may be very easy to have a low ratio as far as deaths and days off are concerned. And as to pollutants, you don't have air pollutants with a nuclear power plant. In some respects, comparing a nuclear power plant to a fossil fuel plant is as illogical as comparing the deaths caused by its radiation to the deaths caused by car accidents. You just can't compare them. They are not similar.

The argument concerning the economic benefits of nuclear power plants is stronger than the health argument. These plants do provide jobs and they could do a lot of good for our economy. But there is also a very valid opposing argument. I will consider it shortly.

The best argument is definitely the fact that we need a new source of energy. Once again, I pose the question: what will you do when the lights go out? But now I shall also add: when the lights go out, do we really want to rely on nuclear power to turn them back on?

Transition to the next section.

Arguments against Nuclear Power Plants

Question: Didn't the Fermi power plant in Detroit, Michigan, have an accident in which the core melted?

Answer: Yes, there was an accident in the Fermi power plant in Detroit in 1966 that resulted in the partial meltdown of two of the fuel elements in the core, but it was not a LOCA. ["LOCA" is a loss of coolant accident, the most dreaded accident. The water cooling system that cools the core of the reactor breaks down, which almost always results in a meltdown.] A piece of metal inside the reactor vessel broke loose and partially blocked the coolant flow to several elements in the core.

Question: Wasn't there nearly a serious nuclear power plant accident at Brown's Ferry in 1975?

6

Answer: Yes. There was an anticipated kind of accident that resulted from a design fault. Two operating power plants at the Brown's
Ferry station shared a common instrument and control cable with a
third plant under construction. A construction worker testing for
air leaks with a candle inadvertently set the control and instrument
cable on fire. In the more damaged plant, the fire incapacitated
two of the eleven cooling systems capable of cooling the reactor
core, four of which could only be operated with nonstandard
procedure.[8]

The writer begins
with counter-
arguments. There
are strong
objections to the
claim that the
plants are safe.

What these two formal answers are saying basically boils down to this:
accidents happen. No matter how many precautions you take against unforeseen
risks, there are always going to be the problems you can't be forewarned
against. The designers and operators of these plants are only human; they
make mistakes. Brown's Ferry could never have happened if we didn't make
mistakes. There are too many risks that can't be safeguarded against. Backup systems, shutdown systems, coolant systems can fail with no explicable
reason. To run this risk in a fossil fuel plant is bad enough; nuclear power
plants jeopardize lives because of the risks they pose. Why? To put it
simply, the whole function of a nuclear power plant rests on the necessity of
the core coolant system. If this breaks down and the backup system fails,
the core gets hotter and hotter. It begins to melt down into the ground. In
the process, it makes the whole plant into concrete, radioactive lava. As
this mixture settles into the ground, it spews out gases containing strong
radioactive particles. The wind can carry this dust over an entire state in
less than a day. There is also the added fact that the ground will be radioactive for hundreds of thousands of years.

Yes, the chances of this happening are slight; they are extremely slight.
But to say there are chances says that it could conceivably happen. And this
is within the realm of what we can foresee! A regular atomic reactor can't

blow up, but it can melt down. A fast-breeder reactor can blow up just like a bomb. Even with the near-perfect record these plants have, it must be remembered they have only been operating since the late 1950s. There have been two accidents so far, and the potential is always there for more. Granted, whenever humans enter into an activity there is the potential for harm. But this potential could result in enormous suffering. Even though the chances are slim, we're still playing Russian Roulette, and the stakes have never been this high.

Safety risks aside, there is also an opposing side to the economic question. The plants do provide jobs, but within this particular industry, lay-offs are extremely common. Providing jobs, then periodically taking them away, is no boost to the economy. It just makes the economic cycle of inflation and recession go up and down more quickly. The Palisades, Michigan, plant is a good example of the problem. Since it was built, it has been riddled with shutdowns because of defects. Building better plants is one cure for this, but only a partial one, because every time a plant has even one small, minute thing go wrong, it must shut down. Besides, coming up with better, desperately needed plants doesn't look very likely.

There are also astronomical insurance costs. "Presently, for each plant, the utility operator <u>must</u> purchase $125 million worth of private liability insurance."[9] The Price-Anderson Act set governmental coverage at $435 million. The Price-Anderson Act is now being reconsidered, and the ceiling on insurance is in the process of being raised because of the risk involved in these plants. Why are they paying such high costs; why must they have so much insurance? Because in the case of an accident they have to pay all the people injured and the estates of people killed. And the number of people hurt and killed could be high. Who eventually pays these costs? We, the consumers, do.

There are other arguments against nuclear power besides these. One of the scariest is the prospect of sabotage and nuclear theft. Like any other industrial facility, a nuclear power plant could be damaged by willful acts of

The writer
introduces new
arguments; she
does not merely
argue against each
of the opposing
arguments.

sabotage. It is true that to damage the plant and endanger the public would require a team of trained people to overpower the guards, disable or destroy all the plant's safety features, and finally blow up the reactor pressure vessel.[10] The plants seem safe from attack. However, there are a lot of people, a lot of activist groups, that have the necessary knowledge for sabotage. History has repeatedly shown us that all the security systems and armed guards in the world can fail. Couple this with the fact that there are a lot of brilliant people around who would be willing to attempt sabotage for one reason or another, and you have a formula for disaster.

There is also the chance that a foreign power could drop a bomb on one of these plants. Scientists aren't certain of how much damage a bomb would cause. Who would be unwise enough to attack us and do something that risky? There are always power-hungry Hitlers in the world. It doesn't even have to be a foreign power; we have plenty of terrorist groups right here in the United States who would have access to the type of aircraft that a plot like this would require.

Nuclear theft is also a risk. With nuclear power plants there is a by-product called plutonium. This is the material used to make atomic bombs. I learned how to make one of these in my physics class. How to make an atomic bomb is easily acquired knowledge, even though it's not supposed to be. The plutonium is placed in safety containers for shipment by train or truck to the site where it is buried. The minute it leaves the plant it is unprotected. The reasoning behind all this is that, because of the type of container it is in, the only way to get it out is by contaminating yourself, eventually leading to your death. I don't know who dreamed up this reasoning, but this is like saying there are only sane people in the world. There are an awful lot of people who wouldn't mind committing suicide if they could take Chicago with them. I think this passage clearly defines the high risks involved:

Question: What could a saboteur do?

<u>Answer</u>: He could precipitate one of these core-melting accidents
with a massive release of radioactivity. Nuclear industry officials
insist that saboteurs would pick easier targets. But those of us
who have been looking into this think that atomic power plants are
fragile and very attractive targets. Successful sabotage would
cause great havoc. That is only part of the safeguards problem.
The rest of it concerns protecting materials in the nuclear-fuel
cycle, particularly plutonium that could be stolen and made into
nuclear weapons of varying degrees of efficiency. Especially
troubling here is the possibility that the Government may well be
forced, in protecting the materials and facilities, to take measures
that would infringe our traditional freedoms.

<u>Question</u>: You feel it is possible that terrorists could seize some
plutonium and fashion a crude atomic bomb--

<u>Answer</u>: That is correct. Then, too, plutonium is so enormously
toxic that it could be used as a radiological weapon to contaminate
a big city's air or water supply. This hazard will intensify if
the industry carries out its plans to start large-scale recycling
of plutonium separated from spent fuel for reuse in present
reactors.[11]

Another problem caused by nuclear power plants is the problem of dispos-
ing of nuclear waste. A fast-breeder reactor recycles the material, but the
other plants in operation don't; they just keep spinning it out. It is as
deadly as a bomb. It is a nuclear time bomb just ticking away in the steel
storage tanks and shallow ditches all across the United States. It contains
enough radioactivity to poison the entire planet. There is presently no way
to defuse it, so it could remain lethal for a million years. Nuclear waste
is a collection of hot, highly radioactive materials created by the chain
reaction of atoms inside nuclear reactors. Thirty years of nuclear weapons

production and other military uses have created around a billion pounds of the waste. More is being produced in commercial electrical generating reactors every day. In my lifetime, in my children's, it is not going to go away.[12]

Besides the problem of nuclear pollution itself, how do we get the waste to the place where it will be buried? Right now we do it by train and truck. In fact, every once in a while one of the trains that comes through this campus carries nuclear waste. If that train were to derail and those cannisters ruptured, we wouldn't be having class for a long, long time. But what other way is there to carry the cannisters? There is no effective way to transport this time bomb. Every time a plant loads a train, car, or truck with those vials, it is taking terrible chances.

Would you want to live near a plant, even if you didn't run the risk of living near a potential meltdown? There are radioactive particles present in the air. The air around a plant has a higher concentration of these particles This is not lethal, but radiation builds up in the body; it doesn't dissipate quickly. There are environmental problems. There have been many fish killed in the Great Lakes by the thermal effects, admittedly caused by these plants, on the waters. There are only three of these plants in Michigan at present. The effects would be intensified if we had an escalation in the number of these plants.

The last major concern with these plants is the effect a natural disaster would have on them. They are built to withstand winds, but they are built by human planners who have the capacity for miscalculation. The Brown's Ferry incident proves the plants are susceptible to fire. What about earthquakes? Although earthquakes usually occur along a fault, they can occur anywhere. Nuclear power plants are built to withstand earthquakes, but once again, human error can occur. And it is admitted that an earthquake could seriously damage a power center. And a seriously damaged nuclear power plant can mean a very high likelihood of a meltdown.

I feel that each and every one of these arguments raises very serious questions as to the reliability and the safety of nuclear power plants. The two that concern me the most are the possibility of a nuclear accident and the possibility of sabotage or theft. Not the least of the problems is what we're going to do with the waste.

Although our economic problems are also serious, they are not really vital concerns compared with other problems. The effects of a natural disaster and the environmental problems also pose questions. But even they are not as pressing as the risk of an accident or theft.

Evaluation of arguments against nuclear power

The strongest arguments are the ones concerning accidents, theft, and storage of waste. These are the questions that greatly concerned me. After seeing the data, my decision is very clear.

Conclusion

Answer to thesis question asked in introduction

I do not want to rely on nuclear power plants for energy. Even though their records so far have been fairly good, we are dealing with something that could cause, very easily, a lot of pain and suffering and death. We are dealing with radioactivity--something that just doesn't "go away." We came terribly close with Detroit and Brown's Ferry, too close. One of these accidents is only too likely to occur, as these plants have proven. Yes, we do need a new energy source, but this is not the answer! We are exposing the population of the United States to a terrible risk.

A very respected judge came up with the following formula for the necessity of a potentially harmful product: "Harm versus the need of the product in society."[13] The need is great, but the harm is greater. The harm is lethal.

One of the books I read before I prepared this paper was written by Thomas Scortia and Frank Robinson. It is an account of what a meltdown would be like. Even though it is fictional, it has all its basis in fact. These two men are educated in science and one is a participant in government (he is trying to stop the building of nuclear power plants). They consulted with

Final quote used
for strong ending

many excellent scientists in the writing of the book. In view of the available evidence, it is hard to disagree with them: "It is our sincere hope that The Prometheus Crisis is not a scenario for such a catastrophic accident in the near future. We are more than a little afraid that it may be."[14] Please, in view of the possible results of nuclear power, if the lights go out, I want to sit in the dark.

Sherryl's thesis concerns a very significant problem: the hazards of nuclear power. As she shows, there are two sides to this problem, two significant sides. It is important to remember here that Sherryl is not writing an argument; instead, she is writing an investigation of an argument. As an objective researcher, it is her job to find the data on both sides of the question and to evaluate the arguments on both sides. Even though this is a controversial subject, Sherryl has done a fine job of isolating and explaining the arguments.

Is Sherryl convincing? Can we trust her analysis of the question? She reasons logically, and her data seem compelling. Perhaps some readers would have more confidence in the analysis if there were more data, more documentation, more source material. It is true that research gains in validity in relation to the amount and quality of the data. Each reader must decide this question for him- or herself. It is clear that Sherryl understands the subject and has done some solid research into the question. Her conclusion seems reasonable, given the data she has. (Her paper was written before the accident at Three Mile Island.)

Note that Sherryl has given careful attention to the introduction of her paper. She begins with a quote containing some surprising figures (see Chapter 7 for other effective introductions) and follows the quote with a long paragraph that explains the problem she is investigating. Sherryl ends her introduction by asking the thesis question, the specific research question she wants to answer: "Are nuclear power plants' hazards greater than their benefits?"

After discussing and documenting the arguments favoring nuclear power, Sherryl begins her evaluation of these arguments: "Such are the arguments for nuclear plants." This is a key component of her research. The presentation of the data amounts to an objective summary, but the *evaluation* of the data is a critique of the facts, of the reasoning, of the quality of the evidence. It is here that the researcher has the opportunity to analyze and validate, and it is here that the researcher has the greatest opportunity for objective insight into the problem. Note that the opportunity arises again after the presentation of the arguments for the other side. In both places Sherryl has given us her interpretation, her view of the data. In short, her research is more than a mere compilation of the facts. She tells us the facts, and she shows us what they mean.

Finally, her paper ends with a reasonable conclusion, in which she answers her research question. This answer is a data-based conclusion; that is, it is not simply Sherryl's "opinion" but a conclusion that she feels is compelled by the data. If she has done a good job of presenting her research, the reader too should feel compelled by the data. Note that Sherryl has saved something for the conclusion. The quote from *The Prometheus Crisis* seems especially relevant and adds further strength to her conclusion that the hazards of nuclear power plants outweigh their benefits.

Popular research topics

You may find the following list helpful in determining a research issue for yourself if you are assigned a research paper for your composition course. These topics are some of the research questions our students have asked in recent years:

1 Should Marijuana Be Legalized?
2 Capital Punishment: Yes or No?
3 Abortion versus Right to Life: Who Is Right?
4 Euthanasia: Do We Have a Right to Death?
5 Is There Too Much Sex in Advertising?
6 Gun Laws: Good or Bad?
7 Hunting: Sport or Massacre?
8 The Resurrection: Hoax or History?
9 Nuclear Waste: Safe?
10 Bermuda Triangle: Natural or Supernatural?
11 Freedom of the Press versus Gag Rule
12 Modern Witches: Neurotics or Mystics?
13 TV Violence: Harmful or Harmless?
14 Legalized Prostitution: Pro and Con
15 Pornography: Harmful or Helpful?
16 Legalized Homosexuality: Pro and Con
17 School Athletics: Good or Bad?
18 Genetic Engineering: Pro and Con
19 Imprisonment versus Rehabilitation
20 ERA: Necessary or Unnecessary?
21 Vegetarianism: Healthful or Harmful?
22 Reincarnation: Fact or Fiction?
23 Malpractice: Patients' Rights versus Doctors'
24 Transcendental Meditation: Real or Gimmick?
25 Biofeedback: Science or Fiction?
26 Nudity: Good or Bad?
27 UFOs: Science or Fiction?
28 John F. Kennedy's Assassination: Lone Assassin or **Conspiracy?**
29 Snowmobiles: Sport or Mayhem?

30 The Army: Volunteer or Conscriptive?
31 Shroud of Turin: Real or Fake?
32 National Health Insurance: Pro and Con
33 American Nazis: A Threat?
34 Women in West Point: Yes or No?
35 Are Fat People Discriminated Against?
36 Hockey Violence: Necessary?
37 Drinking Age: Raise to 21?
38 ESP: Fact or Fiction?
39 Advertising: Pro and Con
40 Cigarettes and Cancer: Proved or Not?
41 Fear of Snakes: Justified or Not?
42 American Funerals: Tragedy or Travesty?
43 Transsexuals: Should They Compete in Sports?
44 The Unborn Fetus: Is It a Person?
45 The Oil Shortage: Real or Contrived?
46 Legalized Gambling: Pro and Con
47 Welfare: Social Benefit or Ripoff?
48 Mandatory Retirement: Pro and Con
49 Women in Management: Pro and Con
50 Police Brutality: Fact or Fiction?

If you keep in mind that a research paper is not a "report," not a mere collection of facts, you will avoid topics like "The History of the Tank," "The Advantages of Dentistry," "The Development of Feminism."

Such one-sided topics are usually well researched in encyclopedias, history books, and elsewhere. They require you only to compile the known facts. To create a topic you can think about, one that will allow you to weigh the evidence and reach conclusions, change such topics into two-sided questions (see page 179). For example: "Are Tanks Essential to Modern Warfare?" "What Are the Advantages and Disadvantages of Dentistry?" "Do Women Still Face Job Discrimination Today?"

KILLS

By being so long in the lowest form (at Harrow) I gained an immense advantage over the cleverer boys . . . . I got into my bones the essential structure of the ordinary British sentence—which is a noble thing.

SIR WINSTON CHURCHILL, *Roving Commission: My Early Life*

To become a competent writer, you must master two closely related skills: the skill of discovering something worthwhile to say, and the skill of discovering how to say it. This chapter focuses on the latter, sentence-level skills; for no matter how interesting your ideas are or how well you organize an essay, your writing appears on the page one sentence at a time. Control over your sentences is essential.

In recent years, researchers have discovered that, by adolescence, almost all people have acquired virtually everything worth knowing about using language. Naturally, you can always expand your vocabulary—there are over 500,000 words in English—but you have known for a very long time how to form a question, state a fact, or put a sentence together. Using language is closely related to the ability to think, and people who say "I ain't got no smarts" are expressing the same *thought* as those who say "I am not very intelligent." If the first speaker used French, for example, the second Chinese, and a translator told you what they said, you would not imagine there was a difference in these speakers' ability to think.

If beginning writers, then, have in their brains the same language patterns that experienced writers have, why does their writing "sound" so different? This has been a central problem in teaching people to express their ideas in writing. The traditional approach was to teach parts of speech and rules of grammar, then to have students practice sentence labeling and sentence diagraming. After as much as twelve years of exposure to this type of language study, students entering college still wrote, more often than not, in short, choppy, immature-sounding sentences.

Furthermore, experienced writers themselves frequently say that they learned to write, not by studying grammar books, but by extensive reading and intensive *practice* at the craft of writing. But there is something confusing about the idea that practice will improve writing. Any language with 500,000 words will permit an almost infinite number of combinations of those words; no human could possibly practice every conceivable combination. It wouldn't do you much good simply to copy sentences written by other writers. The point of effective writing is to write new compositions with original sentences.

Experienced writers are correct, though, when they say that practice is the key to improving sentence-writing skills. With practice, your sentences can become more mature, better crafted, more expressive. The crucial issue is, however, to discover what needs to be practiced: it is the *connecting* devices of language that enable experienced writers to craft good sentences. Though there are thousands upon thousands of words in English, there are astonishingly few ways to connect them to each other. It is this connecting, or *sentence-combining*, skill that experienced writers have mastered and that beginning writers need to practice. Recent composition research shows that if you practice these sentence-connecting skills, you can very quickly become a sentence artist, confident in your ability to express your ideas in a variety of ways, assured when you sit down to write.

You can see this for yourself. Read the following two passages. Passage *B* was written by a professional writer, Sinclair Lewis. How does it differ from passage *A*?

A He dipped his hands in the bichloride solution. He shook them. The shake was quick. His fingers were down. His fingers were like the fingers of a pianist. The fingers of the pianist were above the keys.

B He dipped his hands in the bichloride solution and shook them, a quick shake—fingers down, like the fingers of a pianist above the keys.

Sinclair Lewis's sentence sounds "smoother"; he uses fewer words, is less repetitive, and builds a more consistent image. Passage *A* sounds choppy, wordy, repetitious; it lacks flow. The immature sentences are harder to read, and in fact, reading very many such sentences could become an unpleasant chore.

People are intrigued to discover that both passages contain the same information; the chief difference between them is in the way Lewis has connected up that information. Here's how the first passage can be transformed into the much better sentence in the second passage:

He dipped his hands in the bichloride solution/ ~~He~~ shook them/, ~~The~~
a quick ←— shake ~~was quick~~, ~~His~~ fingers ~~were~~ down/, ~~His fingers were~~ like the fingers of a pianist/ ~~The fingers of the pianist were~~ above the keys.

and (above "He shook them")

Lewis has gained rhythm, emphasis, and power by deleting redundant expressions ("He," "his," "his fingers were") and by using simple connecting devices ("and" and commas). With practice, you can quickly learn to use these sentence-combining devices essential to the writer's craft.

Suppose you were asked to combine the following three sentences into one longer, more mature sentence:

The officer took out his pistol.
The officer calmly pointed it at the prisoner's head.
He then pulled the trigger.

You might come up with the following response:

The officer took out his pistol, calmly pointed it at the prisoner's head, and then pulled the trigger.

Combining these three sentences involved three easy operations: First, you deleted the redundant phrases, "The officer" and "he"; then you added a comma between "pistol" and "calmly"; and last you put ", and" between "head" and "then."

Some people would probably combine the three sentences in different ways. For example:

The officer took out his pistol, calmly pointed it at the prisoner's head, and pulled the trigger.

The officer took out his pistol and calmly pointed it at the prisoner's head before pulling the trigger.

The officer took out his pistol, calmly pointed it at the prisoner's head, then pulled the trigger.

After taking out his pistol, the officer calmly pointed it at the prisoner's head and pulled the trigger.

After taking out his pistol and calmly pointing it at the prisoner's head, the officer pulled the trigger.

And there are still other acceptable combinations. It is obvious, then, that three short sentences can be crafted into a number of different single sentences. A writer can, with relative ease, convey essentially the same information in a variety of ways.

In this chapter, you will work with many of the combining devices experienced writers use, and you will exploit the language ability you already have. As you practice using these combining devices, you will discover a major transformation occurring in your writing: you will begin to produce better-sounding sentences in your own compositions. Remember, though, that because writing is a physical, as well as a mental, act, you must go beyond merely solving the sentence problems in your head. You must practice putting each sentence on paper, one word at a time. Then, these new, more mature language habits/patterns will become imprinted on your mind.

WORKING THE PROBLEMS

In order to accustom you to combining sentences, we will start off by using a series of connection *signals*. These sentence-combining signals show you how you can join several separate sentences into one. Generally, signals to the right of a sentence direct you to add whatever is inside the parentheses to the beginning of the sentence.

EXAMPLE
The armies of Alexander the Great swept through Baktria and Scythia.
The armies invaded India.   (,)
Then they returned to Persia.   (, AND)

The *slash* signal, a diagonal line through a word, means to delete the word in which the slash appears. In the example, the slash signals direct you to delete "The," "armies," and "they."

The *comma* signal (,) means to add a comma at the beginning of the sentence in which the comma signal appears. Since you have deleted "The" and "armies" in the example, you would be left with ", invaded India" after inserting the comma signal.

The *comma-and* signal (, AND) means to put a comma and "and" at the beginning of the sentence in which the signal appears. In the example, put ", and" in front of "then" to complete the solution.

In general, work the problems in your head and then write out the one-sentence answer. In particular:

STEP 1: READ THE WHOLE PROBLEM

The armies of Alexander the Great swept through Baktria and Scythia.

The armies invaded India.   (,)

Then they returned to Persia.   (, AND)

STEP 2: SOLVE EACH LINE OF THE PROBLEM

BEFORE YOU TRY TO SOLVE THE WHOLE PROBLEM

The armies of Alexander the Great swept through Baktria and Scythia.

~~The armies~~ invaded India.   (,)

Then ~~they~~ returned to Persia.   (, AND)

It's usually possible to do step 2 in your head, but write it out if you feel it will help.

STEP 3: WRITE OUT THE NEW SENTENCE

The armies of Alexander the Great swept through Baktria and Scythia, invaded India, and then returned to Persia.

Practice

Write out each of the following five sentence-combining problems as one sentence. You have been given all the necessary signals in the first two and limited assistance with the third; in the last two, combine the sentences in any way you choose.

1 The snowmobile roared through the trees.
  The snowmobile plowed through the brush.   (,)
  The snowmobile disappeared into the wilderness.   (, AND)

2 Set your government's affairs in order.
  The opposing party will do it for you.   (, OR)

3 The drought hung over Oklahoma.
  The drought was drying up rivers.   (,)
  It was emptying ponds and lakes.
  It was parching the land.
  It was threatening the region with another Dust Bowl.

4 Genghis Khan spent his nights in revelry.
  Genghis Khan spent his days in butchery.

5 Peter Frampton sauntered onto the stage.
  Peter Frampton picked up his guitar.
  He played a few casual bars.
  He paused.
  He launched into a song that had his audience murmuring their approval.
  The song then had the audience thundering their approval.

What is gained by connecting up these ideas into one sentence? The answer concerns the power of the period (and the other end marks). The end marks are the most powerful punctuation marks in the language because they indicate that a unit of thought has ended. In the examples you have just completed, the ideas are fairly complex. They are composed of several related thoughts, and to show that these thoughts all add up to one larger, more complex idea, you withheld the period until the end of all those ideas. In short, you *unified* the ideas by connecting up the sentences that expressed them. This does not necessarily mean, of course, that experienced writers have more complex *ideas* than you do; rather, they have simply learned how to *express* their ideas so that the unity and complexity are preserved. Think of someone learning to skate. At first the movements are short, jerky, and uncertain. With practice, these separate, disconnected movements will blend together into the smooth and gracefully flowing motions of the mature skater. So too with sentence combining. With practice, you will rapidly develop the ability to make the disconnected elements of your thoughts flow together into the rhythmically balanced expression of complex ideas. Indeed, sentence combining will help to promote complex and sophisticated thoughts by enabling you to manipulate sentence structures to express these thoughts easily and habitually. As you work the sentence problems, concentrate on creating a better sentence and not merely on getting the problem "right." When you reach the point where you can see several possibilities for a sentence and feel confident enough to choose among them, you will be well on the way to becoming a sentence artist. Mastery over the sentence will free you to concentrate on the larger components of your essay.

COMBINING BY ADDITION

One of the easiest devices for combining ideas is to connect one idea to another, unchanged. You can do this with certain marks of punctuation (comma, semicolon) and/or with one of the many connecting words in the language ("and," "but," "when," "because," "or," "while," "though," "so"). For example:

A At 9 A.M. he assembles his own staff.

Each in turn talks about where difficulties may lie for the President.   (, AND)

At 9 A.M. he assembles his own staff, and each in turn talks about where difficulties may lie for the President.

"Hannibal Astride the Potomac," *Time,* 14 March 1977

B My cells are no longer the pure line entities I was raised with.
   They are ecosystems more complex than Jamaica Bay.   (;)

   My cells are no longer the pure line entities I was raised with; they
   are ecosystems more complex than Jamaica Bay.
   LEWIS THOMAS, *The Lives of a Cell: Notes of a Biology Watcher*

C The writer intends to cut out a piece of his thought.
   He must cut a piece that his reader can perceive as having a kind
   of wholeness.   (, BUT)

   The writer intends to cut out a piece of his thought, but he must
   cut a piece that his reader can perceive as having a kind of wholeness.
   JOHN E. JORDAN, *Using Rhetoric*

D Inflation since 1960 is also taken into account.   (WHEN)
   The retooling costs due to style changes are conservatively estimated to average one billion dollars annually.   (,)

   When inflation since 1960 is also taken into account, the retooling
   costs due to style changes are conservatively estimated to average
   one billion dollars annually.
   RALPH NADER STUDY GROUP ON AIR POLLUTION, *Vanishing Air*

   In these examples, the signal at the end of a sentence moved
to the front of that sentence before it was combined.

Addition practice 1: combining with signals

*Write out each of the following problems as a single sentence, using
the signals to help you re-create the original.*

1 You walk into a room full of people.   (WHEN)
   You communicate with everyone there
   without ever saying a word.   (,)
   ELIZABETH MCGOUGH, "Body Language–It Tells on You," *American Youth
   Magazine*, March/April 1979

2 This poem can help explain Keats' life.
   His life cannot explain the poem.   (;)
   HAROLD BLOOM, *The Visionary Company: A Reading of English Romantic Poetry*

3 An honest man has hardly need to count more than his ten fingers.
   In extreme cases he may add his ten
   toes, and lump the rest.   (, OR)
   HENRY DAVID THOREAU, *Walden*

4 Strolling players like Rueda's company still toured Spain.
   Permanent theaters had been built in
   the sixteenth century.   (EVEN AFTER)
   KENNETH MACGOWAN AND WILLIAM MELNITZ, *The Living Stage*

5 Our profession is young.　(YET BECAUSE)

We feel insecure.　(AND BECAUSE)

We do not like to admit our humanity.　(,)

JEROME BRUNER, "Essay for the Left Hand," *On Knowing: Essays for the Left Hand*

6 In most of Europe the languages of the people developed freely until the Middle Ages.

They were mainly spoken languages.　(BECAUSE)

All learned writings were made in Latin.　(, WHILE)

STANLEY RUNDLE, "Language and Dialect," *A Linguistic Reader*

7 In California, farmers were well equipped to expand their production quickly.

They had already developed one of the most highly mechanized types of agriculture in the nation.　(FOR)

GERALD D. NASH, *The American West in the Twentieth Century: A Short History of an Urban Oasis*

8 They did what they could to break out.

Failing, they clung to life as long as they could.　(;)

THOMAS PYNCHON, *The Crying of Lot 49*

9 You are at the heart of this city.　(WHEN)

You are at the heart of Nature.　(,)

JEAN-PAUL SARTRE, "New York, the Colonial City," *Literary and Philosophical Essays*

10 The President was not a stupid man.

The intricacies of government bored him.　(, BUT)

The dirty work of politics repelled him.　(, AND)

DREW PEARSON, *The Senator*

11 He had a somewhat worn and anxious look.

He was composed and easy.　(, BUT)

He suspected anything.　(, AND IF)

It did not appear in his face or manner.

MARK TWAIN, "A Curious Experience," *The Complete Short Stories of Mark Twain*

12 The fragility of her loveliness was emphasized by the inevitable comparisons with the rose.

She was urged to employ her beauty in lovemaking before it withered on the stem.　(, AND)

GERMAINE GREER, *The Female Eunuch*

13 The noise in the cell quieted.

The door clanked open.　(AS)

The silence deepened.　(, AND)

A quilt had been thrown over the prisoners.　(AS THOUGH)

They watched Yakov enter.　(AS)

BERNARD MALAMUD, *The Fixer*

14 A single-celled animal moves as a whole.
   It has neither cells nor muscles.   (, THOUGH)
   It takes account of its environment.   (;)
   It has no brain.   (, THOUGH)
   CHARLES HARTSHORNE, *Reality As Social Process*

15 The importance of events mounted.   (AS)
   More points on the map needed coverage.   (, AS)
   More reporters were hired.   (AND)
   The *CBS World News Roundup* was born.   (,)
   DAVID HALBERSTAM, "CBS: The Power and the Profits," *Atlantic Monthly*, Jan. 1976

   This practice was designed to demonstrate that ideas can be effectively connected together unchanged. However, the fact that you *can* connect ideas to each other does not necessarily mean that you always *should*. Arbitrarily running sentences together is not the idea; such a practice will often produce baby talk: "I have a dog, and his name is Spot, and he is white, and he follows me, and I play with him." You need not limit yourself to simple concepts that can be expressed in the language of children. Where two ideas complete a single, broader concept, you can express that completeness by connecting the ideas in a single sentence. Effective writing depends on judicious use of the addition skill.

Addition practice 2: creating alternative combinations

Select five of the signaled problems from Addition practice 1. Rework each problem individually this way: ignore the signals, take the base sentences in any order you please, and create a one-, two-, or even three-sentence answer you think is interesting. You may wish to adhere strictly to the words and phrases used in a given problem; or you may prefer a looser answer that adds, deletes, or replaces information contained in a problem; or you may want to try strict versions for some problems and loose versions for others.

MODEL

In most of Europe the languages of the people developed freely until the Middle Ages because they were mainly spoken languages, while all learned writings were made in Latin. (Problem 6, Addition practice 1)

STRICT ALTERNATIVES

A While all learned writings were made in Latin, the languages of the people, because they were mainly spoken languages, developed freely until the Middle Ages in most of Europe.

B Because the languages of the people were mainly spoken languages, they developed freely in most of Europe until the Middle Ages. All learned writings, however, were made in Latin.

LOOSE ALTERNATIVE

Until the Middle Ages, most spoken European languages developed freely simply because they were seldom found in writing.

Addition practice 3: combining without signals

Write out the sentence problems in this exercise in any way you please. Although each problem can be written as one sentence, occasionally you may choose to create answers that consist of more than one sentence. Take the sentences in any order at all, and try to produce as many different answers as you can. Then discuss your preferences. For example, if you were given the following problem, you could easily produce several different answers:

PROBLEM

Victory finds a hundred fathers. Defeat is always an orphan.

SOLUTIONS

Victory finds a hundred fathers; defeat is always an orphan.

Although victory finds a hundred fathers, defeat is always an orphan.

Defeat is always an orphan, but victory finds a hundred fathers.

Victory finds a hundred fathers; defeat, however, is always an orphan.

The ability to recast your sentences is an important rewriting and editing skill.

1 There is some ambiguity about the knowledge an educated man should have. There is none at all about the skills.
BERTRAND RUSSELL, "What Good Is Philosophy?" *The Art of Philosophizing and Other Essays*

2 I'll go in for my chest x-ray. I have finished my tenth cigarette.

3 Speed increases. Involvement falls off. The involvement is sensory. One is experiencing deprivation. The deprivation is real. The deprivation is sensory.
EDWARD T. HALL, "The Automobile Syndrome," *The Hidden Dimension*

4 Even the experienced news reporters were shocked. Several rock fans complained about the rock concert. There were no drug arrests. No one attacked the police.

5 In the northern European cultures the romantic mode is usually associated with femininity. This is certainly not a necessary association.
ROBERT M. PIRSIG, *Zen and the Art of Motorcycle Maintenance*

6 He [Hitler] was financed by the wives of some of the great industrialists. Their husbands had heard of him.
ERIC HOFFER, *The True Believer*

7 In the end we shall make thoughtcrime literally impossible. There will be no words in which to express it.
GEORGE ORWELL, *1984*

8 Her date dropped her off. Agnes slipped up to her room. The dorm supervisor had gone to bed.
SALLY FOSTER

9 Over the referee's face came a look of woe. Some spasm had passed its way through him. He leaped on Griffith to pull him away.
NORMAN MAILER, *The Presidential Papers*

10 It will spread out into space. After four or five years it will reach the next star.
ARTHUR C. CLARKE, "The Star of the Magi," *Report on Planet Three*

11 Its speed slackens. Crests of following waves crowd in toward it. Abruptly its height increases. The wave form steepens.
RACHEL CARSON, *The Sea Around Us*

12 Mistakes are always paid for in casualties. Troops are quick to sense any blunder made by their commanders.
DWIGHT D. EISENHOWER, *Infantry School Quarterly*, April 1953

13 This emulsion has many valuable properties. It penetrates the skin. It does not become rancid. It is mildly antiseptic and so forth.
ALDOUS HUXLEY, *Brave New World Revisited*

14 He is forbidden to kiss his girl in the public parks. He cannot be trusted to stop at kissing.
H. L. MENCKEN, "The American: His Morals," *The Young Mencken: The Best of His Work*

15 The self-educated genius is therefore becoming rarer. He still has not vanished.
ISAAC ASIMOV, *Fact and Fancy*

Addition practice 4: imitation

Imitate at least three of the sentences you created in Addition practices 1, 2, or 3. Create a sentence with a structure similar to that of the model sentence you have selected but on a different *subject. You may wish to do a close imitation or a loose imitation. Write out the model sentence you select* before *you create the loose or strict imitation sentence.*

MODEL

When her date dropped her off, Agnes slipped up to her room after the dorm supervisor had gone to bed. (Problem 8, Addition practice 3)

CLOSE IMITATION

When the police car left the scene, the burglar climbed in through a downstairs window after the unsuspecting couple had retired for the night.

When the police car had left and the residents had retired for the night, the burglar was free to climb through a downstairs window and rob the wall safe.

COMBINING BY DELETING

Instead of connecting whole sentences, experienced writers often delete part of a sentence, especially repetitious words or phrases, and combine the remaining idea. For example:

A Darling trotted back.
    He was smiling.   (,)
    He was breathing deeply.   (,)
    He was breathing easily.   (BUT)
    He was feeling wonderful.   (,)
    He was not tired.   (,)
    This was the tail end of practice.   (, THOUGH)
    He'd run eighty yards.   (AND)

Darling trotted back, smiling, breathing deeply but easily, feeling wonderful, not tired, though this was the tail end of practice and he'd run eighty yards.
IRWIN SHAW, "The Eighty Yard Run"

The slashes direct you to delete repetitious words. Another way to signal deletion is to underline the words to be retained and connected. Underlining directs you to keep the underlined words and delete the words not underlined in that sentence. In example B, for instance, you would delete "He" and "is," move the comma to the front of that sentence, and then combine the remaining idea, ", bruised and aching," with the sentence above.

B Picture poor old Alfy coming home from football practice every day.
    He is bruised.   (,)
    He is aching.   (AND)
    He is agonizingly tired.   (,)
    He is scarcely able to shovel the mashed potatoes into his mouth.   (,)

Picture poor old Alfy coming home from football practice every day, bruised and aching, agonizingly tired, scarcely able to shovel the mashed potatoes into his mouth.

PAUL ROBERTS, "How to Say Nothing in Five Hundred Words," *Understanding English*

Writers often combine their ideas by deleting a repetitious word or phrase and substituting words like "who," "which," "that," "whom," "whose" for the repeated element. In example *C*, the (WHO) signal directs you to delete the repeated phrase "The witnesses" and substitute "who." The (WHICH) signal directs you to delete the repeated element "the facts" and substitute "which." You would then move the phrase "upon which" to the front of its sentence.

C In court cases, considerable trouble is sometimes caused by witnesses.

The witnesses cannot distinguish their judgments from the facts.   (WHO)

Those judgments are based upon the facts.   (UPON WHICH)

In court cases, considerable trouble is sometimes caused by witnesses who cannot distinguish their judgments from the facts upon which those judgments are based.

S. I. HAYAKAWA, "Reports, Inferences, Judgments," *Language in Thought and Action*

In addition to achieving unity and economy of expression, Shaw, Roberts, and Hayakawa have succeeded in creating unified images or ideas, always a difficult task because English is a linear language (it is produced "straight line," one word after another), but reality is seldom linear. In the sentence by Irwin Shaw, there are many separate items, but if we had seen Christian Darling on the football field, we would have perceived these details simultaneously. By deleting repetitious words and using commas to "blend" sentences, Shaw has fused these disparate elements into a single sentence and, more important, into a single *image*. Deleting and connecting, then, are important creative skills that will enable you to make your writing more accurately reflect your perception of reality.

Deletion practice 1: combining with signals

Write out each of the following problems as a single sentence, using the signals to help you re-create the original.

1 He was prone to superstition.

He was <u>not prone to credulity.</u>   (, BUT)
JAMES BOSWELL, *Life of Samuel Johnson*

2 The civilization of Egypt was remarkably homogeneous.

The civilization reached its fullness in the first few dynasties of the Old Kingdom.   (, WHICH . . . ,)
J. KELLY SOWARDS, *Western Civilization to 1660*

The (, WHICH . . . ,) signal means to replace the repeated element "The civilization" with ", which" before "reached" and also to put a comma after "the Old Kingdom." The sentence then ends with "was remarkably homogeneous."

3 The conspirators were to go into action early in November.

The conspirators were to <u>assassinate Hitler.</u>   (,)

The conspirators were to <u>overthrow his regime.</u>   (,)

The conspirators were to make peace with the West.   (AND)
LADISLAS FARAGO, *Burn After Reading*

4 A lawyer without history or literature is a mechanic.

Thȩ lawyȩr is/a mere working mason.   (,)

He possesses some knowledge of these.   (; IF)

He may venture to call himself an architect.   (,)
SIR WALTER SCOTT, *Guy Mannering*

5 Hȩ was living in a feudal age some 2,500 years ago.   (THOUGH)
He sounded the note of wisdom.   (,)
He/uttered dictums of golden truth.   (AND)

The note of wisdom and the dictums of truth have retained their brilliance in spite of time.   (THAT)
WU-CHI LIU, *Confucius, His Life and Times*

6 His glance was quizzical.
His glance was <u>curious.</u>   (,)
His glance was <u>imperative.</u>   (,)
THEODORE DREISER, *An American Tragedy*

7 The tragedy at Kent was partially the result of the current clash between two different life styles.

The life styles are contending for the spirit of America.   (, WHICH)
JAMES A. MICHENER, *Kent State*

8 The voice of science is itself impeccably rational.   (BECAUSE)
Thȩ voiȩe is/insistently reasonable.   (,)
It/is/forever self-correcting.   (, AND)
It cannot be deduced out of existence.   (,)
KENNETH MACCORQUODALE, "Behaviorism Is a Humanism," *The Humanist*, March/April 1971

9 Slow performance may indicate
momentary attention gaps.   (WHILE)

Extremely rapid performance may
be indicative of a person.   (,)

The person sacrifices accuracy to speed.   (WHO)

The person's personality demands a challenge.   (, AND WHOSE)

J. R. BLOCK, "A Test That Tells Who Is Accident-Prone," *Psychology Today*,
June 1975

10 Biological time never creates the same world twice.

Out of its clefts and fissures creep, at long intervals, surprisingly
original creatures.   (, BUT)

The creatures' destinies can never be anticipated.   (WHOSE)

They arrive.   (BEFORE)

LOREN EISELEY, *The Unexpected Universe*

11 More particularly, they rediscovered Panini's magnificent grammar
of Sanskrit.

Sanskrit is the ancient literary dialect of India.   (,)

The grammar was probably written late
in the fourth century, B. C.   (, WHICH)

OWEN THOMAS, *Transformational Grammar and the Teacher of English*

12 Religion and other ways of knowing lost their power to enrich
thought for many.   (WHILE)

Science became the truth of truths.   (,)

Technique became the holy principle.   (, AND)

T. GEORGE HARRIS, "The Religious War Over Truth and Tools," *Psychology
Today*, Jan. 1976

13 The life of Man is a long march through the night.

It is surrounded by invisible foes.   (,)

It is tortured by weariness and pain.   (,)

The march is towards a goal.   (,)

Few can hope to reach the goal.   (THAT)

None may tarry long.   (, AND WHERE)

BERTRAND RUSSELL, "A Free Man's Worship," *Mysticism and Logic*

14 On top of the craft's triangular surface, a 30-inch antenna dish
unfolds.

The antenna dish searches the star-sprinkled sky for homing signals
from earth.   (AND)

It finds them.   (,)

It locks on.   (AND)

K. E. KRISTOFFERSON, "Message From the Surface of Mars," *Reader's Digest*,
Feb. 1976

15 Paley was not a mere corporate figure.

Paley was a total individual.   (BUT)

Paley was a man.   (,)

The man lived a life rich in its texture.　(WHO)

The man knew and enjoyed quality.　(, WHO)

The man demanded it in every aspect
of his own life.　(, AND WHO)

DAVID HALBERSTAM, "CBS: The Power and the Profits," *Atlantic Monthly*, Jan.
1976

Deletion practice 2: creating alternative combinations

*Select five of the signaled problems from Deletion practice 1. Ignore
the signals, take the sentences in any order you please, and create a
one-, two-, or even three-sentence answer that you think is interesting.
You may wish to adhere strictly to the words and phrases used in a
given problem; or you may prefer a looser answer that adds, deletes,
or replaces information contained in the model sentence; or you may
want to try strict versions for some problems and loose versions for
others.*

MODEL

Although living in a feudal age some 2,500 years ago, he sounded the
note of wisdom and uttered dictums of golden truth that have retained
their brilliance in spite of time.　(Problem 5, Deletion practice 1)

STRICT ALTERNATIVES

A The note of wisdom he sounded and the dictums of golden truth he
uttered have retained their brilliance although he lived in a feudal
age some 2,500 years ago.

B Despite his having lived some 2,500 years ago in a feudal age, the
note of wisdom he sounded and the dictums of golden truth he uttered
have retained their brilliance.

LOOSE ALTERNATIVE

Although he lived 2,500 years ago, the wisdom and truth he gave us
then remain as insightful as when they were first spoken.

Deletion practice 3: combining without signals

*Write out the sentence problems in this exercise in any way you please.
Although each problem can be written as one sentence, occasionally
you may choose to create answers that consist of more than one sentence. Take the sentences in any order at all and try to produce as many
different answers as you can. Then discuss your preferences. For example, you could solve the following problem in a number of ways:*

PROBLEM

He made one of the greatest discoveries of all time. Galileo died in

disgrace. He died a man. The man was lonely. The man was disillusioned. He was outlawed by the church.

SOLUTIONS

Although he made one of the greatest discoveries of all time, Galileo
died in disgrace, a lonely, disillusioned man, outlawed by the church.

Galileo, who made one of the greatest discoveries of all time, died in
disgrace, a disillusioned, lonely man, outlawed by the church.

Outlawed by the church, a lonely and disillusioned man, Galileo, who
had made one of the greatest discoveries of all time, died in disgrace.

Galileo made one of the greatest discoveries of all time. But when he
was outlawed by the church, he died in disgrace, a lonely, disillusioned
man.

1 The chapel was full. The chapel was not packed. The chapel was
very quiet.
JAMES BALDWIN, *Notes of a Native Son*

2 The garbage has been burned. The residue is dumped onto barges.
The residue is cooled. The barges are towed off by tugboats to one
of five landfill sites around the city.
KATIE KELLY, *Garbage: The History and Future of Garbage in America*

3 We have probably all met people. The people are intensely educated. The people manage to be abysmally stupid, nevertheless.
ISAAC ASIMOV, *Fact and Fancy*

4 The marriage had just taken place. The bride still wore her dress.
The mother still wore her corsage.
JOAN DIDION, "Marrying Absurd," *Slouching Towards Bethlehem*

5 The movie explored parts of American society. The movie is always
in quest of exoticism. The parts are unknown to the middle class. The
middle class is respectable.
ARTHUR SCHLESINGER, JR., "America at the Movies," *Saturday Review*, 12 Nov.
1977

6 You're going to repair a motorcycle. A supply of gumption is the
first tool. It is the most important tool. The supply is adequate.
ROBERT M. PIRSIG, *Zen and the Art of Motorcycle Maintenance*

7 The couple discharged their obligations. The obligations were religious. The obligations were social. The couple furnished forth a
progeny. The progeny was copious. The couple kept their troubles to
themselves. The couple maintained civility. The civility was public.
The couple died under the same roof. The couple were not always on
speaking terms. It was rightly regarded as a successful marriage.
KATHERINE ANNE PORTER, "The Necessary Enemy," *The Collected Essays and
Occasional Writings of Katherine Anne Porter*

8 All parts of this system interact. Ideally it should be analyzed. It
should be planned. It should be managed as a whole.
NEIL H. JACOBY, "The Environmental Crisis," *The Center Magazine*, Dec. 1970

9 People are to be brought together again. They are to be given a chance to get acquainted with each other. They are to get involved in nature. Some solutions must be found to the problems. The problems are posed by the automobile. The solutions are fundamental.

EDWARD T. HALL, "The Automobile Syndrome," *The Hidden Dimension*

10 The trade advertisements are, however, instructive. They furnish an important clue to the frame of mind. The funeral industry has hypnotized itself into this frame of mind.

JESSICA MITFORD, *The American Way of Death*

11 She is a young woman. She is frank. She is charming. She is fresh-hearted. The young woman married for love.

KATHERINE ANNE PORTER, "The Necessary Enemy," *Collected Essays and Occasional Writings of Katherine Anne Porter*

12 Patriotism can be an asset for any society. The asset is great. The society is organized. It can also be a tool. The tool is manipulated by leaders and elites. They are unscrupulous. They are cowardly.

RALPH NADER, "We Need a New Kind of Patriotism," *Life*, 9 July 1971

13 The bull charges. The banderillero rises to his toes. He bends in a curve forward. Just as the bull is about to hit him he drops the darts into the bull's hump just back of his horns.

ERNEST HEMINGWAY, "Killing a Bull," *By-Line Ernest Hemingway*

14 Iron is strong. Iron is heavy. It is clamorous. It is struck. It is avid of oxygen. It is capable of corruption.

DONALD CULROSS PEATTIE, "Chlorophyll: The Sun Trap," *Flowering Earth*

15 Such is the story of a peasant boy. The boy was Spanish. The boy was drawing with charcoal on a plank. A teacher saw him. The teacher started training him. The teacher helped to make the artist Goya.

GILBERT HIGHET, "Training the Thinker," *Man's Unconquerable Mind*

Deletion practice 4: imitation

Imitate at least three of the sentences you created in Deletion practices 1, 2, or 3. Create a sentence with a structure similar to that of the model sentence you have selected but on a different subject. You may wish to do a close imitation or a loose imitation. Write out the model sentence you select before you create the loose or strict imitation sentence.

MODEL

The conspirators were to go into action early in November, assassinate Hitler, overthrow his regime, and make peace with the West. (Problem 3, Deletion practice 1)

CLOSE IMITATION

The terrorists decided to launch their operation in the spring, kidnap the foreign minister, destroy the main oil pipelines, and seize the nation's radio stations.

The terrorists, whose spring offensive had just been initiated, kidnapped the foreign minister, satchel-bombed several major industrial plants, and launched an all-out attack on the country's radio and television stations.

COMBINING BY EMBEDDING

In order to achieve economy and clarity in their writing, experienced writers often combine their ideas by embedding all or part of one sentence *into* another sentence. Embedding allows them to show that two ideas are not merely related to each other, but that one is actually *part* of the other.

THE (THAT) AND (THE FACT THAT) SIGNALS

When you work on the embedding skill, think of one sentence as having a slot (which we will label SOMETHING) in it. The SOMETHING signal is simply directing you to put a clause or phrase into that slot. For example:

A She knew SOMETHING.

He was going to leave her.   (THAT)

She knew that he was going to leave her.
JAMES BALDWIN, "Come Out the Wilderness," *Fifty Years of the American Short Story*

In example A, THAT moved to the front of its sentence and the clause "that he was going to leave her" was then inserted into the SOMETHING slot.

B The great thing about human language is SOMETHING.

It prevents us from sticking to the matter at hand.   (THAT)

The great thing about human language is that it prevents us from sticking to the matter at hand.
LEWIS THOMAS, *The Lives of a Cell: Notes of a Biology Watcher*

C This is due largely to SOMETHING.

Many writers think, not before, but
as they write.   (THE FACT THAT)

This is due largely to the fact that many writers think, not before, but as they write.
W. SOMERSET MAUGHAM, *The Summing Up*

D She wants me to believe SOMETHING.

The body is a spiritual fact.   (TH/AT)

The body is <u>the instrument of the soul.</u>   (,)

She wants to believe the body is a spiritual fact, the instrument of the soul.

SAUL BELLOW, *Herzog*

The word "that" is often optional in English. In example *D*, Saul Bellow chose to delete "that" and simply embed "the body is a spiritual fact" into the SOMETHING slot in the first sentence. We have signaled the deleted "that" by putting a slash mark through the signal: (TH/AT).

E Fr/eud continued his studies.   (BUT)

Fr/eud denounced religion as an illusion.   (,)

Freud accumulated additional clinical evidence showing SOMETHING.   (, AND)

His patients' immature concepts of God were contributing to their mental illness.   (HOW)

But Freud continued his studies, denounced religion as an illusion, and accumulated additional clinical evidence showing how his patients' immature concepts of God were contributing to their mental illness.

GEORGE CHRISTIAN ANDERSON, *Man's Right to Be Human*

Variations on the (THAT) signal are (HOW), (WHEN), (WHERE), (WHY), (IF), (WHO), (WHAT). In example *E*, (HOW) moved to the front of its sentence and the clause "how his patients' immature concepts of God were contributing to their mental illness" was then inserted into the SOMETHING slot.

THE (IT . . . THAT) SIGNAL

When you encounter the IT . . . THAT signal, remember the following rule: The IT substitutes for the SOMETHING slot above; the THAT goes to the front of its own sentence. For example:

A SOMETHING is incomprehensible.

Such drugs could be dispensed without competent medical advice.   (IT . . . THAT)

It is incomprehensible that such drugs could be dispensed without competent medical advice.

NORMAN COUSINS, "The Toxified Society," *Saturday Review,* 5 March 1977

B   Throughout this book, SOMETHING is important to remember.

We are not considering language as
an isolated phenomenon.   (IT . . . THAT)

Throughout this book, it is important to remember that we are not
considering language as an isolated phenomenon.

S. I. HAYAKAWA, "The Language of Reports," *Language in Thought and Action*

C   SOMETHING was lucky.

We were both of us only fourteen.   (IT . . . TH~~A~~T)

It was lucky we were both of us only fourteen.

WILLIAM GOLDING, "Thinking as a Hobby," *Holiday*, April 1961

It is obvious that embedding (and the other sentence-combining skills) often produces longer sentences. Thus, you may feel
that sentence combining is merely the art of writing longer sentences. While there is some truth to that idea, it is *not* true that
long sentences are better than short ones. Short sentences are
often as effective as long sentences. Variety in sentence *length*
is just as important as variety in sentence *style*. But if you compare them, you will discover that the sentences of experienced
writers are, on the average, substantially longer than those of
beginning writers, and—more important—that beginning writers
use more words to express an idea. Experienced writers are more
economical with their words; they manage to say more in less.
And they achieve this economy of expression by judicious use of
deletions, embeddings, and the other sentence-combining skills.

Embedding practice 1: combining with signals

*Write out each of the following problems as a single sentence, using
the signals to help you re-create the original.*

1   The transactional analyst believes SOMETHING.

Psychiatric symptoms result from some
form of self-deception.   (THAT)

ERIC BERNE, *What Do You Say After You Say Hello?*

2   We can make useful observations from photographs.

We err.   (, BUT)

We forget SOMETHING.   (IF)

The camera is not a complete reproduction of the objects photo-
graphed.   (THAT)

DAVID K. BERLO, *The Process of Communication*

3   SOMETHING seems to be generally taken for granted.

Wife-beaters are not gentlemen in twentieth
century terms.   (IT . . . THAT)

Self-control is expected of a gentleman, under even the most trying circumstances.   (AND THAT)
RUSSELL LYNES, "Is There a Gentleman in the House?" *Look,* 9 June 1959

4 Leeuwenhoek failed to see SOMETHING.   (IF)

Germs cause human disease.   (THAT) .

He did show SOMETHING.   (,)

They could devour and kill living beings.   (THAT)

The beings were <u>much larger than themselves.</u>
PAUL DE KRUIF, *Microbe Hunters*

5 Some thought SOMETHING.

They were the only person to hear the cries.   (TH̸AT)

The rest believed SOMETHING.   (;)

Others heard them, too.   (THAT)
JOHN M. DARLEY AND BIBB LATANE, "Why People Don't Help in a Crisis," *Reader's Digest,* May 1969

6 SOMETHING is belts of Flexten cord, instead of steel.

I̸t makes the Goodyear American Eagle Radial the tire for today.   (WHAT)
ADVERTISEMENT, *People Weekly,* 14 March 1977

7 SOMETHING would put him in an awful spot.

Lois Farrow somehow found out SOMETHING.   (IT . . . IF)

He had let her daughter go to sleep with her legs across Duane's.   (TH̸AT)
LARRY MCMURTRY, *The Last Picture Show*

8 Stimulating the brains of lightly anesthetized patients in the operating room became a most important way to localize functions.

SOMETHING was found.   (SINCE)

Physical landmarks were not sufficiently uniform to be completely reliable.   (IT . . . THAT)
ELLIOT S. VALENSTEIN, *Brain Control: A Critical Examination of Brain Stimulation and Psychosurgery*

9 From the outset, in the sixteenth century, the leaders of European society fervently believed SOMETHING.

A great change in the life of man was about to take place.   (THAT)

The change was <u>cyclic.</u>
LEWIS MUMFORD, "The Pentagon of Power," *Horizon,* Autumn 1970

10 Many students of discrimination are aware o̸f SOMETHING.

The victim often reacts in ways as undesirable as the action of the aggressor.   (THAT)
BRUNO BETTELHEIM, *The Informed Heart*

11 We are told SOMETHING.

The trouble with Modern Man is SOMETHING.   (THAT)

He has been trying to detach himself from nature.   (THAT)
LEWIS THOMAS, *The Lives of a Cell: Notes of a Biology Watcher*

12 The psychological journey into our inner world helps us to experience our emotions without fear.

   It helps us to admit SOMETHING.   (,)

   We have denied.   (WHAT)

   It helps us to deny SOMETHING.   (, AND)

   We once believed.   (WHAT)
   GEORGE CHRISTIAN ANDERSON, *Man's Right to Be Human*

13 We may, of course, be pleasantly (or even unpleasantly) surprised.

   We get to Mars.   (WHEN)

   All the evidence points to SOMETHING.   (; BUT)

   Our little red neighbor is a very much older
planet than Earth.   (THE FACT THAT)

   Any intelligent Martians must have become extinct millions of
years ago.   (, AND)
   ARTHUR C. CLARKE, "To the Stars," *Voices from the Sky*

14 I know SOMETHING.

   You think SOMETHING.   (THAT)

   I'm wasting my time.   (THAT)
   DONALD BARTHELME, "See the Moon?" *Fifty Years of the American Short Story*

15 I suppose SOMETHING.

   Willie had his natural quota of ordinary
suspicion and cageyness.   (THAT)

   Those things tend to evaporate.   (, BUT)

   SOMETHING is SOMETHING.   (WHEN)

   People tell you.   (WHAT)

   You want to hear.   (WHAT)
   ROBERT PENN WARREN, *All the King's Men*

Embedding practice 2: creating alternative combinations

*Select five of the signaled problems from the preceding embedding
practice. Ignore the signals, take the sentences in any order you please,
and create a one-, two-, or even three-sentence answer that you think
is interesting. You may wish to adhere strictly to the words and phrases
used in a given problem; or you may prefer a looser answer that adds,
deletes, or replaces information contained in a problem; or you may
want to try strict versions for some problems and loose versions for the
rest.*

MODEL

She wants me to believe the body is a spiritual fact, the instrument of
the soul.   (Example *D*, page 252)

STRICT ALTERNATIVES

A She wants me to believe that the body, as the instrument of the
soul, is a spiritual fact.

B She wants me to believe that the body is a spiritual fact. To her, the body is the instrument of the soul.

LOOSE ALTERNATIVE

Convinced that the body has spiritual significance, she also believes that it is influenced and controlled by the soul.

Embedding practice 3: combining without signals

Complete the sentence problems using the embedding skills you practiced in the signaled exercises in Embedding practice 1. Although each problem can be combined into one sentence, occasionally you may choose to create answers that consist of more than one sentence. You may take the sentences in any order at all. Try to produce as many different answers as you can, and then discuss your preferences. For example, if you were given the following problem, you could easily produce several different solutions:

PROBLEM

The scientific community was disturbed. It discovered something. A Princeton undergraduate had designed a bomb. The undergraduate was young. The bomb was atomic. He designed the bomb from information. The information was supplied to him by officials. The officials were employed by the federal government.

SOLUTIONS

The scientific community was disturbed when it discovered that a young Princeton undergraduate had designed an atomic bomb from information supplied to him by officials employed by the federal government.

When it discovered that a young undergraduate from Princeton had designed an atomic bomb from information supplied to him by federal government officials, the scientific community was disturbed.

The scientific community was disturbed when it discovered that a young Princeton undergraduate had designed an atomic bomb. He designed the bomb from information that was supplied to him by officials employed by the federal government.

A young Princeton undergraduate designed an atomic bomb from information supplied to him by officials of the federal government. When the scientific community discovered this, it was disturbed.

1 The Yankelovich poll is certainly not wrong. It tells us something. Eighty-two percent of Americans *think* of themselves as "middle-class." ROBERT HEILBRONER, "Middle-Class Myths, Middle-Class Realities," *Atlantic Monthly,* Sept. 1976

2 They were not only able to say something. They were close to dying. Many were able to predict the time of their death. The time was approximate.

ELISABETH KÜBLER-ROSS, "Facing Up to Death," *Today's Education,* Jan. 1972

3 I knew something. I could never win that way. There were whites. They were many. There were blacks. They were but few.

RICHARD WRIGHT, *Black Boy*

4 Starting in 1965, a number of cable-tray fires in plants alerted the AEC to something. The cable-tray fires were serious. The plants were nuclear. To save space and money, plant builders were squeezing the trays so close together. A fire in one could quickly spread to others.

JAMES NATHAN MILLER, "The Burning Question of Brown's Ferry," *Reader's Digest,* April 1976

5 Once I had been taken to one of our old marsh churches to see a skeleton. The skeleton was in the ashes of a rich dress. The skeleton had been dug out of a vault. The vault was under the church pavement.

CHARLES DICKENS, *Great Expectations*

6 Once, in a dry season, I wrote in large letters across two pages of a notebook, something. Innocence ends. One is stripped of the delusion. One likes oneself.

JOAN DIDION, "On Self Respect," *Slouching Towards Bethlehem*

7 She told me one day. She was sweeping my apartment. She was worried about her two sons. She asked something. She might talk with me.

JAMES A. MICHENER, *America Against America*

8 He was addressed by other slaves as Toby. It was the master's name for him. The African said angrily something. His name was Kin-tay.

ALEX HALEY, "My Furthest-Back Person—'The African' "

9 He too found evidence to show something. The evidence was copious. Evolution took place. He too wanted to find a reason.

ISAAC ASIMOV, *Fact and Fancy*

10 I am encouraged to tell myself something. I am enjoying my beverage. It's my favorite. Really, I am only getting sloshed.

DONALD HALL, "An Ethic of Clarity," *Modern Stylists*

11 I have felt compelled to write things down. I was five years old. I doubt something. My daughter ever will do so. She is a child. The child is singularly blessed. The child is accepting. She is delighted with life exactly as life presents itself to her. She is unafraid to go to sleep. She is unafraid to wake up.

JOAN DIDION, "On Keeping a Notebook," *Slouching Towards Bethlehem*

12 Something is fortunate. This is so. The huge masses of water actually moved across the sea. They comprise a wave. Navigation would be impossible.

RACHEL CARSON, *The Sea Around Us*

13 **Ralph Paine used to say something. He managed** *Fortune* **in my time. Anyone who said something was either a writer or a liar. Writing was easy. The writer was bad. The liar was unregenerate.**

JOHN KENNETH GALBRAITH, "Writing, Typing & Economic$," *Atlantic Monthly,* Jan. 1978

14 **I have been assured by an American of my acquaintance in London something. The American is very knowing. A young healthy child if well nursed is at a year old a food, whether it is stewed. It is roasted. It is baked. It is boiled. The food is most delicious. The food is nourishing. The food is wholesome. I make no doubt of something. It will equally serve in a fricassee, or a ragout.**

JONATHAN SWIFT, "A Modest Proposal"

15 **This hypothesis is the work of linguist Benjamin Whorf. Whorf contended something. Different linguistic groups perceive and conceive reality in different ways. The language spoken by the group shapes the cognitive structure of the individual speaking that language.**

E. FULLER TORREY, *The Mind Game: Witch Doctors and Psychiatrists*

Embedding practice 4: imitation

Imitate at least three of the sentences you created in Embedding practices 1, 2, or 3. Create a sentence with a structure similar to that of the model sentence you have selected but on a different *subject. You may wish to do a close imitation, or a loose imitation. Write out the model sentence you select* before *you create the loose or strict imitation sentence.*

MODEL

It would put him in an awful spot if Lois Farrow somehow found out he had let her daughter go to sleep with her legs across Duane's. (Problem 7, Embedding practice 1)

CLOSE IMITATION

It would leave Alex in an awkward position if by chance the judge discovered he had helped a political rival with his campaign.

LOOSE IMITATION

It would have meant instantaneous death to the fugitive couple if the Nazis had discovered that they were not visiting relatives but Jews preparing to escape to Israel.

COMBINING BY TRANSFORMING

Up to this point, you have been practicing sentence-combining skills that focused on how to connect and embed ideas by deleting single words or phrases from a sentence and inserting the remainder into the preceding sentence. In this section, you will expand your repertoire of sentence-combining operations by developing expertise with a variety of sentence-transforming skills. Transforming involves rearranging or changing the insert sentence before connecting it to the preceding sentence.

THE (ING) AND (WITH) SIGNALS

Two of the more effective techniques utilized by experienced writers are "ing" and "with" phrases. In example A, the (ING) signal directs you to change "kept" to "keeping"; "she" is then unnecessary in the first sentence, so you delete it:

A   She kept a firm hand on her committee.   (ING)
    She issued precise instructions.   (,)

Keeping a firm hand on her committee, she issued precise instructions.
CECIL WOODHAM-SMITH, *Florence Nightingale*

B   The trackers scuttled along.
    They stopped.   (, ING)
    They looked.   (, ING)
    They hurried on.   (, AND + ING)

The trackers scuttled along, stopping, looking, and hurrying on.
JOHN STEINBECK, *The Pearl*

C   The children catapulted this way and that across green lawns.
    They shouted at each other.   (, ING)
    They held hands.   (, ING)
    They flew in circles.   (, ING)
    They climbed trees.   (, ING)
    They laughed.   (, ING)

The children catapulted this way and that across green lawns, shouting at each other, holding hands, flying in circles, climbing trees, laughing.
RAY BRADBURY, *The Illustrated Man*

D   The social scientists, especially the economists, are moving deeply into ecology and the environment these days.
    The results are disquieting.   (, WITH)

The social scientists, especially the economists, are moving deeply into ecology and the environment these days, with disquieting results.
LEWIS THOMAS, *The Lives of a Cell: Notes of a Biology Watcher*

E Monterey sits on the slope of a hill.
It has a blue bay below it.   (, WITH)
It has a forest of tall dark pine trees at its back.   (AND WITH)

Monterey sits on the slope of a hill, with a blue bay below it
and with a forest of tall dark pine trees at its back.
JOHN STEINBECK, *Tortilla Flat*

F The room was just as Jake had left it.
The fan was turned on and the pitcher of
ice water was beside the table.   (, WITH)

The room was just as Jake had left it, with the fan turned on and
the pitcher of ice water beside the table.
CARSON MCCULLERS, *The Heart Is a Lonely Hunter*

THE ('s), (OF), AND (L$\not{Y}$) SIGNALS

A SOMETHING enchanted the audience.
Nureyev danced.   ('s + ING)

Nureyev's dancing enchanted the audience.

The sentence is derived like this:

Nureyev + ('s) = Nureyev's
danced + (ING) = dancing

You then insert "Nureyev's dancing" into the SOMETHING slot.

B Alfred Lord Tennyson recalled SOMETHING.
The innumerable bees murmured in
immemorial elms.   (ING + OF)

Alfred Lord Tennyson recalled the murmuring of innumerable
bees in immemorial elms.

C The television audience was delighted by SOMETHING.
Nadia Comanechi won a gold medal at
the 1976 Olympics.   ('s + ING + OF)

The television audience was delighted by Nadia Comanechi's winning of a gold medal at the 1976 Olympics.

D SOMETHING put the class to sleep.
The professor lectured endlessly.   (L$\not{Y}$ + ING + OF)

The endless lecturing of the professor put the class to sleep.

Note that the signals (L$\not{Y}$ + ING + OF) tell you not only what to
do (delete "ly," add "ing," insert "of") but how to change the
order of the words: the deleted "-ly" word comes first ("endless"),

then the "-ing" word ("lecturing"), and finally the "of" insertion ("of the professor").

E SOMETHING was morally outrageous.

He butchered political opponents
mercilessly.   ('s + I/X̶ + ING + OF)

His merciless butchering of political opponents was morally outrageous.

In example *E*,

He + ('s) = His

Similarly, when you add *'s*, "I" should be changed to "my," "we" to "our," "she" to "her," "they" to "their," and "it" to "its." (Note the spelling of "its.")

THE (FOR . . . TO), (IT . . . TO), AND
(IT . . . FOR . . . TO) SIGNALS

The (FOR . . . TO) signal directs you to change a sentence like "John runs" to "For John to run . . . ." The (IT . . . TO) and (IT . . . FOR . . . TO) signals function like the (IT . . . THAT) signal. The "it" replaces the appropriate SOMETHING signal and "to" or "for . . . to" operate on their own sentences. For example:

A SOMETHING is easier than SOMETHING.

A camel goes through the eye of
a needle.   (IT . . . FOR . . . TO)

A rich man enters into the kingdom of God.   (FOR . . . TO)

It is easier for a camel to go through the eye of a needle than for a rich man to enter the kingdom of God.
MATTHEW, 19:24

B SOMETHING won't be easy.

We send him into any of the three phases.   (IT . . . TO)

It won't be easy to send him into any of the three phases.
THOMAS PYNCHON, *Gravity's Rainbow*

THE DISCOVER→DISCOVERY SIGNAL

Certain transformations involve changing the form of a word; thus "discover" can be changed to "discovery," "fail" to "failure," "investigate" to "investigation," and so on. Rather than supply a signal for these changes, we will simply give you the word you need. For example:

A Winston Churchill denounced SOMETHING.

Hitler seized Czechoslovakia.   ('s + SEIZURE + OF)

Winston Churchill denounced Hitler's seizure of Czechoslovakia.

B The nation finally insisted on SOMETHING.

Richard Nixon immediately resigned as
President.   ('s + L̸Y̸ + RESIGNATION)

The nation finally insisted on Richard Nixon's immediate resignation as President.

Transformation practice 1: combining with signals

*Write out each of the following problems as a single sentence, using
the signals to help you re-create the original.*

1 The only thing necessary for the triumph of evil is SOMETHING.

Good men do nothing.   (FOR . . . TO)
EDMUND BURKE, "Letter to William Smith"

2 There was the house.

The house was <u>low</u>.   (,)

It was <u>long</u>.   (AND)

It was <u>obscure</u>.   (AND)

One light burned downstairs, in Sir
Clifford's room.   (, WITH + ING)
D. H. LAWRENCE, *Lady Chatterley's Lover*

3 If possible, SOMETHING is best.

Cast from a bridge abutment.   (IT . . . TO)

The fish can be played at or near water level.   (, SO THAT)
LEE WULF, *The Sportsman's Companion*

4 For a month he had worked on these papers.

He scribbled them during working hours.   (, + ING)

He typed.   (, + ING)

He made carbons on the typewriter at
the New York Café.   (AND + ING)

He distributed them by hand.   (, + ING)
CARSON MCCULLERS, *The Heart is a Lonely Hunter*

5 Most of the early fathers of the Church were subordinationists.

They believed SOMETHING.   (, + ING)

The Son and the Holy Spirit were subordinate in time and in power
to the Father.   (THAT)
JEFFREY B. RUSSELL, *A History of Medieval Christianity: Prophecy and Order*

6 His hands rested on his knees.

His handsome head presented a
rigid profile to the doorway.   (;)

It had big eyebrows.　　(WITH)
JOSEPH CONRAD, *Heart of Darkness*

7 SOMETHING is permissible.
Others seek God by a road less direct.　　(IT . . . FOR . . . TO)
They lead a good life in the world.　　(, TO)
They raise a Christian family.　　(, TO)
THOMAS MERTON, *The Silent Life*

8 Eunice continued to laugh.
She laughed <u>steadily.</u>　　(,)
She laughed <u>hysterically.</u>　　(,)
She clutched her stomach.　　(, + ING)
She collapsed into a chair.　　(, + ING)
HORTENSE CALISHER, "A Christmas Carillon," *Prize Stories 1955: The O. Henry Awards*

9 An aspect of the political change was SOMETHING.
The political change was revolutionizing Europe.　　(WHICH)
They encouraged foreign adventure and exploration.　　(THE ENCOURAGEMENT + OF)
ROBERT L. HEILBRONER, *The Worldly Philosophers*

10 Even she seemed cheered by SOMETHING.
The manager came.　　('s + ING)
She sensed SOMETHING.　　(;)
Her husband had an irrationally light spirit.　　('s + J/Y + LIGHTNESS + OF)
DORIS LESSING, "The Second Hut," *African Short Stories*

11 Essentially, SOMETHING means SOMETHING.
I love my neighbor.　　(ING)
I recognize SOMETHING.　　(ING)
SOMETHING is as real as mine.　　(THAT)
He exists.　　('s + EXISTENCE)
W. H. AUDEN, *Hiroshima Plus 20*

12 SOMETHING would have been impossible.
Someone guesses SOMETHING.　　(IT . . . FOR . . . TO)
James Bond was contemplating the possibility of his own death later that day.　　(THAT)
He felt the soft-nosed bullets.　　(, + ING)
They tore into him.　　(ING)
He saw his body.　　(, + ING)
It jerked on the ground.　　(ING)
His mouth perhaps screamed.　　(, + ING)
IAN FLEMING, *The Man with the Golden Gun*

13 The rocking horse bounded forward on its springs.
It startled the child into SOMETHING.　　(, + ING)

The child scampered noiselessly back
to bed.   (A + I/X + SCAMPER)
DYLAN THOMAS, "The Tree," *Ten Modern Masters*

14 SOMETHING is not the purpose of these comments.

Someone suggests SOMETHING.   (IT . . . TO)

Anything can be done.   (THAT)
CLIFTON FADIMAN, "Party of One," *Holiday*, June 1961

15 I had a strange thought.

I looked at the guardian's body.   (; + ING)

I felt SOMETHING.

Every single part of it was independently alive.   (THAT)

The eyes of men are alive.   (, AS)
CARLOS CASTANEDA, *A Separate Reality*

Transformation practice 2: creating alternative combinations

*Select five of the signaled problems in Transformation practice 1.
Ignore the signals, take the sentences in any order you please, and
create a one-, two-, or even three-sentence answer that you think is
interesting. You may wish to adhere strictly to the words and phrases
used in the model sentence; or you may prefer a looser answer that
adds, deletes, or replaces information contained in the model sentence.*

MODEL

Monterey sits on the slope of a hill, with a blue bay below it and with
a forest of tall dark pine trees at its back.   (Example E, page 260)

STRICT ALTERNATIVES

A With a blue bay below it and with a forest of tall pine trees at its
back, Monterey sits on the slope of a hill.

B Monterey, which sits on the slope of a hill, has a blue bay below it
and a forest of tall dark pine trees at its back.

LOOSE ALTERNATIVE

Situated on the slope of a hill, Monterey looks down to a blue bay
and up to a forest of towering dark pine trees.

Transformation practice 3: combining without signals

*Complete the sentence problems in this practice using the transforming
skills you practiced in the signaled exercises in Transformation practice
1. Although each problem can be combined into one sentence, occasionally you may choose to create answers that consist of more than
one sentence. Take the sentences in any order at all, and try to produce
as many different answers as you can. Then discuss your preferences.*

For example, you could come up with many solutions to the following
problem; three are listed here.

PROBLEM

Albert Einstein was a rarity. He was a scholar. The scholar was
dedicated. The scholar was brilliant. The scholar was creative. He had
a love for humanity. He had a wonderful sense of humor.

SOLUTIONS

Albert Einstein was a rarity, a dedicated, brilliant, creative scholar
with a love for humanity and a wonderful sense of humor.

A dedicated, brilliant, creative scholar with a love for humanity and
a wonderful sense of humor, Albert Einstein was a rarity.

Albert Einstein was a rarity, a dedicated, brilliant, creative scholar
with a love for humanity. He also had a wonderful sense of humor.

1 We were all fanatics about our hair. We worked on it in the school
restrooms. Our arms grew weak.
WILLIAM ALLEN, "Haircut," *Starkweather*

2 They wrenched the flag furiously from the dead man. They turned
again. The corpse swayed forward. It had a bowed head.
STEPHEN CRANE, *The Red Badge of Courage*

3 I went upstairs. I felt like a criminal.
RICHARD WRIGHT, *Black Boy*

4 They were maddened. They were angry. They leaped and howled
round the trunks. They cursed the dwarves in their horrible language.
Their tongues hung out. Their eyes shone as red and fierce as flames.
J.R.R. TOLKIEN, *The Hobbitt*

5 News of the disaster spread quickly to other sports arenas. It started
other panics among the crowds. They tried to get to the exits. They
could buy a paper. They could study a list of the dead.
E.B. WHITE, "The Decline of Sport (A Preposterous Parable)," *The Second Tree*
from the Corner

6 They are surrounded by students. The students have little interest
in acquiring an education. They lack companionship with students.
The students want to learn. They receive no encouragement at home.
These children apply themselves even less than they would. There
were good students in class. They identify with them.
BRUNO BETTELHEIM, "Grouping the Gifted," *NET Journal,* 54 *March* 1965

7 He came home from a day at the hospital. The day was arduous. He
would go straight to his pad. His pad was yellow. He would write
his tensions away.
WILLIAM ZINSSER, "The Transaction," *On Writing Well*

8 Something is easy. Someone says something. Other people are superstitious. They believe something. We regard it to be untrue.
MARGARET MEAD, "New Superstitions for Old," *Redbook,* Jan. 1966

9 Spatially, the urban environment must be viewed as one subdivision of the entire ecosystem. The ecosystem is global. The ecosystem also embraces lands. The lands are rural. It embraces the oceans. It embraces the atmosphere. The atmosphere surrounds the earth. It embraces outer space.

NEIL H. JACOBY, "The Environmental Crisis," *The Center Magazine*, Dec. 1970

10 He whirled back to Yossarian. He sneezed thunderously six times, before he could speak. He staggered sideways on rubbery legs in the intervals. He raised his elbows ineffectively to fend each seizure off.

JOSEPH HELLER, *Catch 22*

11 A town official was crossing a bridge on his bicycle about ten miles from the heart of the city. He felt the right side of his face seared. He thought something. He had sunstroke. He jumped to the ground.

ALEXANDER H. LEIGHTON, "That Day at Hiroshima," *Atlantic Monthly*, Oct. 1946

12 Writers often read aloud at this stage of the editing process. They mutter. They whisper to themselves. They call on the ear's experience with language.

DONALD M. MURRAY, "The Maker's Eye: Revising Your Own Manuscript," *The Writer*, Oct. 1973

13 She is dismayed. She is horrified. She is full of guilt and forebodings. She is finding out little by little something. She is capable of hating her husband. She loves him faithfully.

KATHERINE ANNE PORTER, "The Necessary Enemy," *Collected Essays and Occasional Writings of Katherine Anne Porter*

14 We rush toward superindustrialism, therefore. We find people. They adopt life styles. They discard life styles at a rate. The rate would have staggered the members of any previous generation.

ALVIN TOFFLER, *Future Shock*

15 She came towards me. I held out my hand. I envied her for her dignity. I envied her for her composure. She took my hand. Hers was limp. Hers was heavy. Hers was deathly cold. It lay in mine like a lifeless thing.

DAPHNE DU MAURIER, *Rebecca*

Transformation practice 4: imitation

Imitate at least three of the sentences you created in Transformation practices 1, 2, or 3. Create a sentence with a structure similar to that of the model sentence you have selected but on a different subject. You may wish to do a close imitation or a loose imitation. Write out the model sentence you select before you create the loose or strict imitation sentence.

MODEL

The social scientists, especially the economists, are moving deeply into ecology and the environment these days, with disquieting results. (Example D, page 259)

CLOSE IMITATION

Army generals, especially extreme conservatives, are getting involved in politics and government today, with repressive consequences.

LOOSE IMITATION

Because of economic difficulties and lack of experience in self government, many new democracies in Africa are being taken over by repressive military regimes, with disastrous consequences for individual freedom and universal suffrage.

COMBINING BY PUNCTUATING

You have already had extensive practice with the comma, semicolon, and period. Two punctuation marks favored by many modern writers are the colon and the dash; they allow writers to express their ideas with economy and clarity.

THE COLON (:) AND DASH (—) SIGNALS

Note the use of the colon and dash signals in the following examples:

A In sum, there are at least two types of faith.
   There are <u>possibly many more</u>.   (, THOUGH)
   There is <u>the faith of the true believer</u>.   (:)
   There is <u>the faith of a heretic</u>.   (AND)

   In sum, there are at least two types of faith, though possibly many more: the faith of the true believer and the faith of a heretic.
   WALTER KAUFMAN, *The Faith of a Heretic*

B The pipeline workers were <u>masked</u>.
   The pipeline workers were <u>insulated by down clothing</u>.   (AND)
   These pipeline workers know well the
   same enemy as Jack London.   (,)
   The enemy is <u>killing cold</u>.   (:)

   Masked and insulated by down clothing, these pipeline workers know well the same enemy as Jack London: killing cold.
   EDWARD J. FORTIER, "Jack London's Far North," *National Observer*, 21 June 1975

C Fifty years have expired since this adventure.
   The fear of punishment is no more.   (—)

   Fifty years have expired since this adventure—the fear of punishment is no more.
   JEAN JACQUES ROUSSEAU, *Confessions*

D The hour of Yellow Sky was approaching.   (BUT)

It was the hour of daylight.   (— . . . —)

But the hour of Yellow Sky—the hour of daylight—was approaching.

STEPHEN CRANE, "The Bride Comes to Yellow Sky"

The double-dash signal (— . . . —) in example *D* indicates an interrupter set off on both sides by dashes. The interrupter "the hour of daylight" was inserted into the sentence above, not just attached to the end of it.

E There is, after all, another side to the human spirit, too.

It is a dark side.   (— . . . —)

There is, after all, another side—a dark side—to the human spirit, too.

ERIC SEVAREID, "The Dark of the Moon"

F Nevertheless, character is the source.

Character is the willingness to accept responsibility for one's own life.   (— . . . —)

Self-respect springs from the source.   (FROM WHICH)

Nevertheless, character—the willingness to accept responsibility for one's own life—is the source from which self-respect springs.

JOAN DIDION, "On Self-Respect," *Slouching Towards Bethlehem*

G The crimes have changed in rapid succession.

The Jews have been charged with the crimes in the course of history.   (WITH WHICH)

They were crimes.   (—)

The crimes were to justify the atrocities.   (WHICH)

The atrocities were perpetrated against them.   (. . . —)

The crimes with which the Jews have been charged in the course of history—crimes which were to justify the atrocities perpetrated against them—have changed in rapid succession.

ALBERT EINSTEIN, "Why Do They Hate the Jews?"

The signal (. . . —) instructed you to put a dash at the end of its sentence, immediately after "perpetrated against them" and, of course, immediately in front of "have changed."

Punctuating practice 1: combining with signals

Write out each of the following problems as a single sentence, using the signals to help you re-create the original.

1 Two hours later the loudspeakers sent out an order.
   The order was from the head of the camp.
   All the Jews must come to the assembly place.   (:)
   ELIE WIESEL, *Night*

2 Down drifts the calf.
   The calf is dead.   (—)
   GUNTER GRASS, *Dog Years*

3 The best marriages are the ones.
   The ones are arranged.   (THAT)
   That is, they are the marriages.   (—)
   The marriages aren't rushed into.   (THAT)
   Two foolish people think SOMETHING.   (BECAUSE)
   They can't live without each other.   (THAT)
   LENOR M. WEBER, *My True Love Waits*

4 The phone was downstairs.   (SINCE)
   I didn't see SOMETHING.
   We were going to call the police.   (HOW)
   Nor did I want the police.   (— . . . —)
   Mother made one of her decisions.   (BUT)
   Her decisions were incomparable.
   Her decisions were quick.
   JAMES THURBER, "The Night the Ghost Got In," *My Life and Hard Times*

5 At the age of three the average child moves into a phase.
   The phase is new.
   The phase is graphic.
   It starts to simplify its scribbling.   (:)
   Its scribbling is confused.
   DESMOND MORRIS, *The Naked Ape*

6 He stood for a moment.
   He was a child.   (—)
   He was alien.   (,)
   He was lost in the gloom of the wilderness.   (AND)
   The gloom was green.
   The gloom was soaring.   (AND)
   The wilderness was markless.
   WILLIAM FAULKNER, *The Bear*

7 To understand the physical world, and ultimately man himself, one
   must eliminate the living soul.
   Man himself exists in this world as merely a product of mass and
   motion.   (— WHO . . . —)
   LEWIS MUMFORD, "The Pentagon of Power," *Horizon*, Autumn 1970

8 Now runneth she foolishly in the arid wilderness.
   She seeketh the soft sward.   (, AND)

She is <u>mine wisdom!</u>   (—)

Mine wisdom is <u>wild.</u>

Mine wisdom is <u>old.</u>

FRIEDRICH NIETZSCHE, *Thus Spake Zarathustra*

9 So I would say to the organizations and groups SOMETHING.

They would force integration on the
South by legal process.   (WHICH)

"Stop now for a moment."   (:)

WILLIAM FAULKNER, "A Letter to the North," *Essays, Speeches, and Public
Letters*

10 Above all we need a policy.

The policy concerns <u>world population.</u>

We need it <u>not at some date in the future.</u>   (—)

The date is <u>unspecified.</u>

We need it <u>now.</u>   (, BUT)

JULIAN HUXLEY, "The Crowded World"

11 The modern world *is* a waste land.

The world never has been a flower garden.   (, BUT)

The world <u>surely never will be</u> a flower garden.   (— AND . . . —)

WALTER KAUFMANN, *From Shakespeare to Existentialism*

12 The executive, instead of standing behind his own judgment, makes
the show easier and easier.

Every last one of the testers can understand it.   (UNTIL)

There's nothing left to understand.   (— BECAUSE)

KRISTI WITKER, "The Price is Wrong: Game Shows People Play," *Redbook*, Feb.
1976

13 Many experiences of failure, plus the environmental crisis, have
suddenly brought on the loss of confidence in SOMETHING.

The loss of confidence is <u>deeper.</u>

The loss of confidence is <u>more</u> general.   (,)

I̶t̶ has been man's chief source of certainty.   (WHAT)

The source of certainty is <u>his logical mind.</u>   (:)

The source of certainty is <u>his skill as a toolmaker.</u>   (AND)

GEORGE T. HARRIS, "The Religious War Over Truth and Tools," *Psychology
Today*, Jan. 1976

14 This revolution has resulted in a growing understanding of the
forces.

Th̶is revol̶ution i̶s as profound as the revolution in astronomy 500
years ago.   (—)

Copernicus displaced the Earth from its position at the Center of
the Universe.   (WHEN + . . . —)

The forces shape the continents.   (WHICH)

Th̶e forc̶es set them drifting about the world.   (AND)

JOHN R. GRIBBIN AND STEPHEN H. PLAGEMANN, *The Jupiter Effect*

15 There were stragglers going by.
   The regiment had passed.   (LONG AFTER)
   They were <u>men</u>.   (—)
   The men could not keep up with their platoons.   (WHO)
   ERNEST HEMINGWAY, *A Farewell to Arms*

Punctuating practice 2: creating alternative combinations

*Select five of the signaled problems from the preceding punctuation
practice. Ignore the signals, take the sentences in any order you please,
and create a one-, two-, or even three-sentence answer that you think
is interesting. You may wish to adhere strictly to the words and phrases
used in a given problem; or you may prefer a looser answer that adds,
deletes, or replaces information contained in a problem; or you may
want to try strict versions for some problems and loose versions for the
rest.*

MODEL

In sum, there are at least two types of faith, though possibly many
more: the faith of the true believer and the faith of a heretic.
(Example A, page 267)

STRICT ALTERNATIVES

A In sum, there are at least two—though possibly many more—types
of faith: the faith of the true believer and the faith of a heretic.

B Though there are possibly many more, there are, in sum, at least
two types of faith: the faith of a heretic and that of the true believer.

LOOSE ALTERNATIVE

Among the many possible types of faith, two stand out. The first is
obvious—the faith of a true believer; the second is less apparent—the
faith of a heretic.

Punctuating practice 3: combining without signals

*Complete the sentence problems using the punctuating skills you prac-
ticed in the signaled exercises in Punctuating practice 1. Although each
problem can be combined into one sentence, occasionally you may
choose to create answers that consist of more than one sentence. You
may take the sentences in any order at all. Try to produce as many
different answers as you can, and then discuss your preferences. For
example, if you were given the following problem, you could easily
produce several different solutions:*

PROBLEM

The Population Reference Bureau announced something. Women in
the third-world countries have a life expectancy of only fifty-six years.

The third-world countries are the poorest nations on earth. The average American woman can expect to live. She is seventy-seven years old.

SOLUTIONS

The Population Reference Bureau announced that women in the third-world countries—the poorest nations on earth—have a life expectancy of only fifty-six years, whereas the average American woman can expect to live until she is seventy-seven years old.

The Population Reference Bureau announced that women in the third-world countries have a life expectancy of fifty-six years. The average American woman can expect to live until she is seventy-seven years old—very different from women in the poorest nations on earth.

The Population Reference Bureau announced that American women have a life expectancy of seventy-seven years, whereas the average woman in the third-world countries—the poorest nations on earth—can expect to live only until she is fifty-six years old.

The Population Reference Bureau announced that women in the third-world countries—the poorest nations on earth—have a life expectancy of only fifty-six years. The average American woman, on the other hand, can expect to live to be seventy-seven years old.

1 Here man attains the ultimate in fear. He fears himself.
NORMAN COUSINS, "Where Hell Begins," *Present Tense: An American Odyssey*

2 There are two types of connotation. One is personal. One is general.
RICHARD D. ALTICK, *Preface to Critical Reading*

3 For the scientist, there is only "being." There is no wishing. There is no valuing. There is no good. There is no evil. There is, in short, no goal.
ALBERT EINSTEIN, "Science and Ethics," *Relativity: A Richer Truth*, edited by Phillip Frank

4 He was a little man. The man was undersized. He had a head. It was too big for his body. He was a sickly little man.
DEEMS TAYLOR, "The Monster," *Of Men and Music*

5 Uranium produced energy for mankind. It underwent fission. The fission was controlled. The energy was useful. The ash is still produced. The ash is radioactive. It is still there.
ISAAC ASIMOV, "Tomorrow's Energy," *The American Way*, Feb. 1975

6 Futurism is also an attitude. It is a perspective toward change.
ALVIN TOFFLER, "What Futurists Can Do," *The Futurist*, April, 1976

7 So in recent times we have seen a split develop between a culture and a counterculture. The split was huge. The culture was classic. The counterculture was romantic. The two worlds were growingly alienated. They were hateful toward each other. Everyone wondered

something. It will always be this way. It is a house divided against itself.

ROBERT M. PIRSIG, *Zen and the Art of Motorcycle Maintenance*

8 He had one mistress. He was faithful to the mistress to the day of his death. It was Music.

DEEMS TAYLOR, "The Monster," *Of Men and Music*

9 The classic mode, by contrast, proceeds by reason. It proceeds by laws. They are themselves forms of thought and behavior. The forms are underlying.

ROBERT M. PIRSIG, *Zen and the Art of Motorcycle Maintenance*

10 He finds himself shackled to a tyranny. It is more absolute than any he has known outside himself. It is an inner tyranny. It enfeebles the conscience. It dictates over it.

NORMAN COUSINS, "Where Hell Begins," *Present Tense: An American Odyssey*

11 Finally, one coach brought in the last straw. It was the two-platoon system. The two-platoon system is unfair to the opponents. They cannot muster a double team. It obliges a university's first team to play only a half a game.

ALLEN JACKSON, "Rugby is a Better Game," *Atlantic Monthly*, Nov. 1952

12 Something is often said. Stoicism was un-Greek. It suited Romans far better. Something is true. It had won its most distinguished and conspicuous success in Rome. It won over two men of genius. They were the slave and the emperor.

EDITH HAMILTON, *The Echo of Greece*

13 What we are trying to picture here is the whole of space. It is expanding. Yet it is not expanding *into* anything. It is simply expanding.

JACOB BRONOWSKI, "The Imaginative Mind in Science," *Imagination and the University*

14 He was clearly depressed by something. He saw it. It is a feeling. He means us to have the feeling, too.

RICHARD D. ALTICK, *Preface to Critical Reading*

15 They all said the same thing. He took no notice of you. You left him alone. He might charge. You went too close to him.

GEORGE ORWELL, "Shooting an Elephant," *Shooting an Elephant and Other Essays*

Punctuating practice 4: imitation

Imitate at least three of the sentences you created in Punctuating practices 1, 2, or 3. Create a sentence with a structure similar to that of the model sentence you have selected but on a different subject. You may wish to do a close imitation or a loose imitation. Write out the model sentence you select before you create the loose or strict imitation sentence.

MODEL

Above all we need a world population policy—not at some unspecified date in the future, but now. (Problem 10, Punctuating practice 1)

CLOSE IMITATION

Most important we need a nuclear energy policy—not at the end of this century, but right now.

LOOSE IMITATION

If mankind is to survive nuclear annihilation, we must strive for an enlightened policy on nuclear energy that can be efficiently and safely implemented—not at some vague future date—but now, when we so desperately need it.

BEYOND THE SENTENCE

In the following pages, you will concentrate on discourse beyond the sentence, on the interesting interplay that occurs between and among sentences. Sentences are the building blocks of effective writing, and with the exception of extremely informal messages, a single sentence rarely accomplishes the writer's purpose; effective writing depends on a series of sentences working together smoothly. We are interested here in the cement that binds units of discourse together, in the interrelationships of structure and meaning—the syntactic and semantic devices—that help the reader sustain interest and comprehension from one sentence to the next.

SENTENCE CHUNKS

In earlier exercises in this chapter, you were sometimes given the option of solving a combining problem by creating an answer consisting of two or more sentences. Now you will extend your experience with cohesion in writing by focusing on multisentence structures we have named *chunks*. A sentence chunk is any group of two or more sentences isolated from a paragraph, whose meaning and structure combine to form a discrete unit, or whole, *within* the paragraph. The chunks in this section have all been extracted from paragraphs by experienced writers.

Sentences can surprise you. Looked at in isolation, a single sentence may be uninteresting, even boring. Used with other sentences, that same sentence can come alive. It can gain much of its meaning and considerable power from the surrounding sentences. For example, a short sentence can have a strong impact if you place it after or between long sentences. A long sentence can attract and hold the reader's attention if you contrast it with a short sentence. Rhythm, variety, meaning, and structure all contribute to cohesive discourse, not merely within a single sentence, but within longer units of writing.

Look, for example, at the following sentence:

It happens in an instant.

If you were asked whether you find that sentence interesting or well written, you might reply that the sentence isn't especially interesting and you have no idea what "It" refers to. But if you were provided with a limited context for the sentence—if you were given the sentence immediately preceding "It happens in an instant"—and then asked to comment, your reaction would probably be very different:

Most people tend to think of going to sleep as a slow slippage into oblivion, but the onset of sleep is not gradual at all. It happens in an instant.

In this context, "It happens in an instant" is a very effective piece of writing because it plays off the first, longer sentence. It is short, sharp, and to the point. The first sentence provides "going to sleep" and "the onset of sleep" as referrents for "It" in the second sentence. The length of the first sentence (25 words) sets up a sharp contrast with the length of the second sentence (5 words). "It happens in an instant" gains most of its meaning and effect not because of its inherent merit but because it works as a unit with the preceding sentence.

The third sentence in this chunk locks into the unit:

Most people tend to think of going to sleep as a slow slippage into oblivion, but the onset of sleep is not gradual at all. It happens in an instant. One moment the individual is awake, the next moment not.

The last sentence clearly relates to the second sentence by describing exactly how fast "happens in an instant" is. Can you find less obvious examples of the interplay between this sentence and the two that precede it?

You may wonder why this set of sentences is not a paragraph. Indeed, if a short paragraph suited the writer's purpose in a specific composition, these three sentences would make an effective one. But, in this case, the writer uses the paragraph unit to say more about the onset of sleep than that it is sudden. Notice how smoothly the chunk coheres with the rest of the paragraph:

A number of curious experiences occur at the onset of sleep. A person just about to go to sleep may experience an electric shock, a flash of light, or a crash of thunder—but the most common sensation is that of floating or falling, which is why "falling asleep" is a scientifically valid description. A nearly universal occurrence at the beginning of sleep (although not everyone recalls it) is a sudden, uncoordinated jerk of the head, the limbs, or even the entire body. Most people tend to think of going to sleep as a slow slippage into oblivion, but the onset of sleep is not gradual at all. It happens in an instant. One moment the individual is awake, the next moment not.

PETER FARB, "The Levels of Sleep," *Humankind*

Working with chunks as discrete units can help you to extend your writing proficiency beyond the sentence. As sentence-combining practice improved the maturity of your own sentences, practice with sentence chunks will translate into a noticeable improvement in longer stretches of your writing. Practicing, recreating, and rewriting structures longer than one sentence will give you skills that will be especially useful when you are at the rewriting and editing stages of the composing process.

SENTENCE CHUNKS WITH SIGNALS

As you work on the signaled sentence chunks below, make use of the skills you acquired in the first part of this chapter. One signal, the double slash (//), has been added. This new signal simply directs you to begin a new sentence at the point where it appears. In the example, the *two* double slash signals indicate that this chunk of discourse will consist of *three* sentences. The first sentence ends with "must not be denied." The second sentence begins with "It is permissible" and ends with "so parcelled out." The third sentence begins with "It is a whole" and ends with "mother of consciousness."

EXAMPLE

The wheel of history must not be turned back.

Man's advance towards a spiritual life must not be denied.   (, AND)

The advance towards a spiritual life began
with the rites of initiation.   (, WHICH . . . ,)

The rites were primitive.

//SOMETHING is permissible.

Science divides up its field of inquiry.   (IT . . . FOR . . . TO)

Science operates with hypotheses.   (AND TO)

The hypotheses are limited.

Science must work in that way.   (, FOR)

The human psyche may not be so parcelled out.   (: BUT)

It is a whole.

The whole embraces consciousness.   (WHICH)

It is the mother of consciousness.   (, AND)

CARL GUSTAV JUNG, "Freud and Jung: Contrasts"

Following the combining signals, you would produce this group of sentences taken from a paragraph by Carl Jung:

The wheel of history must not be turned back, and man's advance towards a spiritual life, which began with the primitive rites of initiation, must not be denied. It is permissible for science to divide up its field of inquiry and to operate with limited hypotheses, for science must work in that way: but the human psyche may not be so parcelled out. It is a whole which embraces consciousness, and it is the mother of consciousness.

Sentence chunks practice 1: combining with signals

Use the combining signals on the groups of sentences below to help you create the original sentence chunks written by the various writers cited below each set.

1 He was a tackle on the football team.

He was named Bolenciecwcz.   (,)

// Ohio State University had one of the best football teams in the country.   (AT THAT TIME)

Bolenciecwcz was one of its stars.   (, AND)

The stars were outstanding.

// In order to be eligible to play SOMETHING was necessary.

He had to keep up in his studies.   (IT . . . FOR . . . TO)

It was a very difficult matter.   (,)

He was not dumber than an ox.   (, FOR WHILE)

He was not any smarter.   (,)

JAMES THURBER, "University Days," *My Life and Hard Times*

2 You will reject it now.

At a later period some of it may come back to you as truth.   (, BUT)

// I'm talking to you.   (WHEN)

You think of me as an older person.   (,)

You think of me as an "authority."   (,)

I speak of my own youth.   (, AND WHEN)

SOMETHING becomes unreal to you.

I say it.   (WHAT)

The young can't believe in the youth of their fathers.   (— FOR)

//Perhaps this little bit will be understandable.   (BUT)

I put it in writing.   (IF)

F. SCOTT FITZGERALD, "Dearest Scottie," *The Letters of F. Scott Fitzgerald,* Andrew Turnbull, ed.

3 My dad was always on the run from the cops.

I never saw him out of disguise.   (AND)

I was twenty-two.   (TILL)

//I thought he was a man with glasses and a limp.   (FOR YEARS,)

The man was <u>short</u>.

The man was <u>bearded.</u>   (,)

The glasses were <u>dark.</u>

Actually, he was tall.   (;)

He was <u>blond.</u>   (AND)

He resembled Lindbergh.   (AND)

WOODY ALLEN, "Confessions of a Burglar," *The New Yorker,* 18 Oct. 1976

4 In the technological systems of tomorrow machines will deal with the flow of materials.

The technological systems of tomorrow will be <u>fast, fluid and self-regulating.</u>   (— ... —)

The materials are <u>physical.</u>

Men will deal with the flow of information and insight.   (;)

//Machines will increasingly perform the tasks.

The tasks are <u>routine.</u>

Men will perform the tasks.   (;)

The tasks will be <u>intellectual.</u>

The tasks will be <u>creative.</u>   (AND)

ALVIN TOFFLER, *Future Shock*

5 By 1915 Vachel Lindsay anticipated Marshall McLuhan.

Vachel Lindsay was <u>the first theoretician of the movies.</u>   (, ... ,)

The theoretician was <u>significant.</u>

The theoretician was <u>American.</u>

He wrote SOMETHING.   (WHEN)

"Edison is the new Gutenberg.   (,)

//He has invented the new printing."

ARTHUR SCHLESINGER JR., "America at the Movies," *Saturday Review,* 12 Nov. 1977

6 The earth grew warmer.

Its body exhaled moisture and gases.   (;)

Water collected on the surface.   (;)

The first molecules struggled across the threshold of life.   (; SOON)

//Some survived.

Others perished.   (;)

The law of Darwin began its work.　　(; AND)

//The pressures of the environment acted ceaselessly.

The forms of life improved.　　(, AND)

ROBERT JASTROW, "Man of Wisdom," *Until the Sun Dies*

7　Meanwhile the wasp moves off a few inches.

The wasp digs the spider's grave.　　(TO)

The wasp has satisfied itself [of] SOMETHING.　　(, + ING)

The victim is of the right species.　　(THAT . . . ,)

//The wasp works vigorously with legs and jaws.　　(ING)

It excavates a hole.　　(,)

It has a diameter.　　(WITH)

The diameter is slightly larger than the spider's girth.

The wasp pops out of the hole.　　(NOW AND AGAIN)

It makes sure [of] SOMETHING.　　(TO)

The spider is still there.　　(THAT)

ALEXANDER PETRUNKEVITCH, "The Spider and the Wasp," *Scientific American*,
Aug. 1952

8　The best place to write is by yourself.

Writing becomes an escape from the boredom
of your own personality.　　(, BECAUSE)

//SOMETHING's the reason.

For years I've favored Switzerland.　　(IT . . . THAT)

In Switzerland I look at the telephone.　　(, WHERE)

/ yearn to hear it ring.　　(AND)

JOHN KENNETH GALBRAITH, "Writing, Typing and Economic$," *Atlantic
Monthly*, Jan, 1978.

SENTENCE CHUNKS WITHOUT SIGNALS

The groups of sentences you will be working with in this section
have been extracted from the paragraphs of experienced writers.
These sentence chunks are groups of two, three, or more sentences
that go together in some way; they form a subset within a
paragraph.

Unlike the problems in Sentence chunks practice 1, the
sentences in this section do not contain combining signals. In the
following exercises, you will practice creating your own units of
discourse from the information in the sentence sets. From your
previous experience with combining, you know that each set of
sentences has many possible solutions. It is challenging to create
your own sentence chunks and then compare them with those of
your fellow writers and, of course, with the original version.
Sentence chunks without signals resemble a hurriedly written first
draft of a composition, an invitation to rewrite, re-create, and edit.

There are, then, no right answers to these problems, only better or more interesting ones.

Examine the following combining problem, create an effective chunk of discourse based on the problem set, and compare your version with the original, written by John Leonard.

PROBLEM

There are no books. There are no newspapers. There are no magazines. There are no pictures on the wall. There is a television set. He watches the television set all day long. He drinks beer. He smokes cigarettes. I am sufficiently familiar with the literature. It is on schizophrenia. I realize something. This room is a statement. He is making the statement about himself.

Following are three of the many possible solutions to this problem:

SOLUTIONS

A There are no pictures on the walls. There is a television set, and he spends his whole day watching it, drinking beer and smoking cigarettes. There are no newspapers; no magazines; not even a book. I am familiar enough with the literature on schizophrenia to perceive that the room is a reflection of what he thinks of himself.

B I am reasonably familiar with the literature on schizophrenia and, as I understand it, this appears to be a classic case. He sits in front of a television set all day long, watching, smoking cigarettes, drinking beer. There are no pictures on the walls. There is nothing to read—no newspapers; no magazines; not even a single book. This room—how he lives in it—is a statement about the self.

C There are no books, no newspapers or magazines, no pictures on the wall. There is a television set, which he watches all day long while drinking beer and smoking cigarettes. I am sufficiently familiar with the literature on schizophrenia to realize that this room is a statement he is making about himself.

As you may have guessed, version *C* is the John Leonard original ("An Only Child," *The New York Times*, 27 July 1977). It stays closer to the problem set. Notice that the other two are fairly competent pieces of writing; they have pretty much the same message as that of John Leonard. Note especially that version *B* reflects a radical change in the order of the information sentences. As you work the problems in the following practice, take the sentences in any order you please.

Sentence chunks practice 2: combining without signals

Combine the following unsignaled sentence chunks into effective, interesting pieces of writing.

1 The dog backed up. It did not yield. A rumbling began to rise in his chest. The rumbling was low. The rumbling was steady. It was something out of a midnight. The midnight was long gone. There was nothing in that bone to taste. Shapes were moving in his mind. The shapes were ancient. They were determining his utterance.
LOREN EISELEY, "The Angry Winter," *The Unexpected Universe*

2 Students complete a first draft. They consider something. The job of writing is done. Their teachers too often agree. Professional writers complete a first draft. They usually feel something. They are at the start of the writing process. A draft is completed. The job of writing can begin.
DONALD M. MURRAY, "The Maker's Eye: Revising Your Own Manuscripts," *The Writer*, Oct. 1973

3 I can think back over more than a hundred nights. I've slept a hundred nights in the truck. I sat in it. A lamp burned. I was bundled up in a parka. I was reading a book. It was always comfortable. It was a good place to wait out a storm. It was like sleeping inside a buffalo.
BARRY LOPEZ, "My Horse," *North American Review*

4 A commencement orator advises students. They enrich themselves culturally. Chances are something. He is more interested in money than he is in poetry. A university president says something. His institution turned out 1,432 B.A.'s last year. He tells us something. He thinks something. He is running General Motors. The style is the man.
DONALD HALL, "An Ethic of Clarity," *Modern Stylists*

5 Mental retardation occurs in some parts of your city. It occurs at a rate. The rate is five times higher than it is in the remainder of your city. Twenty-five per cent of some prison populations are mentally retarded. Mental retardation does not just happen. It is caused.
RAMSEY CLARK, *Crime in America*

6 It is on Ellis Island. They pile into the hall. The hall is massive. It occupies the entire width of the building. They break into dozens of lines. The lines are divided by railings. The railings are metal. There they file past the first doctor.
IRVING HOWE, *World of Our Fathers*

7 Once, I entered a mansion. I blew the safe. I removed six thousand dollars. A couple slept in the same room. The husband woke up. The dynamite went off. I assured him. The entire proceeds would go to the Boys' Clubs of America. He went back to sleep. Cleverly, I left behind some fingerprints of Franklin D. Roosevelt. He was President then.
WOODY ALLEN, "Confessions of a Burglar," *The New Yorker*, 18 Oct. 1976

8 Velva has no organized charity. A farmer falls ill. His neighbors get in his crop. A townsman has a catastrophe. The catastrophe is finan-

cial. His personal friends raise a fund. It is to help him out. Bill's wife, Ethel, lay dying. She lay so long in the Minot hospital. Nurses were not available. Helen and others took their turns. They drove up there just to sit with her. She would know in her gathering dark something. Friends were at hand.

ERIC SEVAREID, "Velva, North Dakota," *This Is Eric Sevareid*

9 Many recounted their own experiences. The experiences were bitter. They were at the hands of funeral directors. Hundreds asked for advice on something. It was to establish a consumer organization in communities. None exists in the communities. Others sought information about pre-need plans. The membership of the funeral societies skyrocketed.

JESSICA MITFORD, *The American Way of Death*

10 He [Richard Wagner] had the emotional stability of a six-year-old child. He felt out of sorts. He would rave. He would stamp. He would sink into gloom. The gloom was suicidal. He would talk darkly of going to the East. It was to end his days as a Buddhist monk. It was ten minutes later. Something pleased him. He would rush out of doors. He would run around the garden. He would jump up and down on the sofa. He would stand on his head.

DEEMS TAYLOR, "The Monster," *Of Men and Music*

PARAGRAPHS: COMBINING WITH SIGNALS

The signal system we have been using to create single sentences and groups or chunks of sentences can also give you practice in creating paragraphs. Again we will use the double slash signal (//). This signal simply means to begin a new sentence. In the following example, the one double slash signal indicates that this paragraph will consist of two sentences:: the first ends with "the most grisly tourist center on earth"; the second begins with "They come for a variety of reasons . . . ."

Every day, people come to Brzezinka.   (AND YET,)

The people are from all over the world.

Brzezinka is quite possibly the most grisly tourist center on earth.   (,)

//They come for a variety of reasons.

They come to see SOMETHING.   (—)

It could really have been true.   (IF)

They remind themselves not to forget.   (, TO)

They pay homage to the dead by the act of looking upon SOMETHING.   (, TO)

The act is <u>simple</u>.

They suffered at the place.   ('S + OF + ING)

A. M. ROSENTHAL, "There Is No News from Auschwitz," *The New York Times Magazine*, 16 April 1961

If you followed each combining signal, you would produce A. M. Rosenthal's paragraph:

And yet, every day, people from all over the world come to Brzezinka, quite possibly the most grisly tourist center on earth. They come for a variety of reasons—to see if it could really have been true, to remind themselves not to forget, to pay homage to the dead by the simple act of looking upon their place of suffering.

Paragraphs practice 1: combining with signals

Use the combining signals on the groups of sentences below to create the original paragraphs written by the various writers cited below each set of sentences.

1 Mistakes are at the very base of human thought.
   Mistakes are <u>embedded there</u>.   (,)
   Mistakes are <u>feeding the structure like root nodules</u>.   (,)
  // We were not provided with the knack of being wrong.   (IF)
   We could never get anything useful done.   (,)
  // We think our way along.
   We choose between alternatives.   (BY + ING)
   The alternatives are <u>right</u>.
   The alternatives are <u>wrong</u>.   (AND)
   The wrong choices have to be made as
   frequently as the right ones.   (, AND)
  // We get along in life this way.
  // We are built to make mistakes.
   We are <u>coded for error</u>.   (,)
   LEWIS THOMAS, "Why Can't Computers Be More Like Us?" *The Saturday Evening Post*, Oct. 1976

2 People were moments later decapitated.
   People were cut to ribbons by flying glass.   (OR)
   The people were in buildings.   (WHO)
   The buildings sheltered them from the effects.   (THAT)
   The effects were <u>instantaneous</u>.
   The effects accompanied the flash.   (THAT)
  // Others were crushed.
   Walls and floors gave way even in buildings.   (AS)
   The buildings maintained their outer shells erect.   (THAT)

// In the thousands of buildings that fell, people were pinned below the wreckage.

They were not killed in many cases.   (,)

They were held there.   (, BUT)

The fire caught up with them.   (TILL)

The fire swept the city.   (THAT)

The fire put an end to their screams.   (AND)

ALEXANDER H. LEIGHTON, "That Day at Hiroshima"

3 The day my son Laurie started kindergarten he renounced overalls.

The overalls were corduroy.

The overalls had bibs.   (WITH)

He began wearing jeans.   (AND)

The jeans were blue.

The jeans had a belt.   (WITH)

// I watched him go off the first morning with the older girl.

The older girl lived next door.

I saw clearly SOMETHING.   (AND)

An era of my life was ended.   (THAT)

// My tot had been replaced by a character.

My tot was sweet-voiced.

My tot was nursery-school.

The character was long-trousered.

The character was swaggering.

The character forgot to stop at the corner and wave good-bye to me.   (WHO)

SHIRLEY JACKSON, *Charles*

4 He [Richard Wagner] had a genius for making enemies.

// He would insult a man.

The man disagreed with him about the weather.   (WHO)

// He would pull endless wires in order to meet some man.

The man admired his work   (WHO)

The man was able and anxious to be of use to him.   (, AND)

He would proceed to make an enemy of him with some exhibition of arrogance and bad manners.   (— AND)

The enemy was mortal.

The exhibition was idiotic.

The exhibition was wholly uncalled for.   (AND)

// A character was a caricature of one of the critics of his day.

The character was in one of his operas.

The critics were the most powerful.

// He was not content with burlesquing him.

He invited the critic to his house.   (,)

He read him the libretto aloud in front of his friends.   (AND)

DEEMS TAYLOR, "The Monster," *Of Men and Music*

5 I watched the flight of the ball.

It went straight down the middle. (AS)

// Then I dropped back a few steps.

I began the sprint across field. (AND)

// My man must have thought SOMETHING.

Someone had missed their blocking assignment. (THAT)

Maybe SOMETHING was. (OR)

He was a rookie. (IT . . . BECAUSE)

Whatever the reason, he was making a bad mistake. (, BUT)

He was running full speed. (:)

He was not looking to either side. (AND)

// I knew SOMETHING.

He didn't see me. (THAT)

I decided to take him low. (AND)

// I gathered all my force.

I hit him. (AND)

// I did. (AS)

I heard his knee explode in my ear. (,)

There was a sound of muscles and ligaments separating. (,)

The sound was jagged.

The sound was tearing. (,)

// The next thing, time was called.

I knew the thing. (THAT)

He was writhing in pain on the field. (AND)

// They carried him off on a stretcher.

I felt sorry. (AND)

At the same time, I knew SOMETHING. (—BUT)

It was a block. (THAT)

The block was tremendous.

That was SOMETHING. (AND)

I got paid for SOMETHING. (WHAT)

DAVE MEGGYESY, *Out of Their League*

6 A majority was needed to enact the program.

The majority was two-thirds.

Seven votes would kill it. (, SO)

The votes were negative.

// It was on May 10, 1976.

The plan came before the legislature for the first time. (, WHEN)

All six representatives from the sewer
district stood opposed. (,)

// They had more than enough support to get the plan blocked.

Several northwestern and central Suffolk
legislators said SOMETHING. (;)

"We can't afford this program now."   (,)

// The meeting took place in an auditorium in Hauppauge.

The auditorium was windowless.

The auditorium was theaterlike.   (,)

Hauppauge is located in west central Suffolk.   (,)

West central Suffolk is suburbanized.

// The discussion turned into a shouting match between East and West End legislators.

// One of the program's supporters shut down the debate.   (THEN)

// He accepted the inevitable.   (-ING)

He moved SOMETHING.   (,)

The program should be neither voted down nor approved.   (THAT)

It should be tabled indefinitely.   (BUT)

// That is SOMETHING.   (AND)

It happened.   (WHAT)

// The legislature had fixed on a course of action.   (AT LAST)

// They had chosen not to decide.

TRACY KIDDER, "The Battle for Long Island," *Atlantic Monthly*, Nov. 1976

7 War it has been indeed.   (AND)

It has been the long war of life against its environment.   (—)

The environment is inhospitable.

It has been a war.   (,)

The war has lasted for perhaps three billion years.   (THAT)

// It began with strange chemicals.

The chemicals were seething under a sky.

The sky was lacking in oxygen.

It was waged through ages.   (;)

The ages were long.

The first plants learned to harness the light of the nearest star.   (UNTIL)

The plants were green.

The nearest star was our sun.   (,)

// The human brain burns by the power of the leaf.

The brain is so frail.   (,)

The brain is so perishable.   (,)

The brain is so full of dreams and hungers.   (,)

The dreams and hungers are inexhaustible.

LOREN EISELEY, *The Unexpected Universe*

8 No two classes of object could be more different.

// A meteor is a speck of matter.

The speck is usually smaller than a grain of sand.   (,)

The speck of matter burns itself up by friction.   (, WHICH)

It tears through the outer layers of Earth's atmosphere.　(AS)

//A comet may be millions of times larger
than the entire Earth.　(BUT)

A comet may dominate the night sky for weeks on end.　(, AND)

//A comet may look like a searchlight.

The comet is <u>really great</u>.

The searchlight shines across the stars.　(ING)

//SOMETHING is not surprising.　(AND)

Such an object always caused alarm.　(IT . . . THAT)

The object was <u>portentous</u>.

It appeared in the heavens.　(WHEN)

//Calpurnia said to Caesar SOMETHING.　(AS)

Beggars die.　(: "WHEN)

There are no comets seen. /

The heavens themselves blaze forth the death of princes."　(;)
ARTHUR C. CLARKE, "The Star of the Magi," *Report on Planet Three*

Note the slash mark (called a "virgule") at the end of the line "There are no comets seen." This virgule should be incorporated into the sentence, for it is a conventional way to separate two quoted lines of poetry. The sentence should be written out like this:

As Calpurnia said to Caesar: "When beggars die there are no comets seen; / the heavens themselves blaze forth the death of princes."

9 Columbus kidnapped ten of his Taino hosts.

The Taino hosts were <u>friendly</u>.

He carried them off to Spain.　(AND)

They could be introduced to the white
man's ways in Spain.　(, WHERE)

//One of them died.

He arrived there.　(SOON AFTER + ING)

He was baptized a Christian.　(, BUT NOT BEFORE)

//The Spaniards were so pleased.

They had made SOMETHING possible.　(THAT)

The first Indian entered heaven.　(IT . . . FOR . . . TO)

They hastened to spread the news
throughout the West Indies.　(THAT)

The news was <u>good</u>.
DEE BROWN, *Bury My Heart at Wounded Knee*

10 He falls back upon the bed awkwardly.

//His stumps rise in the air.

The stumps are <u>unweighted by legs and feet</u>.　(, . . . ,)

They present themselves.　　(-ING)

//I unwrap the bandages from the stumps.

/I begin to cut away the scabs and the fat
with scissors and foreceps.　　(, AND)

The scabs are black.

The fat is dead.

The fat is glazed.　　(,)

//A shard of bone comes loose.

The bone is white.

//I pick it away.

//I wash the wounds with disinfectant.

/I redress the stumps.　　(AND)

//He does not speak.　　(ALL THIS WHILE,)

//What is he thinking behind those lids?

Those lids do not blink.　　(THAT)

//Is he remembering a time?

He was whole.　　(WHEN)

//Does he dream of feet?

//Does he dream of SOMETHING?

His body was not a log.　　(WHEN)

The log is rotting.

RICHARD SELZER, "The Discus Thrower"

PARAGRAPHS: COMBINING WITHOUT SIGNALS

The paragraphs in this section were selected from a variety of works written by experienced writers. They were broken down into shorter sentences to provide you with practice in creating paragraphs.

Examine each set of sentences and then construct an interesting paragraph of your own. As you know from your previous experience, many different answers are possible when you combine. The point of this exercise is to give you intensive experience in manipulating sentence structures in larger pieces of discourse, an important rewriting and editing skill. Share your paragraphs with your fellow students. Comparing and contrasting versions will increase your flexibility in producing effective paragraphs in your own writing.

Read the following problem, create an effective paragraph based on the problem set, and compare your version with the original, by David Shub.

PROBLEM

Lenin was now forty years old. He was at the very prime of his powers. The structure was still quite feeble. He had spent years to perfect the structure. The strain was telling. He looked worn. He was harassed more than ever by headaches. He was harassed by insomnia. He continued to work with energy. The energy was furious.

Following are three of the many possible solutions to this problem:

SOLUTIONS

A Lenin was now forty years old, at the very prime of his powers, but the structure he had spent years to perfect was still quite feeble. The strain was telling. He looked worn. He was harassed more than ever by headaches and insomnia, but continued to work with furious energy.

B Now forty years old and at the very prime of his powers, Lenin continued to work with furious energy. But the strain was telling. The structure he had spent years trying to perfect was still quite feeble. He looked worn, harassed more than ever by headaches and insomnia.

C Lenin continued to work with furious energy on the structure he had spent years perfecting. But it was still quite feeble. Although forty years old now and at the very prime of his powers, Lenin looked worn. Harassed more than ever by headaches, he suffered increasingly from insomnia. The strain had begun to tell.

David Shub's original, from *Lenin*, is version *A*.

Paragraphs practice 2: combining without signals

Work on the following sentence sets to create interesting and well-written paragraphs. Take the sentences in any order you please.

1 Europeans and Indians met for the first time. They met in the Western Hemisphere. They met 450 years ago. Neither side was prepared for the event. The Europeans were looking for a quite different land. It was a land of spices. It was a land of shimmering silks. It was a land of dancing girls. It was the Indies! Quite naturally, Columbus and his followers insisted something. Indeed this is what they had found. The Indians, for their part, had no expectations. They were hopeful at first. The creatures would go away. The creatures were strange.
HAROLD E. FEY AND D'ARCY MCNICKLE, *Indians and Other Americans*

2 Over the years we have tried every technique of coexistence with the rabbit hordes. The coexistence was peaceful. We built a Berlin Wall. It was made of chicken wire. We put it around the vegetable garden. They scorned it. They tunneled under the wall. They climbed over it. They climbed like Marines up a rope ladder. They hurled themselves against the wall. They breached the barricade. They laughed! Have you ever been snickered at by fifteen rabbits? They

were knee-slapping rabbits. Few sneers are more contemptuous.
JAMES J. KILPATRICK, "Waste No Pity Upon These Foxes," *Psychology Today,*
Aug. 1977

3 The ascent of Man covered tens of thousands of years. It was described by Jacob Bronowski. The reshaping of Man can occur within a few decades. The reshaping of Man is now underway.
VANCE PACKARD, *The People Shapers*

4 The integration of her colored and white citizens is thought by many people to be America's most intractable problem. Some even think something. It is insoluble. There are both blacks and whites. They will tell you something. Harmony is actually impossible. They say something. The two groups must be parted. They sound like the ancient emperor Alexander. He was asked to solve the problem of a rope. It was tied with the Gordian Knot. The Gordian Knot was fantastically complicated. He "unravelled" it in the most arrogant yet pessimistic way imaginable. He slashed it through. He did it with one sweep of his sword. The sweep was mighty.
DAVID FROST, *The Americans*

5 Some New Yorkers become morose with rain. Others prefer it. They like to walk in it. They say something. On rainy days the city's buildings seem somehow cleaner. The buildings seem washed in opalescence. The buildings are like a Monet painting. There are fewer suicides in New York. It rains. The sun is shining. New Yorkers seem happy. The depressed person sinks deeper into depression. Bellevue Hospital gets more calls. They are suicide calls.
GAY TALESE, "New York," *Esquire,* July 1969

6 Is a wife the new status symbol for the power-driven man? The wife has a career. Perhaps she is for the next generation of top executives. She is not today, according to psychologists David Winter, Abigail Stewart, and David McClelland. In this study they found something. The study was of fifty-one college graduates ten years later. The wife is still a sign of success. The wife is at home.
MARY MARCUS, "My Wife the Homemaker: Still a Status Symbol," *Psychology Today,* Oct. 1977

7 Despite this need for public approval, football does not demand a discriminating public. It doesn't welcome a discriminating public. The football fan is an absolute oaf. He is compared to the baseball fan or the tennis fan. The baseball fan, particularly, is a man of perceptivity. His perceptivity is high. The baseball fan has learning. He has memorized a quantity of statistics. The quantity is staggering. He can recognize each player. He knows what each batted last year. He knows when each broke which clavicle. He knows where. He knows why. He knows how good the prospects are for each rookie. The rookie comes along. The football fan knows nothing. He can't recognize one player from another, except by the number on the uniform. He can't tell a right guard from a left kidney. It is all he can do to follow the ball. Often he can't even do that.
WADE THOMPSON, "My Crusade Against Football," *The Nation,* April 1959

8 The maker's eye is never satisfied. Each word has the potential to ignite meaning. The meaning is new. This article has been twice written all the way through the writing process. It was published four years ago. Now it is to be republished in a book. The editors made a few suggestions. The suggestions were small. I read it with my maker's eye. It has been re-edited. It has been re-revised. It has been re-read. It has been re-re-edited. Each piece of writing to the writer is full of potential. It is full of alternatives.

DONALD M. MURRAY, "The Maker's Eye: Revising Your Own Manuscripts," *The Writer*, Oct. 1973

9 It was exactly as Monsignor Cardinale had predicted. More than a hundred people were waiting in the audience. The Pope arrived. He quickly demonstrated a remarkable ability for making each person feel something. He was the recipient of individual Papal attention. The Pope sat in his chair. It was high backed. It was velvet lined. His head was resting lightly against the frame. He spoke easily. He spoke informally about the meaning to him of Christmas. He related incidents. The incidents were drawn from his pastoral life. His pastoral life was long. He said something. Peace in our time had to be more than inspiration. It had to be a reality. He blessed his audience. He stepped down. He was assisted through a side door to his office.

NORMAN COUSINS, "The Improbable Triumvirate: Khrushchev, Kennedy and Pope John," *Saturday Review*, 30 Oct. 1971

10 The howlers clambered grumpily up to the network of branches at the summit of the oak. The oak was next to their quarters. The howlers were early rising. The branches were leafless. They were keeping a rendezvous with the first sun. The sun was burning through the winter mist. They were huddled motionless. They were in silhouette against the brilliance of the sky. The brilliance was icy. They looked to the casual visitor like so many squirrels' nests. Up close, though, they were yawning. They were scratching. They were thinking about breakfast. It was the beginning of another day at the Verlhiac Primate Center. It is one of the most personalized institutions. It is one of the most innovative institutions of behavioral research anywhere in the world.

RUDOLPH CHELMINSKI, "The Lindberghs Liberate Monkeys from Constraints," *Smithsonian*, March 1977

11 Pushing the expenses off on the consumer goes back at least as far as the *ancien régime* in France. The peasants were subjected to taxation to support the aristocracy. The taxation was grinding. The aristocracy were not taxed. The system of government encroached upon them. At its basis it is a system for protecting the people. It became their worst oppressor. In the United States, the Internal Revenue Service collect our taxes. They also make us compute the tax for them. This is an activity. It exacts a cost in sweat, tears, and agony. The cost is incalculable. It takes years off our lives. We groan over their forms. Their forms are complicated.

JOHN GALL, "Systematics: How Systems Work and Especially How They Fail"

12 Most tarantulas live in the tropics. Several species occur in the temperate zone. A few are common in the southern U.S. Some varieties are large. They have fangs. The fangs are powerful. They can inflict a wound with the fangs. The wound is deep. These spiders do not, however, attack man. The spiders are formidable looking. You can hold one in your hand. You are gentle. You won't be bitten. Their bite is dangerous only to insects and mammals such as mice. The mammals are small. For man it is no worse than a hornet's sting.

ALEXANDER PETRUNKEVITCH, "The Spider and the Wasp," *Scientific American,* Aug. 1952

13 Institutions other than schools are now recognizing the need for sex education. The sex education should be more adequate. They are beginning to assume responsibilities in this area. This is particularly true of institutions. They are religious. A number of organizations have begun to discuss sexuality seriously. The organizations are religious. Several are active in producing sex education materials. They are active in disseminating the materials.

COMMISSION ON OBSCENITY AND PORNOGRAPHY, *The Report of the Commission on Obscenity and Pornography*

14 For a quarter of a century, American, British and Soviet scientists have been trying to design magnetic fields. They have been trying to produce magnetic fields. The magnetic fields are strong. The magnetic fields will hold atom fragments in place. The atom fragments are electrically charged. The temperature is raised to the necessary high figure to start fusion going. Some of the most advanced devices can be found at Princeton University. The devices are for producing such magnetic fields. Here and elsewhere on Earth, scientists have come steadily closer to their goal. Even now they are not quite there.

THOMAS GRIFFITH, "Equality's Uneven Hand," *Atlantic Monthly,* Jan. 1978

15 Thomas Hudson shot again. He was behind with another spurt of water. He felt sick at his stomach. Something had hold of him inside. It was gripping him there. He shot again. He shot as carefully as he could. He shot as steady as he could. He knew fully well what the shot meant. The spurt of water was ahead of the fin. The fin kept right on. It made the same motion. The motion was slicing. David had the fish off the spear. It was in his hand. The mask was up on his forehead. He was looking steadily toward the shark. The shark was coming.

ERNEST HEMINGWAY, *Islands in the Stream*

The English sentence, as Churchill said, is a noble thing. A writer needs to master the sentence. We all appreciate, of course, that experienced writers have read a great deal and spent countless hours writing. But often what distinguishes them from beginning writers is the control these experts have gained over their sentences. They have mastered the art of putting words down on paper. As you become increasingly proficient at sentence combining, you will find that you no longer have to worry about your sentences, and you can instead concentrate on organizing your ideas. Soon you will find that you can really write; ideas, images, details, specific words will come to mind more easily, and you will be capable of crafting them into mature and graceful sentences. It is as if sentence combining removes a barrier, a psychological tangle of nouns and verbs and modifiers. Once you reach that stage, you will know it, and your readers will know it too. Your writing will acquire new rhythms, texture, and power. All it takes is practice.

Y

ou write with ease to
show your breeding.
But easy writing's curst hard reading.

RICHARD SHERIDAN, *Clio's Protest*

Beginning writers are often uncertain about what paragraphs are supposed to accomplish and how to make them effective. It is important to realize then that, as divisions of the whole composition, paragraphs must develop from your overall decisions about purpose, audience, self, experience, and code. Paragraphs become the natural divisions of your purpose, and they are judged to be effective or ineffective on the basis of how well each contributes to the overall purpose of the composition.

Indenting to indicate the beginning of a new paragraph is a convention of writing, like punctuating or starting a new sentence with a capital letter. Hundreds of years ago, writers did not indent to signal paragraph divisions. Instead, they used a signal (¶) in the left-hand margin; the word "paragraph," meaning "write beside," is derived from that practice. In modern writing, however, indenting has become a firmly established convention, and the modern reader *expects* paragraph indentations to signal breaks in units of thought or divisions in a composition's organization. Consequently, two common problems of paragraphs must be avoided: paragraphs that ramble, sometimes for entire pages or more, and paragraphs that appear to be arbitrary indentations after every sentence or two. Obscuring the writer's ideas, rambling paragraphs often confuse readers, and short, single-sentence paragraphs usually distract them.

Each writing situation and each writer are different, and no one can say that all paragraphs must be written this way or that. Paragraphs can be written any way that serves your overall purpose. The challenge is to learn to write (and rewrite) paragraphs with all your prior decisions about purpose in mind. This chapter offers you much useful advice to help you meet that challenge.

In the following pages, we are imagining an idealized paragraph, a kind of general paragraph that might or might not appear in a specific writing situation. We are not talking about a paragraph that might be found with several others in a composition, one paragraph among many. Instead, we are talking about a one-paragraph composition. When there is only one paragraph in the whole composition, most of the traditional advice applies. And if we are talking about the one-paragraph composition, most of our advice will be the same for the paragraph as for the whole composition. You cannot just write a paragraph (except for practice) any more than you can just write a composition; you must first consider purpose, self, audience, experience, and code.

When you have enough prewriting material to begin writing your paragraph, traditional advice concerning the idealized paragraph calls for the following:

1 A paragraph often has a *topic sentence*.
2 A paragraph should have a *plan of development*.
3 A paragraph should have *supportive details*.
4 A paragraph should be *unified*.
5 A paragraph should be *coherent*.

TOPIC SENTENCE

Since we are talking about an idealized paragraph here, one that is especially suited for semiformal or formal writing, we will specify a kind of paragraph that does have a topic sentence. Some paragraphs do not have topic sentences, and some paragraphs do not place the topic sentence first; but we will treat these as variations of the ideal paragraph. Paragraphs have a controlling, central idea—all paragraphs are *about* something—and thus most paragraphs have a *topic idea*, with or without a topic sentence. (Semiformal writing and formal writing differ from experimental and creative writing in which authors may deliberately set out to ignore conventional structures and patterns.) Thus, our idealized paragraph will have a topic sentence stating what the paragraph is about. The topic sentence is the italicized first sentence in the following example:

Hayman nightlife is pure potpourri. The Cabaret Lounge is cosmopolitan, Hernando's Hideaway leans to the romantic, the Tapa Lounge is for conversation. A different "night" happens almost every evening of the week. There's Old Time Music Hall Night. Oriental Night imports a thirty-foot Chinese dragon, dressed in flamboyant silks. Right Bank Night aspires to be like a night at Maxim's. Left Bank Night strives mightily to simulate basic bohemian. Hayman's Calypso Night gives you an Australian version of Jamaica at carnival time. New Year's Eve calls itself a New Orleans Mardi Gras Gala.

FRANK RILEY, "A Quiet Place to Fossick," *Saturday Review*, Oct. 1971

The word "potpourri" refers to a jar of flower petals or spices, a mixture of sweet-smelling aromas. Here it is being used in the sense of a collection of miscellaneous things. Thus the intention of this paragraph, its design, is to tell us how varied and pleasant the nightlife is at Hayman's. The author begins with the topic sentence, which suggests what the paragraph will be about.

PLAN OF DEVELOPMENT

The plan of development of your whole composition is likely to become the plan for your paragraphs too. If you are writing a story, you are likely to use chronological development throughout. But paragraphs shouldn't just "happen." Plan each paragraph as carefully as you plan an entire composition. The wandering, rambling, confused paragraph may appear in an early draft of your work, but the finished paragraph should be carefully shaped according to a logic the reader can see. As you read the following paragraph, ask yourself whether it demonstrates that its authors had an overall purpose or design in mind as they wrote the paragraph. Do you think that the design occurred to them first and then the supplementary details? Or did thinking of the events (details) that comprise the stampede lead the authors to the realization that it is "the greatest Wild West show since Buffalo Bill"?

This elemental drama, pitting man against beast (with the beast triumphant as often as not) is merely one small act in a ten-day-long program of lusty, free-swinging, dizzying madness—a Western extravaganza called the Calgary Stampede. No matter the big ones in Madison Square Garden and Cheyenne or the National Finals; the stampede is the grandpa and predecessor of them all: the biggest rip-snortin' reincarnation of the Old West anywhere. Incorporating street dances, frontier gambling, gawking cowboys and Indians in from the plains, grand parades, fireworks displays, livestock competitions, red-coated Mounties, flapjacks served at curbside, a giant midway, thoroughbred horse racing and enough linament to soothe the pain of a regiment, the Calgary Stampede is, surely, the greatest Wild West show since Buffalo Bill first bedazzled the jaded East.

RICHARD AND MARY MAGRUDER, "Stampede," *Ford Times*, June 1976

Some people are convinced that the details led to the generalizations; others that the generalizations led the Magruders to search for supportive details; still others that the search for details and the refining, or narrowing in on a controlling idea, occurred simultaneously, each influencing the other. In any event, at some stage in the act of composing, details and generalizations melded in an overall design that produced a lively paragraph, satisfying to the reader, one that appears to have been designed to proceed from specific details to final generalization. We will have more to say about development in the section on paragraph structure.

SUPPORTIVE DETAILS

Details are at the heart of all good writing. A series of paragraphs containing unsupported generalizations and unexplained abstractions soon becomes tedious to read. To develop an idea, to explain a concept, requires supportive details that expand and illustrate the idea. A paragraph must do more than make an interesting assertion—a paragraph must *show* as well as *tell*. Most paragraphs are ineffective when they lack details. For example:

Man is ill-adapted to his environment. There is nothing man can do that some other creature cannot do better. It is true, of course, that man's brain has allowed him to cope with the environment; unfortunately, that same brain has done little to protect the environment.

This paragraph is trying to make a point about the relationship of human beings to their environment, but the reader gets only a general impression. *Why* are humans "ill-adapted" to their environment? *How* has the human brain enabled people to cope? All these informative, supportive *details* are missing. The reader can see in a general way what the writer is trying to say, but the message does not sink in. The passage fails to convince the reader because it contains no support for its generalizations. Contrast the preceding underdeveloped paragraph with the one below:

When you watch a bird over the beach or a fish along the reef, you realize how ill-adapted man is to this environment anyway. Physically there is nothing he can do that some other creature cannot do better.

Only his neocortex, the "thinking cap" on top of his brain, has enabled him to invent and construct artificial aids to accomplish what he could not do by himself. He cannot fly, so he has developed airplanes that can go faster than birds. He is slower than the horse, so he invented the wheel and the internal combustion engine. Even in his ancestral element, the sea, he is clumsy and short of breath. Without his brain, his artificial aids, his technology, he would have been unable to cope with, even survive in, his environment. But only after so many centuries is his brain dimly realizing that while he has managed to control his environment, he has so far been unable to protect it.

A. B. C. WHIPPLE, "An Ugly New Footprint in the Sand," *Life*, 20 March 1970

The fully developed paragraph by Whipple fleshes out the bare skeleton of ideas with specific data; it is the specific details that convince the reader Whipple's argument is sound.

UNITY

The term "unity" comes from the Latin word *unus,* meaning "one." A paragraph is therefore described as "unified" if all its sentences develop *one* concept or idea. Irrelevant sentences tend to distract the reader and should be edited out of the final draft. A good rule is to delete any sentence or detail that does not advance the topic. If in doubt, leave it out.

A renowned contemporary author, Suzanne Langer, wrote one of the following paragraphs. The other two contain irrelevant, distracting information that intereferes with the development of the paragraph.

A The momentous difference between us and our animal cousins is that they do not know they are going to die. Animals spend their lives avoiding death, until it gets them. They do not know it is going to. Neither do they know that they are part of a greater life, but pass on the torch without knowing. We have always feared death. The great poets have often alluded to the awesome finality of death, calling it "the great leveller." Death has been called the "ultimate joke" and religion "the opiate of the masses." The aim of animals, then, is simply to keep going, to function, to escape troubles, to live from moment to moment in an endless Now.

B The momentous difference between us and our animal friends is that they do not know they are going to die. Of course, plants don't know that they are going to die either, but neither do they know they are alive. Animals spend their lives avoiding death, until it gets them. They do not know it is going to. Neither do they know that they are part of a greater life, but pass on the torch without knowing. Their aim, then, is simply to keep going, to function, to escape troubles, to live from moment to moment in an endless Now.

C The momentous difference between us and our animal cousins is that they do not know they are going to die. Animals spend their lives avoiding death, until it gets them. They do not know it is going to. Neither do they know that they are part of a greater life, but pass on the torch without knowing. Their aim, then, is simply to keep going, to function, to escape troubles, to live from moment to moment, in an endless Now.

SUZANNE K. LANGER, *Man and Animal: The City and the Hive*

In paragraph *A* there are a few extraneous sentences, as if the writer, in thinking about the difference between the way animals and people die, decided to remind the reader about the human fear of death. Having started in this direction, the irrelevant sentences wander away from the subject, until they end with a statement about religion. In paragraph *B* there is an irrelevant sentence about plants, as if the writer had thrown in a contrastive statement about other nonhuman forms of life. Paragraph *C*, as written by Langer, is a unified paragraph about animal life; specifically it is about one way animal life differs from human life. A paragraph should not be "more or less" unified, nor "sort of" about its topic, but rather, specifically and only about that topic.

COHERENCE

Beginning writers sometimes produce incoherent paragraphs because they forget that the audience doesn't share their own thorough grasp of the subject. You yourself may have a clear sense of the interrelationships among the details in your paragraph; having already thought your ideas through, you begin to see the paragraph as an organic whole. "It's perfectly clear to me," you may think. The question is, of course, Is it clear to the reader? The writer is responsible for making clear to the reader the relationships between and among the sentences in a paragraph. The reader needs clues in order to follow what the writer has to say. Are the interrelationships clear in the following paragraph?

Is the funeral inflation bubble ripe for bursting? A few years ago, the United States public suddenly rebelled against the trend in the auto industry towards ever more showy cars, with their ostentatious and nonfunctional fins, and a demand was created for compact cars patterned after European models. The all-powerful auto industry, accustomed to *telling* the customer what sort of car he wanted, was suddenly forced to *listen* for a change. Overnight the little cars became for millions a new kind of status symbol. The American public is becoming sickened by ever more extravagant and costly funerals.

You may have to read the paragraph more than once to realize what it is about. The author is attempting to draw a comparison between the automobile industry and the funeral industry. But there are no clues *in* the sentences to show this connection. Even though a skilled reader might guess the relationship between these ideas, it is the writer's job to make all the relationships as clear as possible (crystal clear, not "sort of" clear), as in the following:

Is the funeral inflation bubble ripe for bursting? A few years ago, the United States public suddenly rebelled against the trend in the auto industry toward ever more showy cars, with their ostentatious and nonfunctional fins, and a demand was created for compact cars patterned after European models. The all-powerful auto industry, accustomed to *telling* the customer what sort of car he wanted, was suddenly forced to *listen* for a change. Overnight, the little cars became for millions a new kind of status symbol. Could it be that the same cycle is working itself out in the attitude toward the final return of dust to dust, that the American public is becoming sickened by ever more ornate and costly funerals, and that a status symbol of the future may indeed be the simplest kind of "funeral without fins"?
JESSICA MITFORD, *The American Way of Death*

Exploiting a logical relationship, such as the comparison Mitford suggests, is only one among many devices used by experienced writers to create coherent paragraphs. The aim is to help the reader follow as the writer moves from sentence to sentence. Another, simpler, device of coherence is the *transition*.

Transitions are signals indicating where the writer is going and how the reader should follow. These signals not only identify the relationships between the sentences, they actually help to connect one sentence to another. They are the mortar used by experienced writers to ensure that the ideas or details in a paragraph stick together. In the following paragraphs the transitional words and phrases are italicized:

A Kudirka was thrown into a cell with five other newly arrived dissidents. *After three weeks*, the youngest of the five, Mikhail Jacysin, a twenty-four-year-old Ukrainian nationalist, was called out for what he

supposed to be a physical examination. *When* he was returned to the cell, he stood motionless and glassy eyed for several moments. *Then* he broke into uncontrollable sobs and began pounding on the door, screaming over and over, "They will not make me into a swine."
KENNETH Y. TOMLINSON, "A Man Called Simas," *Reader's Digest*, August 1975

B A growing phenomenon among the nation's labor force, job-sharing —in which two part-time employees divide the duties of one full-time position—is fast shaping up as the best of all possible working worlds. *First*, it features many of the advantages—shorter hours, more flexible schedules—of traditional part-time work, which means that housewives, students, and the retired can pursue careers that might otherwise have been incompatible with previous commitments. *Second*, it encompasses a much wider range of job types and opportunities than part-time workers—usually relegated to clerical work—have enjoyed in the past. *And third*, it offers a prorated full-time salary (generally much higher than part-time wages), as well as extended benefits such as medical coverage, vacation pay, sick leave, and life insurance.
CHARLOTTE MACDONALD, "Job Sharing," *Woman's Day*, 28 June 1977

In paragraph *A*, the author's overall plan was to develop the paragraph chronologically. However, he did more than arrange the events in the order of their occurrence; he added specific transitional devices to help the reader follow the developments in time. The topic sentence in paragraph *B* promises the reader a catalog of the advantages of job sharing. The transitional expressions "First," "Second," "And third," help to deliver on that promise by providing the framework on which the details (advantages) are hung.

COMMON TRANSITIONAL SIGNALS

FOR ADDITION
again, also, and, and then, besides, finally, first, further, furthermore, in addition, lastly, moreover, next, second, secondly, too

FOR COMPARISON
also, as, by the same token, in comparison, likewise, similarly

FOR CONTRAST
after all, although, and yet, but, by contrast, however, nevertheless, on the contrary, on the other hand, otherwise, still, yet

FOR SUMMARY
as I have said, in brief, in conclusion, in other words, in short, on the whole, to conclude, to summarize, to sum up

FOR EXAMPLES AND ILLUSTRATIONS

by way of illustration, for example, for instance, incidentally, indeed, in fact, in other words, in particular, specifically, that is

FOR RESULT

accordingly, as a result, consequently, hence, in short, then, thereafter, therefore, thus, truly

FOR TIME

afterwards, at last, at length, immediately, in the meantime, lately, at length, meanwhile, of late, presently, shortly, since, soon, temporarily, thereafter, thereupon, until, while

FOR CONCESSION

after all, although it is true, at the same time, granted, I admit, I concede, naturally, of course, while it is true

In addition to these transitional signals, skilled writers make use of association chains—repetitions of key words and concepts and synonyms or pronouns that substitute for these key terms. We have italicized the various terms used in the following paragraph to indicate the *people* mentioned in the story.

Every 12 years, on auspicious days chosen by astrologers, *pilgrims* come to the junction of the Ganges and Jumna Rivers to bathe away *their* sins. At the appointed moment, the *throng* surges forward into the waters. In 1954, a February day was selected as the most favorable in 144 years and *four million Hindus* came to the holy spot. In the onrush about *five hundred persons* were crushed to death. But relatives consoled themselves with the thought that of all times and places to die, this was the best.
SAM WELLES, editor, *The World's Great Religions*

You can create coherent paragraphs by establishing relationships within sentences and between and among sentences and chunks in a paragraph. (See Chapter 6 for a detailed look at these sentence-combining devices.) The reader encounters the sentences of your paragraph one at a time, and only as each sentence repeats or varies some element of a preceding sentence can the reader understand how they relate to each other. You can, of course, use several techniques in each paragraph. For example, the preceding paragraph describing the death of the five hundred pilgrims is developed by time signals as well as the association chain based on "pilgrims." Notice the different strands of coherence running through the John Steinbeck paragraph that follows:

Two rangy shepherd dogs trotted up pleasantly, (until) they caught the scent of strangers, (and then) they backed cautiously away, watchful, their tails moving slowly and tentatively in the air, but their eyes and noses quick for animosity or danger. *One of them*, scratching his neck edged forward, ready to run, and little by little he approached Tom's legs and sniffed loudly at them. (Then) he backed away and watched Pa for some kind of signal. *The other pup* was not so brave. He looked about for something that could honorably divert his attention, saw a red chicken go mincing by, and ran at it. There was the squawk of an outraged hen, a burst of red feathers, and the hen ran off, flapping stubby wings for speed. *The pup* looked proudly back at the men, (and then) flopped down in the dust and beat its tail contentedly on the ground.

JOHN STEINBECK, *The Grapes of Wrath*

The italicized words indicate the subjects of the paragraph, the dogs. The parentheses indicate the specific transitional devices signaling chronological sequence. And the chain of pronouns referring to the dogs differs in color. As you can see, Steinbeck succeeded in producing a coherent paragraph by skillfully interweaving several different kinds of transitional devices.

PARAGRAPH STRUCTURE

A paragraph should not be an accident; it should be carefully thought out and polished. As you examine many different ways to design paragraphs, keep this in mind: following specific patterns is not as important as the general habit of designing your paragraphs.

A word of caution: beginning writers sometimes become disheartened when they examine a well-constructed model paragraph by an accomplished writer. They find its inner logic, its coherence, its perfection forbidding, and doubt that they'll ever be able to produce a comparable paragraph. But you must not assume that well-constructed, beautifully developed paragraphs simply flow from the pens of experienced writers. Most writers write and then laboriously rewrite; they edit and polish (see Chapter 1). Think of a favorite television show, movie, or record album. What actually happens in the studio is often quite different from the finished product. You never see or hear the dozen retakes, the tape that is discarded, the careful editing. In reading, you see a well-developed, effective paragraph, but what you never know is how that paragraph was actually produced—how it happened or "grew." The writer may have tried several alternative methods of developing the paragraph before discovering the one preserved for the reader. What is rejected is often as important as what is finally retained. Having alternative methods of paragraph development to choose from will enrich your final choice.

One useful method for looking at paragraph structure defines a paragraph as a sequence of structurally related sentences (Francis Christensen, "A Generative Rhetoric of the Paragraph," *College Composition and Communication,* Dec. 1965). In terms of logic and reasoning, the topic of a paragraph is a *generalization* and the development of a paragraph is usually made up of one or more *specific instances* of the generalization. In other words, a paragraph makes a general statement that is illustrated with specific statements as the paragraph develops.

The "topic + development" structure is generated by addition. Notice in the following example how many specifics (illustrations) have been added to the topic sentence:

TOPIC (GENERALIZATION)
Dr. Steele points to a number of characteristics most abusive parents have in common.

DEVELOPMENT (SPECIFIC INSTANCES)

1 They are immature.

2 They lack self esteem; they feel incompetent as parents.

3 They have trouble finding pleasure and satisfaction in the outside world.

4 They possess a strong fear of spoiling their children and hold an equally strong belief in the efficacy of corporal punishment.

5 Finally, they are markedly deficient in the ability to empathize with, and respond to, their children's needs.
MYRON BRENTON, "What Can Be Done About Child Abuse?" *Today's Education,* Sept./Oct. 1977

This simple paragraph illustrates the basic topic plus development structure of the ideal paragraph, in which the topic sentence expresses some generalization and the development is made up of specifics (illustrations) within the generalization. We have numbered five sentences, but there are six illustrations (sentence 2 contains two closely related illustrations punctuated with a semicolon).

Thus we can state a second rule about our ideal paragraph: the topic sentence and the developmental sentences stand in a relation of general to specific with respect to each other. All the sentences in the Brenton paragraph are generalizations in the *logical* sense, but with reference to each other, the topic sentence is more general. It names a category (parental characteristics). The details in the developmental sentences are included in this category. They are, in fact, specific instances (immaturity, incompetence, dissatisfaction, and so on).

The Brenton paragraph also illustrates a paragraph moving *from* generalization *to* specification, but the possibilities for movement can be quite complex. Another movement is from specific to general, in which the topic sentence comes last:

DEVELOPMENT (SPECIFIC INSTANCES)

   1 I remember disliking Harvey Anderson, who was handsome and Negro and good in arithmetic and an incredible show-off.

   2 And there was Henry Marshall, who was tall and blond and a constant bully.

TOPIC (GENERALIZATION)

As adults will do, I assign each of my friends and acquaintances a race today; I didn't then.

GILBERT MOORE, "No One Has Ever Called Me a Nigger," *Life*, 15 Oct. 1967

In the Brenton and Moore examples, the developmental sentences *add* illustrations to the topic sentences. In each case, the illustration sentences are related to the topic sentence but not to each other. However, notice in the next example how each of the developmental sentences adds to the sentence it follows:

TOPIC (GENERALIZATION)

The film director's desire for a more flexible and mobile instrument that would enable the camera to move freely about the set led to more sophisticated machinery.

DEVELOPMENT (SPECIFIC INSTANCES)

   1 One such device is the crab dolly, a steel cart mounted on heavy pneumatic tires.

   2 This type of dolly can be steered noiselessly and abruptly and contains a pedestal upon which the camera is placed.

   3 The pedestal can be raised and lowered during the shot.

LEE R. BOBKER, *Elements of Film*

These examples represent two basic paragraph patterns: the sentences added directly to the topic sentence comprise a *coordinate* pattern; added to each other, a *subordinate* pattern. The sentences in a coordinate pattern all have the same relationships to each other; they are all of the same order and bear the relationship of addition to the topic sentence. The sentences in a subordinate pattern are not parallel to each other, and each makes a comment on only the sentence immediately preceding it. In the Bobker paragraph, development sentence 1 comments on the topic sentence, providing an illustration of the sophisticated machinery mentioned in the topic sentence. But sentence 2 adds to sentence 1, giving a detail about the crab dolly mentioned in sentence 1; and sentence 3 adds a detail about the pedestal mentioned in sentence 2.

These examples illustrate what is meant by "unity" and "coherence" in a paragraph. Because the sentences are held together in one or the other pattern of relationship, the paragraph becomes a unit (or unified); because the sentences are related to each other, the reader is able to follow a coherent flow of information from one sentence to the next. Thus, any sentence that breaks the pattern or seems not to be clearly related to either a sentence above or the topic sentence breaks the unity of the paragraph and may cause the reader to lose the thread of coherence.

The most common type of paragraph mixes coordinate and subordinate patterns, as in the following example:

TOPIC (GENERALIZATION)
The baboon, of course, is not without resource.

DEVELOPMENT (SPECIFIC INSTANCES)
1 He is fairly formidable.

  2 Like all primates he lacks claws but his nails are formidable.

  2 He has canines like daggers.

  2 And he has wits.

    3 If, while he is plundering, a man comes out of a farmhouse, he will flee.

    3 If a woman comes out, he will ignore her.

    3 But if a determined male human enemy dresses in woman's clothes, the baboon will instantly take to the woods.

  2 And South African farmers are convinced that the baboon can count to three.

3 When a troop of chacma baboons raids an orchard and the enraged farmer appears, the troop will withdraw, to return of course the instant he leaves.

3 If three farmers enter the orchard, and two withdraw, the baboons are not deceived; they will keep their distance.

3 Only if four farmers enter the orchard, and three withdraw, will the baboon's mathematics fail him.

4 He will return to the orchard and fall into an ambush.

ROBERT ARDREY, *African Genesis*

This paragraph by Robert Ardrey has many levels of generalization and specification. (There is no real limit to the number or complexity of the levels possible in a paragraph.) All the development sentences illustrate the topic sentence, supporting the statement that the baboon has resources. But, as you can see from the numbering system, there are several coordinate-pattern sentences, sentences that are at the same level of specification; and the whole paragraph is built on a pattern of subordination.

Thus we have the basic paragraph patterns: coordinate, subordinate, and mixed. And you can see that by relating your sentences to each other in these ways, you can generate very complex paragraphs. To illustrate the possibility for complex relationships among sentences in a paragraph, we have provided a paragraph by Bruno Bettleheim about a little boy who suffered the delusion that he was not human but mechanical:

TOPIC (GENERALIZATION)

During Joey's first weeks with us we would watch absorbedly as this at once fragile and imperious nine-year old went about his mechanical existence.

DEVELOPMENT (SPECIFIC INSTANCES)

1 Entering the dining room, for example, he would string an imaginary wire from his "energy source"—an imaginary electric outlet—to the table.

2 There he "insulated" himself with paper napkins and finally plugged himself in.

3 Only then could Joey eat, for he firmly believed that the "current" ran his ingestive apparatus.

1(a) So skillful was the pantomime that one had to look twice to be sure that there was neither wire nor outlet nor plug.

2 Children and members of our staff spontaneously avoided stepping on the "wire" for fear of interrupting what seemed the source of his very life.

BRUNO BETTLEHEIM, *Joey, A "Mechanical Boy"*

In this paragraph, sentence 1 illustrates (gives an example of) the topic sentence. Sentence 2 adds a detail to this example, and sentence 3 adds to sentence 2. So far, this paragraph looks like a subordinate pattern, with each sentence related to the one immediately above it. But sentence 4 refers back not only to the sentence above it but to sentences 1, 2, and 3—the example plus its added details, the expanded illustration. And for this reason we have labeled it 1(a). The last sentence adds a comment to sentence 1(a) the same way that sentence 2 adds to sentence 1, and so we have labeled it 2.

Paragraph development analysis

Describe the pattern of development in each of the following paragraphs. How are the sentences related to each other? It may be helpful to write out the paragraphs, showing the coordinate or subordinate relationships and numbering the levels of generality.

1 Giraffes are well adapted for reaching up, awkwardly built for reaching down. To feed on a bush, drink from a pool, or lick the salt in the dirt, they have to spread their front legs wide apart. Water holes are notorious hideouts for predators, and in their spraddled drinking position, giraffes are vulnerable. When a three-hundred-pound lion fixes itself to the end of a giraffe's six-foot neck, the victim is more than likely doomed to die by strangulation.

BRISTOL FOSTER, "Africa's Gentle Giants," *National Geographic*, Sept. 1977

2 No country can touch us when it comes to heartburn and upset stomachs. This nation, under God, with liberty and justice for all, neutralizes more stomach acid in one day than the Soviet Union does in a year. We give more relief from discomfort of the intestinal tract than China and Japan combined.

ART BUCHWALD, "Acid Indigestion," *Esquire*, Dec. 1975

3 Several years ago I was hired by a bank in the Chicago area to test a variety of uniforms. The vice-president in charge of this operation favored a uniform in several shades of green; he thought banks should remind people of money. We tested not only his uniform but several other colors. We outfitted a team of researchers in dresses, shirts, and suits of different colors and had them go into stores to cash checks. We discovered that when they showed up in green clothing they invariably were questioned more thoroughly and their IDs were checked more closely than when they appeared in other colors.

JOHN T. MOLOY, "Wearin' o' the Green Makes Mistrust," *Detroit Free Press*, 7 Jan. 1979

4 A woman teacher ate the flesh of her own dead beloved sister. For this she was taken by the Khmer Rouge guards and beaten in front of the entire village. They beat her without mercy from the morning until the evening, when, thank God, she died. And all this time her own child sat weeping, helpless and baffled, beside her.

PIN YATHAY, "Escape from Cambodia," *National Review*, 22 Dec. 1978

VARIATIONS ON PARAGRAPH BEGINNINGS

We have been using the term "topic sentence" to mean the sentence that states what the paragraph is about and also to mean the sentence in the paragraph to which the others are related. But we said earlier that some paragraphs don't have topic sentences. In fact, there are three variations on the way paragraphs begin.

THE TRANSITIONAL SENTENCE

It is very common to start a paragraph with a sentence that relates back to the preceding paragraph. The transitional sentence does for the paragraph what the transitional signal does for the sentence; it establishes coherence between paragraphs. Note the following example:

TRANSITIONAL SENTENCE
At Moreton Drive peace was pouring in a bland golden flood out of the park opposite.

TOPIC SENTENCE
1 There were birds in mother's garden.

DEVELOPMENT SENTENCES
2 Somebody had put out seed for them, in a little terra cotta dish suspended from the branch of a tree.

3 Sparrows and finches were fluttering, flirting; a rain of seed scattered from the swaying dish.

3 From the lawn at the foot of the tree, a flight of blue pigeons took off clattering, and away.

PATRICK WHITE, *The Eye of the Storm*

In this paragraph by Patrick White the first sentence is not the topic of the paragraph. It is a transitional sentence relating this paragraph to the preceding one. The topic sentence is the one we have numbered 1. Notice that if you remove this sentence, the rest of the sentences have nothing to attach to.

TOPIC + RESTRICTION

Sometimes the topic of a paragraph is first stated in a general way and then restricted immediately by a more specific sentence. Often the decision to write a "topic + restriction" beginning is simply a decision in favor of readability—the topic may be easier to read if written as two sentences instead of as one long one.

TOPIC SENTENCE

1 The LSD state varies greatly according to the dosage, the personality of the user and the condition under which the drug is taken.

TOPIC-RESTRICTION SENTENCE

1R Basically, it causes changes in sensation.

DEVELOPMENT SENTENCES

2 Vision is markedly altered.

3 Changes in depth perception and the meaning of the perceived object are most frequently described.

3 Illusions and hallucinations can occur.

2 Thinking may become pictorial and reverie states are common.

3 Delusions are expressed.

3 The sense of time and of self are strangely altered.

2 Strong emotions may range from bliss to horror, sometimes within a single experience.

2 Sensations may "crossover," that is, music may be seen or color heard.

2 The individual is suggestible and, especially under high doses, loses his ability to discriminate and evaluate his experience.

NATIONAL CLEARING HOUSE FOR DRUG ABUSE INFORMATION, *A Federal Source Book: Answers to the Most Frequently Asked Questions about Drug Abuse*

The topic sentence, number 1, identifies the subject of the paragraph, the LSD state, which differs from person to person. The next sentence, number 1R, restricts the topic of the paragraph to the basic changes in sensation caused by LSD. All the level 2 sentences, then, refer to the topic and restriction in 1 and 1R.

IMPLIED TOPIC SENTENCE

Although some paragraphs have no topic sentence, they must have a topic idea that is clearly implied.

2 Her person was short, thin, and crooked.

2 Her forehead projected in the middle, and then descended in a declivity to the top of her nose, which was sharp and red, and would have hung over her lips, had not nature turned up the end of it.

2 Her lips were two bits of skin, which, whenever she spoke, she drew together in a purse.

2 Her chin was peaked; and at the upper end of that skin which composed her cheeks, stood two bones, that almost hid a pair of small red eyes.

2 Add to this a voice most wonderfully adapted to the sentiments it was to convey, being both loud and harsh.

HENRY FIELDING, *Joseph Andrews*

We have labeled these sentences 2 because they are all second-level examples of an implied topic sentence (I shall describe the woman). Since the examples themselves clearly make the point, there is no need for a topic sentence here.

Coordinate-subordinate paragraph practice

Practice writing coordinate and subordinate sequences. Write paragraphs of your own in which the subsequent sentences are specific instances of the topic sentence; and paragraphs in which each sentence comments on the one above it. Note the following two paragraphs:

COORDINATE

1 You can buy practically anything in a supermarket today.

2 Naturally there is food: meat, fruit and vegetables, dairy products, and anything else you can think of to eat or drink.

2 But you can also buy pots and pans and mops and flyswatters, and other household goods.

2 You can also buy books and magazines and records.

2 And any large market will have a drug and medicine section where you can get your Dristan and nasal spray.

2 Some stores even have a clothing section, or at least a rack full of panty hose.

IRENE SMALL

SUBORDINATE

1 The common table lamp is composed of a shade and some kind of base.

2 The shade diffuses the light; the base contains the electrical components.

3 The electrical components are composed of a socket and a cord running through the lamp and ending in a plug.

4 The socket has an opening for the bulb and a switch for opening and closing the contacts with the cord.

LON GWAINER

We have said that the patterns of development for the paragraph are the same as those for the full composition. Thus, paragraphs can be developed by thesis and support, by chronological and spatial order, by comparison and contrast, cause and effect, question and answer, definition, classification, and a number of other developmental plans that come about as a result of the overall design of your composition rather than as special requirements of paragraph writing. (To review some of these patterns, see Chapter 3.) Two kinds of paragraphs, however, demand special attention: *introductory* and *concluding* paragraphs.

INTRODUCTORY PARAGRAPHS

The first paragraph is often the most important. You may win or lose your reader right at the beginning of your composition; therefore, the extra time it takes to write an effective beginning is well spent. The beginning is usually the hardest part in writing, so we recommend that you postpone serious work on the introductory paragraph until after you have completed a rough draft of the entire paper. With a clear sense of the overall scope of your paper —its details, its method of development, its conclusion—you will be in a better position to shape an effective introduction.

The introduction should convince the reader that you offer an original approach to an interesting topic in a lively style. A well-crafted introduction must be accurate; it is disconcerting to discover that the subject of a composition is something other than what the writer suggested in the introduction. Finally, the introduction should lead the reader smoothly into the body of the paper.

PROBLEMS TO AVOID

The one-sentence introduction There is almost no occasion in formal writing for the one-sentence introduction. Usually, these one-sentence paragraphs ("Fishing is a very interesting sport") are empty statements, and they must be edited out. The true introduction is likely to be found in the next paragraph. Either remove these one-liners entirely, connect them to the next paragraph, or build them into more substantive introductions.

The empty introduction   Papers sometimes begin with several sentences that wander around the subject without really saying anything. Often these sentences are simply variations on the title of the paper: "Fishing can be a very interesting sport. There are many people who take it up as a hobby. The rewards of fishing are great. There is no doubt that fishing can be a fulfilling and meaningful experience for all concerned." In this introduction, the writer is displaying little concern for the reader. And most readers, anticipating that the body of the paper is likely to be as empty as the introduction, will simply stop reading.

The assumption-of-knowledge introduction   The writer assumes the reader knows the subject and, as a consequence, the writer fails to include important information. Your introduction must stand on its own, *informing,* as well as interesting and encouraging, the reader. Avoid references to the assignment: "This is a very difficult subject." "I am not really an expert on this topic." Avoid starting off with pronouns whose antecedents are assumed: "It is a very sad play" (reference to *Hamlet*). Avoid references to the title of your paper: "Yes, he certainly was!" (title: Was Hamlet Crazy?). Though every paper should have a title, the title is not *part* of the introduction.

EXAMPLES OF INTRODUCTORY PARAGRAPHS

The following introductory paragraphs come from fiction and nonfiction works of writers with widely different styles. As you read them, decide why at least some deserve to be called effective introductions, using the following criteria:

1 Who is the likely audience? The general reader? Young people? Sports enthusiasts? The academic community? Do you think the introduction will appeal to its audience?

2 What personality does the writer project? Does the author sound intelligent, bland, humorous, superior, knowledgeable, sarcastic? Is the author's tone suitable for subject and audience?

3 Is the introduction interesting? Informative? Does it lead the reader smoothly into the paper?

START WITH A DRAMATIC INCIDENT

It looked as ridiculous as a dead shark on horseback—a snub-nosed, thick-bodied, powerless rocket ship called *Enterprise* perched on three struts atop a Boeing 747, five miles up in the bright California sky.

Suddenly the 747 dipped and gunned its engines. Inside the *Enterprise*, Cmdr. Fred Haise punched the disconnect button, and the stocky craft popped free of its ferry. "She's flying good," Haise yelled jubilantly. He pushed the ship through two ninety-degree turns, then pointed its nose downward toward the salt-and-clay flatbed of Edwards Air Force Base, where he glided into a landing five minutes later.

RICHARD BOOTH, "Free Enterprise," *Newsweek*, 22 Aug. 1977

START WITH A CONTRAST

Women are expected to behave differently from men in trying to get their way, and so they do, most of the time. Although feminine strategies often work, their use can seriously damage a woman's self esteem and diminish the respect she gets from others. But if she adopts the more effective techniques used mostly by men, she may be called pushy or aggressive.

PAULA B. JOHNSON AND JACQUELINE D. GOODCHILDS, "How Women Get Their Way," *Psychology Today*, Oct. 1976

START BY TELLING A STORY

I have seldom had the chance to meet the scientists who work a few buildings away from my own or live just doors away in this small college town, but I remember a neighboring physicist who came to the door once and asked if I would look at his refrigerator, which had gone off while his wife was making toast. I was still making uncomfortable apologies for my ignorance when snapping his circuit breaker off and on, I heard the refrigerator begin to purr.

STERLING EISEMINGER, "On Parblind Scholars," *Phi Kappa Phi Journal*, 1977

START BY SETTING THE SCENE

During the whole of a dark, dull and resoundless day in the autumn of the year, when the clouds hung oppressively low in the heavens, I had been passing alone, on horseback, through a singularly dreary tract of country, and at length found myself, as the shades of evening drew on, within view of the melancholy House of Usher. I know not how it was—but with the first glimpse of the building, a sense of insufferable gloom pervaded my spirit. I say insufferable; for the feeling was unrelieved by any of that half-pleasurable, because poetic, sentiment with which the mind usually receives even the sternest natural images of the desolate or terrible. I looked upon the scene before me—upon the mere house, and the simple landscape features of the domain—upon the bleak walls—and upon the vacant eye-like windows—upon a few rank sedges—and upon a few white trunks of decayed trees—with an utter depression of soul, which I can compare to no earthly sensation more properly than to the after-dream of the reveller upon opium—the bitter lapse into everyday life—the hideous dropping of the veil.

EDGAR ALLAN POE, "The Fall of the House of Usher," *The Works of Edgar Allan Poe*

START WITH A QUESTION OR PROBLEM

What is it like to die? That is a question which humanity has been asking itself ever since there have been humans. I have had the opportunity to raise this question before a sizable number of audiences. These groups have ranged from classes in psychology, philosophy and sociology through church organizations, television audiences and civic clubs to professional societies of medicine. On the basis of this exposure, I can safely say that this topic excites the most powerful of feelings.

RAYMOND A. MOODY, "Is There Life After Death?" *Saturday Evening Post,* May/June 1977

START WITH A DESCRIPTION

Mr. Frost came into the front room of his house in Cambridge, Massachusetts, casually dressed, wearing high plaid slippers, offering greetings with a quiet, even diffident friendliness. But there was no mistaking the evidence of the enormous power of his personality. It makes you at once aware of the thick, compacted strength of his body, even now at eighty-six; it is apparent in his face, actually too alive and spontaneously expressive to be as ruggedly heroic as in his photographs.

"Robert Frost," *Writers at Work,* George Plimpton, ed.

START BY EXPLAINING THE THESIS

Critics of the Equal Rights Amendment contend that ratification of the ERA will result in women being subject to the military draft and having to fight in the front lines of any future war. With or without the ERA, it is very difficult to postulate in this era that women should not be drafted into a peacetime Army.

YVONNE BRAITHEWAITE, "Let's Play Taps For an All Male Army!" *Saturday Evening Post,* Oct. 1977

START WITH A BRIEF HISTORICAL BACKGROUND

The Constitution of the United States of America was drafted between May 14 and September 17, 1787, by fifty-five men meeting in the city of Philadelphia. It was made effective on June 21, 1788, by the vote of nine state ratifying conventions. Under the governmental system set up by this document, a group of thirteen sparsely populated states strung out along the Atlantic Ocean from Massachusetts to Georgia has developed into one of the greatest powers of world history. Appropriately, the parchment sheets on which the Constitution was written are preserved as a national shrine in the National Archives at Washington, and the document has come to be regarded with the awe and reverence reserved for religious objects.

C. HERMAN PRITCHETT, "The American Constitution," *The American Constitutional System*

START WITH UNUSUAL FACTS AND FIGURES

The lowest natural temperature ever recorded on earth was registered in Antarctica at the Soviet scientific station Vostok on August 26, 1960:

−126.94° Fahrenheit. Vostok, however, is an anomaly, an observation post manned in the same occasional way as a spacecraft and standing at 11,500 feet above sea level. The coldest place where people choose to live year-round is a village of six hundred souls in a mountain valley 2,300 feet above sea level on the banks of the Indigirka River in Northeastern Yakutia. It is named Oymyakon.

RUDOLPH CHELMINSKI, "Polus Kholodo: The Coldest Place," *Atlantic Monthly*, Oct. 1977

START WITH A QUOTATION

"The world isn't used to your open diplomacy. It stiffens the back of Israel and raises the expectations of the Arabs, which, once frustrated, will retard rather than bring peace." During a week of buffeting over US-Soviet relations, Jimmy Carter hardly needed that sober assessment of his Middle East Policy. But it came last Wednesday from Rabbi Alexander Schindler, one of the 53 Jewish leaders invited to a dialogue with the President at the White House.

"Jimmy Woos the Jewish Leaders," *Time*, July 1977

START WITH A DEFINITION

First of all for the sake of clarity, I must say that the term "oriental medicine" is in fact too broad to be strictly meaningful, but I use it in a special—and today generally accepted—sense to mean medicine that originated in China and travelled to Japan by way of Korea. Chinese medicine—or Kampo—may be divided into two major streams of development. Therapeutical systems arising in the area of the Yellow River include acupuncture, mox, and amma massage, all of which are widely practiced in Japan.

KATSUSKE SERIZAWA, "The Philosophy of Chinese Medicine," *Massage: The Oriental Method*

START WITH AN IDEA TO BE REFUTED

"One of the most common errors of modern folklore is that because of our advanced technology, people in America today have more leisure time than anybody anywhere before," said Struever. "That's baloney. The hardest workers the world has ever seen could be today's Americans. People think primitive peoples like those at Koster struggled from dawn to dusk simply to survive. Not true. How hard a man works depends a lot on what he considers necessary goals in life, and at that time there was no environmental imperative in the valley requiring man to work hard. The large river valleys of the Midwest probably had the heaviest plant and animal population in North America, and therefore could support large human populations, and did. In 4200 B.C. man lived in a land of milk and honey, with tremendous food resources all around him in this valley, and the taking was easy.

FELICIA HOLTON, "Seven Thousand Years of Prehistoric Man in Illinois," *Vista*, Spring 1975

CONCLUDING PARAGRAPHS

It is important to keep in mind that the function of the conclusion is to bring the paper to an end. Papers should not arbitrarily and abruptly stop. Especially in nonfiction, the reader expects the writer to round the paper off, to give a clear signal that the final point has been made.

A detailed summary is the most common technique used by beginning writers to conclude their essays—and the most boring. Certainly you may briefly summarize the highlights covered in detail in the body of your paper, but a detailed review of every point made may insult your readers' intelligence, thus alienating them at a crucial stage in the writer-reader transaction. Since the conclusion is the last thing your readers encounter, it tends to have a disproportionate impact on them. A weak conclusion can too often spoil an otherwise competent paper.

The conclusion is your final chance to establish the significance of what you have to say; therefore, it should be the high point of your essay. End on a strong, lively note, leaving the reader something to remember, satisfied that you have delivered what you promised in the introduction.

PROBLEMS TO AVOID

The one-sentence ending   "I never dreamed Look-out Point could be so breathtaking on a moonlit night in October."

The tacked on moral or lesson   Especially in personal experience stories, readers should *know* from what has been said what the moral is. An ending like "I'll never again take Dead Man's Curve at ninety miles an hour in my father's station wagon" can ruin the impact of a strongly written paper. A lesson or moral should go without saying. Also avoid "hokey," contrived endings: "I woke suddenly; it had all been a dream!"

Trite concluding phrases   "To sum up," "In conclusion," "I will now conclude by . . . ," and so on.

Introducing new problems or subjects   "Yes, there are many joys to fishing, but our fishing areas are in danger!"

The weak ending   Don't use up all your material in the body of the paper; save something interesting for the conclusion.

EXAMPLES OF CONCLUDING PARAGRAPHS

The following passages are concluding paragraphs from articles, essays, books, and chapters in books, written by a variety of authors. First of all, note the specific techniques used to develop each paragraph; then decide what is effective about each paragraph.

END WITH A CALL FOR ACTION

The Communists disdain to conceal their views and they openly declare that their ends can be attained only by the forcible overthrow of all existing social conditions. Let the ruling classes tremble at a Communist revolution. The proletarians have nothing to lose but their chains. They have a world to win. Working men of all countries, unite!
KARL MARX, *Manifesto of the Communist Party*

END WITH A PREDICTION

The victories bode well for the future of women in politics. Women overcame such problems as underfinanced campaigns to achieve an across-the-board fifty-percent win-rate equal to that of male candidates, points out NWPC political action coordinator Fredi Wechsler. "One of our handicaps has been inexperience, coupled with poor timing," explains Jan McMichael, NWPC executive director. But, she says, women are now seeing politics as a full-time career. "They're preparing for their campaigns by building political bases early on instead of waiting until the 'nest empties.' Many of the women who ran this time and lost," she adds, "are the first ones we'll be looking to for '76."
CAROL DANA, "Win Some, Lose Some, and On to '76," *Ms.*, March 1975

END BY DRAWING A DEDUCTION FROM THE FACTS

Finally, the several classes of facts which have been considered in this chapter, seem to me to proclaim so plainly that the innumerable species, genera and families, with which this world is peopled, are all descended, each within its own class or group, from common parents, and have all been modified in the course of the descent, that I should without hesitation adopt this view, even if it were unsupported by other facts or arguments.
CHARLES DARWIN, "Mutual Affinities of Organic Beings," *On the Origin of Species*

END WITH A QUESTION

In asking whether the equal protection clause really requires all this, I have found myself rereading two of the most famous of all judicial comments on the Constitution—what it is and what it permits. They both came from the pen of John Marshall in 1819.

In considering this question, then, we must never forget, that it is a *constitution* we are expounding.

And later in the same opinion:

Let the end be legitimate, let it be within the scope of the constitution, and all means which are appropriate, which are plainly adapted to that end, but consistent with the letter and spirit of the constitution, are constitutional.

If the Constitution is read in this grand manner, can it truly be *unconstitutional* to make room for qualified members of racial minorities on the staircase to the professions?

MCGEORGE BUNDY, "The Issue Before the Court: Who Gets Ahead in America?" *Atlantic Monthly*, Nov. 1977

END ON A STRONG CONTRAST

The United States Supreme Court has always been a political institution. There is ample precedent and high-minded language to support both sides in this case. I am not overly sanguine about the outcome of the Bakke case. The public mood is against affirmative action, and the Burger Court has not always been sensitive to minority interests. Still, there is reason to hope that the Court will have the foresight to understand that no one's interest will be served if we continue to exist as two nations divided by color and opportunity.

CHARLES LAWRENCE III, "The Bakke Case: Are Racial Quotas Defensible?" *Saturday Review*, 15 Oct. 1977

END WITH A QUOTATION THAT ESPECIALLY ILLUSTRATES YOUR POINT

Farber's dream will not be easy to realize. But it may not be impossible, either. *Fortune* magazine, in a recent article documenting the many problems in using solar energy, concluded that "if . . . costs could be brought down, the move to solar energy just might grow into the biggest economic development since the automobile revolution." Outright enthusiasts have no such reservations. "There are no ifs involved with solar energy anymore," says Professor Y. B. Sofdari, of Bradley University. "It's merely a question of when."

C. P. GILMORE, "Sunpower!" *Saturday Review*, 30 Oct. 1976

END BY DISMISSING AN OPPOSING IDEA

Cloning of animals, particularly livestock, may, on balance, be a worthwhile idea deserving thorough investigation. But for humans, cloning would be, on balance, unjustifiable. The hazards, the ethics, the meager chances for any significant gain for mankind, should impel us to reject it as anything but a challenging stunt.

VANCE PACKARD, *The People Shapers*

END WITH A FINAL ILLUSTRATION

The real lesson of the week of October 22, 1962, was that the cause of life on earth is too important to be left to the national aggregations. That lesson will make its mark only when a genuine world order comes into being that is able to resolve disputes on the basis of justice and codified law and that is responsible not just to national governments but to the society of humans on earth.

NORMAN COUSINS, "The Cuban Missile Crisis: An Anniversary," *Saturday Review*, 1 Oct. 1977

Writing activities

Before starting the paragraph-writing activities here, reread Chapter 1. The considerations that inform effective paragraph writing are the same as those that govern the whole composition: purpose, audience, experience, self, code; and prewriting, writing, rewriting, proofreading.

1 Write a letter for a future generation, an unborn grandchild who will never know the energy-rich world of the twentieth century. Try to explain what ordinary life was like, when there was ample energy, to a child who must live without fossil fuel.

2 Prepare a piece for the school newspaper about some aspect of college that annoys students: application and registration procedures, cafeteria food, parking fees, class hours, dorm regulations, and so on.

3 Write a paragraph to be put up on the public memo board, advertising a room for rent. Describe the room for prospective renters.

4 An application form for a job asks you to describe either the one aspect of your previous work (including chores at home) you liked best or the one aspect you liked least. Illustrate in detail for an employer who wants to see how you handle language.

5 The school yearbook invites you to compose a piece on "someplace special." Write a description of a place special to you.

6 A television survey requests your view of television programs' and advertisements' insult to the viewer's intelligence. Write a paragraph illustrating the "insult" of just one program or ad.

7 You must return to your high school to deliver a short speech on the question, Do Americans admire conformity and obedience more than individuality and creativity? Illustrate one incident of conformity and/ or obedience you have observed or experienced.

8 Your animal husbandry final exam asks you to speculate about why Americans spend so much money on the care and feeding of their pets. Illustrate one aspect of the appeal pets have for people.

9 Write a paragraph to be added to your lawyer's directions in case of accident or death concerning euthanasia. From a personal point of view, describe any situation in which you would, or would not, want the doctors to "pull the plug."

10 You are a case worker for the Office of Student Affairs. You must write a paragraph for the files reporting the facts in an incident in which a student was disorderly at a party you attended. Write a second paragraph describing the same incident in a letter to a friend back home.

11 You have failed your earth sciences final exam; write a paragraph to the Dean of Students explaining why that happened. (Do you, for example, need a tutor or a reduced work load?) Write another letter explaining the failure to a friend at a distant school.

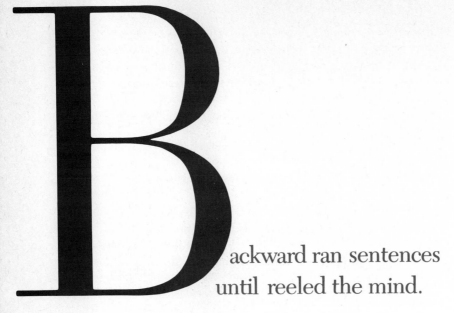

Backward ran sentences
until reeled the mind.

WOLCOTT GIBBS, *More in Sorrow*

In Chapter 6, you learned to combine and rewrite sentences to make your writing more effective. Chapter 8 describes other challenges you may face in producing well-crafted sentences: how to avoid common sentence flaws and how to create particular effects. Both of these skills will be especially useful when you revise and polish. To write effective sentences you must present ideas clearly and accurately, without wasted words. To make your ideas stand out for the reader you must give your sentences emphasis and variety.

CLARITY

Clear writing is a fulfilled transaction between you and your reader. The sentence faults discussed in this section tend to obscure your ideas from the reader. At the writing and rewriting stages, in each draft of a composition, edit and revise so that each sentence is clear in itself and in the way it reflects your overall purpose.

ILLOGICAL SENTENCES

Sometimes, beginning writers will write one sentence while thinking of another, putting parts of both of them on the paper. The result usually doesn't quite make sense. For example, imagine a writer thinking, "The story contains many good details. I admire the outcome of the story." But instead of writing two sentences, the author writes, "The details of the story admire the outcome." This is an illogical sentence (*details*, inanimate, can't *admire*), the result of faulty combining of ideas.

In the following pairs, why is sentence *B* illogical?

A From seventy throats, ugly howls and infernal laughter break the darkness of an African night.

VITUS B. DRÖSCHER, *The Friendly Beast*

B From seventy throats, ugly howls and infernal laughter examine the darkness of an African night.

A Few, if any, of the underdeveloped societies have the technical knowledge or the personnel to solve their problems.

ALAN WOLFE AND CHARLES MC COY, *Political Analysis*

B The technical knowledge or the personnel to solve their problems incorporate few, if any, of the underdeveloped societies.

A After turning off the ignition and sitting behind the wheel for five minutes trying to get my head together, I slowly open the car door and step out into the thirty-degree cold.

V. RAMIREZ

B After turning the engine off in which I am sitting behind the wheel for five minutes by trying to get my head together, I slowly open and step out the door in the thirty-degree cold.

RAMBLING SENTENCES

It is possible to get carried away with sentences. Sentences that ramble on and on, especially when they cause the reader to lose the main idea, should be broken up into shorter units.

What is the effect of writing the sentences of *A* as one long sentence in *B*?

A His last stop was his doctor's office. Complaining of chest pains, Daley, who had suffered from angina for several years, dropped by for a check-up—and collapsed. Ninety minutes of effort by medical teams could not revive him. After twenty-two years as mayor, at the head of a political machine without parallel in America, Daley was dead at seventy-four.

"The Man Who Made Chicago," *Time*, 3 Jan. 1977

B His last stop was his doctor's office, where, complaining of chest pains, Daley, who had suffered from angina for several years, dropped by for a check-up—and collapsed, so that even ninety minutes of efforts by medical teams could not revive him, and therefore after twenty-two years as mayor, at the head of a political machine without parallel in America, Daley was dead at seventy-four.

ECONOMY

Economical writing wastes neither words nor the reader's time. Whether an idea is simple or complex, it should be expressed in economical sentences.

WORDINESS

A good rule of thumb for any writer is *don't waste words*. The idea is not simply to use as few words as possible, but to use only as many words as necessary to express what you mean. If any words *can* be removed without changing the meaning of your sentences, they *should be*.

What is the effect of adding words to the original versions of the following sentences?

A President Ford announced today that Ronald Reagan would be an acceptable vice-president.
BILL WALSH

B President Ford, whose home is in Grand Rapids, announced today that Ronald Reagan would be an acceptable vice-president.

A In slow pulses the thick plume of fountain rose, fell upon itself, and slapped the pool in lazy rhythms.
THOMAS WOLFE, *Look Homeward Angel*

B In slow pulses the thick plume (that is, it looked like a plume) of fountain rose, fell upon itself, and slapped the pool in lazy rhythms.

A There are at least three parts to all interviews—the opening, the substantive, and the closing.
PETERSON, GOLDHABER, PACE, *Communication Probes*

B No doubt anyone would agree to the notion that there are in effect really just three parts to all interviews—the first being the opening, the second being the substantive, and of course the third and last being the closing.

REDUNDANCY

Redundant expressions are phrases like "repeat again," "completely unique," and "hurry quickly." Explain the redundancy in sentence *B* in the following:

A For months he would demand the same meal every day.
JAMES PHELAN, *Howard Hughes: The Hidden Years*

B For months he would demand the same identical meal every day.

A King Pellinore, who had been run away with, vanished altogether behind his back.
T. H. WHITE, *The Sword in the Stone*

B King Pellinore, who had been run away with, vanished altogether from view behind his back.

EXCESSIVE "WHO," "WHICH," "THAT"

The use of "who," "which," or "that" is often optional. Where such words are necessary to make the meaning of the sentence clear, they should be used. But when the sense is clear without them, they can be removed. In most cases, the result will be a more economical, more natural-sounding sentence. "Jane is a girl who likes cigars" is more economically expressed "Jane likes cigars." "Lucas knows exercise is good for him" is equivalent to "Lucas knows that exercise is good for him."

What is the effect of adding "who," "which," or "that" in sentence *B*?

A The art of management has been defined as getting things done through other people.
JOHN CAREY, *Getting Acquainted with Accounting*

B The art of management has been defined as that of getting things done through other people.

A When he looked out the window, the snow was still falling, but there were signs of a moon, a circle of dim light within the falling snow.
BERNARD MALAMUD, *The Fixer*

B When he looked out the window, the snow was still falling, but there were signs of a moon, which was a circle of dim light within the falling snow.

EMPHASIS

As you begin to write longer, more sophisticated sentences, you must craft them consciously to give the right emphasis to your ideas. Even in short sentences a writer must make clear for the reader which ideas are to be emphasized.

EFFECTIVE REPETITION

Deliberate repetition of words or phrases is one way to achieve emphasis within a sentence. What would be the effect of substituting *B* for *A* in the following?

A In every time, in every tongue, in every lonely troubled corner on earth, this bewilderment has been uttered.
BENJAMIN KOGAN, *Health*

B In every time, tongue, and troubled corner on earth, this bewilderment has been uttered.

A Society is sustained by communication: communication makes life possible.
PETERSON, GOLDHABER, PACE, *Communicaton Probes*

B Society is sustained by communication; and this makes human life possible.

PARALLELISM

Parallelism is a basic concept in writing, much like consistency, to which it is related. It is a convention that similar concepts should be written in similar forms; that is, they should be parallel. Parallelism is a form of repetition. Thus, "I like fishing and skiing," not "I like fishing and to ski."

Explain the parallelism in the following examples. What would be the effect of substituting sentence B for sentence A?

A But perhaps more important, the future home will provide room and equipment for drying, cleaning, canning and other food processing chores.
ROBERT RODALE, "Gardens of the Future," *Organic Gardening and Farming*, Jan. 1977

B But perhaps more important, the future home will provide room and equipment for drying, cleaning, and canned foods and other processed food chores.

A Imagine that we stand on an ordinary seaside pier, and watch the waves rolling in and striking against the columns of the pier.
SIR JAMES JEANS, *The Stars in Their Courses*

B Imagine that we stand on an ordinary seaside pier, and are watching the waves rolling in and strike against the iron columns of the pier.

INVERTED SENTENCES

One way of achieving emphasis is to invert your sentences. (Inverting your sentences is one way to achieve emphasis.) However, one kind of inversion is not much admired: the *backward* sentence, a sentence whose inverted structure sounds unnatural or obscures meaning (Learning English are the students).

How does the inverted sentence change the emphasis in the following?

A Excessive debt is engulfing thousands of families.
U.S. News and World Report, 20 June 1970

B Engulfing thousands of families is excessive debt.

A Leonardo the man appears more clearly and variously in his drawings than in his paintings or his notes.

WILL DURANT, *The Renaissance*

B In his drawings and more clearly and variously than in his paintings or his notes appears Leonardo the man.

PASSIVE SENTENCES

A passive sentence is one in which the doer of the action is invisible (The bear was shot), or the doer is hidden behind the word "by" (The bear was shot by the hunter). Whether there is any real need for the passive depends on whether the doer or the receiver of the action is being emphasized. The most direct statement is, of course, "The hunter shot the bear"; but if we ask what happened to that bear, the correct answer may be, "The bear was shot by the hunter." Even so, some passives are more awkward than others, and many sound pointlessly indirect by comparison with the active voice: "The paper was received by him" as opposed to "He received the paper."

In the following sentences, why does the passive seem less effective than the active?

A Miranda leaped into the pit that had held her grandfather's bones.

KATHERINE ANNE PORTER, "The Grave"

B The pit that had held her grandfather's bones was leaped into by Miranda.

A The boy's mind fumbled at little things.

THOMAS WOLFE, *Look Homeward Angel*

B Little things were fumbled at by the boy's mind.

SENTENCE RHYTHM

Just as you have learned to recognize the flat intonation of a recorded telephone message, and just as you know when someone is reading "without expression," you can learn to tell when there is something wrong with the rhythm of a sentence. It is very difficult to describe poor sentence rhythm; teachers usually just mark such sentences "awkward." But you can probably already tell when a sentence doesn't sound right. Something halting, unnatural, or awkward announces that the rhythm is off beat. Or the rhythm may be so homogenized, without variation or motion or emphasis, that it sounds flat, dead—a robot sentence.

What is the matter with the rhythm in sentence *B* of the

following? What do the *A* sentences achieve that the *B* sentences do not?

A Stormgren spun on his heels and stared into the shadowy corridor.
ARTHUR C. CLARKE, *Childhood's End*

B On his heels Stormgren spun, and into the shadowy corridor stared.

A They were feeding among the dew and the long shadows, with twilight already in the fields below.
RICHARD ADAMS, *Watership Down*

B Where there was dew they were feeding where the long shadows were above the fields below which already had twilight on them.

OTHER OPTIONS

Inexperienced writers sometimes use exclamation points, underlining, and quotation marks to show emphasis (This *is* important!), but there are other options.

Emphasis through structure

She reacted *sarcastically* to his proposal.   (Single word)

She reacted *with sarcasm* to his proposal.   (Phrase, more emphatic)

As she reacted to his proposal, *her sarcasm was evident.*   (Clause, most emphatic)

Emphasis through position   Moving things around usually causes a change in emphasis. There is no hard rule about position except that ideas gain emphasis when they show up in unexpected places. Modifiers tend to be most emphatic at the beginning of the sentence; independent clauses tend to be most emphatic at the end.

She reacted to his proposal sarcastically.

She sarcastically reacted to his proposal.

Sarcastically she reacted to his proposal.

While he was making his proposal, she reacted sarcastically.

How does the *B* sentence change the emphasis in the following?

A When Goldmund first came to his senses on his bed of straw in the stable, he missed the gold piece in his pocket.
HERMANN HESSE, *Narcissus and Goldmund*

B Goldmund missed the gold piece in his pocket when he first came to his senses on his bed of straw in the stable.

A If you blame yourself for knowing less than everything about imported wines, stop.
Mademoiselle, Oct. 1975

B For knowing less than everything about imported wines, stop blaming yourself.

A He was carrying two guns, big capable forty-fives, in the holsters hung fairly low and forward.
JACK SCHAFER, *Shane*

B He was carrying in the holsters, hung fairly low and forward, two big, capable forty-fives.

Emphasis through contrast   It is not always sufficient to say what a thing is; it is sometimes necessary to say what a thing is *not*. Furthermore, contrast is an excellent way of achieving emphasis.

What do the contrastive sentences below accomplish that the others do not?

A She handled her brushes with a certain ease and freedom which came, not from long and close acquaintance with them, but from a natural aptitude.
KATE CHOPIN, *The Awakening*

B She had been painting for a short time and had little acquaintance with her brushes, which she handled with a certain ease and freedom from a natural aptitude.

A And so we smile our way through the day, though in fact we may feel angry and annoyed beneath the smile.
JULIUS FAST, *Body Language*

B And so we smile our way through the day, and in fact we may feel angry and annoyed beneath the smile.

VARIETY

Avoid monotony in writing. The normal order for an English sentence is *subject—verb—object,* but if every sentence in your paper runs in normal order, you will put your reader to sleep. To achieve variety, use the techniques described in this section.

VARIED BEGINNINGS

Begin with a prepositional phrase   See page 374 for list of prepositions.

In the tumultuous business of cutting-in and attending to a whale, there is much running backwards and forwards among the crew.
HERMAN MELVILLE, *Moby Dick*

In the exciting business of registering for classes, there is much running backwards and forwards among the freshmen.
YVETTE WILLIAMS

Begin with more than one prepositional phrase

On this public holiday, as on all other occasions, for seven years past, Hester was clad in a garment of coarse gray cloth.
NATHANIEL HAWTHORNE, *The Scarlet Letter*

On this exam day, as on all other exams, for the whole semester, I was half asleep from studying all night.
FOSTER RANDOLPH

Begin with a simile

Like a razor also, it seemed massy and heavy, tapering from the edge into a solid and broad structure.
EDGAR ALLAN POE, "The Pit and the Pendulum"

Like a steam hammer, Professor Haroldson kept pounding away at Aristotle and the Sophists.
DAN LING

Begin with an adjective or several adjectives

Silent, grim, colossal—the big city has ever stood against its revilers.
O. HENRY, "Between Rounds," *The Four Million*

Wet, tired, hungry—I stood in the rain in front of the Union waiting for Felicia.
LUANA JOHNSON

Begin with an appositive

The elephant, the slowest breeder of all known animals, would in a few thousand years stock the whole world.
CHARLES DARWIN, *The Descent of Man*

Bubbles Revere, the fastest talker on campus, would in a few minutes wear out any listener.
RON SEVEILLE

Begin with an infinitive

To see her, and to be himself unseen and unknown, was enough for him at present.
THOMAS HARDY, *Jude the Obscure*

To know Bentley, and to be in his company for very long, was one of life's least rewarding experiences.
LARRY TATE

Begin with a modifying clause   Start with a subordinator (after, although, as, as if, because, before, if, since, though, unless, until, when, whenever, where, wherever, while):

When little boys have learned a new bad word, they are never happy till they have chalked it up on a door.
RUDYARD KIPLING, "The Phantom 'Rickshaw"

When teachers make a point, they are never happy till they see you scribble it in your notes.
SUE DEWITT

Begin with a noun clause   Start with a relative pronoun or certain of the subordinators (that, what, whatever, when, where, wherever, which, who, whoever, whom, whomever, whose, why):

What was meant by this ceremony the reader may imagine, who has already gathered some idea of the reckless irreverence of Roaring Camp.
BRET HARTE, "The Luck of Roaring Camp"

What was meant by chug-a-lug the reader may imagine, who has already gathered some idea of the rowdy uproar of a kegger.
RON LIEBERMANN

Begin with a participle

Crawling on all fours, I made steadily but slowly toward them; till at last, raising my head to an aperture among the leaves I could see clear down into a little dell beside the marsh, and closely set about with trees, where Long John Silver and another of the crowd stood face to face in conversation.
ROBERT LOUIS STEVENSON, *Treasure Island*

Creeping up to the door, I made steadily but slowly toward them; till at last, peeking through the glass in the door I could see clear into the foyer of the dorm, where Big Mother Maisy and her Little Snitch were blabbing away at each other.
SALLY NEWTON

Begin with a suspended transition

Scientists, furthermore, had succeeded in creating life, so that human evolution need no longer be left to chance.
ALVIN C. EURICH, "Higher Education in the Twenty-First Century," in *The Campus in the Modern World*, John D. Margolis, ed.

Heinie, furthermore, had succeeded in getting his boot stuck in the latrine, so that there was no possibility of getting it out without falling over backward.
JACK STOWKOWSKI

VARIED TYPES OF SENTENCES

The cumulative sentence   The cumulative sentence is built by addition; it adds details either before or after the main idea has been established. For example:

He showed up in a new car, a brand new Italian sports car, a roaring red sex symbol.
MERRIAM COLLINS

Set up as a problem in sentence combining, the sentence looks like this:

He showed up in a new car.
~~It was~~ a brand new Italian sports car.   (,)
~~It was~~ a roaring red sex symbol.   (,)

The two modifying sentences are reduced to descriptive phrases and added to the main clause. Since these cumulative modifiers are nonrestrictive (they can be removed without changing the main idea of the sentence), they must be set off with commas. Notice too that the modifiers add not only descriptive details, they add specificity. The main clause here tells us only that there was a new car; the added modifier specifies that it was an Italian sports car; the last modifier adds the specific details of red color and sex symbol.

Note the same additive process in the following sentence, in which we get a specific detail about a woman's appearance added to the main clause:

The confused shouting that rose so suddenly brought her to her feet and across the front porch without her slippers, hair half braided.
KATHERINE ANNE PORTER, *Noon Wine*

The cumulative sentence permits you to add more and more specific details, building highly descriptive pictures for the reader. The more specific details you add, the more highly textured your sentence will become, as in the following:

He watched them holding themselves with their noses into the current, many trout deep, fast moving water, slightly distorted as he watched

them far down through the glassy convex surface of the pool, its
surface pushing and swelling smooth against the resistance of the
log-driven piles of the bridge.
ERNEST HEMINGWAY, "Big Two-Hearted River"

The balanced sentence The balanced sentence is very formal
and elegant, it is often used in public oratory. It is crafted by
balancing two similar ideas in similar words and structures. For
example:

And so my fellow Americans, ask not what your country can do for
you; ask what you can do for your country.
JOHN F. KENNEDY, Inaugural Address

What does the balanced sentence achieve that the other
sentences do not in the following pairs?

A Extremism in the defense of Liberty is no vice; and . . . modera-
tion in the pursuit of Justice is no virtue.
BARRY GOLDWATER, Acceptance speech, Republican National Convention, 1964

B It is no vice to be extreme in defending liberty; and . . . to pursue
justice only moderately lacks virtue.

A Winners never quit; quitters never win.

B The only way to win is through perseverance; however, if you quit,
you obviously cannot win.

A When the going gets tough, the tough get going.

B Those who are successful are at their best when they are faced with
adversity.

The periodic sentence The periodic sentence builds to a climax:
the reader must wait for the end of the sentence before he or she
can get the meaning. The periodic sentence is created by suspending part of the sentence, frequently the verb, until the end. Technically, even a short sentence could be called "periodic" if it were
properly constructed, but the term usually applies to long sentences in which there is a clear sense of *waiting* for the end.
For example:

If Beethoven had been restricted to a less enlightened court circle,
had not known the Breunings, had not been exposed to the repercus-
sions of the French Revolution, he might have remained a talented
and serious musician but not much more.
FRIDA KNIGHT, *Beethoven and the Age of Revolution*

What do the periodic sentences achieve in the following pairs? What would be the effect of substituting sentence *B* for *A*?

A In that instant, in too short a time, one would have thought, even for a bullet to get there, a mysterious, terrible change had come over the elephant.
GEORGE ORWELL, "Shooting an Elephant"

B A mysterious and terrible change had come over the elephant in that instant, which was too short a time, one would have thought, even for a bullet to get there.

A From this dream and its associations with a number of rather ordinary childhood memories and several fairy tales familiar to the patient during his early years, some remarkable conclusions are derived.
C. H. THIGPEN AND HERVEY CLECKLY, *The Three Faces of Eve*

B Some remarkable conclusions are derived from this dream and its associations with a number of rather ordinary childhood memories and several fairy tales familiar to the patient during his early years.

Long and short   There is no rule about length of sentences in English. Long sentences are not better than short sentences; short sentences are not better than long. This book teaches beginning writers to combine short sentences because new writers tend to write many more short than long ones. A paper made up of too many short sentences may sound immature, and a paper made up of too many lengthy sentences is likely to sound boring. Note the variety and emphasis gained by juxtaposing long sentences and short in the following examples:

To raise morale and get rid of the troublemakers, he now planned a second reconnaissance under Hojeda, consisting of four hundred men with orders to march to Santo Thomás, relieve Margarit's garrison, and then explore the country and live off the natives. This was one of Columbus's worst decisions.
SAMUEL ELIOT MORISON, *Christopher Columbus, Mariner*

There was absolutely no end to that awful song with its eternal "I will kiss thee!" and at last neither I nor Sir Henry, whom I had summoned to enjoy the sight, could stand it any longer; so, remembering the dear old story, I put my head to the window opening and shouted, "For Heaven's sake, Good, don't go on talking about it, but *kiss* her and let's all go to sleep!" That choked him off, and we had no more serenading.
H. RIDER HAGGARD, *Alan Quatermain*

Sentence evaluation practice

In each of the following pairs, one sentence is thought to be better than the other in one or more aspects of sentence effectiveness. Which is the better sentence?

1[1] **A** My wife was overwhelmed by the number of things she had to do that seemed to have nothing to do with teaching when she first taught.

B When my wife first taught, she was overwhelmed by the number of things she had to do that seemed to have nothing to do with teaching.

2[2] **A** I believe the President, who is elected every four years, has an obligation to lay before the American people and its Congress the basic premises of his policy and to report fully on the issues, developments, and prospects confronting the nation.

B I believe the President has an obligation to lay before the American people and its Congress the basic premises of his policy and to report fully on the issues, developments, and prospects confronting the nation.

3[3] **A** ORU exists to serve the whole body of Christ, worldwide.

B To serve the whole body of Christ, worldwide, exists ORU.

4[4] **A** The boys were a more rowdy lot, and no teacher in her right mind would have turned her class over to them.

B They were boys who were such a rowdy lot that no teacher who was in her right mind would have turned her class over to them.

5[5] **A** Leroy was the best athlete, the best whistler, the best horseshoe player, the best marble shooter, the best mumblety-pegger, and the best shoplifter in our neighborhood.

B Leroy was the best athlete, whistler, horseshoe player, marble shooter, mumblety-pegger and shoplifter in our neighborhood.

6[6] **A** The medulla is laid just inside the skull, just above the large hole at the bottom of it.

B The medulla lies just inside the skull, just above the large hole at the bottom of it.

7[7] **A** Edison developed a 100-watt carbon-filament lamp having an efficiency of 1.61 p.w. and a life of 600 hours.

B A 100-watt carbon-filament lamp having an efficiency of 1.61 p.w. and a life of 600 hours was developed by Edison.

8[8] **A** Presidents Roosevelt and Johnson were good examples of articulate speech and using plain language to get their ideas across to the American public.

B Presidents Roosevelt and Johnson were articulate speakers who used plain language to get their ideas across to the American public.

9⁹ A A curious choice for a starring role in Disney's bright, upbeat world Mickey Mouse may have seemed at first.

B At first glance Mickey Mouse may have seemed a curious choice for a starring role in Disney's bright, upbeat world.

10¹⁰ A Teachers accept the concept of the whole child; this concept includes the child's social immaturities, his feelings of inadequacy, his anger, his joy and his exuberance, which must be dealt with.

B Teachers accept the concept of the whole child, but they are not ready to deal with the child's social immaturities, his feelings of inadequacy, his anger, his joy and his exuberance.

11¹¹ A When Father Cassidy drew back the shutter of the confessional, he surprised the appearance of the girl at the other side of the grille.

B When Father Cassidy drew back the shutter of the confessional, he was a little surprised at the appearance of the girl at the other side of the grille.

12¹² A Before the rich man was a fish casserole, baked in a cream sauce and garnished with parsley.

B There was a casserole in front of the man who was rich; it was a fish casserole, baked in a sauce of cream, and garnished with parsley.

13¹³ A A star crept out from among the overhanging grasses as the time passed.

B As the time passed, a star crept out from among the overhanging grasses.

14¹⁴ A He had come to avoid a scandal, to make plain the danger, and to offer the truth.

B He had come not to make a scandal but to avoid it; not to raise a danger but to make one plain; not to oppose a truth but to offer it.

15¹⁵ A Sex can be an exaggeration to a point where it becomes dull.

B Sex can be exaggerated to a point where it becomes dull.

16¹⁶ A You should report any lost keys at once to the head resident.

B Any lost keys should be reported by you at once to the head resident.

17¹⁷ A Of the four, Peanuts, who was the quiet one, was living in a land of silence.

B Of the four, Peanuts was the quiet one, living in a land of silence.

18¹⁸ A All week long I lived for the blessed sound which was the dismissal gong at three o'clock on Friday afternoons.

B All week long I lived for the blessed sound of the dismissal gong at three o'clock on Friday afternoons.

19[19] *A* Denied political freedom and economic capability, a man can accomplish little in his home or community.

B A man can accomplish little in his home or his community denied political freedom and economic capability.

20[20] *A* She demanded from those who surrounded her a rigid precision in details and being preternaturally quick in detecting the slightest deviation from the rules which she laid down.

B She demanded from those who surrounded her a rigid precision in details, and she was preternaturally quick in detecting the slightest deviation from the rules which she laid down.

21[21] *A* More than the traditionally enumerated five senses are the way man knows his world.

B Man knows his world through more senses than the five that are traditionally enumerated.

22[22] *A* A dog is an animal of much greater intelligence than a chick, and in Pavlov's laboratory, dogs require long series of repeated experiences for learning to relate certain perceptual signals to the imminence of food.

B A dog is an animal of much greater intelligence than a chick, and yet in Pavlov's laboratory, dogs require long series of repeated experiences for learning to relate certain perceptual signals to the imminence of food.

23[23] *A* With her marriage, Tehani seemed to take on a new dignity and seriousness, though in the privacy of our home, which had a thatched roof, she showed at times that she was still the same wild tomboy who had beaten me at swimming at Matavai.

B With her marriage, Tehani seemed to take on a new dignity and seriousness, though in the privacy of our home she showed me at times that she was still the same wild tomboy who had beaten me at swimming in Matavai.

24[24] *A* Let us never negotiate out of fear, but let us never fear to negotiate.

B Fear should never be the motivation behind our negotiations and so we should always be brave enough to negotiate.

25[25] *A* The course of the *Mayflower* was now in mid-Atlantic and making steady headway.

B The *Mayflower* was now in mid-Atlantic and making steady headway.

[1] HERBERT R. KOHL, *The Open Classroom*

[2] RICHARD NIXON, *U.S. Foreign Policy for the 1970's, Building for Peace*

[3] ORAL ROBERTS, *ORU Catalogue*, 1973–1974

[4] JAMES MICHENER, *Hawaii*

[5] ED LUDWIG and JAMES SONTIBANE, *The Chicanos*

[6] GUSTAV ECKSTEIN, *The Body Has a Head*

[7] "Lighting," *Encyclopaedia Britannica*

[8] GEORGE A. HOUGH, *News Writing*

[9] ANTHONY LUCAS, "The Alternative Life-Style of Playboys and Playmates," *New York Times Magazine*, 11 June 1972

[10] DON DINKMEYER, *Understanding Self and Others*

[11] FRANK O'CONNOR, "News for the Church"

[12] CARSON MC CULLERS, "The Jockey"

[13] RICHARD ADAMS, *Watership Down*

[14] GIORGIO DE SANTILLANA, *The Crime of Galileo*

[15] EDWARD FORD, *Why Marriage?*

[16] *CMU Residence Hall Handbook*, 1975

[17] THOMAS THOMPSON, *Richie*

[18] ALFRED KAZIN, *A Walker in the City*

[19] JOSEPH R. BRANDT, *Why Black Power?*

[20] LYTTON STRACHEY, *Queen Victoria*

[21] ROBERT WHITMAN, *Understanding the Behavior of Organisms*

[22] ARTHUR KOESTLER, *The Act of Creation*

[23] CHARLES NORDHOFF and JAMES NORMAN HALL, *Mutiny on the Bounty*

[24] JOHN F. KENNEDY, Inaugural address, 20 Jan. 1961

[25] GEORGE F. WILLISON, *Saints and Strangers*

The difference between the almost right word and the right word is really a large matter—'tis the difference between the lightning-bug and the lightning.

MARK TWAIN, *The Art of Authorship*

No two words in English have exactly the same meaning; no two words carry exactly the same ideas or attitudes or values. For the writer this means choosing exactly the right word for any situation. Like everything else in writing, choosing words means considering your audience, knowing the effect you want to make, understanding the words you might use. In short, word choice is directly related to a writer's purpose. An effective writer must consider all the shades of meaning and subtleties of context our language has to offer.

CONNOTATION AND DENOTATION

Words do not automatically "mean" what the dictionary says. There are two kinds of meaning: connotation and denotation. When people ask for the "definition" of a word, they are usually asking for the denotation of the word: its generally accepted meaning. Words do not fall out of heaven, with definitions attached to them. The dictionary maker must do what you and I would do upon encountering a new word—see how people use it and then *deduce* its meaning. Thus the denotation of a word becomes a generalization, the *general* definition of the word. The denotation of "sear" for example, is "to cause to wither or dry," or in some cases "to burn or scorch," as when we sear meat to trap the juices inside. It is this general definition that we all more or less agree to, and we say that the word "sear" denotes (means) to dry, parch, or burn.

However, our language is old, and many words have long histories. Words change over the course of time. They pick up "extra" meanings, or they acquire particular associations. Very often words acquire emotional or attitudinal labels (some words are "bad" and some are "good"). These additional meanings and associations, connotations, can cause problems for writers. Non-English speakers have particular difficulty with the connotations of words. For example, we can accept "sear the meat," "sear the cloth with the iron," "the sun will sear the flowers," and even "her kisses will sear his lips!" But most native speakers of English will not accept "sear the wood in the fireplace," "sear the garbage," nor "fell and seared my knee," though in every case the meaning "to burn" is intended. We don't use "sear" that way. Historically, the word has come to be used in some contexts and not in others, so we say that the word *denotes* burning and scorching perhaps, but it *connotes* the effect of heat on moisture, and our use of the word is more or less limited to that concept. (When we speak of a "searing pain" we have in mind the kind of pain caused by touching a hot stove: scorched flesh.)

Thus, knowing the denotation of a word is usually not enough; you need to be aware of its connotations as well to avoid the kind of language error involved in an old story about the first translating computer, which, when translating the English "Out of sight, out of mind" into Chinese, came up with "Absent idiot." A good place to begin this kind of analysis of language is in your dictionary.

USING THE DICTIONARY

In order to make effective word choices, you need a thorough understanding of at least one good dictionary. Since dictionaries vary considerably, it may be worth your while to become familiar with several. A little investigation will reveal that there is much more to most dictionaries than definitions of words. The dictionary can provide an astonishing amount of information if you know how to use it. For example, *Webster's New Collegiate Dictionary*, in addition to the definitions of words, contains a detailed explanatory chart to show what all the parts of the definitions mean; additional notes that explain each element of the entries (pronunciation, spelling, usage, and so on); a brief essay on the English language and its history by W. Nelson Francis; a list of abbreviations and pronunciation symbols used in the dictionary; a long list of biographical names (famous and important people); an equally long list of geographical names; an exhaustive list of the names and addresses of colleges and universities in English-speaking North America; a list of signs and symbols; and even a handbook of style. Thus the writer can have a small encyclopedia of useful information in a good dictionary.

READING THE ENTRIES

The entry for "choreography" shows a number of features of the dictionary:

cho·re·og·ra·phy \\ˌkōr-ē-ˈäg-rə-fē, ˌkȯr-\\ *n, pl* **-phies** [F *chorégraphie,* fr. Gk *choreia* + F *-graphie* -graphy] **1** : the art of symbolically representing dancing **2** : stage dancing as distinguished from social or ballroom dancing **3 a** : the composition and arrangement of dances esp. for ballet **b** : a composition created by this art — **cho·reo·graph·ic** \\ˌkōr-ē-ə-ˈgraf-ik, ˌkȯr\\ *adj* — **cho·reo·graph·i·cal·ly** \\-i-k(ə)lē\\ *adv*

Note that the word is given with dots between the syllables (for the purpose of word division). It is followed by a guide to pronunciation with a secondary accent on the first syllable and a primary accent on the third. The vowel chart at the bottom of the page explains the umlaut (ä) and the schwa (ə). Note that the first syllable is pronounced with either a long *o* (kōr) or an *aw* sound (kȯr). In this dictionary, variant pronunciations are equally valid unless specifically marked otherwise. Note that the syllabication marked with dots does not exactly correspond to the divisions of pronunciation marked with hyphens (see Word Division in Chapter 11).

Following the pronunciation guide is the part of speech *n* (noun) and the spelling of the plural. In this dictionary, plural forms are not usually given unless the plural requires some change in the root word; in "choreography," *y* changes to *i*.

The etymology of the word (history of its development) is given in reverse order. The immediate ancestor of "choreography" is the French word "chorégraphie," which is itself formed from the Greek word "choreia" (dance) and the French "-graphie" (write). The word has its origin, then, in the two concepts, dancing and writing.

The dictionary shows three meanings for this word. They are given in order of development; that is, the oldest meaning is given first. And you can see from this that "choreography" originally referred to pictures or diagrams of dances. The third meaning has two submeanings, marked *a* and *b,* relating to either the art of composing or the composition of a dance.

Last, the dictionary gives an adjective and an adverb form for this word, and the pronunciations of each of them.

Other entries show various other kinds of information about words. For example:

civ·il \ 'siv-əl\ *adj* [ME, fr. MF, fr. L *civilis,* fr. *civis*]   1 a : of or relating to citizens <~liberties>   b : of or relating to the state or its citizenry   2 a : CIVILIZED <~society>   b : adequate in courtesy and politeness : MANNERLY   3 a : of, relating to, or based on civil law   b : relating to private rights and to remedies sought by action or suit distinct from criminal proceedings   c : established by law   4 *of time* : based on the mean sun and legally recognized for use in ordinary affairs   5 : of, relating to, or involving the general public, their activities, needs, or ways, or civic affairs as distinguished from special (as military or religious) affairs

syn CIVIL, POLITE, COURTEOUS, GALLANT, CHIVALROUS *shared meaning element* : observant of the forms required by good breeding. CIVIL is feeble in force, often suggesting little more than avoidance of overt rudeness. POLITE is more positive and commonly implies polish of manners and address more than warmth and cordiality <the cultured, precise tone, *polite* but faintly superior — William Styron> COURTEOUS implies an actively considerate and sometimes rather stately politeness <listened with *courteous* attention> *Gallant* and *chivalrous* imply courteous attentiveness esp. to women but GALLANT is likely to suggest dashing behavior and ornate expression <ever ready with *gallant* remarks of admiration> while CHIVALROUS tends to suggest high-minded and disinterested attentions <felt at once *chivalrous* and paternal to the lost girl> *ant* uncivil, rude

Note the context aids for this word <~ liberties> and <~ society>. Note too the presentation and discussion of synonyms. Here all the synonyms more or less "denote" the shared meaning element: "observant of the forms required by good breeding." But notice too the connotative explanations provided for each of them. The context aid <the cultured, precise tone, *polite* but faintly superior—William Styron> indicates a quote from the author Styron. Note the antonyms at the end of the entry.

If you have a good college dictionary and understand how to use it, you can improve the quality of your diction. This does not mean finding "fancier" words but rather the words best suited to what you are trying to say. As a general rule, it is a mistake to ransack the dictionary for new words; a writer needs to be thoroughly familiar with a word before using it in a composition. This kind of familiarity is gained from reading, or hearing the word used, in context. You're likely to find that you use the dictionary most often to help you avoid some of the problems that writers face with word choices.

USING WORDS

Most readers would surely agree that clear, concise, and accurate language is the preferred style for semiformal or formal writing, but even these simple guidelines must be interpreted in the light of an author's purpose. A letter to the President of the United States should not be written in street slang. On the other hand, there may be times when street slang is the most effective language to use. The true guide, then, seems to be that the best language is whatever is appropriate and effective for an author's purpose.

In the following sections, we discuss some stylistic problems good writers avoid and some options you may wish to incorporate into your writing. By comparing well-written sentences to poorly written ones, you will begin to develop a sense of the kinds of choices skilled writers make.

To help you develop a writer's sensitivity to words, sentences are presented in pairs throughout this chapter. Sentence *A* in any pair demonstrates good writing, usually by a professional writer. Sentence *B*, on the other hand, is less accurate, less concise, or just less clear than *A*.

ABSTRACTIONS

"Abstract" means removed from physical reality; it refers to qualities and ideas. Abstractions are necessary and worthwhile aspects of language; they carry our intellectual concepts. Few writers can do without them entirely, but to write only in the abstract, without tying ideas to concrete reality now and then, bores and frustrates the reader. Abstractions can also contribute to dishonesty in writing, as for example when a salesperson claims to want to discuss your "insurance needs" but actually wants to sell you a policy.

In the following pairs, why is the more concrete original better than the abstract sentence? Or why would the second sentence be less effective in the context for which *A* was written?

A People are licensed to drive cars, and should be licensed to possess firearms.
Towne Courier, 24 Sept. 1975

B That a governmental agency should exercise regulatory influence over private transportation is analogous to the same extension of power over private possession of weaponry.

A Anyone who can live on welfare should be courted by Wall Street.
JOANNA CLARK, "Motherhood," in Judith Carnoy and Marc Weiss, *A House Divided*

B There need be no more effective demonstration of financial competency than successful self-maintenance on government benefits and compensation.

CLICHÉ

A cliché is a worn-out word or phrase, some expression so familiar that it no longer has any force: "She's as pretty as a picture, as smart as a whip, as cute as a button," and so on. These tired old expressions are poor substitutes for more forceful, direct ways of saying things.

In what ways are the *A* sentences more effective than the *B* sentences? What would be the effect of replacing *A* with *B*?

A It's tiresome as hell to lose, but I still enjoy the game.
"Limping for Life," *Time*, 11 Nov. 1975

B It's not whether you win or lose, it's how you play the game that matters.

A Her answer was short but accurate.
LEN BRAVELL

B Her answer was short but hit the nail on the head.

CONFUSING NEGATIVES

Avoid the double negative (I don't have none). Any time a sentence contains more than one negative, there is likely to be confusion: "It is by no means not shameful not to stand up to a bully!" "They didn't realize that they were not the ones who wouldn't be going!" For clarity, these should be made into positive statements. Do each of the negatives in the following pairs mean the same thing? Why is *A* preferable to *B*?

A We cannot directly observe what happened in the past.
THOMAS C. PATTERSON, *America's Past: A New World Archeology*

B There is no reason not to suppose that we cannot directly observe what happened in the past.

A Initially, I assume that any physician I go to will teach me as much about my health as my garage mechanic teaches me about my car.
MANUEL J. SMITH, *When I Say No, I Feel Guilty*

B Initially, I never fail to assume that any physician I go to will not refrain from teaching me any less about my health than my garage mechanic teaches me about my car.

EFFECTIVE MODIFIERS

Not every sentence requires modifiers, but when you do use modifiers, you will gain clarity and accuracy by choosing carefully. It is not just more "interesting," it is more accurate to describe things with the most specific modifiers. In the following sentences, try to determine what the *A* sentence gains through modifiers that the other sentence lacks. Why wouldn't *B* work as well in the same context as *A*?

A The fish turned, banking as smoothly as an airplane, and followed the receding sound.
PETER BENCHLEY, *Jaws*

B The fish turned in an even movement and followed the sound that was growing dim.

A A night watchman adopted a tiny orange-and-white kitten he had found lying exhausted and half starved on an onion bag.
JEAN BURDEN, *Woman's Day*, 1975

B A watchman adopted a small parti-colored kitten he had found lying tired and hungry on a vegetable bag.

EFFECTIVE NOUNS

Searching for the right word is the mark of a skilled writer. The right word is the one that is most specific for your meaning; given the context of why you are writing, who you are writing to and what you are writing about, any word ought to be selected because it is the clearest, most concise, most accurate word. Students sometimes hunt through dictionaries to come up with a *new* word for a familiar concept, but this can be dangerous if the word has subtle connotations. Whether you find them in a book or dredge them up from your memory, good nouns can powerfully influence your writing. Why are the nouns in *A* better in the following? What would you lose if you substituted *B* in the context of *A*?

A It was like a furnace outside, with the sunlight splintering into flakes of fire on the sand and sea.
ALBERT CAMUS, *The Stranger*

B It was like a griddle outside, with the light splintering into shiny places on the ground and water.

A To emphasize his point, Dr. Straith even included a photograph of the interior of his car showing the padding he had installed.
ROBERT CIRINO, *Don't Blame the People*

B To emphasize his notion, Dr. Straith even included a picture of the interior of his own automobile showing the stuff that he had installed.

A The Russians were on the edge of Hungary.
WINSTON CHURCHILL, *Triumph and Tragedy*

B The Russians were on the verge of Hungary.

EFFECTIVE VERBS

While some textbooks advise beginning writers to select "colorful" or "vivid" verbs, keep in mind that *accuracy* is the best guideline. "She passed out" may be more vivid than "she fainted," but the difference between the verbs in those phrases isn't just a matter of degree. The danger of overstatement often accompanies such efforts to be colorful. Thus a hunting paper may speak of "blasting to bits" when, in fact, the less vivid "shooting" may be more accurate. Nevertheless, most readers prefer vivid verbs, so you should try for the most vivid *and* the most accurate language. Why are the verbs better in the *A* sentences below? What would be the effect of writing *B* in place of *A*?

A Inside the plane, the handful of boys who were able tried to prize away the seats which trapped so many of the wounded.
PIERS PAUL READ, *Alive*

B Inside the plane, the handful of boys who were able took a shot at getting up the seats which held so many of the wounded.

A Horses clopped along, shuffling up dust.
RAY BRADBURY, *The Martian Chronicles*

B Horses moved along, lifting up dust.

A William now directed his archers to shoot high into the air, so that the arrows would fall behind the shield wall, and one of these pierced Harold in the right eye, inflicting a mortal wound.
WINSTON CHURCHILL, *A History of the English Speaking Peoples: The Birth of Britain*

B William now gave it to be known that his archers should make their arrows go high into the air, so that the arrows would be right behind the shield wall, and one of these went into Harold's right eye and gave him a mortal wound.

Note that the forms of "to be" (am, is, are, was, were, be, being, been) are the weakest verbs of all.

EMOTIONAL LANGUAGE

Emotional language reveals that a writer's feelings have gained too much control. Instead of calm and objective reporting, the reader finds name calling, exaggeration, and unfair and unreasonable language abuse. Such emotionalism may be intentional in satiric or polemic writing, but for most nonfiction writing more objective language is preferred. What would be the effect of writing *B* in place of *A* in the following pairs?

A The market place will tend to pay women less than men as long as wives give priority to their husbands' jobs.
GEORGE E. GILDER, *Sexual Suicide*

B The market place will tend to pay women less than men as long as wives kowtow to their lord-and-masters' jobs.

A This sort of financial legerdemain clearly showed that tricky minds were at work on this project in order to avoid legislative consideration of it at all, and public review and understanding.
FERDINAND LUNDBERG, *The Rockefeller Syndrome*

B This sort of financial flim-flammery clearly showed that evil and vicious minds were at work on this project in order to tie the legislature in red tape and bamboozle the public.

EUPHEMISM

Using pleasant words, or inoffensive ones, to cover hard truths is generally considered evasive writing. There are legitimate uses for euphemism (when trying to spare someone's feelings perhaps), but in general, authors avoid them. Common euphemisms, such as "pass on" for "die," are easy to spot because they have obvious plain English equivalents. What is the effect of substituting the euphemism for the more direct original in each of the following?

A You see, sir, we spent those two hours telling dirty jokes.
MURRAY LEINSTER, "First Contact," *Science Fiction Hall of Fame*

B You see, sir, we spent those two hours telling ribald stories.

A Many men decided that laws forbidding introduction of African slaves were unjust to newly settled areas; a few, believing the laws unconstitutional or not legally enforceable, determined to violate them.
TOM HENDERSON WELL, *The Slave Ship Wanderer*

B Many men decided that laws forbidding introduction of African labor were unjust to newly settled areas; a few, believing the laws were lacking in the force of law, determined to test them.

FIGURES OF SPEECH

A figure of speech should be fresh, clear, and should make an image for the reader. The purpose of the figure of speech is to create a picture, to make an idea clear and forceful through comparison. An effective figure pleases the reader, brings the "well said" reaction. Writers must judge whether their images will work for the reader. "She's as graceful as a squirrel," for example, would probably fail. The squirrel may be graceful to some, but to most people it is a symbol of quickness; using it to evoke gracefulness may not work very well. Does the following figure work for you? "The sun came up in the morning like a huge grapefruit."

METAPHOR

A metaphor makes an implied comparison, as in this description of tuna:

Powerful torpedoes of shining silver and steel, with perfect proportions and streamlined shape, they had only to move one or two fins slightly to set their 150 to 200 pounds gliding about in the water with consummate grace.
THOR HEYERDAHL, *Kon-Tiki*

SIMILE

An expressed comparison, a simile uses the words "like" or "as."

The train was curving the mountain, the engine loping like a great black hound, parallel with its last careening cars, panting forth its pale white vapor as it hurled us even higher.
RALPH ELLISON, *The Invisible Man*

PERSONIFICATION

In this form of comparison, some object or animal is given human qualities.

An occasional timid horn squeaked off in the distance.
JACQUELINE SUSANN, *Once Is Not Enough*

MIXED METAPHORS

These metaphoric comparisons are illogical or inconsistent; the writer mixes more than one idea into an image.

The lightning stabbed at the ground with long tentacles of light.
JOHN TUTTLE

DEAD METAPHORS

These metaphors have become part of the language and are no longer considered figures of speech. Too many of them make your writing trite. They can sometimes create accidental humor:

You have to wear heavy shoes on the foot of the mountain.

In the following pairs, the original contains an effective figure of speech. What does the *B* sentence in each pair lose by comparison?

A Then the lids opened, revealing pale pools of blue vagueness that finally solidified into points that froze upon the vet, who looked down unsmilingly.
RALPH ELLISON, *The Invisible Man*

B Then the lids opened, revealing pale pools of blue vagueness that finally cleared into horizons that hung over the vet, who looked down unsmilingly.

A She would look for dark spots in his character and drill away at them as relentlessly as a dentist at a cavity.
MARY MCCARTHY, *Cruel and Barbarous Treatment*

B She would analyze his character for any evidence of weakness and finding any, would exploit them without regard for his discomfort.

A She wore her hair in two braids wound tight around her head like pale silk ropes.
PAUL DARCY BOLES, "The House Guest," *Seventeen*, Oct. 1975

B She wore her hair in two braids wound tight around her head like pale silk strings.

A The rising moon was beginning to light up the eastern sky with a pale, milky glow.
ARTHUR C. CLARKE, *Childhood's End*

B The rising moon was beginning to light up the eastern sky with a pale, ermine glow.

JARGON

Jargon covers all specialized vocabulary and terminology, but it very often means overdone or unnecessary technical language. Most readers would call the following *necessary* jargon; it is very difficult to express this idea in simpler words.

The photons which strike a crystal on the stage of a light microscope do not alter the crystal's position.
A. TRUMAN SCHWARTZ, *Chemistry: Imagination and Implication*

Why is the technical language in the following pairs jargon? Why is the *A* sentence better?

A By two months of age, the average child will smile at the sight of his mother's face.
ATKINSON AND HILGARD, *Introduction to Psychology*

B By two months of age, the child at the developmental median will smile at his maternal parent's face.

A I followed a simple plan. I studied what the public schools and teachers do and did the opposite.
LESTER VELIE, "Give Us This Day Our ABC's," *Reader's Digest*, Aug. 1975

B The development of my educational innovation was founded on the simple expedient of inverting the prevailing curricular design and pedagogy of the public schools and teachers.

NEOLOGISMS

Inventing new words is one of the privileges of those who write, but there is no point to creating new words when old ones will serve as well. In general, most readers expect a new word to achieve something that old words do not. In this example—"The team's attackage strength was low"—"attackage" isn't an improvement over existing words such as "attack" or "offensive": it adds nothing to the concept.

Are the neologisms in the following pairs an improvement over the original words? Could you substitute the *B* sentence for the *A* sentence? What would be the effect of substituting the *B* sentence for the *A* sentence?

A The great smooth trunks stood motionless in their green shade, the branches spreading flat, one above the other in crisp, light dappled tiers.
RICHARD ADAMS, *Watership Down*

B The great smooth trunks stood motionless in their green shade, the branches spreading flat, one above the other in crisp, light besquinched tiers.

A She held out her hands to him and he kissed her.
PAT FRANK, *Alas Babylon*

B She held out her hands to him and he lipped her.

A Although skier injuries have been on the decline in recent years, one statistic hasn't changed: the incidence of heart failure on the hill.
Ski, Sept. 1975

B Although skier injuries have been on the decline in recent years, one statistic hasn't changed: the incidence of death on the hill heart-failurewise.

OVERSTATEMENT

Using excessive or unnecessary intensifiers, exaggerating, or over-dramatizing with language strikes most readers as amateurish. For example: "The *worst* day of my life was the day Buffy Allen discovered I had been seeing her steady! I was just *devastated* when she found out!" This writer is trying to make a relatively unimportant event sound more important than it could possibly be.

Some intensifiers to use with restraint

basically, certainly, definitely, incredibly, intensely, perfectly, unbearably, totally, positively, absolutely, passionately, quite, really, simply, very

Some dramatic modifiers to use with caution

fantastic, terrific, sensational, fabulous, awful, horrible, horrid, terrible, unbelievable, incredible, stupendous, gigantic

What does overstatement do to reader reaction in the following sentences?

A The small plane flew over square fields, all of them flooded—it had been raining here recently.
SVETLANA ALLILUYEVA, *Only One Year*

B The darling little plane zoomed back and forth over the ever so neatly square fields, all of them terribly flooded—it had actually been raining here quite recently.

A When we look at the stars, we see them arranged in the form of geometrical figures—lines, semicircles, triangles, squares.
ROBERT S. RICHARDSON, *The Fascinating World of Astronomy*

B When we really look at the stars, we definitely see them arranged in the form of perfect geometrical figures—lines, semicircles, triangles, squares.

SWITCHING TENSE

Writers may write in any tense that suits their purpose; the rule is to be consistent. Write in the present tense or in the past, but not both. Present tense is very difficult to manage (the writer must somehow account for the fact that words appear on the page while, for example, "I am running for my life"). For semiformal or formal writing, you would do well to write in the past tense only. What is the effect of the tense shift in the following?

A He lived then in a home which, though cheap and unfashionable, possessed its picturesque distinction.
REBECCA WEST, *The New Meaning of Treason*

B He lived then in a home which, though cheap and unfashionable, possesses its picturesque distinction.

A She'd attached herself to Fred the moment he arrived at the party and saw to it that his glass was filled with punch whenever it was even a quarter empty.
JOHI MAURA AND JACKIE SUTHERLAND, *If It Moves, Kiss It*

B She'd attached herself to Fred the moment he arrives at the party and sees to it that his glass is filled with punch whenever it is even a quarter empty.

SWITCHING VOICE

SWITCHING FROM PERSONAL TO IMPERSONAL

The rule is to be consistent. Switching from personal "I" to impersonal "one," for no apparent reason, sounds as though the writer has forgotten who he/she is. What is the effect of the voice shift in the following?

A When I came back, she had the pillow off her head all right—I knew she would—but she wouldn't look at me, even though she was laying on her back.
J. D. SALINGER, *The Catcher in the Rye*

B When I came back, she had the pillow off her head all right—one could have predicted it—but she still wouldn't look at me, even though she was laying on her back.

A Later that evening, I walked through a hotelroom door and there they were—all lazing around drinking up the evening's profits, laughing and jiving with the assembled multitudes and being generally happy . . . .
BEN EDWARDS, "Bastard Children of Gordon Sinclair," *Creem*, April 1974

B Later that evening, one walked through a hotelroom door and there they were—all lazing around drinking up the evening's profits, laughing and jiving with the assembled multitudes and being generally happy . . . .

The same fault sounds equally inconsistent the other way around—switching from impersonal "one" to personal "I"; some readers feel "one" is too impersonal and vague to be used at all. To avoid the choice between "I" and "one," writers sometimes substitute the editorial "we" or the all-purpose "you":

The change, we may notice, had to be made by the state.
C. B. MACPHERSON, *The Real World of Democracy*

If your credit card is only good for charging things, it's only half a card.
Advertisement, *Time*, Sept. 1975

Other voices include the *invisible writer:* "The experiment was conducted under difficult conditions" (by a phantom?); and the *masked writer:* "This researcher believes the evidence will show . . ." "This reporter was present when . . ." "The present writer is of the opinion . . . ."

Each of these voices has its uses as long as the writer is consistent in presenting that voice. What voice you use depends on what and to whom you are writing. The question of voice is closely related to the degree of formality of your writing.

SWITCHING FROM FORMAL TO INFORMAL

In the following pairs, consider the effect of the switch from formal to informal or from informal to formal:

A The prospect of being left alone with the young man seemed suddenly unendurable.
MARY MCCARTHY, *Cruel and Barbarous Treatment*

B The prospect of being left alone with the young man seemed all of a sudden like a bummer.

A I pictured a noisy all-night blast . . . a lot of drinking and tons of drunken conversation.
ROBERT H. RIMMER, *The Harrad Experiment*

B I pictured a noisy all-night blast . . . a lot of drinking and inordinate amounts of inebriated discourse.

CHOOSING A STANCE

"Stance" refers to the author's point of view, a complex of attitudes toward self, subject, and audience (see Chapter 1). The author may be serious, humorous, sarcastic, and so forth; personal or impersonal; formal or informal. The range of stances in English is very broad. It covers everything from the hip, cool, half-secret lingo of the streets to the difficult, technical, half-secret jargon of scholarly writing. For most writers, the best stance is somewhere in the middle between too personal and too impersonal, too formal and too informal. Whatever level you choose, your reader will expect you to stick with it. Switching back and forth is a fault except when done deliberately for humor or irony.

Why might a writer choose one stance over another? You will be able to answer that question for yourself if you can determine what each of the following writers achieves with stance:

A writer choosing the most formal English

Russian physiologists, including Lebeden, have emphasized an inter-active relationship with visceral pathology and cortical centers.
JAMES C. COLMAN, *Abnormal Psychology and Modern Life*

A writer choosing informal English

The boomerang is a neat weapon for streetfighting and is as easy to master as a Frisbee.
ABBIE HOFFMAN, *Steal This Book*

A writer choosing a middle level, on the formal side

British colonial rule varied greatly from colony to colony, partly de-pending on the interest of Europeans in settlement.
R. HARPER AND T. SCHMUDDE, *Between Two Worlds*

A writer choosing a middle level, on the informal side

Quite frankly, we don't know what is happening in the so-called Bermuda Triangle.
ADI-KENT THOMAS JEFFREY, *The Bermuda Triangle*

A writer deliberately mixing diction

If the other parts of the books aren't so great, here's where the real value lies—every picture tells a story, don't it?
TONY GLOVER, *Creem*, Sept. 1972

UNCONSCIOUS ECHOES

People who "read with their ears" often pick up things that others miss, such as the jingle-jangle noise of unconscious rhymes and alliterations and other echoes. Why is unconscious echo irritating in the following *B* sentences?

A The payroll data are prepared on punched cards each week for each employee.
DONALD H. SANDERS, *Computers in Society*

B The payroll plans are prepared on punched cards each pay period for each person.

A His arm is still sound; it is the Namath knees that are gone.
"Limping for Life," *Time*, 24 Nov. 1975

B His arm is still sound; it is the Namath knees that are bound.

UNDERSTATEMENT

Understatement is the fine art of restraint in language. The good writer knows when to restrain the impulse to hammer home a point. The more the point seems worthy of heavy emphasis, the more it achieves by understatement. A famous example is attributed to Mark Twain: "The reports of my death have been much exaggerated."

What does the understated sentence achieve in each of the following pairs? What is the effect of sentence *B*?

A When she heard Paula's car rattle and pop out back, she closed the book she hadn't really been reading and darted joyfully toward the door.
ARTHUR LAURENTS, *The Way We Were*

B She had been trying to read, though she was really too anxious to concentrate, and when she heard Paula's car rattle to a stop out back, she closed the book and darted joyfully toward the door.

A Mumbles taught us to drive in a '65 Nova which had only two options—an AM radio and an overflowing ashtray.
"Drive He Said," *CM Life*, 12 Nov. 1975

B Mumbles taught us to drive in a '65 Nova which was pretty much stripped down to bare necessities and showed its use.

WORD PLAY

In informal essays and personal-experience stories, you may have the opportunity to play with words. A cleverly turned phrase can often be highly effective—as the world of advertising has discovered. Explain the play on words in the following. What does the *A* sentence achieve that the version in *B* does not?

A Try the light, smooth whiskey that's becoming America's favorite Canadian.
Advertisement, *Time*, 22 Sept. 1975

B Try the light, smooth whiskey that's becoming America's favorite import from Canada.

A Not long ago, most people dismissed vegetarians as weird people who just drank juice and ate nuts, but now, no-meat cookbooks are selling very well and vegetation restaurants are sprouting up all over.

CLAIRE HENDRICKS

B Not long ago, most people dismissed vegetarians as weird people who just drank juice and ate nuts, but now, no-meat cookbooks are selling very well and vegetarian restaurants are opening for business all over.

Diction evaluation practice

In each of the following pairs, one sentence is thought to be better than the other in some aspect of diction. Which is the better sentence?

1[1] **A** The hoses were attached at water pipes that stood out of the brick bases of the houses.

B The hoses were attached at spigots that stood out of the brick foundations of the houses.

2[2] **A** He was placed in a drunk tank with two other men, neither of whom he has ever seen before in his life.

B He was placed in a drunk tank with two other men, neither of whom he had ever seen before in his life.

3[3] **A** A district's sports programs may be ripe for a penalty call from the courts if those programs deny participation to an individual because of dress or hair styles, marital status, or sex.

B It is possible that judicial intercession may be required where there is a conflict between the requirements of athletic activities and the civil liberties of participants.

4[4] **A** I don't suppose anybody ever deliberately attunes a watch or a clock.

B I don't suppose anybody ever deliberately listens to a watch or a clock.

5[5] **A** It's really happening, Serpico thought, and identified himself as a police officer.

B It's really happening, Serpico thought, and nommed himself as a police officer.

6[6] **A** That spring when I had a great deal of potential and no money at all, I took a job as a janitor.

B That spring when I had a great deal of potential and was living from hand to mouth, I took a job as a janitor.

7[7] **A** Those who own the land shall govern it.

B Government is the prerogative of ownership.

8[8] A She pulled on her overshoes, wrapped a large tartan shawl around her, put on a man's felt hat, and ventured out along the causeways of the first yard.

B She put on her overshoes, put a large tartan shawl around her, put on a man's felt hat, and went out along the causeways of the first yard.

9[9] A As soon as the seat-belt sign goes off and people began to move about the cabin, I glanced around nervously to see who's on board.

B As soon as the seat-belt sign goes off and people begin to move about the cabin, I glance around nervously to see who's on board.

10[10] A We were going to The Cabin when Bernie suddenly doubled over with a cramp.

B We were going to The Cabin when Bernie suddenly doubles over with a cramp.

11[11] A I knew she was guilty; I could feel it in my bones.

B I knew she was guilty; one could feel it in his bones.

12[12] A There's not much better you can call the color of an orange than orange.

B It is likely that the best description available for the color of the orange fruit is simply that which is customarily given it, namely, and simply, orange.

13[13] A He had red hair and a cute face and I couldn't help staring at him.

B He had deep dark red hair falling in waves into a face that was pure elf, and I couldn't do anything but moon after him.

14[14] A As the P.M. walked very slowly to the aircraft there was a grey look on his face that I did not like, and when he came at last to this house he collapsed wearily into the first chair.

B As the P.M. dragged himself to the aircraft, there was a grey look on his face that terrified me, and when he came at last to this house, he keeled over with exhaustion into the first chair.

15[15] A He was laughing, and he took a gulp of whiskey and handed the bottle to Muldoon.

B He was consumed with mirth and permitted himself to imbibe of whiskey and extended the decanter to Muldoon.

16[16] A He got off the trunk and leads the way across the clinking cinders into the dark, and the others follow.

B He got off the trunk and led the way across the clinking cinders up into the dark, and the others followed.

17[17] A The faces blow past in the fog like confetti.

B The faces blow past in the fog like shredlings.

18[18] A Just as ghastly were the illegal tortures, which included smoking the suspect's head in a cylinder, or burning the skin off his torso by winding a soft pewter pipe around it like some great serpentine musical instrument and then pouring boiling water through its convolutions.

B Just as bad were the tortures, which included smoking the person's head or burning the skin off his torso with hot water running through a pipe around his body.

19[19] A Bowling Green was well fortified, and Johnson thought he could hold the place if Buell made a frontal assault, but there was little chance that Buell would do anything so foolish.

B It was certainly true that Bowling Green was a well fortified place, and Johnson was pretty sure that if he had to he could probably hold it if it should happen that Buell would make an assault from the front, but—of course—it was rather unlikely that Buell would do such a thing, since it was so foolish.

20[20] A Her normally peach-blush pink cheeks were blazing-fire red from the early morning wind; her hands were ugly lobster claws as if they had just been burned in harsh chemicals, and she had the foul reek of sheep-dip about her.

B Her normally pink cheeks were polished pippin by the early-morning breeze; her hands were wrinkle-red as if they had just been washed in strong soap, and she smelled of sheep.

21[21] A She would step out of her shoes and kick them into a corner, step out of her flimsy frock and expose her bony legs in their short pink pants and flesh-colored stockings.

B She would step out of her shoes and kick them into a corner, step out of her light as a feather frock, and expose her long bony legs in their pink pants and flesh-colored stockings.

22[22] A She couldn't decide whether she shouldn't go or not.

B She couldn't decide whether she should go.

23[23] A There is little reason not to doubt that your watch is not keeping correct time, that is, correct sun time.

B The chances are excellent that your watch is not keeping correct time, that is, correct sun time.

24[24] A He put a handful of coffee in the pot and was putting a lump of grease out of a can and was making it slide across the hot skillet.

B He put a handful of coffee in the pot and dipped a lump of grease out of a can and slid it sputtering across the skillet.

25[25] *A* Carla was brave as a lion and spoke right up to the Dean.

B Carla was scared but stubborn and spoke right up to the Dean.

1 JAMES AGEE, *A Death in the Family*

2 CARYL CHESSMAN, *Cell 2455 Death Row*

3 DAVID L. MARTIN, "Schoolboy Sports a Bone-Crushing Financial Problem," *Los Angeles Times*, 9 July 1972

4 WILLIAM FAULKNER, *The Sound and the Fury*

5 PETER MAAS, *Serpico*

6 JAMES ALAN MC PHERSON, "Gold Coast"

7 JOHN JAY, in MICHAEL PARENTI, *Democracy for the Few*

8 D. H. LAWRENCE, "The Blind Man"

9 ERICA JONG, *Fear of Flying*

10 SANDRA DROTT

11 KATHY SMITH

12 TONY HARMON

13 JULIE MASTERSON

14 LORD MORAN, "Churchill," taken from *The Diaries of Lord Moran*

15 JOHN O'HARA, *From the Terrace*

16 WILLIAM GOLDING, *Lord of the Flies*

17 KEN KESEY, *One Flew over the Cuckoo's Nest*

18 DENNIS BLOODWORTH, *The Chinese Looking Glass*

19 BRUCE CATTON, *Terrible Swift Sword*

20 ROBERT RUARK, *Uhuru*

21 KATHERINE ANNE PORTER, *Ship of Fools*

22 DONNA BLAIR

23 MICHAEL P. MC INTYRE, *Physical Geography*

24 ERNEST HEMINGWAY, "Big Two-Hearted River"

25 STANLEY YANKLEVITCH

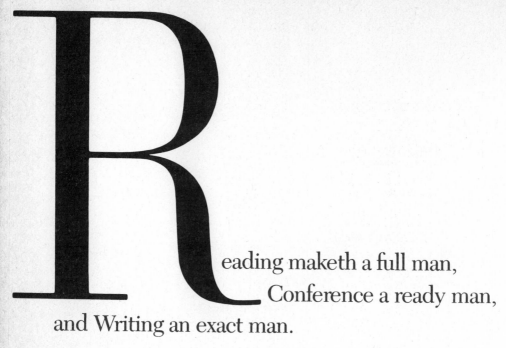

eading maketh a full man,
Conference a ready man,
and Writing an exact man.

FRANCIS BACON, *Of Studies*

The "rules" of English are not really rules at all; they are only customs or conventions. They grew out of the history of the English-speaking peoples. And throughout history these conventions have changed as writers have changed with the times. Today, it is nearly impossible to describe all the varieties of the English language.

You do not need to learn any rules about slang or informal English. Very few people worry about mistakes in informal English. But most educated readers are concerned when they find "mistakes" in formal writing. Therefore, this chapter on usage will help you review those problems that sometimes come up in formal writing.

Formal English is, in general, the language used in printed works today: newspapers, magazines, books, and other writing aimed at the educated public. It is the language of schools, businesses, science, and the professions. Formal English does not mean "fancy" or pretentious language; it means having a standard *form*. It is the language you yourself use when you are conscious of *how* you are writing as well as *what*. If you scribble a telephone message for a roommate, you probably don't care whether your words are precise. But if you take a message for your employer, you may be very conscious of *how* your writing looks. For example, here is a telephone message written in three different styles:

INFORMAL
B call'd, call him back tonite, he's at joans.

FORMAL
Bruce called. Call him back tonight. He is at Joan's.

PRETENTIOUS

Mr. Bruce Watson telephoned while you were absent. He requests that you return his call at your convenience this evening. He is presently visiting at the dormitory of Miss Joan Dawkins.

Your roommate would accept either the formal or the informal message without question. But the pretentious message would very likely cause him or her to assume that you were joking or being stuffy. The pretentious message attempts to be more important than the situation warrants.

The rule of thumb for the usage guidelines in this chapter is not what is "right" according to some arbitrary authority, but what educated readers are accustomed to. Not every authority agrees on just what these expressions are, but this chapter presents the majority opinion on most of the common problems in formal writing.

AGREEMENT

Educated readers expect things to *agree*. Mixing singulars and plurals distracts the reader. In most cases, you just have to remember how many things you are writing about, but you must handle a few cases in agreement with special care.

GROUP WORDS

Words like the following are considered *singular* in form.

the army	the faculty
the band	the generation
the body (of students)	the group
the class	the majority
the company	the minority
the crowd	the part (of the group)
the enemy	the portion

Conventional usage Group words take *singular* verbs and *singular* pronouns:

The company *has its* work to do.

The band *is* playing *its* introduction.

Optional usage Group words *may* be given plural verbs and pronouns if you intend to emphasize the actions of each member of the group. (Many people think this usage sounds unnatural.)

The orchestra *are* tuning *their* instruments.

The class *are* studying *their* books.

CONFUSING SINGULARS

anyone, everyone, no one, one	a man who
a box of, a cup of, a trainload of	none (of these students)
each (student), each of (the students)	the number of (students)
	physics
everybody, nobody, somebody	that she likes milk and pickles
either Jack or Jill, neither Jack nor Jill, either person	two plus six
fifteen miles	Jack as well as Jill
five minus three	Jack together with Jill
ham and eggs	this kind (of apple)
mathematics	that kind (of apple)

Conventional usage These expressions are confusing because they often sound plural—they are frequently followed by a plural phrase—but they are all *singular* and take *singular* verbs and *singular* pronouns.

Each of them *has his* book.

A box of strawberries *is* all she had.

Electronics *is her* major.

Five cents *doesn't* buy much these days.

Special note: gender-specific references The use of masculine pronouns when *both* sexes are referred to or implied is unacceptable in modern writing. For example, when a group of students contains both men and women, "Each student should have *his* work finished on time" can be rephrased "Each student should have *his or her* work finished on time" or "Students should have *their* work finished on time."

Agreement practice 1

Select suitable forms from the choices in parentheses.

1 **Neither of these courses** (have/has) **enough material in** (them/it) **to do you any good.**
LIZ FULTON

2 **One of the pleasantest moments of my life** (was/were) **at a grand gala at the electoral Palace, where I had the honor of walking a**

polonaise with no other than the Margravine of Bayreuth, old Fritz's own sister . . . .

WILLIAM MAKEPEACE THACKERAY, *The Memoirs of Barry Lyndon*

3 They had come thither, not as friends nor partners in the enterprise, but each, save one youthful pair, impelled by (his/their) own selfish and solitary longing for this wondrous gem.

NATHANIEL HAWTHORNE, "The Great Carbuncle"

4 Every individual within the system (has/have) (his/their) unique role, and each role (is/are) different and indispensable.

DON ROOTE

5 Neither Senator Thomas Hart Benton nor Sam Huston (was/were) dwarfed by the towering reputation of (his/their) three colleagues.

JOHN F. KENNEDY, *Profiles in Courage*

6 Twenty dollars (is/are) a lot of money for a textbook.

VIRGINIA HOWELL

7 "It is required of every man," the Ghost returned, "that the spirit within (him/them) should walk abroad among (his/their) fellowmen, and travel far and wide; and if that spirit goes not forth in life, (they/it) (is/are) condemned to do so after death."

CHARLES DICKENS, *A Christmas Carol*

8 Neither the rain nor the cold (was/were) going to keep me from that party at the lake.

IRENE ABLER

9 Practically everybody who (has/have) found the place, after the switch to Stinson Beach, (is/are) far enough into the thing to know what the "acid" in the Acid Test means.

TOM WOLFE, *The Electric Kool-Aid Acid Test*

10 Anyone coming into the basement for the first time would have thought (himself/themselves) in a den of maniacs.

GEORGE ORWELL, *Down and Out in Paris and London*

CONFUSING PLURALS

Words and phrases like the following are considered *plural* in form:

both the girls and the boys	neither the girls nor the boys
both (men), both of (the men)	a number of (students)
the boys as well as the girls	one of those who (study), one of those girls who (study)
either the boys or the girls	
eleven assignments	these kinds (of apples)
girls and boys	those kinds (of apples)
Jack and Jill	those days, those years, the years
men who, men and women who, people who, those who	two sixes (2 × 6)

Expressions like these are all *plural* and take *plural* verbs and *plural* pronouns.

An odd number of girls *have their* books.

She is one of those girls who *have their* books.

Neither the girls nor the boys *are* ready.

These kinds of apples *are* good.

Agreement practice 2

Select suitable forms from the choices in parentheses.

1 The years I spent in school (was/were) a waste of time.
LINDA HALL

2 His tunic and breeches (was/were) so thickly soakéd through with Italian blood that they thought at first he had been shot through the chest.
CARLOS BAKER, *Ernest Hemingway*

3 Ten assignments in one semester (is/are) too much.
VAL DINAN

4 My uncle, however, was one of those men who (is/are) always prepared with expedients.
JULES VERNE, *A Journey to the Center of the Earth*

5 Gardenias and the peerage (was/were) his only weaknesses.
OSCAR WILDE, "The Canterville Ghost"

6 Those who call themselves intelligent (is/are) vain.
ANNETTE FRELING

7 Tailoring and weaving, though qualitatively different productive activities, (is/are) each a productive expenditure of human brains, nerves, and muscles, and in this sense (is/are) human labour.
KARL MARX, *Capital*

8 Now therefore why tempt ye God, to put a yoke upon the disciples, which neither our fathers nor we (was/were) able to bear?
Acts 15:10

9 The difficulties of casting and staging six Strauss operas in a dozen days (make/makes) this a rare and spectacular event.
MARCIA COLMAN MORTON, "Cities in Winter: Vienna," *Saturday Review*, 8 Jan. 1977

10 Either the students or their teachers (is/are) responsible for the so-called grade inflation.
MARCIE BRONSON

IRREGULAR PLURALS

SINGULAR	PLURAL
alumna	alumnae (f.)
alumnus	alumni (m.)
analysis	analyses
bacterium	bacteria
cactus	cactuses, cacti
crisis	crises
criterion	criteria
curriculum	curriculums, curricula
datum	data
formula	formulas, formulae
index	indexes, indices
medium	media
nucleus	nuclei
octopus	octopuses, octopi
parenthesis	parentheses
stimulus	stimuli
stratum	strata
thesis	theses
die	dice

As a matter of fact when data are [not "is"] of this type, all of the usual mathematical and statistical implications may be made.
N. M. DOWNIE AND R. W. HEATH, *Basic Statistical Methods*

In man, with his highly developed nervous system, emotional stimuli *are* in fact the most common stressors—and of course, *these* would be encountered most frequently in psychotic patients.
HANS SELYS, *Stress without Distress*

SPECIAL PROBLEMS IN AGREEMENT

Mixed compound subject It is possible to write a compound subject that is part singular and part plural. The rule is, the verb agrees with the part closest to it.

Neither Jack nor his sisters *have* the answer.

Neither the space nor the things in it *were* in the room before.
SUSANNE K. LANGER, *Problems in Art*

Separated subject and verb In a long or complicated sentence, words may get between the subject and the verb, causing you to "lose" the subject. Figure out who is doing what in a sentence before you decide whether the verb should be singular or plural.

The superiority of stockades built by the Union Troops over those built by the Confederates *was* striking.
OTTO EISENSCHIML AND RALPH NEWMAN, *Eyewitness: The Civil War As We Lived It*

Atypical word order   Usually, the subject comes first in the sentence, before the verb:

```
       1       2
    SUBJECT  VERB
```
The   *dog*   *was*   young and healthy.

But writers sometimes change the order of their sentences:

```
              2          1
            VERB      SUBJECT
```
Young and healthy   *was*   the   *dog.*

Put the sentence in normal order before deciding whether the verb should be singular or plural. Why is the verb singular in each of these examples?

There *is*, so far as I know, no good reason for these excuses.

For the many, there *is* a hardly concealed discontent.
STUDS TERKEL, *Working*

***Does* each of the boys belong to the club?**

Agreement and logic   Because educated readers expect things to *agree* in formal writing, certain expressions sound illogical:

The sophomores are clever as foxes [not "a fox"].

The frat brothers made up their minds [not "mind"] in a hurry.

The verb agrees with its *subject,* not with what comes after the verb:

The best bargain for lunch *is* sandwiches and a cup of soup.

Sandwiches and a cup of soup are the best bargain for lunch.

Agreement review

Select suitable forms from the choices in parentheses.

1 As I walked along, it occurred to me that the two children's behavior (was/were) a true reflection of all mankind.
THEODOR REIK, *Of Love and Lust*

2 A number of people (is/are) coming to the dance.
JEFF WRIGHT

3 The number of days left till Christmas (is/are) twelve.
ELAINE DIAMOND

4 Each kind of bacteria (produce/produces) a juice that creates the kind of fermentation that is necessary to do the work.
ALLAN L. BENSON, *The Story of Geology*

5 Every generation (has/have) (its/their) styles of living.
SUSANNE K. LANGER, *Problems of Art*

6 There (was/were) usually several reasons for his behavior.
FRANK ANSON

7 It is the government's policies which (cause/causes) the problem.
NANCY DESOTO

8 Neither stress nor syllabic weight (is/are) a very keen psychologic factor in the dynamics of French.
EDWARD SAPIR, "Language and Literature," *Language*

9 The implications of this argument (has/have) been examined.
JESUS CASTELLANO

10 These (sort/sorts) of ideas are what started him thinking in the first place.
JIM STRONG

11 She is one of those girls who (enter/enters) too many activities.
REBECCA SOLSTEIN

12 Intellectually, these include the elements of myth, magic, empiricism, and scientific attitude . . . . Each of these (has/have) a role in helping to answer the question "Who or what is man?" and in coping with the exigencies of existence.
CARL P. SWANSON, *The Natural History of Man*

13 Neither for the Catholic, the Protestant, nor for the Jew (is/are) the world a *good* place in which an enduring happiness is to be expected.
NORBERT WIENER, *The Human Use of Human Beings*

14 Every one of the guys in my dorm (has/have) different ideas about dating.
LARRY OLIVER

15 If anyone wants good grades (he or she/they) should stay out of the bars.

PRONOUNS AS SUBJECTS AND OBJECTS

Subjects and objects can cause problems for writers using pronouns.

The typical order of the English sentence is:

1	2	3
SUBJECT	VERB	OBJECT
The man	shot	the bear.

The subject does the acting, the verb names the action, and the object receives the action.

However, sentences are not always in standard order. You must turn the sentence around in your mind before deciding which word is the subject and which is the object:

Jazz I love, but opera I hate.

SUB	OB		SUB	OB	
I	love	jazz, but	I	hate	opera.

Passive sentences   Passive sentences have been changed so that the object becomes the subject: "The bear which the man shot was huge." Technically, "the bear" is the subject of this sentence, but *logically* it is "the man" who is (or was) doing the shooting. The passive tends to hide the logical subject, and its use can neutralize the sense of action or create an impression of evasiveness in writing.

Sentence combining for subject-object discovery   If the preceding sentence were set up as a sentence-combining problem, it would look like this:

The bear was huge.
The man shot i̶t̶.   (WHICH)

This problem indicates that "The bear was huge" is the base of the sentence; it is the part that could stand alone. The second part—"which the man shot"—is a "which" clause being used to modify "bear." Separating the parts of the sentence in this way reveals where the subjects and objects are and also where the pronouns belong. ("Which" takes the place of "it," the object, in this sentence.) Notice in the following example that figuring out the parts of the sentence helps to select the right pronoun: "She is the girl whom I invited."

She is the girl.

I invited her. (WHOM)

"She is the girl" is the part of the sentence that can stand alone. The "whom" clause is a modifier for "girl," and in this sentence "whom" replaces "her" (even though the clause is inverted). Figure out which part of the sentence is the *base* and which is the modifying clause before trying to pick a pronoun for the subject or object.

SUBJECT PRONOUNS

I, you, we, he,
she, it, they, who

OBJECT PRONOUNS

me, you, us, him,
her, it, them, whom

Why are the object pronouns required in the following?

They have known *her* for years.

She is the one *whom* they know.

It is difficult for *us* students to study at night.

Objects with prepositions Prepositions are followed by objects: *for* him, *to* us, *with* us, *by* her, *between* them, *between* you and me, *after* him, *near* whom. Most prepositions are words of position that tell the reader where something is:

PREPOSITIONS OF POSITION

above	before	from	through
across	behind	in	to
after	below	into	toward
against	beneath	near	under
along	beside	of	unto
amid	between	off	up
among	beyond	on	upon
around	by	over	with
at	for	past	within

Though not position words, "but," "except," "since," "until," and a few others are considered prepositions; they can take objects. When these words join with a noun or pronoun to make a modifying phrase (in the winter, for him, to the store) they are called prepositions, and the noun or pronoun after them is considered an object. But note a different use for these words: "She stepped onto the ice and fell *through*." Here, "through" has no noun or pronoun after it; it acts like an independent modifier. Some of the other words you will recognize as conjunctions: "She laughed, *but* I didn't see the joke."

The "to be" exception to the subject-object rule   Forms of "to be" (am, is, are, was, were, be, being, been) do not take objects in formal writing.

It is *I* [not "me"].

The girl who said it was *she* [not "her"].

It was *who*?

Subject-object practice 1

Select suitable forms from the choices in parentheses.

1 **My wife and** (I/me), **on our later study of chimpanzees right inside the forest, found the same thing: noisy, mobile males, and quiet, slow mothers.**
VERNON REYNOLDS, *The Apes*

2 **Digestion is a problem for** (we/us) **Americans.**
DAN JONES

3 **Then, as he thought, he realized that if there was any such thing as ever meeting, both** (he/him) **and his grandfather would be acutely embarrassed by the presence of his father.**
ERNEST HEMINGWAY, *For Whom the Bell Tolls*

4 **There followed a weighty correspondence between** (he/him) **and the King, and the King at last relented to the change in the plan, thanking his minister for his advice . . . .**
CHARLES W. FERGUSON, *Naked to Mine Enemies: The Life of Cardinal Wolsey*

5 **Few of us remember that the decrepit Old Year,** (who/whom) **we picture in cartoons as a bowed and bald Father Time with sickle, is also a figure of death; or that the baby New Year, chubby and smiling as Cupid, is also a symbol of love and light.**
MARGARET MEAD AND RHODA METRAUX, *A Way of Seeing*

6 **Let's just keep this between you and** (I/me)
BETTY TRAVEN

7 **As he played, empty bottles went sailing through the gathering darkness to explode and tinkle on the cobblestones, but, so far, none were directed toward** (he/him) **or the girl.**
BOYD UPCHURCH, *The Slave Stealer*

8 **Such advocates of obfuscation apparently teach fairly well, if it is** (they/them) **who have instructed my graduate students.**
WENDELL JOHNSON, "You Can't Write Writing," in *Language, Meaning and Maturity*, S. I. Hayakawa, ed.

9 I'm damned if I'm going to have people walking by and seeing you sit here as if this division were a partnership between you and (I/me).
NORMAN MAILER, *The Naked and the Dead*

10 I hope they invite you and (I/me) **to the party.**
JANE STEIL

"WHO" AND "WHOM"

The difference between "who" and "whom" causes more trouble than it is worth. "Whom" has almost completely disappeared from informal English. (No one asks "Whom did you see?" except those who habitually speak formal English.) But the distinction between the two forms of "who" is still important in formal written English.

"Who" is the subject form (it can be the subject).

"Whom" is the object form (it can be the object).

It is necessary to figure out who is doing what in the sentence to know which word is the subject and which is the object. Why is the object form required in the following?

Whom are you discussing?

Whom are you looking for?

Whom did you see?

Whom does he want to marry?

With *whom* were you dancing?

Sometimes, words get between the subject and the verb, changing the appearance of the sentence but not the grammar. Treat these sentences as combining problems—break the sentences down into basic sentences to see what goes where (see page 373).

WHO/WHOM PROBLEM SENTENCE	SOLUTION WITH SENTENCE COMBINING
The girl (who/whom) they think was in the car has escaped	The girl has escaped. They think *she* was in the car.
	She = who
	The girl *who* they think was in the car has escaped.
Laura pointed out a boy (who/whom) she said was the team captain.	Laura pointed out a boy. She said (that) *he* was the team captain.
	He = who

Laura pointed out a boy *who* she said was the team captain.

He is the thief (who/whom) the police agree is the most clever.

He is the thief. The police agree (that) *he* is the most clever.

He = who

He is the thief *who* the police agree is the most clever.

A related substitution trick can help you figure out "who" or "whom" problems. Substitute some other pronoun (he, she, they, him, her, them) into the sentence:

I know (who/whom) phoned this morning.

I know *he* phoned this morning.

He = who

I know *who* phoned this morning.

Subject-object practice 2

Which is the right word? How do you know?

1 He is a man (who/whom) everyone should know.

2 (Who/Whom) does he think he is?

3 To (who/whom) did he refer?

4 Anyone (who/whom) you pick will have to work hard.

5 She is one person (who/whom) should be invited.

6 (Who/Whom) are you?

7 He might not be the one (who/whom) you think he is.

8 List the ones (who/whom) you think should come.

9 She is the kind of leader (who/whom) we want for president.

10 (Who/Whom) do you think is the best candidate?

11 (Who/Whom) shall I say called?

12 We have the man (who/whom) we were looking for.

13 I wonder (who/whom) is in there.

14 You should see (who/whom) is standing outside.

15 For (who/whom) is this intended?

16 You must be (who/whom) they think you are.

17 A student (who/whom) we all know, is failing.

18 (Who/Whom) it is, I think I know.

19 (Who/Whom) do you think she is calling?

20 (Who/Whom) do you think you are fooling?

21 It was she (who/whom) we wanted to question.

22 (Who/Whom) **do you think you are?**

23 You are the ones (who/whom) **the committee selected.**

24 I have to find out (who/whom) **she is.**

25 (Who/Whom), **they asked, did this?**

PRONOUN REFERENCE

AMBIGUOUS

A pronoun must not appear to refer to two words simultaneously: "The President told the vice-president *he* couldn't make the speech." What does "he" refer to? Clear up such confusing references when you revise:

AMBIGUOUS
Don't touch the dishes with your hands when *they* are dirty.

REVISED
Don't touch the dishes when your hands are dirty.

When the dishes are dirty, don't touch them.

VAGUE

It should always be *perfectly* clear to the reader what your pronouns refer to. The farther away the pronoun gets from its referent, the greater the possibility that the reader and perhaps the writer too will "lose" the referent:

VAGUE
Helen is giving a party, *which* is a good idea.

What is good, the fact that it is Helen giving the party or the fact that she is giving a party instead of a speech? Often, you'll find that the best solution for vague pronoun references is to recast the thought, getting rid of the pronoun completely:

REVISED
We've all been studying too hard for exams, so Helen's decided to give a party.

ILLOGICAL

In this situation, a pronoun refers to something missing from the sentence—an implied idea that must be expressed for the sentence to be understood:

ILLOGICAL

Although my school gave much attention to reading, *they* didn't do me any good.

The reading exercises didn't do any good? The teachers didn't do any good? Again, the best course is to rewrite the sentence so that you convey a precise idea to the reader:

REVISED

Although my school gave much attention to reading, even remedial classes didn't prepare me for college reading assignments.

EXCESSIVE

A proliferation of pronouns usually creates childish-sounding sentences:

EXCESSIVE

Science has always been my worst subject and it is hard to study it when it isn't taught very well and when it comes so early in the day and especially when it is so hard to understand it anyway!

Using the skills you learned in Chapters 6 and 8, rewrite such sentences for better clarity and emphasis:

REVISED

Science—scheduled at eight in the morning before I'm really awake, hard to understand if not taught well, and almost impossible for me to comprehend in any case—continues to be my worst subject.

Pronoun reference review

Which is the better sentence? Why?

1[1] A Cunegonde fainted; as soon as she recovered, she slapped her face; and everything was confusion in the most beautiful and agreeable of all possible castles.

   B Cunegonde fainted; as soon as she recoverd, the Baroness slapped her face; and everything was confusion in the most beautiful and agreeable of all possible castles.

2[2] A His new car was my father's pride, which he polished every Sunday.

   B His new car, which he polished every Sunday, was my father's pride.

3³ A Its front foot caught a piece of quartz and little by little the shell pulled over and flopped upright.

B Its front foot caught a piece of quartz and little by little it pulled over and flopped upright.

4⁴ A Her thin musical voice died away over the water; Leon could hear the wind blown trills pass by him like a fluttering of wings.

B Her thin musical voice died away over the water; Leon could hear it pass by him like a fluttering of wings.

5⁵ A Now Gregor's sister had to cook too, helping her mother; true it didn't amount to much, for they ate scarcely anything.

B Now Gregor's sister had to cook too, helping her mother; true the cooking didn't amount to much, for they scarcely ate anything.

6⁶ A In vain I told him in English that boys were the most dangerous creatures; and if once you begin with it, it was safe to end in a shower of stones.

B In vain I told him in English that boys were the most dangerous creatures; and if once you begin with them, it was safe to end in a shower of stones.

7⁷ A I was in my room waiting for the phone to ring when suddenly it started raining.

B While I was in my room waiting for the phone to ring, the rain suddenly started.

8⁸ A She pretended to make light of his genius and I took no pains to defend him.

B She pretended to make light of his genius and I took no pains to defend this.

9⁹ A Subjectivity is a journalistic principle among the underground press staffers and they care much more about opinion than fact.

B Subjectivity is a journalistic principle among underground press staffers and it cares much more about opinion than fact.

10¹⁰ A He used the wild country as the Indians do, in cooperation and communion with it, which finds any form of noise a baneful disharmony.

B He used the wild country as the Indians do, in cooperation and communion with it, finding any form of noise a baneful disharmony.

VERBS

Every verb has four forms: "write," "wrote," "written," "writing"; a few have alternate forms; a few have repeated forms. Check the dictionary if you have any doubts about the form of a verb. A few of the more troublesome ones are listed for you here:

PRESENT	PAST	PERFECT [°]	PROGRESSIVE [°]
awake	awoke, awaked	awaked, awoke, awaken	awaking
awaken	awakened	awakened	awakening
begin	began	begun	beginning
break	broke	broken	breaking
bring	brought	brought	bringing
buy	bought	bought	buying
dive	dived, dove	dived	diving
draw	drew	drawn	drawing
drink	drank	drunk	drinking
freeze	froze	frozen	freezing
get	got	got, gotten	getting
go	went	gone	going
know	knew	known	knowing
lay	laid	laid	laying
lie (*recline*)	lay	lain	lying
lie (*tell a lie*)	lied	lied	lying
make	made	made	making
set	set	set	setting
sing	sang	sung	singing
sink	sank	sunk	sinking
sit	sat	sat	sitting
take	took	taken	taking
wake	woke, waked	waked, woken	waking
wear	wore	worn	wearing

[°] The perfect and progressive forms are used with forms of "to be" (am, is, are, was, were, be, being, been) and with forms of "to have" (have, has, had): "am writing," "was beginning," "has begun," "had known," "have been singing," and so on.

SLANG VERBS

In informal writing and personal-experience stories, slang may be both appropriate and desirable, but in formal writing, slang verbs should be avoided: "We was busted by the fuzz last night. We was just sittin' around rappin', ya know, like it was so cold I nearly frosted my butt. My old lady's all busted up about it."

UNCONVENTIONAL VERB FORMS

Within formal English, inexperienced writers sometimes use the wrong verb form:

It was so cold that we were *frozen* [not "froze"] by noon.

I have *woken* [not "woke"] up at eight o'clock every morning since the semester started.

The ship *sank* [not "sunk"] in minutes.

They have *gone* [not "went"] to the library together for months.

Equally unconventional, and unacceptable in semiformal or formal writing, is the creation of new forms by mixing parts of verbs:

I have *tooken* this course twice now, and I still don't get it.

He has *drunken* so many beers he can't stand up.

"LIE" AND "LAY"

The difference between "lie" and "lay"—like the difference between "who" and "whom"—often causes trouble. The words are different in *meaning*. "To lie" (lie, lay, lain, lying) means to be at rest; this word only tells you *where* something is. "To lay" (lay, laid, laid, laying) means to put something somewhere.

The words are different in *grammar*. "Lie" never takes an object; it is usually followed by a *place* expression (lie *down*, lie *on the bed*). "Lay" always takes an object: lay *the book* down; lay *it* on the bed.

The problem is in the past tense of "lie."

Today I lie down; yesterday I *lay* down [not "laid"].

To decide which verb is needed, you must either be certain of the meaning you intend, or you must check to see whether the verb has an object (lay) or not (lie). But remember that writers don't always use normal order in their sentences: subject—verb—object.

He—laid—*the book* down.

The book was laid down by him.

Remember, in a passive sentence, the object is put into the subject slot. Figure out who is doing what before you decide whether the sentence has an object in it.

Verb practice 1

Select suitable forms from the choices in parentheses.

1 Teachers should not (lay/lie) hands on students.
2 The report has been (laying/lying) there all day.

3 (Lay/Lie) the carpeting straight.

4 They (lay/laid) in bed until noon yesterday.

5 That dog has (laid/lain) there all day.

6 If you're tired, you ought to (lie/lay) down for a while.

7 The letter is (lying/laying) right there in front of you.

8 They have (laid/lain) tracks right across our field.

9 I (lie/lay) here daydreaming all through yesterday's test.

10 Better let sleeping dogs (lie/lay).

11 The treasure (lies/lays) buried six feet under.

12 They (lay/laid) the child on the back seat when they went shopping.

13 The leaves were (lying/laying) all over the yard.

14 She (lay/laid) awake all night worrying.

15 You need to (lie/lay) aside your fears.

16 The ship (lay/laid) at anchor all week.

17 The book has (laid/lain) on the shelf for weeks.

18 She is (lying/laying) on the cot.

19 (Lie/Lay) the towels on the counter.

20 Could it have (lain/laid) there all this time?

21 By tomorrow, it will have (laid/lain) there a month.

22 Can you (lay/lie) brick in your spare time?

23 Time (lays/lies) heavily when you're bored.

24 The laws were (lain/laid) down by Moses.

25 They will (lie/lay) there for hours if you let them.

DOUBLE PAST TENSE

Much prose is written in the past tense, and this sometimes makes a problem for writers. How do you refer to a past or prior event when you are already writing in the past? Use the past perfect:

He *said* that he *had seen* her.

"He said that he *saw* her" and "He said that he *seen* her" are both unacceptable in this case.

He knew that he *had passed* [not "passed"] the test when he saw his mark.

Putting both verbs in simple past sounds all right in informal English, but doing so fails to make the distinction in time clear enough for most educated readers.

CONDITIONAL STATEMENTS

People sometimes use a redundant conditional (If you *would* do it, you *would* be sorry). Use "will" verb forms to express only the consequences, not the condition. (The "if" statement is the condition.) Formal writing requires the following:

If you *do* it, you *will be* penalized.

If you *did* it, you *would be* penalized.

If you *hadn't done* it, you *wouldn't have been* penalized.

STATEMENTS OF DOUBT, WISHES, PROBABILITY, CONDITIONS CONTRARY TO FACT

The rule on "was" and "were" for statements of doubt, probability, and so on, is changing. It is disregarded by many modern writers; but the distinction is still important to most educated readers.

I wish I *were* [not "was"] dead.

If it *were* [not "was"] true, I could forgive her.

Would you do it if it *were* [not "was"] possible?

Verb review

Select suitable forms from the choices in parentheses.

1 It (sits/sets) pretty well back from the road, in a lawn gone sparse and rusty in the late season.
ROBERT PENN WARREN, *All the King's Men*

2 The jailers fed us in the morning, and it tasted good because some of us hadn't (ate/eaten) in twenty-four hours.
DICK GREGORY, WITH ROBERT LIPSTYE, *Nigger: An Autobiography*

3 We all (lay/lie) there, my mother, my father, my uncle, my aunt, and I too am (laying/lying) there.
JAMES AGEE, *A Death in the Family*

4 He said, if it (was/were) possible that there could be any country where Yahoos alone were endued with reason, they certainly must be the governing animal, because reason will always in time prevail against brutal strength.
JONATHAN SWIFT, *Gulliver's Travels*

5 At daylight, Rainsford (lying/laying) near the camp, was awakened by a sound that made him know that he had new things to learn about fear.
RICHARD CONNELL, "The Most Dangerous Game"

6 Gurov (lay/laid) **awake all night, raging, and went about the whole of the next day with a headache.**
ANTON CHEKHOV, "The Lady with the Dog"

7 If he (would break/broke) **into a run, they'd chase him.**
JOHN DOS PASSOS, *Forty-Second Parallel*

8 Unless there is a remarkable biological breakthrough in geriatrics, we have (gone/went) **just about as far as we can go in raising life expectancy.**
ISAAC ASIMOV, "The Slowly Moving Finger," *Of Time and Space and Other Things*

9 The cries of the dying were (drownded/drowned) **in the martial music of trumpets and drums.**
WILL DURANT, *The Reformation*

10 And even if it (was/were) **possible to devise a method for maintaining an innocent vacuity of mind, the wisdom of such a policy is surely questionable.**
LUCIUS GARVIN, *A Modern Introduction to Ethics*

11 One event that (takes/taken) **me by surprise every year is the announcement of a new Miss Rheingold.**
WILLIAM K. ZINSSER, "There Are Smiles," *The Haircurl Papers*

12 If a modern-day Rip Van Winkle (would go/went) **to sleep and didn't wake up for 100 years, how well would he be able to understand an American of 2061?**
MARIO PEI, "English 2061: A Forecast," *Saturday Review*, 14 Jan. 1961

13 A series of tests which gave this kind of interesting evidence was (undertook/undertaken) **by the well-known American author Upton Sinclair.**
SUSY SMITH, *ESP for the Millions*

14 The people who have (manage/managed) **to get off the block have only got as far as a more respectable ghetto.**
JAMES BALDWIN, *Nobody Knows My Name*

15 The world in twenty or forty years—let us say thirty-six—has (come/came) **to the point where without an atomic war, without even a hard or furious shooting war, it has** (gave/given) **birth nonetheless to a fearful condition.**
NORMAN MAILER, "The Last Night: A Story"

DANGLING PARTS

Some modifiers seem to "dangle" when they do not modify anything in the sentence. Often these modifiers produce humor by accidentally attaching to something unintended: "Riding my bike through the woods, the bear suddenly appeared in front of me." The modifier attaches to the *nearest* noun, and therefore "the bear" is "riding my bike." Move modifiers next to what you intend them to modify to avoid the problem: "Riding my bike through the woods, *I* suddenly saw the bear in front of me."

Practice

Which is the better sentence in the following pairs?

1[11] A Reading carefully through the text, several concepts appeared.

   B As I read carefully through the text, several concepts began to appear.

2[12] A Seeing him beside his wife, I understood why people said he came from a good family and had married beneath him.

   B Seeing him beside his wife, he looked like he had come from a good family and had married beneath him.

3[13] A Having departed from my friend, some remote spot in Scotland was selected where I could finish my work in solitude.

   B Having departed from my friend, I determined to visit some remote spot in Scotland, and finish my work in solitude.

4[14] A Reaching the boulevard, the desire to run was overcoming him.

   B By the time he reached the boulevard, he was fighting the desire to run.

5[15] A Long and tangled and hanging down, his eyes were shining through his hair like he was behind vines.

   B His hair was long and tangled and hung down, and you could see his eyes shining through like he was behind vines.

6[16] A They spread the skin out and trimmed the fat from it, and then they were faced with the question of what to do with the tail.

   B Spreading the skin out and trimming the fat from it, the tail posed a question.

7[17] A Holding the bolts with a wrench, the plate will slowly rotate to the left.

   B Holding the bolts with the wrench, you can slowly rotate the plate to the left.

8[18] A As he swept his long arms, as though brushing aside some impalpable object, the wolves fell back and back further still.

   B Sweeping his long arms, as though brushing aside some impalpable object, the wolves fell back and back further still.

9[19] A Watching Dr. Ferris watch him, the sudden twitch of anxiety appeared, the look that precedes panic, as if a clean card had fallen on the table from a deck Dr. Ferris had never seen before.

   B Watching Dr. Ferris watch him, Rearden saw the sudden twitch of anxiety, the look that precedes panic, as if a clean card had fallen on the table from a deck Dr. Ferris had never seen before.

10[20] A Squealing and kicking in his father's arms with all his might, his yells redoubled when he carried him upstairs and lifted him over the bannister.

B Poor Hareton was squealing and kicking in his father's arms with all his might, and redoubled his yells when he carried him upstairs and lifted him over the bannister.

MISPLACED PARTS

MOVABLE MODIFIERS

Movable modifiers (only, just, almost) usually come before the verb. But in some cases an ambiguity can arise. For example, "I only lost the money" can be interpreted "I only lost the money [I didn't steal it]" or "I lost only the money [I still have the receipts]." Avoid ambiguity by placing the modifier next to the word it modifies and, when necessary, giving the reader additional information to make your meaning clear:

AMBIGUOUS	CLEAR
I just earned three dollars.	I earned just three dollars [not four or five dollars].
	I earned three dollars just now.
I only looked at the shirt.	I only looked at the shirt; I didn't buy it.
	I looked at only the shirt [not at slacks, shoes, or socks].
School begins again after the summer vacation in September.	School begins again in September, after the summer vacation.

NEGATIVES

Informally, many people accept the movable "not," as in "Everyone can't [cannot] be rich." But formally, you gain greater precision by placing the "not" next to the word it negates: "*Not everyone* can be rich."

INFORMAL	MORE FORMAL
Everyone doesn't have to hold the same opinion.	Not everyone has to hold the same opinion.
Everybody doesn't own a Cadillac.	Not everybody owns a Cadillac.

You may want to reread the "Not Every" section in Chapter 4.

SQUINTING MODIFIERS

"Squinting" modifiers seem to modify in two directions at once, modifying two words at once. To clear up any doubts in the reader's mind, move the squinting modifier next to the word you intend to modify.

AMBIGUOUS

The coach told them often to jog.

REVISED

The coach told them to jog often.

The coach often told them to jog.

AWKWARD SPLIT INFINITIVES

An infinitive is the word "to" plus a verb (to run, to go, to think). Putting a word or words between "to" and its verb is called "splitting the infinitive" (to quickly run, to slowly go, to really think). Often, the split infinitive sounds perfectly natural, but sometimes it can sound unnecessarily awkward.

AWKWARD

You have to usually read with care in his class.

They liked to seldom dance together at parties.

REVISED

You usually have to read with care in his class.

They seldom liked to dance together at parties.

Practice

Which is the better sentence?

1[21] A Brandy tasters tell almost as much from bouquet as from tastes that are professional.

B Professional brandy tasters tell almost as much from bouquet as taste.

2[22] A And now there are gas water heaters with double-density insulation and improved utilization that save gas.

B And now there are gas water heaters that save gas with double-density insulation and improved utilization.

3[23] A She liked to before dinner read in the evening and she drank Scotch and soda while she read.

B She liked to read in the evening before dinner and she drank Scotch and soda while she read.

4[24] A At the end of the corridor a door stood open, down which M. Chasle made his way on stumbling feet.

B A door stood open at the end of the corridor, down which M. Chasle made his way on stumbling feet.

5[25] A Apart from "Super Fly" midi-coats and the like, there is little tangible evidence so far that life on the street has begun to imitate art.

B There is little tangible evidence so far that life has begun to imitate art on the street apart from "Super Fly" midi-coats and the like.

6²⁶ *A* We sat and listened while the professor droned on with our eyes on his face.

B With our eyes on his face, we sat and listened while the professor droned on.

7²⁷ *A* But as time went on, he manifested some anxiety and surprise, glancing at the clock more and more frequently and at the window less hopefully than before.

B But as the time went on glancing at the clock more frequently and at the window less hopefully than before, he manifested some anxiety and surprise.

8²⁸ *A* I travel not to go anywhere, but to go for my part.

B For my part, I travel not to go anywhere, but to go.

COMPARISONS

ILLOGICAL

"She is taller than any girl in the class" is illogical since it seems to imply that she is taller than herself, or that she is not part of the class. "She is the tallest girl in the class" or "She is taller than any other girl in the class" each solves this problem.

ILLOGICAL
Corky was faster than anyone on the team.

REVISED
Corky was the fastest runner on the team.

INCOMPLETE

A comparison is meaningful only if its terms are adequately expressed. For example, in "She is young, if not younger, than you are," the parenthetic phrase, "if not younger," not only interrupts, it disconnects the first part of the sentence from the rest (She is young . . . than you are). The full comparison requires "She is *as young as,* if not younger than, you are."

INCOMPLETE
You need math more than Jim.

REVISED
You need math more than Jim does.

You need math more than you need Jim.

"-*LY*" WORDS

Much informal writing, especially in advertising, dispenses with the -*ly* on modifiers, and thus it is easy to drop the -*ly* in your own writing: "His trouble is that he can't think logical." Most verbs, however, express action (*drive* slowly) and require *-ly* modifiers:

Think *carefully* [not "careful"] before you answer.

The grand major domo, white plumes on his head, knocked *loudly* [not "loud"], but there was no response.

STANLEY B. TROUP AND WILLIAM A. GREENE, *The Patient, Death and the Family*

Usage review 1

Select the formal English alternative in the following sentences.

1[29] Everyone wants to surround (himself/theirself) and (his/their) family with objects of lasting beauty, meaning and value—objects to be owned now with pride and passed on as valuable heirlooms to future generations.

2[30] Rushed by ambulance to Harlem Hospital, I (lay/laid) in bed for hours while preparations were made to remove the keen-edged knife from my body.

3[31] A "The Alteration" starts out far better than it ends.
B "The Alteration" starts out well, if not better than, it ends.

4[32] I am being (make/made) witness to matters no human being may see.

5[33] You're one of those charming women with (who/whom) it's nice to talk, and nice to be silent.

6[34] American blacks had (become/became) recognized as a species of human being by amendments to the Constitution shortly after the Civil War.

7[35] You have to adjust your scope extra (careful/carefully) or you won't see anything but your own eye.

8[36] If man (was/were) forced to demonstrate for himself all the truths of which he makes daily use, his task would never end.

9[37] They find so often that instead of having (laid/lain) an egg, they have (laid/lain) a vote, or an empty ink-bottle, or some other absolutely unhatchable object, which means nothing to them.

10[38] A modern poet has characterized the personality of art and the impersonality of science as follows: Art is (I/me): Science is (we/us).

11[39] Hail, Emperor, we (who/whom) are about to die salute you.

12[40] It was one of those swift dramas which (is/are) played only in Italy or Paris.

13⁴¹ *A* Coming down the slope, my skis suddenly started to ripple.

B As I was coming down the slope, my skis suddenly started to ripple.

14⁴² Each of their friends (was/were) going to bring part of the dinner.

15⁴³ The fact is that the number of the officials and the quantity of the work (is/are) not related to each other at all.

16⁴⁴ *A* Whistling bravely, the dark didn't scare me at all.

B By whistling bravely, I tried to keep from being scared of the dark.

17⁴⁵ (Who/Whom), then, was the forger?

18⁴⁶ It is even possible that the first genuine thinking machines may be (growed/grown) rather than constructed; already some crude but very stimulating experiments have been carried out along these lines.

19⁴⁷ Jesus may have expressed the feeling that, if this Temple made with hands (was/were) destroyed, real religion might not lose much.

20⁴⁸ It's better to (answer quickly/quickly answer) even if you don't know the question.

21⁴⁹ But if the open air and adventure mean everything to Defoe (it/they) (mean/means) nothing to Jane Austen.

22⁵⁰ I am apt to fancy I have contracted a new acquaintance (who/whom) it will be no easy matter to shake off.

23⁵¹ The only difference between (he/him) and (they/them) was that he had lost his all.

24⁵² Professor Smile ought to retire; he's (older than any/the oldest) professor in the department.

25⁵³ The gate itself, or what remained of it, (lay/laid) unhinged to one side, the interstices of the rotted palings choked with grass and weeds like the ribs of a forgotten skeleton.

26⁵⁴ In this real world his horse danced as if it (were/was) wild or crazy, and this is the reason why he called himself Crazy Horse.

27⁵⁵ But Henry James and Mrs. Wharton (was/were) our most interesting novelists, and most of the young writers followed their manner, without having their qualifications.

28⁵⁶ One of my fondest recollections (is/are) of an outhouse in Virginia.

29⁵⁷ One of the biggest problems of the Carter advisors (has/have) been how to sort out all the widely varying estimates of the number of people in the affected categories.

30⁵⁸ Perhaps she pitied most not those (who/whom) **she aided in the struggle, but the more fortunate** (who/whom) **were preoccupied with themselves and cursed with self-deceptions of private success.**

DICTIONARY OF USAGE PROBLEMS

Abbreviations Avoid abbreviations in formal writing. "Etc." should not be used. You may instead write "and so on" or "and so forth," but it is often better to list the additional items, rather than to imply to the reader that there is more to the sentence than you have written.

Accept, except "Accept" means to take or receive: "I accept the responsibility." "Except" means to exclude or "but": "Everyone left except Bill."

Affect, effect "Affect" means to influence: "Your health affects your personality." It also means to pretend or take on airs: "He affects indifference to her rejection." "Effect" means to bring about directly or to change: "I will effect the repairs on your car immediately." "An effect" is a result: "One effect of not studying is poor grades."

Alot Not recognized in formal writing as a spelling of "a lot." Compare with "a little."

Already, all ready "Already" means previously: "You have already explained that answer." "All ready" means everything is ready: "They are all ready for the exam."

Alright Not recognized in formal writing as a spelling of "all right." Compare with "all wrong."

All of a sudden "Suddenly" is less wordy.

Allusion, illusion "Allusion" means a reference to something: "Your allusion to Shakespeare should be documented." "Illusion" means ghost, imaginary vision, false appearance: "He created the illusion of prosperity by living on credit."

Among, between Use "among" when you are writing about more than two things: "There are many differences among students." Use "between" for two items only: "A comparison between apples and oranges is futile."

Amount, number "Number" is used for things that can be counted (number of trees). "Amount" is used for things that are measured by volume (amount of corn, amount of noise). Note: *amount of* money and *number of* dollars.

At this point in time "Now" or "at this time" is less wordy.

A while, awhile Following a preposition, "while" is a noun: "Let's sit for a while and think about our plans." "Awhile" is a modifier: "We sat awhile and then left."

Being, being as, being that Poor substitutes for the more precise "since" or "because." "Since [not "Being"] I knew the way, I drove."

Bad, badly Formal writing requires "bad" to express emotion or illness: "Students feel bad when they get low grades."

Can, may Not considered interchangeable. "You can pass the test" is not the same as "You may pass the test." But the distinction between "can" and "may" when making a request—"Can I leave the room?" "May I leave the room?"—depends on how polite the writer wants to sound.

Cite, site "Cite" means to refer to: "Your paper cites Hemingway." "Site" means place: "This is a good site for the picnic."

Compliment, complement To "compliment" is to flatter: "I won't compliment him for that terrible pun." To "complement" is to balance or complete. "The professor's handouts complement the text."

Consensus of opinion Redundant. "The consensus is that smoking is bad for you."

Continuous, continual "Continuous" means without interruption: "A continuous supply of electricity is essential to industry." "Continual" means happening frequently but not continuously: "The continual ringing of the phone kept me from studying."

Contractions Usually not found in very formal writing, but otherwise acceptable if they serve the writing purpose ("I'll," "haven't," "don't," "can't," and so on).

Contrast from One thing contrasts *with* another.

Could of Not recognized in formal writing as a form of "could have."

Credible, credulous "Credible" means that which sounds believable, such as a witnesss or testimony. "Credulous" means believing too easily, gullible: "Inga is so credulous she'll believe anything you tell her."

Desert, dessert "Dessert" is the last course of a meal. "Desert" means arid land, and "to desert" means to abandon: "She deserted him in the desert after dessert."

Differ/different—from/than Very formal writing requires "from": "She is different from other girls." But "than" is widely used in less formal writing.

Disinterested, uninterested "Disinterested" means impartial: "A referee must be disinterested in the outcome." "Uninterested" means not interested: "She was uninterested in his proposal."

Double negative Not acceptable in formal writing (can't hardly): "He can't manage the budget" or "He can hardly manage the budget."

Enthuse, enthused, enthusing Informal derivatives from "enthusiasm." Not recognized in formal writing.

Few, less "Few" should be used with countable items: few people. "Less" should be used with items measured by volume or degree: less milk, less noise.

Fun Not accepted as a modifier in formal writing: "Waterskiing is a thrilling [not "fun"] sport." "She is an enjoyable [not "fun"] person to be with."

Go and, take and, try and Wordy. "Go [not "Go and"] see the nurse if your throat is still sore."

Farther, further In very formal English, "farther" is used for physical distance: "Her room is farther down the hall." "Further" is used for degree: "You should pursue your studies further." Less formally, the words are interchangeable, except when you mean "additional." For "additional," "further" is required: "No further applications can be accepted."

Hanged, hung "Hanged" means executed by hanging: "He was hanged by a mob of racists." For any other kind of hanging, use "hung": "The stockings were hung by the chimney with care . . . ."

Himself, herself, myself Not acceptable as substitutes for "him," "her," "me," and so on. "The class couldn't decide between Alice and *me* [not "myself"]." However, "-self" words are correct when they are used to refer back to a pronoun. "She gave herself a shock." "Alice decided she would do the work herself."

Hopefully Weak substitute for "maybe" or "I hope." "I hope [not "Hopefully"] this report will be finished on time." "Hopefully" is acceptable to convey "with hope": "Despite her problems, she faces the future hopefully."

How In formal writing "how" means procedure or manner. It cannot be a substitute for "that": "The book shows *that* [not "how"] the NFL is quick to act when a player or coach is suspected of wrong-doing."

If, whether, whether or not Use "whether" to express doubt: "She wondered whether she should go." "Whether or not" is redundant.

In back of, behind "Behind" is less wordy: "The broom is behind the door."

In, into Most educated readers believe "He fell in the closet" is illogical or ambiguous if the writer means "He fell into the closet."

Infer, imply "Imply" means to suggest. "Infer" means to deduce. "I infer that you are implying I am dishonest."

Inside, inside of "Inside" is less wordy: "She is inside the house."

In this day and age Wordy for "now" or "today."

Irregardless Not recognized in formal writing. Use "regardless": "Regardless of what you think, she is a good teacher."

Its, it's "It's" means it is. "Its" means belonging to it: "It's time to give the dog its annual bath."

Like, as "Like" should not be used in place of a conjunction, connecting two sentences. "They did things *as* [not "like"] their ancestors had done them." Less formally, the two words are interchangeable: "Winston tastes good like a cigarette should."

Lots of Not recognized in formal writing as a substitute for "many" or "much": "There are *many* [not "lots of"] reasons for going to school."

Mad Not recognized in formal writing as a substitute for "angry."

Might of Use "might have" in formal writing.

Most every Informal for "almost every" or "nearly every." "Nearly everyone [not "Most everyone"] approves of charity." "He hits the ball almost every [not "most every"] time."

Numbers In general, any number that can be expressed in one or two words should be written out (ninety-nine, two thousand, five million). But in technical reports and informal writing, numerals are usually preferred (99, 2,000, 5 million). Avoid starting a sentence with a numeral: "Nine thousand seventy-six people went to the game." Even better, rewrite the sentence so that the number does not come first: "Attendance at the game was 9,076."

Off of Redundant. "Get off [not "off of"] the couch."

Ourself Not recognized in formal writing, except for royalty. Unless you are a king or a queen, use "ourselves."

Particular Usually unnecessary modifier, especially in the presence of "this," "that," "these," or "those." "This type [not "this particular type"] of person should be watched closely."

Pretentious language Pompous, stuffy writing intended to impress the reader with the writer's intelligence. (See the example on page 38.)

Prevalent The word has positive connotations: widespread, widely accepted. It should not be used to mean common or big, especially in a negative sense: "A big [not "prevalent"] problem today is alcoholism in school."

Principal, principle The principal is the head of the school. The word can be used to designate any main or chief thing: "The principal cause of poverty is unemployment." "Principle" refers to ethics, theories, guidelines, moral quality: "His actions seem good, but his principles are suspect."

Proceed Pretentious when the context requires "go": "He went [not "proceeded"] to the library to do some studying."

Prophecy, prophesy A "prophecy" is a prediction. To "prophesy" is to make a prediction.

Real, really Unacceptable for "very." "The show was very [not "real"] good."

Rarely ever Redundant. "I rarely [not "rarely ever"] go out at night."

Reason is because Formal writing requires "reason is that": "The reason for the fire was that [not "because"] the wiring was defective."

Shall, will The distinction between these words is seldom observed. Some writers still use "shall" when they want to be especially formal or emphatic: "We shall surely die." But generally, "shall" is no longer used except for formal requests: "Shall we go?"

Theirself, theirselves, themself None of these is recognized in formal writing. Use "themselves."

Today's modern world, today's modern society, modern world of today Wordy for "now" or "today."

Use to Informal for "used to": "We used to live in the gray house."

Where Informal for "in which": "This is a book in which [not "where"] the crooks get away with the crime."

Where to, where at Redundant. "Where are you going [not "going to"]?" "Where is my pencil [not "Where is my pencil at"]?"

Usage review 2

Select the formal English alternative in the following sentences.

1 The reason is (that/because) **they are overladen with ideas.**
ALFRED NORTH WHITEHEAD, *The Aims of Education*

2 The old idea that the hen deliberately selects the male she thinks the most beautiful is putting the matter in human terms which certainly do not apply to a bird's mind; but it seems certain that the brilliant and exciting display does have an (affect/effect) **on the hen bird, stimulating her to greater readiness to mate.**
JULIAN HUXLEY, *On Living in a Revolution*

3 It is only with science that the (allusion/illusion) **exists; the** (allusion/illusion) **of a neutral, inhuman activity separate from the world of "telegrams and anger."**
JOHN H. STEELE, "The Fiction of Science," *The Listener*

4 The (amount/number) **of college bulletins and adult-education come-ons that keep turning up in my mailbox convinces me that I must be on a special mailing list for dropouts.**
WOODY ALLEN, *Getting Even*

5 (Suddenly/All of a sudden) **the superintendent made up his mind.**
GEORGE ORWELL, "A Hanging," *Shooting an Elephant and Other Essays*

6 Let's (accept/except) **115 as man's maximum age, then, and ask** (whether/if) **we have a good reason to complain about this.**
ISAAC ASIMOV, "The Slowly Moving Finger," *Of Time and Space and Other Things*

7 I (hardly/don't hardly) **remember getting** (in/into) **bed and to sleep, but all night in my dreams I thought I could hear a wolf calling and singing and sobbing in a voice of exquisite tenderness.**
THEODORA C. STANWELL-FLETCHER, *Driftwood Valley*

8 (Already/All ready) **it has created a situation where parents and children find it hard to communicate on social matters.**
CHARLES W. COLE, "American Youth Goes Monogamous," *Harper's Magazine*, March 1957

9 **But according to the rules, it is** (alright/all right) **to kid him a little.**
BENJAMIN SPOCK, *Baby and Child Care*

10 **If she had never, from the first, regarded her marriage as a full cancelling of her claims on life, she had at least, for a number of years,** (accepted/excepted) **it as provisional compensation . . . .**
EDITH WHARTON, "Souls Belated"

Revision practice

Revise any of the following sentences that contain a problem in usage. Some of the sentences may not require revision.

1 In our modern world of today, drugs have become quite a problem.

2 Adreen stepped into her closet.

3 They didn't know whether they shouldn't ask for permission.

4 The one who always has the answer is she.

5 Their racing shell sunk in six feet of water.

6 No one can lay in bed forever, Manny.

7 I knew he was guilty when I seen him look away.

8 Professor Hasty sometimes gets a look on his face that is disturbing.

9 Speak soft or she will hear you.

10 I felt so badly about missing the test that I went back to sleep.

11 Irregardless of the time it takes, you must keep hunting data.

12 I wonder whether or not it will snow by Christmas.

13 I had been reading for an hour when suddenly I find this marvelous quote.

14 It's easy to guess whom you mean.

15 At this point in time, I'm not prepared to answer the question.

16 No one understands why this data is so unusual; its totally unique.

17 The men all have their mind made up.

18 This is one of those schools which provide financial aid to students.

19 The reason grammar is so hard is because it seems so arbitrary.

20 The party was quite a surprise for her and me.

1 FRANÇOISE-MARIE DE VOLTAIRE, *Candide*

2 BETTY PIERCE

3 JOHN STEINBECK, *The Grapes of Wrath*

4 GUSTAVE FLAUBERT, *Madame Bovary*

5 FRANZ KAFKA, *The Metamorphosis*

6 ROBERT LOUIS STEVENSON, *An Inland Voyage*

7 MARK SILVERS

8 HENRY JAMES, *The Aspen Papers*

9 ROBERT J. GLESSING, *The Underground Press in America*

10 OLIVER LA FARGE, *Old Man Facing Death*

11 HOWARD ADAMS

12 ALBERT CAMUS, *The Stranger*

13 MARY WOLLSTONECRAFT, *Frankenstein*

14 NATHANAEL WEST, *The Day of the Locust*

15 MARK TWAIN, *Huckleberry Finn*

16 ROBERT MURPHY, *A Certain Island*

17 DAN THOMPSON

18 BRAM STOKER, *Dracula*

19 AYN RAND, *Atlas Shrugged*

20 EMILY BRONTË, *Wuthering Heights*

21 "Choose from a World of Brandies," *House Beautiful,* Nov. 1976

22 Advertisement, American Gas Association

23 ERNEST HEMINGWAY, "The Snows of Kilimanjaro"

24 ROGER MARTIN DU GARD, *The Thibaults*

25 CHARLES MICHNER, "Black Movies: Renaissance or Ripoff?" *Newsweek,* 23 Oct. 1972

26 BONNIE SULLIVAN

27 CHARLES DICKENS, *The Old Curiosity Shop*

28 ROBERT LOUIS STEVENSON, *Travels with a Donkey*

29 Advertisement, *The Saturday Evening Post,* Jan./Feb. 1977

30 MARTIN LUTHER KING, JR., *Why We Can't Wait*

31 "Now and Forever," *Newsweek,* 17 Jan. 1977

32 JAMES AGEE AND WALKER EVANS, *Let Us Now Praise Famous Men*

33 LEO TOLSTOY, *Anna Karenina*

34 VINE DELORIA, JR., *Custer Died for Your Sins: An Indian Manifesto*

35 VALLERIE ENSON

36 ALEXIS DE TOCQUEVILLE, *Democracy in America*

37 D. H. LAWRENCE, *Cocksure Women and Hensure Men*

38 CLAUDE BERNARD, *Bulletin of the New York Academy of Medicine,* IV, 1928

39 SUETONIUS, *Life of Claudius*

40 HONORE DE BALZAC, *The Imaginary Mistress*

41 DEANNA CROSS

42 MAE SHIPERS

43 C. NORTHCOTE PARKINSON, *Parkinson's Law and Other Studies in Administration*

44 FELICIA STRAUSS

45 RICHARD D. ALTIC, *The Scholar Adventurer*

46 ARTHUR C. CLARKE, *Profiles of the Future*

47 HENRY SLOAN COFFIN, *The Meaning of the Cross*

48 GRETCHEN FUNNEL

49 VIRGINIA WOOLF, "How Should One Read a Book?"

50 OLIVER GOLDSMITH, *The Citizen of the World*

51 JOSEPH CONRAD, "The End of the Tether"
52 WHITNEY SODER
53 WILLIAM FAULKNER, *The Hamlet*
54 DEE BROWN, *Bury My Heart at Wounded Knee*
55 WILLA CATHER, *Willa Cather on Writing*
56 MARJORIE KINNAN RAWLINGS, *Cross Creek*
57 "Pardon: How Broad a Blanket?" *Time*, 17 Jan. 1977
58 ADLAI E. STEVENSON, *Looking Outward*

Y ou have to really work at it to write. I guess there has to be talent first; but even with talent you still have to *work* at it to write.

JAMES JONES, *Writers at Work*, George Plimpton, ed.

By comparison with larger matters of purpose and substance and structure, such things as punctuation, spelling, and capitalization may seem trivial. But all these mechanics of writing are tools the writer uses to signal the reader. An occasional error may be excused, but writers cannot afford to ignore the effect of mistakes on the reader. At the least, mistakes are distracting and interrupt the train of thought; at the worst, mistakes may *change* the thought: faulty punctuation, a mistaken spelling, even a word not capitalized may create a meaning unintended by the writer. Careful writers take pains to ensure that the effect of their words is not distorted by faulty mechanics.

Beyond the mere avoidance of error, mechanics can give you greater facility and maturity of expression. Beginning writers frequently avoid all but the few marks of punctuation they know well—the end marks and the comma—or avoid words they cannot spell readily. All this has the effect of limiting the signals of expression available to you as a writer. With some review and practice with the mechanics of writing, you will be able to increase your use of them and your skill with them.

PUNCTUATION GUIDE

One of the best tools a writer has is punctuation. With a few small signals, the writer can tell the reader how to interpret the ideas on the page and how to understand the relationships among them. There are about a dozen significant marks in the punctuation system; many of them you already know well.

USE A COMMA TO SEPARATE TWO SENTENCES JOINED BY "AND," "BUT," "OR," "NOR," "SO," "FOR"

He had not the energy to put the sound plug in his ear, and the silent motion of the cartoon figures had suddenly become horrid.
LARRY NIVEN, "The Jigsaw Man," *Dangerous Visions*, Harlan Ellison, ed.

All of us could hear somebody moving around in the dark, but nobody had the courage to strike a match or yell out at the intruder.
KAREN FRENCH

And Midge and Emma danced every dance together, for though every little onestep seemed to induce a new thirst of its own, Lou Hersch stayed too sober to dance with his own sister.
RING LARDNER, "Champion"

Reminder The rule does not say to use a comma every time you use the words "and," "but," and so on. Use a comma *only* when these words (conjunctions) join complete sentences. No comma is needed in the following sentence; it does not contain two complete sentences:

Those who saw the kite and fell under its abiding spell would have to be trusted to have sense and eyesight keen enough to follow the kite-string earthward to me and my diffident display.
BARRY FARRELL, "Confessions of a Kite Hustler," *Life*, 19 Sept. 1969

Option Two very short and closely related sentences may be joined by commas alone or by conjunctions alone:

You stick to your side, I'll stick to mine!
D. H. LAWRENCE, *Lady Chatterley's Lover*

It was important to be heard or nothing could be accomplished.
ROBERT COLES, *Children of Crisis*

ERRORS TO AVOID: COMMA SPLICE AND FUSED SENTENCE

It is usually a fault, called a *comma splice*, to join two sentences with a comma only. (See the preceding "Option" for the exception.)

COMMA SPLICE
Holmes tended to use his brains more than his brawn, he was the first literary detective to use chemistry in his work.

Two or more sentences joined without punctuation of any kind create the *fused,* or *run-on,* sentence:

FUSED SENTENCE
Two hours later I came out of the hospital I was equipped with crutches my left leg was in a cast above the knee.

These faults can be fixed in several ways: by adding conjunctions, by using semicolons or colons rather than commas, or by separating the sentences with periods and capital letters:

PUNCTUATION REVISIONS
Holmes tended to use his brains more than his brawn, and he was the first literary detective to use chemistry in his work.

Holmes tended to use his brains more than his brawn; he was the first literary detective to use chemistry in his work.

Holmes tended to use his brains more than his brawn. He was the first literary detective to use chemistry in his work.

Comma splices and fused sentences fail to make clear to the reader the relationships between and among your ideas. When you revise such sentences, decide first whether the ideas are equally important or whether your purpose is better served by emphasizing one idea and deemphasizing others. A revision more extensive than merely changing punctuation and/or conjunctions may be preferable:

SENTENCE REVISIONS
The first literary detective to use chemistry in his work, Holmes counted on brains more than brawn.

When I came out of the hospital two hours later, my left leg was in a cast above the knee, and I was equipped with crutches.

Two hours later I finally hobbled out of the hospital on crutches, my left leg in a cast above the knee.

USE A COMMA AFTER INTRODUCTORY CLAUSES AND PHRASES

Although the existence of creatures too small to be seen with the eye had long been suspected, their discovery was linked to the invention of the microscope.
THOMAS D. BROCK AND KATHERINE M. BROCK, *Basic Microbiology with Applications*

When she had gone, he fumbled for the jug and drank again.
THOMAS WOLFE, *Of Time and the River*

Option   If the introductory element is very short, the comma is optional:

On the second day I recognized defeat and finally unpacked the suitcase I had carried away from Kloten.
IRWIN SHAW, *Nightwork*

In Iowa the cattle waste half their feed just keeping warm in the wintertime.
RICHARD RHODES, "Watching the Animals," *Harper's Magazine,* March 1970

USE COMMAS TO SEPARATE THREE OR MORE ITEMS IN A SERIES

I climbed to the top of a hill and gazed out over the narrow rose-colored beaches, the sea, the faintly out-lined islands.
NIKOS KAZANTZAKIS, *Report to Greco*

I had brought her diapers, nightgowns, blankets, bunting, and bottles for his formula.
BERNARD BARD AND JOSEPH FLETCHER, "The Right to Die," *Atlantic Monthly,* April 1968

Reminder   A series calls for commas *between* the items. Ordinarily, there is no reason for putting a comma at the end of a series. Note in the following sentence that there is no comma after "geology."

Chemistry, anatomy, and geology were three sciences Holmes practiced.

Option   Some writers omit the final comma in a series. This style, although acceptable (many magazines and newspapers use it), can cause confusion. It may not be perfectly clear to the reader how many items you are listing without the final comma:

The Polish authorities are concerned about thievery, graft, corruption, drunkenness and the weakening of family ties . . . .
ABRAHAM BRUMBERG, "The Pope's Divisions," *The New Republic,* 16 June 1979

Does the writer mean that drunkenness concerns the authorities only when it causes the weakening of family ties, or does he mean that drunkenness and the weakening of family ties are separate items of concern? The reader cannot be certain which idea is intended.

Option   Another option is to join the items in a series with conjunctions instead of commas:

Holmes' scholarship includes books he wrote on tobacco and handwriting and footprints.

USE COMMAS TO SET OFF EXPLANATORY AND PARENTHETICAL ELEMENTS

In his smaller works, however, Dostoevsky was singularly free from partisanship.
DAVID MAGARSHACK, *The Best Short Stories of Dostoevsky*

The Peloponnesian War, for example, was little more than a skirmish by modern standards.
ALVIN TOFFLER, *Future Shock*

A glass-bottomed boat, or at least a glass-bottomed bucket, is a great aid in locating the best fishing grounds.
OWEN LEE, *Snorkel and Deep Diving*

USE COMMAS TO SET OFF NAMES AND TITLES IN DIRECT ADDRESS

"Did you cut the telephone wire, George?"
HAROLD MACGRATH, *The Green Stone*

"I know how to dance now, Papa."
HERMAN RAUCHER, *Ode to Billy Joe*

USE COMMAS TO SET OFF APPOSITIVES

Appositives are words that identify a noun or pronoun preceding or following them.

But that couldn't happen because he, an astronaut, is supposed to be one of the most sane people in the world.
ALAN D. FOSTER, *Dark Star*

There was a final touch from Hauptsturmfuehrer Lutz Kroll, the head of the Gestapo in Randers.
ELLIOTT ARNOLD, *A Night of Watching*

Option   The comma may be omitted from common expressions in which appositives are not emphasized: "My friend Harold" or "Fran's brother Claude."

USE COMMAS TO SET OFF ELEMENTS OF WHOLE DATES AND ADDRESSES

Wally died in his padded cell on January 18, 1923, at age thirty.
KENNETH ANGER, *Hollywood Babylon*

At Bell Labs, Buenos Aires, down Earthside, they've got a thinkum a tenth his size which can answer almost before you ask.
ROBERT A. HEINLEIN, *The Moon Is a Harsh Mistress*

Reminder   Partial dates and addresses should not be set off: "May 4 was a terrible day"; "They lived in Virginia for years."

USE COMMAS TO SET OFF SPEAKER TAGS

Speaker tags are the identifiers in dialogue: "he said," "she replied," and so on.

"No, I don't want a raise," I said.
ROBERT PENN WARREN, *All the King's Men*

"Oh Mother," he said, smiling and gently touching the tip of a finger to a tear as it rolled downward, "don't cry."
THOMAS TRYON, *The Other*

Reminder   The comma is not needed if some other mark of punctuation has already been used to set off the actual words of the speaker:

"What's the story?" asked the schoolmaster.
ALBERT CAMUS, "The Guest," *Exile and the Kingdom*

USE COMMAS TO SET OFF CONTRASTIVE ELEMENTS

This difference was a question of brain, not voice.
DESMOND MORRIS, *The Naked Ape*

The coast seems clear, save for that lad in the smithy.
ARTHUR CONAN DOYLE, "The Priory School"

USE COMMAS TO SET OFF NONRESTRICTIVE MODIFIERS

If a modifier is necessary to tell "which one" or "how many individuals," it is restrictive (essential) and should not be set off. Nonrestrictive clauses are set off with commas. Note the difference:

NONRESTRICTIVE
The police, who had guns, were waiting outside.

The "who" clause is nonessential; it doesn't identify or limit the number of police. It only adds extra information and can be removed without changing the idea of the sentence.

RESTRICTIVE
The police who had guns were waiting outside.

This clause is essential; it identifies which police are meant—*only* the ones with guns.

RESTRICTIVE
Those who got out always left something of themselves behind, as some animals amputate a leg and leave it in the trap.
JAMES BALDWIN, "Sonny's Blues"

NONRESTRICTIVE
Howe nodded to the boy, who pushed his head forward and then jerked it back in a wide elaborate arc to clear his brow of a heavy lock of hair.
LIONEL TRILLING, *Of This Time, Of That Place*

Note in the Trilling example that even though the nonrestrictive "who" clause is long, it doesn't affect the basic idea of the sentence: Howe's nodding to the boy. Thus, a comma goes before "who."

USE COMMAS IN PLACE OF "AND" BETWEEN MOVABLE ADJECTIVES

If the order of the adjectives is unimportant, so that the adjectives could be arranged in some other order, separate them with a comma:

He could have carried her about under his coat and brought her out suddenly, a little, brown-skinned, toothless, hunchbacked woman with a cracked, sing-song voice.
DYLAN THOMAS, *Portrait of the Artist as a Young Dog*

He had an old, battered felt hat turned inside out, the upside-down brim tilted at a dashing angle, and a pair of jeans six inches too short.
ELLEN DOUGLAS, "Jesse," *Black Cloud, White Cloud*

They had fried chicken and corn pudding and rich, glazed candied sweet potatoes.
CARSON MCCULLERS, "The Sojourner"

Reminder Use a comma in place of the word "and" between adjectives, but no comma should be used when the second adjective forms a unit with the noun: "He is an intelligent young man." Note in the examples by Douglas and McCullers, "felt hat" and "candied sweet potatoes" are considered units.

USE A COMMA FOR CLARITY

Commas can help the reader to avoid possible misreading:

When she dressed, her dog sat on the bed and watched.

Hunting is good here, for horses can get through the brush easily.

Gurov stopped, and wound the clock.

SEMICOLON

USE A SEMICOLON TO CONNECT TWO CLOSELY RELATED SENTENCES

The isolated kid developed a neurosis; the one with its mother did not.
EZRA STOTLAND, *The Psychology of Hope*

Raymond the Wolf passed away in his sleep one night from natural causes; his heart stopped beating when the three men who slipped into his bedroom stuck knives in it.
JIMMY BRESLIN, *The Gang That Couldn't Shoot Straight*

USE A SEMICOLON TO SEPARATE TWO SENTENCES JOINED WITH A CONJUNCTIVE ADVERB

Conjunctive adverbs include the following:

accordingly	furthermore	later	then
afterwards	hence	moreover	therefore
besides	however	nevertheless	thus
consequently	indeed	otherwise	yet
earlier	in fact	still	

He played but very indifferently; however, my eldest daughter repaid his former applause with interest, and assured him that his tones were even louder than those of her master.
OLIVER GOLDSMITH, *The Vicar of Wakefield*

Plato is imagining a polis on the normal Hellenic scale; indeed he implies that many existing Greek poleis are too small—for many had less than 5,000 citizens.
H. D. F. KITTO, *The Greeks*

USE A SEMICOLON IN A SERIES BETWEEN ITEMS CONTAINING COMMAS

Such modalities as bleeding (in a single year, 1827, France imported 33 million leeches after its domestic supplies had been depleted); purging through emetics; physical contact with unicorn horns, bezoar stones, mandrakes, or powdered mummies—all such treatments were no doubt regarded by physicians at the time as specifics with empirical sanctions.

NORMAN COUSINS, "Anatomy of an Illness," *Saturday Review*, 28 May 1977

Option   Sentences joined by "and," "but," "or," "nor," "so," or "for," usually need a comma before the connective. But when there are other commas in the sentences, you may substitute a semicolon for the comma before the connective:

Except to remark that I was small for my age, a runt, no one had ever paid any attention to me; but now people pointed me out, and said wasn't it sad? that poor little Collin Fenwick.

TRUMAN CAPOTE, *The Grass Harp*

COLON

USE A COLON TO INTRODUCE A SERIES

It contained what he presumed to be pirate plunder: silver and gold plate, cups, candelabra and ornaments, some religious paintings in ornate frames.

JAMES CLAVELL, *Shōgun*

I collect my tools: sight, smell, touch, taste, hearing, intellect.

NIKOS KAZANTZAKIS, *Report to Greco*

Reminder   The colon introduces a series when there is a clear signal, such as "including the following," "as follows," and so on, or when the colon takes the place of an expression like "such as" or "namely": "I collect my tools: [namely] sight, smell . . ." However, when the series is incorporated into a sentence without a signal or break, no introductory mark should be used. Avoid using a colon after any form of "to be" (am, is, are, was, were, be, being, been).

Nearly any journey goes through clusters and groves of banyan, banana, bamboo, jak, cadju, teak, eucalyptus, guava, plantain, mango, manosteen, breadfruit, sugarcane, and terraces of soggy rice.

PETER A. ISEMAN, "Sri Lanka," *Atlantic Monthly*, April 1974

All was poised, chill, and alone.
LOREN EISELEY, *The Immense Journey*

USE A COLON TO EMPHASIZE AN APPOSITIVE

Appositives are words that identify a noun or pronoun that precedes or follows them:

Look at its chief exponent today: Ho Chi Minh, a dried up old man, dreaming the weary dreams of the aged.
NORMAN VINCENT PEALE, *Enthusiasm Makes the Difference*

About ten more years elapsed before investigations were able to determine its chemical identity: indolitic acid.
FULLER, CAROTHERS, et al., *The Plant World*

USE A COLON BEFORE AN EXAMPLE OR ILLUSTRATION

This diminution of self-esteem is not limited to blacks: it affects other oppressed groups as well.
ELIOT ARONSON, *The Social Animal*

Its effect on Cromis was hypnotic: as the syllables rolled, he found himself sinking into a reverie of death and spoliation.
M. JOHN HARRISON, *The Pastel City*

USE A COLON BEFORE A FORMAL QUOTATION

After his oration on the two hundredth founding of Plymouth Colony, a young Harvard scholar wrote:

I was never so excited by public speaking before in my life. Three or four times I thought my temple would burst with the rush of blood . . . . I was beside myself and am so still.
JOHN F. KENNEDY, *Profiles in Courage*

One of the shortest Amendments in American history, it reads: "Equality of rights under the law shall not be denied or abridged by the United States or by any State on account of sex."
CLARE BOOTH LUCE, "When Women Will Be Superior to Men," *McCall's*, April 1976

PARENTHESES

Use parentheses to set off clarifying information and information not grammatically connected to the rest of the sentence:

The square of the time of revolution of a planet about the sun (expressed in years) is equal to the cube of its average distance from the sun (expressed in astronomical units).

MILES, SHERWOOD, AND PARSONS, *College Physical Science*

The white kids were going to have a chance to become Galileos and Madame Curies and Edisons and Gauguins, and our boys (the girls weren't even in on it) would try to be Jesse Owenses and Joe Louises.

MAYA ANGELOU, *I Know Why the Caged Bird Sings*

OTHER PUNCTUATION WITH PARENTHESES

If the parenthetic material is less than a full sentence, the sentence period falls outside the parenthesis, as it does in the example from *College Physical Science* above. Even if the parenthetic material should be a full sentence, as it is in the Maya Angelou example, you do not need either a capital letter to begin it or a period to end it.

If it should happen that the parenthetic material is a question or exclamation, you must still provide an end-of-sentence period:

Hearing that the new faith had made converts in Damascus, he obtained authorization from the high priest to go there, arrest all "who belonged to the Way," and bring them in chains to Jerusalem (A.D. 31?).

WILL DURANT, *Caesar and Christ*

The only time the end-of-sentence period falls within parentheses is when the entire sentence is written as a separate, parenthetic sentence:

Then we express our ideas by transforming what we mean into what we say. (In the case of writing, it's obviously a matter of selecting letters rather than sounds to express our meanings.)

WILLIAM S. CHISHOLM AND LOUIS T. MILIC, *The English Language: Form and Use*

Reminder Punctuation is not used before an opening parenthesis, but it is sometimes necessary after the closing parenthesis:

Diphtheria—Pertussis (Whooping cough)—Tetanus is one of the most reliable vaccinations.

BESSIE HEAD, "The Woman from America," *Classic Magazine*, vol. 3, no. 1, 1968

DASH

USE DASHES TO INDICATE A SUDDEN BREAK IN THE THOUGHT OF A SENTENCE

And Gabriel loved her—if he loved her—only because she was the mother of his son, Ray.

JAMES BALDWIN, *Go Tell It on the Mountain*

Naomi somebody—a close friend of his—told him she had a worm in her thermos bottle.

J. D. SALINGER, "Down at the Dinghy"

USE A DASH FOR A DRAMATIC PAUSE
OR TO EMPHASIZE A POINT

"Now, Doris," he tried to speak lightly, "you can't do that here—not to the ship's surgeon."

A. J. CRONIN, *The Judas Tree*

You've got enough facts—or is it that you don't want to face facts?

ALEXANDER KEY, *The Forgotten Door*

USE A DASH AFTER AN INTRODUCTORY SERIES

Sandbanks, marshes, forests, savages—precious little fit for a civilized man, nothing but Thames water to drink.

JOSEPH CONRAD, *Heart of Darkness*

Salary checks, withholding deductions, mortgage payments—the major items in middle-class finances are firmly geared to a thirty-day cycle, and any dissonant peaks and valleys are anathema.

WILLIAM H. WHITE, JR., *The Organization Man*

USE A DASH IN DIALOGUE WHEN A
SPEAKER'S WORDS END ABRUPTLY

"Because when I went downstairs half an hour ago I met Lady Susan on the way—"

EDITH WHARTON, "Souls Belated"

"For us, our love is our life, not for the ladies. In the ghetto they—"

BERNARD MALAMUD, "The Magic Barrel"

Reminder In typing, make a dash with two hyphens (--) and leave no space before, between, or after them.

BRACKETS

USE BRACKETS TO SET OFF CLARIFYING
MATERIAL INSERTED INTO QUOTATIONS

By autumn the poet [Poe] was again destitute and Mrs. Clemm now exerted herself to secure him some salaried work.

HERVEY ALLEN, "Introduction," *The Works of Edgar Allan Poe*

The 28 limestone figures above the portals [of Notre Dame] actually represented the kings of Judea, but the mob [in 1793], thinking they represented French monarchs, cheered as fellow citizens tied ropes around the statues' necks, pulled them down and guillotined them in Cathedral Square.

PAMELA ANDRIOTAKIS, "After 184 Years a Cousin of the French President Finds Notre Dame's Missing Stone Heads," *People Weekly*, 4 July 1977

Note If material you quote contains an error made by the original author, you may insert "sic" in brackets immediately after the error. "Sic," which means "thus," indicates to the reader that the error in logic or language appears "thus" in the original. Don't use "sic" merely to impress readers with your ability to recognize variant spellings or unconventional punctuation. Instead, reserve it to signal that special care is needed to avoid a misreading:

Oliver raced toward the plain [sic] that moved slowly, steadily away from him as it taxied down the runway.

ITALICS (UNDERLINING)

Underlining, a convention of hand- or typewritten material, indicates words that would be set in italics if the material were to be type-set.

USE ITALICS FOR TITLES OF LONG WORKS

The titles of books, magazines, newspapers, long poems, plays, operas, films, works of art, and the names of radio or television series (as distinct from the titles of individual episodes of such programs) should be underlined in your compositions:

There is another book on the shelf in Kesey's living room that everybody seems to look at, a little book called *The Journey to the East*, by Herman Hesse.

TOM WOLFE, *The Electric Kool-Aid Acid Test*

"It might even get me into the *Saturday Evening Post*," Colonel Cathcart boasted in his office with a smile, swaggering back and forth convivially as he reproached the chaplain.

JOSEPH HELLER, *Catch-22*

USE ITALICS FOR EMPHASIS

"But what *do* you believe in?"

D. H. LAWRENCE, *Lady Chatterley's Lover*

I'm a fair mountain man in spite of my foot, but when we head for home it won't be *that* way.

ALEXANDER KEY, *The Forgotten Door*

Reminder The best way to show emphasis is by means of careful word choice and sentence structure. Italics should be used sparingly to show emphasis; they soon lose effect. Doubling up on punctuation (He never said that!!) is amateurish overkill. Avoid it.

USE ITALICS FOR THE NAMES OF SHIPS, PLANES, AND TRAINS

Her name—*Bethia*—had been painted out, and at the suggestion of Sir Joseph Banks she was rechristened *Bounty*.

CHARLES NORDHOFF AND JAMES HALL, *Mutiny on the Bounty*

The *Enterprise* is the largest man-made vessel in space.

STEPHEN E. WHITFIELD AND GENE RODDENBERRY, *The Making of Star Trek*

USE ITALICS FOR FOREIGN WORDS AND PHRASES

"*Ichi Ban?*" Blackthorne had asked, wanting to know if he was all right.

JAMES CLAVELL, *Shōgun*

"You make me sick, *Herr Doktor*," he told the older man.

FREDERICK FORSYTHE, *The Odessa File*

APOSTROPHE

USE AN APOSTROPHE FOR SINGULAR POSSESSIVES

Add *'s* unless the word already ends in *s*, in which case just add the apostrophe (Watson's hat, corpse's hand, iris' color).

Miss Gollum's father was to be played by Joseph W. Grossman.

JOHN O'HARA, *The Instrument*

She spoke in a whisper, but Moller's doctor's ear detected the hysteria.

ELLIOT ARNOLD, *A Night of Watching*

USE AN APOSTROPHE FOR PLURAL POSSESSIVES

Add *'s* to the *plural form* of the word, unless the plural ends in *s*, in which case just add the apostrophe (policemen's whistles, children's shoes, dogs' tails).

A Martian dies when he decides to, having discussed it with friends and received consent of his ancestors' ghosts to join them.

ROBERT A. HEINLEIN, *Stranger in a Strange Land*

We were coming down on the hemisphere opposite the Taurans' outpost.

JOE HALDEMAN, *The Forever Man*

Option   If you wish to indicate that the possessive is to be pronounced as a separate syllable, you have the option of adding an extra *s* to a word ending in *s* (Holmes's, James's, Lois's, Jones's).

USE AN APOSTROPHE FOR ABSTRACT AND INANIMATE POSSESSIVES

Be careful to treat such terms (day's wages, life's troubles, investigation's conclusion, countries' citizens) as possessives; they can be more difficult to recognize than concrete and/or animate possessives such as "Jean's emotions" and "Darwin's finches."

It was clean—clean in the absolute sense, because it had no capacity to conceive of the world's ugliness.

AYN RAND, *The Fountainhead*

"Franco, for heaven's sake."

JACQUELINE SUSANN, *Once Is Not Enough*

USE AN APOSTROPHE TO FORM A CONTRACTION

If contractions serve your writing purpose, use them. Usually, they will be suitable for informal or semiformal writing. The apostrophe takes the place of the missing letter or letters in the contracted word form.

"So you've been here for a whole hour? Oh, poor fellow!" Zverkov cried ironically, for to his notions this was bound to be extremely funny.

FYODOR DOSTOEVSKY, *Notes from Underground*

QUOTATION MARKS

USE QUOTATION MARKS FOR TITLES OF SHORT WORKS

Most poems, short stories, magazine and newspaper articles, book chapters, the names of specific episodes of continuing television and radio programs, and popular songs take quotation marks:

In 1956, when rock and roll was just about a year old, Frankie Lymon, lead singer of Frankie Lymon and the Teenagers, wrote and recorded a song called "Why Do Fools Fall in Love?"
MICHAEL LYNDON, *Rock Folk*

"The Fall of the House of Usher," by Poe, first appeared in *Burton's Gentleman's Magazine*, September, 1839.

Once a week he watched "The Best of Carson" on the *Tonight Show.*

USE QUOTATION MARKS AROUND ODD OR INVENTED WORDS OR WORDS USED WITH SPECIAL MEANING

I began playing a game in which I had to choose between jobs with imaginary titles like "torpist" and "varisator."
MARVIN GROSSWIRTH, "Let This Computer Plan Your Future," *Science Digest,* Jan. 1977.

Instead, applicants for teacher in New York City spend months or years learning a peculiar "correct" pronunciation that is heard nowhere else on land or sea.
PAUL GOODMAN, *People or Personnel*

USE QUOTATION MARKS AROUND WORDS REFERRED TO AS WORDS

When you write about a word, referring to it as a word instead of for its meaning, use quotation marks around it:

The real problem with "ripoff" is that it's used indiscriminately, to characterize anything from the price of hamburger to the treatment of the Vietnamese boat people.

Option You can use italics instead of quotation marks to distinguish words used as words:

Philanthropist is derived from the Greek words *philein* and *anthropos.*

Whichever treatment you use—quotation marks or italics—follow the style consistently throughout a composition.

USE QUOTATION MARKS AROUND DIRECT QUOTES

"Awww," Pinback groaned, shuffling one foot and looking down at the floor.
ALAN D. FOSTER, *Dark Star*

Arthur replied, "God is total awareness."
RUTH MONTGOMERY, *A World Beyond*

Reminder In dialogue, indent for each new speaker:

"Well, Sonny," I said gently, "you know people can't always do exactly what they *want* to do—"

"*No*, I don't know that," said Sonny, surprising me. "I think people *ought* to do what they want to do, what else are they alive for?"
JAMES BALDWIN, "Sonny's Blues"

USE QUOTATION MARKS FOR SOURCE MATERIAL INCORPORATED INTO YOUR OWN SENTENCES

Incorporating a quote does not create the need for a comma. If the sentence would not require a comma without the quotation marks, it will not require a comma with them: Shakespeare referred to the world as "a stage." According to Shakespeare, "All the world's a stage."

John Diebold, the American automation expert, warns that "the effects of the technological revolution we are now living through will be deeper than any social change we have experienced before."
ALVIN TOFFLER, *Future Shock*

HOW TO HANDLE LONG QUOTES

If you quote more than three typewritten lines, indent all lines of the quotation on the left side and, like the rest of your paper, type the quote double-spaced. For specifics about typing long quotes, see the format guidelines inside the back cover of this book. No quotation marks are required unless they appear in the original.

Fortunately, some scientists seem to be aware of the dangers:

> Difficult as it is to put into words, there is a deep and abiding aesthetic and spiritual need, indeed a love, in the individual man for the unplanned formlessness, the unexpected beauty, and the unhurriedness of life that exists outside of that area controlled by man. To deny that need, that love, is to diminish each of us, to make us the captives, not the masters, of the technological civilization in which we live . . . . The Tin Woodsman in The Wizard of Oz knew whereof he spoke. "To love," he said, "one must have a heart." And that love must encompass all things that re-lease and give expression to the humanity of man. A future in which man replaces all other living things is no future at all.[7]

[7] Carl P. Swanson, The Natural History of Man (Englewood Cliffs, N.J.: Prentice-Hall, Inc.), pp. 374-75.

QUOTATION MARKS AND OTHER PUNCTUATION

Commas and periods always go inside the quotation marks

He believed that Zionism was one of the world's greatest revolutionary movements, and he described it as the "plot on which contemporary Jewish history hinges."
GOLDA MEIER, *My Life*

"I hope to give glory to God, but not to gratify the devil," retorted Alden.
MARION L. STARKEY, *The Devil in Massachusetts*

Colons and semicolons always go outside the quotation marks

Upon some essay which I had to write for him he wrote the comment "childlike and bland"; and, in order to help me to be less childlike, he lent me, to read in the holidays, Saintsbury's book of selections from English prose-writers . . . .
G. E. MOORE, *The Philosophy of G. E. Moore*

They "run away," they "get out of hand": they are creations inside a creation, and often inharmonious towards it . . . .
E. M. FORSTER, *Aspects of the Novel*

Question marks and exclamation points go inside or *outside the quotation marks*   If the matter inside the quotes is a question or an exclamation, the mark goes inside too. If the matter inside the quotes is not a question or exclamation, but the rest of the sentence is, the mark goes outside.

"And see, have I not here my faithful dog to protect me also? My excellent and loyal Hastings!"
AGATHA CHRISTIE, *Curtain*

What do you mean, "I never sent the invitations"?
TIM COO

USE SINGLE QUOTES TO INDICATE A QUOTE WITHIN A QUOTE

"I can't go," Loren pouted. "My father's exact words were, 'I forbid you to see that movie!' and there's no way to get around that."

The tension builds to a climax: "At this instant a horrible change came over his expression; his eyes stared wildly, his jaw dropped, and he yelled, in a voice I can never forget, 'Keep him out! For Christ's sake, keep him out!' "
ARTHUR CONAN DOYLE, *The Sign of the Four*

Note On rare occasions a third set of quotation marks may be needed. Use the third set to indicate a speaker (double quotes) quoting another speaker (single quotes) who in turn is quoting a third speaker (double quotes within the single quotes).

Irwin Shaw, in "The Eighty Yard Run," uses dialogue to reveal character, as in this sentence: " 'When I was waiting for you at the library yesterday two girls saw you coming and one of them said to the other, "That's Christian Darling. He's an important figure." ' "

DO NOT USE QUOTATION MARKS
FOR INDIRECT QUOTES

He said Izzarra was made of the flowers of the Pyrenees.
ERNEST HEMINGWAY, *The Sun Also Rises*

I said there was a society of men among us, bred up from their youth in the art of proving by words multiplied for their purpose, that white is black, and black is white, according as they are paid.
JONATHAN SWIFT, *Gulliver's Travels*

Reminder Although indirect quotes do not need quotation marks, they may require documentation. See pages 195–204.

ELLIPSIS POINTS

USE ELLIPSIS POINTS TO SHOW THAT YOU
HAVE OMITTED ONE OR MORE WORDS
FROM QUOTED MATERIAL

ORIGINAL QUOTE
After luncheon, when I was not going to roam about Venice by myself, I went up to my room to get ready to go out with my mother.
MARCEL PROUST, *The Sweet Cheat Gone*, C. K. Scott Moncrieff, trans.

QUOTE WITH OMISSION
After luncheon . . . I went up to my room to get ready to go out with my mother.

Note Type ellipsis points with three periods, a single space before and after each one. When the omission involves the last part of a quoted sentence use four spaced periods; the fourth dot becomes the sentence period.

After luncheon . . . I went up to my room . . . . In the abrupt angles of the walls I could read the restrictions imposed by the sea, the parsimony of the soil.

USE ELLIPSIS POINTS TO INDICATE BREAKS IN DIALOGUE AND INTERRUPTED OR UNFINISHED THOUGHTS

The 10:35 express stops at Galesville, Selby, and Indiana City, except on Sundays and holidays, at which time it stops at . . . and so it goes.
HARLAN ELLISON, *"Repent Harlequin," Said the Tictockman*

So he gave me two hundred a month and told me I could do my worst on that . . . . This your little girl?
F. SCOTT FITZGERALD, "Babylon Revisited"

FRAGMENTS

The fragment is a stylistic device. Some authors use fragments; some do not. However, anything which slows or prevents the reader's comprehension should be considered a flaw in writing; and in academic and other formal writing situations, many readers always count the fragment as an error.

One Saturday we took a rusty old bus that clanked over the mountains to a small hilled-in village. Where a saw mill made up the public square.

Whether anything useful is achieved by this kind of fragmentation depends on your purpose in writing. While some readers would read the sentence without difficulty, others might stumble over the fragment—especially those who read very much in academic and otherwise formal English. Such readers will prefer a more conventional treatment:

One Saturday we took a rusty old bus that clanked over the mountains to a small hilled-in village where a saw mill made up the public square.
ELLINGTON WHITE, "The Sergeant's Good Friend," *Sewanee Review*, Winter 1957

ABBREVIATIONS

Use a period after common abbreviations: U.S.A., Mrs., Mr., Dr. In a paper in which you make several references to some organization with a long name, such as the National Council of Teachers of English, you may introduce an abbreviated form of the name (NCTE) after using the full name once. Such abbreviations are customarily given without periods: AFL-CIO, UNICEF, UAW, and so on. Except for scientific papers, in which abbreviations are customary, avoid abbreviations other than for names and titles; do not abbreviate words like "pound" (lb.), "ounce" (oz.), "inch" (in.), and so on. See "Abbreviation" in the usage dictionary.

NUMBERS

Use commas and periods (decimal points) to make numbers, percentages, and amounts of money clear: 1,000,000 (one million); $10.95 (ten dollars and ninety-five cents). You must be especially careful when indicating percentages as decimals to get the decimal point in the right place. Three percent is written as .03; thirty percent is equivalent to .30. Increasingly, writers in scientific and technical journals use a zero to "anchor" two-place decimals: 0.23; 0.01. See "Numbers" in the usage dictionary for basic guidelines concerning when to use figures and when to write numbers out in words.

Punctuation proofreading practice

Suggest a revision for any sentence whose punctuation is likely to distract the reader.

1 Hamlet's dilemma is Freudian; what to do with a wayward mother?

2 And so we see that, the idea of universal education is noble but, how many lives are in fact, ruined by it?

3 Surely everyone has heard of journalists like Murrow, Thomas, and Woodward and Bernstein.

4 Jack and Jill went up the hill to fetch a pail of water; and Jack fell down and broke his crown, and Jill came tumbling after.

5 A college degree, which once promised high paying jobs, now promises only a college education.

6 Tennis, swimming, and football, were Dale's favorite sports.

7 Macbeth describes life as "a tale told by an idiot."

8 She can usually be called upon to ask, "Who says we need 'Education' "?

9 "Can any nation," the commentator wanted to know, "survive the death of its own myths?"

10 "Whose opinion is it that we are" merely pawns?

11 The average freshman sleeps much, drinks much, and studies little.

12 The economic theory of supply and demand is just that—a theory, it works only when the cost of production is low.

13 It is possible that the character of education is changing, the costs of going to school may soon create an educated aristocracy.

14 A homeowner feels lucky if he hits water at thirty feet, however, a sixty-foot well is not uncommon.

15 The course catalog listed "Freshman English, Dr. Bowman"; "Advanced Creative Writing, Dr. Bowman"; "Shakespeare's Tragedies, Dr. Bowman"; and "Seminar in Middle English Poetry, Dr. Bowman."

16 Of course no one can write anymore no one ever could!

17 When it became clear that the President had been lying the mood of the nation turned sour.

18 Inevitably that preciseness of mind which has for so long characterized the flavor of our best scholarship.

19 "No, Dinsmore, you may not run your rat tonight," he said.

20 "Open the door," she yelled, "and stand out of the way."

21 Nobody can put up with governmental lying for long—not even governmental "apologists"—without losing touch with reality or becoming very cynical.

22 "Only a language purrist [sic] would wince at a split infinitive today," Clayton asserted in his essay.

23 It isn't just that he has no time for it, he really has no talent for Oriental war poetry.

24 "Attack!" she uttered succinctly and quietly.

25 What do you mean, "He's an 'atheist'?"

26 "A days work for a days wages" is an American cliché.

27 I would certainly be the last one to tell you about your halitosis, but since you ask me . . . .

28 There are just so many sacrifices one can make (dating Professor Piddlemeyer isn't one of them) in pursuit of higher education.

29 Armstrong has been here just long enough to go around saying how *outré* everything is.

30 Certainly you should apply for a tax rebate otherwise you encourage governmental give-away of illegal tax money!

31 There is really only one thing I can't stand about Melinda: her presence.

32 Everyone in the dorms is wondering whether to study for the exam.

33 After lengthy discussion and procedural debates, the trustees have arrived at their conclusion: tuition must be increased.

34 "Candy is nice but liquor is quicker", is a chauvinist myth.

35 I don't care *what* she told you!!!

36 "Come along Miss Van Tassle; the doctor will see you now," she said.

37 Henry James's *Turn of the Screw* poses interesting questions about the narrator's reliability.

38 The truth is that "hip" isn't hip anymore.

39 The Constitution is our chief defense against tyranny, "he said."

40 Dale asked, "Professor Emmett, did you say, 'Shakespeare said, "All the world's a stage" ' ?"

41 Churchill ought to be remembered for his eloquence for his speeches carried Britain through her darkest hours.

42 Convinced of the shoddiness of American cars, Nader made others believe it.

43 You are a natural athlete, but to play a good game of tennis you'll need practice.

44 We protested that the engine used too much oil, that the brakes were worn out, and that the tires were dangerous.

45 "If it rains," said Miss Prescott, "the picnic will be postponed".

46 They had covered the country in the campaign: Trenton, New Jersey; Scranton, Pennsylvania; Chicago, Illinois; and points west.

47 Merl said, "I don't think she's the one who said, 'What did you say?' "

48 "I can think of nothing better," she said, "than sitting here on the deck of the Sea Hawk, sailing along, reading *Yachting*."

49 Any ideas implementation is likely to be more time consuming than the generation of the idea itself.

50 Many people have wondered why the apteryx didn't survive.

SPELLING

Misspelled words are a distraction to the educated reader. Except for people who compete in spelling bees, however, misspelling need not create an obvious problem. A poor speller's first step should be to learn to proofread compositions carefully for misspellings. If you can correct the misspelled words in your finished writing, your "spelling problem" will be at least partly solved, because it won't be apparent to readers.

There is probably no more effective method for improving spelling than simply memorizing the words you can't spell. However, there are a number of things you can do to improve your proofreading abilities.

PRACTICE

Most beginning writers do not proofread as much or as carefully as they should. Proofreading calls for careful scrutiny of each line of a composition, virtually character by character. A quick rush-through before handing in your paper will catch only the most obvious errors. You need time to do a thorough job.

GET SOMEONE TO HELP YOU

A roommate or classmate may not know much more than you, but a fresh pair of eyes may see things yours have missed. Sensible writers ask for help in areas where they are weak. If you and a friend regularly proofread for each other, you will both get better at it and will be able to do a more thorough job on your own manuscripts.

LET YOUR MANUSCRIPT COOL OFF

The paper that is finished the night before it is due will almost always look rushed. If you can give yourself at least twenty-four hours' cooling-off time, you will have a more objective view of your writing. Mistakes that were invisible before will be easier to spot a day or so later.

MEMORIZE THE CORRECT SPELLING OF WORDS YOU HABITUALLY MISSPELL

Except for careless mistakes, most people misspell only certain words. A little memory work will help reduce the list of words you habitually mistake. Little tricks like remembering the "iron" in "environment" and "a rat" in "separate" may help you.

LEARN TO USE A SPELLING DICTIONARY

Unlike standard dictionaries, spelling dictionaries have no definitions in them, just lists of words; thus, they are small and easy to use *quickly* when looking up words. You will still need to use a standard dictionary when you write, but most of your spelling problems can be solved with a small spelling dictionary. (We have provided a very small spelling dictionary for you in this book.) If there is any doubt in your mind whether "receive" or "recieve" is the correct spelling, the spelling dictionary will tell you immediately. You might also find it useful to create your own spelling dictionary. Every time you check the spelling of a word, copy the correct spelling into a notebook. Keep the words in alphabetical order. Study these words specifically; they are the ones *you* dont' know.

LOOK FOR TROUBLE SPOTS IN YOUR WORDS

Most people know which problems they have; with a spelling dictionary you can quickly check out things like the *-able/-ible* and the *ei/ie* combinations. If you can build the habit of checking out troublesome words, you will find yourself beginning to remember the correct spelling of more and more of these words.

REVIEW OF TROUBLE SPOTS IN SPELLING

"ei"/"ie"   *I* before *e* except after *c* or when pronounced as *a*, as in "neighbor" and "weigh." This jingle used to be taught in the elementary schools. It works pretty well, but there are a number of exceptions ("leisure," "seize," and so on). Check any *ei/ie* combinations; memorize the ones that cause you trouble ("friend," "fiend").

"-able"/"-ible"   These two endings (suffixes) are generally pronounced alike, and there are no very useful rules about them. By far, *-able* is the more common spelling, and *-ible* frequently follows an *s* sound ("flexible," "sensible"). However, there is no good substitute for looking these words up and memorizing them.

"-ant," "-ance"/"-ent," "-ence"   As with *-able* and *-ible*, these endings are generally pronounced alike: "abundant," "existent"; "abundance," "existence." Look up any word you are not certain about.

Final "e"   Final *e* is usually dropped to avoid doubling up vowels: "hop[e]ing," "scrap[e]ing." But in some cases it is kept: "changeable," "peaceable." And it is always kept when the suffix begins with a consonant: "hopeful," "boredom." Check any word you are not certain about; many words today are spelled either way ("livable," "liveable"), but some are not.

Double consonants   Many words double the final letter (consonant) before adding a suffix: "hop-ping," "scrap-ping." But "long-vowel" words do not: "hōping," "scrāping." And there are exceptions to the rule ("benefited"). To say it another way, doubling the last consonant has the effect of changing long vowels to short ones, so "hopping" could not be pronounced as the *-ing* form of "hope."

"Pre-"/"Per-"/"Pro-"   Check words with these beginnings (prefixes) (*"per*spiration," *"per*formance," *"pre*pare," *"pro*tect"). Don't spell them by the way you hear them spoken. Many people pronounce them all alike; others interchange them (*"pre*spiration," *"per*tect").

Plurals of "-y" words   Most words that end in *y* change to *ie* for the plural: "babies," "families." When the *y* follows a vowel ("monkey") the plural is formed by adding *s* only ("monkeys").

Suffixes with "-y" words   Change -*y* to *i* before all suffixes (endings) except -*ing*: "beauty," "beautiful"; "noisy," "noisily"; "buy," "buying."

"-ery"/"-ary"   The more common ending, by far, is -*ary*, but a few words end with -*ery*: "cemetery," "stationery" (paper).

"-or"/"-er"/"-ar"   All these endings sound alike ("author," "painter," "grammar"). The safest practice is to check a spelling dictionary.

"-ceed"/"-cede"/"-sede"   Check any words ending with the "eed" sound. "Supersede" is the only word ending in *sede;* "exceed," "proceed," and "succeed" are the only words ending in *ceed.* All the rest of the "eed"-sounding words are spelled -*cede:* "precede," "secede."

Look-alikes and sound-alikes   Homonyms and near-homonyms account for a large number of spelling mistakes. Writers who "spell with their ears" are likely to mistake words like *"board"/ "bored," "stare"/"stair,"* and so on. In many cases readers feel these errors are worse than spelling errors because the writer appears to have used the wrong word, instead of misspelled the right word. Be sure you have the right form with very common words like "there"/"their"/"they're" and "your"/"you're"/"yore."

HYPHENS IN COMPOUND WORDS

Check your dictionary for the spelling of any compound word. Many are spelled as two words, "high school"; others as one word, "coffeepot"; and still others as hyphenated words, "half-dollar."

Compound-word modifiers before a noun   These compounds should generally be hyphenated: "high-school graduate," "left-wing politics," "round-trip ticket." This guideline does not apply to -*ly* words, which are never hyphenated:

"-LY" COMPOUND	HYPHENATED COMPOUND
roughly cut diamond	rough-cut diamond
softly spoken words	soft-spoken words

Compound-word modifiers after a noun Modifiers that are hyphenated when they precede the noun do not need hyphens when they come after the noun: "She is a graduate of high school," "their politics are left wing," "his ticket was round trip."

Prefixes and suffixes The prefixes *all-, cross-, ex-, half-,* and *self-* and the suffix *-elect* are usually hyphenated: "all-important," "ex-governor," "self-pity," "senator-elect." When "self" is the root of the word, however, it is not hyphenated: "selfhood," "selfish."

The prefixes and suffixes listed below form words that are spelled as one word ("overburdened," "substandard," "reread," "tenfold," "animallike"):

anti	non	pseudo	supra
co	over	re	ultra
extra	post	semi	un
infra	pre	sub	under
intra	pro	super	fold
			like

Note When you use a prefix to form a compound word that is spelled exactly like an existing single word, it's necessary to hyphenate. "The new prime minister intends to re-form the cabinet" means that the prime minister is going to get rid of the people in the cabinet and start afresh. "The new prime minister intends to reform the cabinet," however, means that the cabinet members aren't in imminent danger of losing their jobs.

WORD DIVISION

Dividing words at the ends of lines is primarily a printer's device for making all the lines look even. Typed papers have much less need for such uniformity, and for the most part writers can avoid dividing words. However, there are times when word division is hard to avoid; you should follow established practice when you do divide a word.

Always divide between syllables only The syllables of English words have been established by tradition and may not correspond to the actual sound units of words the way you pronounce them: "wa-ter" is the traditional syllabication, although many people pronounce the word "wat-er." Many words seem to contradict pronunciation: "weap-on," "lim-it," "dis-sect." All standard dictionaries show syllabication.

Words containing double letters usually divide between the double letters

com-mon   lit-tle   es-say

Prefixes usually form syllables and can be divided

ex-cite   de-fault   con-vince

COMMON PREFIXES

ab	(absent)	ob	(obtuse)
ad	(admit)	mis	(mistake)
bi	(biceps)	non	(nonsense)
com	(commit)	per	(percolate)
con	(content)	pre	(prevent)
de	(detour)	pro	(proceed)
dis	(discuss)	re	(return)
ex	(extend)	sub	(submarine)
in	(insert)	trans	(transfer)
		un	(uncertain)

Suffixes starting with consonants always form syllables

ful	(helpful)	tion	(action)
ness	(goodness)	wise	(crosswise)
ship	(friendship)		

Other word-division guidelines   The surest guide to syllabication is the dictionary, but you can avoid most errors by remembering the following:

1 Never divide a one-syllable word or a word that is pronounced as one syllable: "through," "school," "width," "rhythm," "stretched."

2 Never leave or carry to the next line a single letter, even if the letter forms a syllable: "a-bout," "e-vict," "man-y," "jerk-y."

3 Hyphenated words must be divided only at the hyphen: "pistol-whip," "all-star."

4 Avoid dividing proper names: "Robert," "Carter," "Rockefeller."

5 The verb ending *-ing* is a separate syllable when it is merely added to a word: "wish-ing," "sew-ing," "pass-ing," "sell-ing." When *-ing* causes a doubling of consonants in the root word, the rule for double letters applies: "run-ning," "step-ping," "hop-ping."

6 The suffixes *-able* and *-ible* should not be divided (*-a-ble, -i-ble*) into two syllables. Take the entire suffix to the next line.

7 Avoid dividing the last word of a paragraph or the last word of a page.

8 Avoid dividing at the end of more than two lines in succession.

Word division practice

How should these words be divided?

apologetic	differentiation	immobilizing	pacification
appreciate	do-gooder	jujitsu	punctuation
backbone	dreadful	keenness	quadrangular
baldheaded	exterminate	label	rehabilitation
clairvoyant	fearsome	Massachusetts	sissy
clergy	governmental	misapplication	thorough
contrary	grinned	nonpartisan	tyrannosaurus
decompose	heavy-duty	ownership	virtuosity

SPELLING DICTIONARY

If you do not find the *form* of the word you are looking for, you may assume that it is a *regular* formation in English ("abacus*es*," "abandon*ed*") or that it may be readily inferred from the form given ("academician"). The abbreviation *cf.* means "compare with" and is used to indicate a homonym or another word similar to the given word.

abacus	accessible	acreage	alcohol
abandon	accidentally	across	alleviate
abdomen	acclaim	actuality	all ready (*cf.* already)
abdominal	accommodate	actually	
ably	accompanied	address	all right (*cf.* all wrong)
abortion	accompaniment	adequate	
abridgment (*or* abridgement)	accompanying	adjacent	allege
	accomplish	admission	alley (*cf.* ally)
absence	accumulate	admittance	allotted
absorption	accuracy	adolescence	allowed (*cf.* aloud)
absurd	accurate	adolescent	
abundance	accuses	advantageous	allude (*cf.* elude)
academic	accusing	advertisement	
academically	accustom	advice (*noun*)	allusion (*cf.* illusion)
academy	achievement	advise (*verb*)	
accelerate	acknowledg-ment (*or* ac-knowledgement)	affect (*cf.* effect)	ally (*cf.* alley)
accept (*cf.* except)			almost
		afraid	a lot (*cf.* a little)
acceptable	activities	against	
acceptance	acquaintance	aggravate	aloud (*cf.* allowed)
access (*cf.* excess)	acquire	aggressive	
	acquitted	aging	already (*cf.* all ready)

altar
alter
altogether
always
amateur
amendment
among
amount
analysis
analyze
angel
angle
annual
annul
anonymous
anticipate
antidote
anxiety
anxious
apiece
apologetically
apparatus
apparent
appearance
applying
appreciation
approach
appropriate
approximate
aquarium
aquatic
arctic
argue
arguing
argument
argumentative
arithmetic
arouse
arousing
arrangement
article
artistically
ascent (cf. assent)

assassin
assent (cf. ascent)
assistance
assistant
atheist
athletic
attempt
attendance
attitude
audience
author
authoritative
auxiliary
available

badminton
bachelor
balloon
barbiturate
bare (cf. bear)
bargain
barrel
basically
basis
beachhead
beauteous
beautiful
bear (cf. bare)
becoming
before
beginning
behavior
belief
believe
believing
beneficial
benefited
biased
bigoted
biscuit
board
bored
born

borne
bouillon (cf. bullion)
bounce
boundary
bourgeois
bourgeoisie
brake (cf. break)
breadth
break (cf. brake)
breath
breathe
breeze
bridal
bridle
brilliance
Britain
bulletin
bullion (cf. bouillon)
buoy
buoyant
bureau
bureaucracy
bureaucratic
burial
buried
busing
business
busyness

cafeteria
calendar (cf. colander)
Calvary (cf. cavalry)
camouflage
campaign
candidate
cannon
canon
cantaloupe
canvas

canvass
capital
capitol
careful
career
carriage
carrier
carrying
casserole
cataract
category
cavalry (cf. Calvary)
ceiling
cemetery
centuries
censor
censure
census
certain
chagrined
challenge
champagne
changeable
characteristic
chassis
chauffeur
chief
children
chimney
choose
chose
chord (cf. cord)
Christian
cigarette
cinnamon
cite (cf. site)
cliché
climactic
climatic
clique
clothes
coarse (cf.

course)
cocoa
coconut
colander (cf.
calendar)
collaborate
collage
collegiate
colonel
colossal
column
comfortable
comfortably
coming
commercial
commission
commit
committee
communist
comparative
compete
competent
competition
competitor
complementary
(cf.
complimentary)
completely
comprehension
complexion
complexioned
complimentary
(cf.
complementary)
concede
conceit
conceive
conceivable
concentrate
concern
concert
consider
condemn
conferred

confidant
confident
confusion
congratulate
connoisseur
connotation
conqueror
conscience
conscientious
conscious
consensus
consequently
considerably
consistent
consistency
consul
consummate
contact
contemporary
continuously
contractual
control
controlled
controversy
controversial
convenience
convenient
coolly
cord (cf.
chord)
corduroy
core (cf.
corps)
corollary
corporate
corps (cf.
core)
corpse
correlate
corroborate
corruptible
council (cf.
counsel)
counselor

counterfeit
courageous
courtesy
criticism
criticize
critique
crochet
crotchety
cruelly
cruelty
cumbersome
curiosity
curious
currant
current
curriculum
cushion
customer
cylinder

dealt
debatable
deceive
decent (cf.
descent, dissent)
deception
decided
decision
defendant
defense
defensible
definite
definition
delirious
democracy
dependent
derelict
descendant
descendent
descent (cf.
decent, dissent)
description
desirable
desirability

despair
desperate
despite
destroy
destruction
detriment
devastating
develop
developed
development
device
devise
die (cf. dye)
difference
difficult
dilemma
diligence
dining
diphtheria
disappear
disappoint
disastrous
discernible
disciple
discipline
discriminate
discussion
disease
disgusted
disillusioned
dissatisfied
dissent (cf.
decent, descent)
dissipate
divide
divine
dominant
doesn't
drunkenness
dual
duel
duly
during

dwarfs
dye (*cf.* die)
easily
ebullient
echoes
ecstasy
education
effect (*cf.* affect)
efficient
effort
eighth
eighteen
elective
elicit (*cf.* illicit)
eliminate
elude (*cf.* allude)
embarrass
embarrassed
embarrassing
emigrant (*cf.* immigrant)
eminent (*cf.* imminent)
emperor
emphasize
encourage
endeavor
enemy
enough
ensure (*cf.* insure)
entertain
enthusiasm
enthusiastic
envelop
envelope
environment
equip
equipped
equivalent
erroneous

escapade
escape
especially
espionage
euthanasia
evenness
evidently
exaggerate
exceed
excellent
excellence
except (*cf.* accept)
excess (*cf.* access)
excitable
excruciating
executive
exercise
exhaust
exhilarate
existence
exorbitant
expel
expense
experience
experiment
explanation
explicit
extraordinary
extremely
exuberant
faint (*cf.* feint)
fallacy
familiar
fantasies
fascinate
favorite
faze (*cf.* phase)
February
feint (*cf.* faint)

fictitious
fiend
fiery
finally
financially
financier
fluorescent
forehead
foreign
foreseeable
forfeit
forth (*cf.* fourth)
fortunate
forty
fourth (*cf.* forth)
fragrance
friend
fulfill
fundamental
futility
gaiety
gases (*or* gasses)
gaseous
gauge
generally
genius
ghost
glamour
glamorous
goddess
gorilla (*cf.* guerrilla)
government
governor
graduation
graffiti
grammar
grammatically
grievance
grievous
gruesome

guarantee
guard
guerrilla (*cf.* gorilla)
guidance
gym
gymnasium
gypsy
handkerchief
hangar
hanger
happily
happiness
harass
headache
hear (*cf.* here)
height
heir
hemorrhage
here (*cf.* hear)
heroes
heroine
high school
hindrance
hoping
hopping
hospitalization
huge
humor
humorous
hundred
hunger
hungrily
hurriedly
hygiene
hypocrisy
hypocrite
ideally
ignorance
ignorant
illicit (*cf.* elicit)
illegitimate

illusion (*cf.* allusion)

imagery

imagination

immediate

immense

immigrant (*cf.* emigrant)

imminent (*cf.* eminent)

immobilize

impaired

impel

impervious

implicit

impress

inadvertent

incidentally

increase

incredible

indefinite

independence

independent

indestructible

indispensable

individually

inevitable

infinitely

inflammable

influence

influential

ingenious

ingenuous

ingredient

initiative

innuendo

inoculate

inquire

insistence

insistent

instance

insure (*cf.* ensure)

intellectual

intelligence

intelligent

intensity

interest

interfere

interfered

interference

interfering

interpretation

interrupt

involve

involvement

iridescent

irrefutable

irrelevant

irreparable

irreplaceable

irresistible

irritable

its (*possessive*)

it's (*or* it is)

jealous

jeopardy

judgment (*or* judgement)

juror

kidneys

knowledge

knowledgeable

laboratory

laborer

laboriously

labyrinth

lama (*cf.* llama)

languor

larynx

lavender

led

legitimate

leisure

length

lengthening

lessen

lesson

liaison

library

license

lightening

lightning

likelihood

literature

livable (*or* liveable)

livelihood

llama (*cf.* lama)

loath

loathe

loneliness

loose

lose

losing

luxury

lying

magazine

magnificence

magnificent

maintain

maintenance

management

maneuver

manual

manufacturer

marriage

marshmallow

material

mathematics

meant

mechanics

medicine

medieval

mediocre

Mediterranean

melancholy

merchandise

mere

mileage

millennium

millionaire

mimic

mimicked

miner (*cf.* minor)

miniature

ministerial

minor (*cf.* miner)

mischief

mischievous

misshapen

misspell

monstrosity

moral

morale

mortgage

mountain

muscle

mussel

mysterious

mythology

naive

napping

narrative

naturally

naval

navel

necessary

neighborhood

nickel

niece

ninety

noncommittal

noticeable

noticing

numerous

obstacle

obtrusive

occasion

occur
occurred
occurrence
occurring
omission
omitted
operate
opinion
opossum
opportunity
opponent
oppose
optimist
original
oscillate
override
overrun
paid
pain (*cf.* pane)
pair (*cf.* pare, pear)
pajamas
pamphlet
pane (*cf.* pain)
panicked
paraffin
parallel
paralleled
paralysis
paralyze
pare (*cf.* pair, pear)
parliament
partially
particular
partner
passed
past
pastime
patent
patient
pavilion
peace (*cf.* piece)

peal (*cf.* peel)
pear (*cf.* pair, pare)
peculiar
peel (*cf.* peal)
peer (*cf.* pier)
pejorative
perceive
perennial
perfectible
performance
periodically
permanent
persistent
personal (*cf.* personnel)
perspiration
persuade
phase (*cf.* faze)
phenomenon
philosophy
phony
phosphorous
physical
physician
piece (*cf.* peace)
pier (*cf.* peer)
pigeon
pirouette
plain
plane
plausible
playwright
pleasant
pleasurable
poignant
poison
poisonous
politician
pore (*cf.* pour)
possess
possession
possible

pour (*cf.* pore)
practically
practice
prairie
precede (*cf.* proceed)
precinct
predator
predominant
prefer
preference
preferred
preferring
prejudice
prepare
prescribe
presence
prestige
pretense
prevalent
priest
primitive
principal
principle
prisoners
privilege
probably
procedure
proceed (*cf.* precede)
professor
prominent
prompt
pronunciation
propaganda
prophecy
prophesy
prostrate
psychiatry
psychoanalysis
psychology
psychosomatic
pumpkin
pursue

pursuit
quantity
quay
queue
quiet
quizzes
rain (*cf.* reign, rein)
rarefied
rarity
realize
really
recede
receipt
receive
receiving
recipe
recognizable
recommend
refer
referee
referred
referring
regard
regretted
regretting
reign (*cf.* rain, rein)
relief
relieve
religion
remember
remembrance
reminisce
rendezvous
repellent
repentance
repetition
representative
reptile
resemblance
reserved
resilience

resilient

resistance

resource

response

restaurant

revise

revolution

rhetoric

rheumatism

rhinoceros

rhyme

rhythm

rhythmically

ridicule

ridiculous

roommate

sacrifice

sacrilege

sacrilegious

said

sandwich

sapphire

satellite

satire

satisfactorily

satisfied

scene

schedule

secretary

seize

sense (cf. since)

sentence

separate

sergeant

sever

several

severe

severely

shear (cf. sheer)

shepherd

sheriff

shining

shiny

shriek

siege

sieve

signaled (or signalled)

significance

silhouette

similar

sincerely

site (cf. cite)

skeptic

ski

skiing

skis

society

sociology

soliloquy

sophomore

source

sovereign

sovereignty

speak

speech

specimen

sponsor

stabilize

staccato

stair

stare

stationary

stationery

steely

stomach

stomachache

straight

strength

stretch

strict

stubborn

studying

stupefy

stupid

substantial

subterranean

subtle

subtlety

succeed

success

succinct

succumb

sufficient

suffrage

summary

superintendent

supersede

suppose

suppress

surprise

surround

susceptible

suspicion

syllable

symbol

symmetry

sympathize

synonym

synonymous

tariff

technique

temperament

temperature

tendency

tendon

testament

than (cf. then)

their (cf. there, they're)

themselves

then (cf. than)

theory

theoretically

therefore

thinness

thorough

threw

through

throughout

to (cf. too, two)

too (cf. to, two)

tomorrow

track (cf. tract)

traffic

trafficked

tragedy

tranquil

tranquillity (or tranquility)

transcendental

transferred

tremendous

tried

tries

truly

turkeys

two (cf. to, too)

tyranny

ukulele

unanimous

undoubtedly

unmistakable

unnecessary

unshakable

unusually

unwieldy

useful

using

vacillate

vacuum

valuable

various

vegetable

vengeance

venemous

vice (cf. vise)

view

vilify

village

villain	wear (*cf.* where)	whole	write
vise (*cf.* vice)		whose	writing
waive (*cf.* wave)	weather (*cf.* whether)	wield	written
warrant	Wednesday	withhold	yield
warring	weird	woeful	yore
wave (*cf.* waive)	whether (*cf.* weather)	women	your
	whisper	worshiped (*or* worshipped)	you're

Spelling proofreading practice

Some of the following sentences contain spelling errors. Correct any misspelled words you find. (Use the spelling dictionary in this book to help you.)

1 In our soceity some form of contack with relegion is bound to touch each of us.

2 The principle had paniced when he saw all of us staying out after the last bell.

3 With four bigger brothers to compeat with at meals, you sort of learn to eat quickly, and eat alot.

4 When I was in high school, I looked towards graduation with enthusiasm.

5 The temperture in the gym was near a hunderd.

6 A soft whisper of breeze cools my body as the sun warms the earth and wakes it's worshipers.

7 Most users think that there are no harmful effects from marijuana.

8 "O.K.," I said to myself, "now your on your own."

9 Well, the concert went fairly well dispite a few seemingly disasterous ocassions.

10 Before she could finish, the anger was already beginning to swell up inside me.

11 The Education Amendment Act of 1972 signaled the start of a revalution in intercollegiate and highschool sports.

12 Because of an imobilizing snow storm one night last March, I was forced to spend the night at my girl's house.

13 I was not impressed by the government's promtness.

14 The other guys were quite though restless, periodicly naping to pass time.

15 It felt strange being able to streach out in front of the T.V. and just forget everything.

16 Hurryedly I threw some water on my face and draged a comb threw my hair.

17 When I opened the door the driver pointed to a sign on the window apearantly meaning, reserved.

18 As I moved slowly out onto the pier, which was partially damaged by weather, I could look down and view beds of seaweed.

19 Maintaining your own aquarium can be a rewarding experience if you follow certain guidelines and instructions.

20 Now the only lights noticable are occassional cigarettes casting minute red sparks like fireflies in the night.

21 Everybody can remember a freind they grew up with, faced hell and damnation with, and yet in the end everything turned out alright.

22 The artical listed several ways in which people have evaded there taxes.

23 I could have walked for an age and not have lost sight of that monsterosity.

24 We desparately didn't want to get wet—that water was cold!

25 I was embarassed, my mother was embarassed, everyone was embarasssed.

26 While the other branches of service are attempting to make life for there troops more liveable, the Marine Corpse is maintaining its standards and disipline.

27 This summer I tried to corrupt the efforts of a committee project to revise one of the English electives.

28 With my stomache in my throat, I sat next to my window and watched the road scampering below the bus.

29 By the third day, when we went to feed the children, we had to take an armed guard with the food.

30 Espionage activities and corporate funding of political parties most clearly surpress and override the will and voice of the people.

31 At this point in life I am finely able to admit to a suspision of nearly every person I've met.

32 My roomates mean well, but I wish they would just let me go to bed.

33 When a bunch of people get togather for a party or just to get togather, various games and devises are used for entertainment.

34 It was a small doe lying on its side, bloated and mishapen, its open eyes glazed.

35 Females have to deside what mood they are in so they can deside the colors and intencities of their make-up.

36 The Bic Mac sandwich is finally prepared and ready to sell to some very fortunant customer.

37 For instance, a senior may decide to sing in the libary for the shear intent of remaining impervious to the libarian's scornful stare.

38 I was never much for pulling pranks, braking miner laws, or being plain mischivious.

39 I first noticied the haircut on a cover model of a November issiue of a familiar high fashion and glamour magazine.

40 Ever since I was in the eighth grade, I have experienced numerous headaches acompanied by impared vision.

Spelling-in-context practice

One problem in proofreading is how to avoid being carried along by what you are saying *instead of attending to* how *you are saying it. Letting your manuscript cool off for a day or two will help, but even then you must force yourself to read slowly and carefully, looking for mistakes. Practice the technique by finding and correcting the spelling errors in the following passages.*

After about an hour or so of bounsing up and down in the truck, we arrived at the mountian that we wished to assend by foot. It didn't look to steep until we began to climb it. The air was thin and our legs grew sore as Marilyn and I struggled with the big canvass back pack that contained our sandwiches and pop. Every three or four minutes we'd have to sease moving and locate a peace of ground that wasn't to rocky to rest on. As we slouched down, we noticed tiny red flowers that apeared to be bright stars in the wild green grass that grew between the pebbles. We even attemted to collect differnt types of rocks, but we had to empty most of them out from our pockets because they were too combersome.

My tame mongoose became famous in the neighberhood. The constant battles mongooses wage so couragously against the deadly cobras have earned them a kind of mythalogical prestege. I believe in this, having often seen them fight these snakes, whom they defeat thruogh sheer agilaty and because of their thick salt-and-pepper coat of hair, which decieves and confuses the reptiles. The country people beleive that, after battling its poisinous enemy, the mongoose goes in search of antidotal herbs.
PABLO NERUDA, *Memoirs*

CAPITALIZATION

The basic rule, to which there are very few exceptions, is to capitalize "first" words and words that are considered proper names or titles.

CAPITALIZE THE FIRST WORD OF A SENTENCE
AND THE FIRST WORD OF A DIRECT QUOTE

Shakespeare said, "All the world's a stage."

Do not capitalize the first word of an incorporated quote:

Shakespeare referred to the world as "all . . . a stage."

CAPITALIZE THE NAMES AND TITLES OF PEOPLE, PLACES, AND THINGS

Mr. V. Guinn	Mt. Everest	Christmas
Aunt Ellen	England	the Renaissance
Jane	the Whitney Museum	the *U.S.S. Forrestal*
Fido	Hammond High School	World War II
Sheriff Gregg	Riverfront Stadium	the Atlantic Ocean

CAPITALIZE WORDS FORMED FROM PROPER NOUNS

English	Shakespearean	Indian

CAPITALIZE TITLES

Except for the small connective words, capitalize the words in titles of books, magazines, films, and so on. Note that the word "the" is ordinarily not treated as part of a newspaper title.

War and Peace	*All in the Family*	the *New York Times*

CAPITALIZE REGIONS BUT NOT DIRECTIONS

the Far East	the North	go west

DO NOT CAPITALIZE THE NAMES OF SEASONS

winter	summer	spring
autumn	fall	

CAPITALIZE THE TITLES OF HEADS OF STATE

Even when personal names do not follow the titles, it is acceptable to capitalize the titles:

the President	the Queen	the Pope

CAPITALIZE THE NAMES OF POLITICAL PARTIES

Communist party	Republican party	Labour party

Do not capitalize these names when you use them as adjectives or when you are referring to a member of the party:

Canada is a democratic nation.

They are known communists.

DO NOT CAPITALIZE SCHOOL SUBJECTS EXCEPT LANGUAGES

math	psychology	Latin

When you are writing the title of a specific course, capitalize it:

Speech 101	Earth Science 300	Art 219

CAPITALIZE BRAND NAMES BUT NOT PRODUCTS

Wrangler jeans	Big Macs	Sony radio

CAPITALIZE THE NAMES OF GOD, DEITIES, AND REVERED FIGURES

God	Allah	Buddah
the Lord	the Virgin Mary	the Apostle Paul

CAPITALIZE KINSHIP TITLES WHEN THEY ARE USED WITH A NAME

Aunt Ellen	Cousin Fred	Grandmother Jones

Capitalize the title alone when it is a substitute for the name of the family member: Is Mother here? Do not capitalize kinship titles alone after articles or possessive pronouns like "a," "the," "my," "your": My mother is sixty-three years old.

CAPITALIZE THE SIGNIFICANT WORDS IN A GREETING OF A LETTER

Dear Ed,	Dear Sir or Madam:	My Dear Mr. Smith:

In the closing of a letter, capitalize only the first word:

Yours truly,	Very sincerely yours,	Very truly yours,

DO NOT CAPITALIZE THE COMMON NAMES OF ANIMALS AND PLANTS

oak tree	cardinal	grizzly bear

Practice

Supply capitalization where necessary in the following sentences.

1 chippewa hills superintendent lavern alward has said the 20 mill request on monday's ballot is necessary.
PAM KLEIN, "It's Decision Time at Polls Monday," *Cleveland Morning Sun*, 10 June 1977

2 for instance, kikkoman's soy sauce has a very strong flavor while la choy's is more mellow.
NANCY SELIGMAN, *Homesteading in the City*

3 and on a january morning in 1945, in fifteen-inch snow in the vosges mountains, by order of the man who is now president of the united states, private slovik was marched out and bound to a post.
WILLIAM BRADFORD HUIE, *The Execution of Private Slovik*

4 starting point of the international quasar hunt is the molonglo observatory in new south wales.
SIMON MITTON, "Mysteries of Quasar Redshifts," 1975 *Yearbook of Astronomy*, Patrick Moore, ed.

5 there were not nearly enough life boats, and, for reasons never explained, several of those that got away were barely filled, and passengers who were left on board when the ship sank were frozen in the icy water before captain rostrum of the *s.s. carpathia* could come to their rescue.
PEGGY GUGGENHEIM, *Confessions of an Art Addict*

6 the city university of new york, the country's third largest university system, sits these days like a giant battered orphan amid the financial ruins of new york city.
LARRY VAN DYNE, "City University of New York," *Atlantic Monthly*, June 1977

7 either the thread has snapped, or the muscle wall has broken through, but the moment the tube was extracted there appeared an open hole and, out of it, a spurt of blood a meter high!
NIKOLAI AMOSOV, *The Open Heart*

8 as dr. winnicott has put it: "at origin, aggressiveness is almost synonymous with activity."
ANTHONY STORR, *Human Aggression*

9 about thirty years ago, miss maria ward, of huntingdon, with only seven thousand pounds, had the good luck to captivate sir thomas bertram, of mansfield park, in the county of northampton, and to be thereby raised to the rank of a baronet's lady, with all the comforts and consequences of an handsome house and large income.
JANE AUSTEN, *Mansfield Park*

10 greek wisdom, she declares in her great essay on the *iliad*, has been taken from us because the twin roman and hebrew world views supplanted it.
EDWARD GROSSMAN, "*Simone Weil: A Life*, by Simone Petrement," *Commentary*, June 1977

11 I can remember now, quite vividly, the eighteen months my uncle angelo, an ordained priest, spent as a special visitor to the united states, serving as an adjunct assistant pastor with a church in brooklyn.
NINO LO BELLO, *The Vatican Empire*

12 now that may look to us like a stock piece of emotional blackmail—like the woman who whimpers that if sonny doesn't do as she wants him to do, mother's going to have one of her nasty turns.
ELAINE MORGAN, *The Descent of Woman*

13 two of england's leading opinion journals—*the tablet*, catholic; *the economist*, general—have taken remarkably contrasting positions on the recent meeting in rome of the anglican archbishop of canterbury, dr. coggan, and pope paul vi.
"Reunion's Detour," *Commonweal*, 10 June 1977

14 normally, sheep breed only once a year, when the autumn days begin to shorten.
BEATRICE TRUM HUNTER, *Consumer Beware!*

15 besides the hosts there was a middle-aged couple, the ralph lewins—he was a colleague of harris's at the columbia university school of architecture; and maybe to balance off adler, harris's secretary, shirley fisher, had been invited, a thin-ankled, wet-eyed divorcee in a long bright-blue skirt, who talked and drank liberally.
BERNARD MALAMUD, "Notes from a Lady at a Dinner Party," *Rembrandt's Hat*

16 gordon lightfoot comes to pine knob tuesday and wednesday, bringing with him the melodic voice and gentle, yet stirring, music that has made him one of the few folk artists to outlast the '60s and prosper in the '70s.
"A Gentle Survivor," *Detroit Free Press*, 14 June 1977

17 in 1972, dr. harry e. simmons, director of the bureau of drugs in the fda, estimated before a senate subcommittee that "superinfections" may be killing tens of thousands of persons yearly in this country.
RUTH MULVEY HARMER, *American Medical Avarice*

18 my companion at the press drank everyday a pint before breakfast, a pint at breakfast with his bread and cheese, a pint between breakfast and dinner, a pint in the afternoon about six o'clock, and another when he had done his day's work.
BENJAMIN FRANKLIN, *The Life of Benjamin Franklin*

19 the tactics of a sneak raid on pearl—crippling the formidable u.s. fleet based there and freeing the japanese navy to dominate the pacific—had been a standard part of both tokyo's and washington's strategic thinking for a decade.
This Fabulous Century, 1940–1950

20 the human species, according to the best theory I can form of it, is composed of two distinct races, *the men who borrow*, and *the men who lend*.
CHARLES LAMB, "The Two Races of Man"

MANUSCRIPT CONVENTIONS

The following general guidelines tell you how to prepare a paper to hand in. Specific format instructions for typed papers (line spacing, indentations, and so on) are inside the back cover.

1 If at all possible, type your papers. If you can't type or don't have a machine, it may be to your advantage to become friends with someone who does. Even if your handwriting is quite legible, most readers will prefer typewritten papers. If you must write by hand, take great care to be neat and legible. Use only dark blue or black ink. If your typewriter ribbon has gone gray, replace it.

2 Use standard typing paper only. You need not buy expensive, heavyweight paper, nor should you use onion skin paper, nor easy-to-erase paper (it smudges). Use inexpensive typing paper of medium weight and learn to use Liquid Paper or Correction Tape for errors. Type or write on one side of the paper only.

3 Type double-spaced. On most machines there is a setting for double space at the left end of the platen (the roller). Double space everything, but triple space above and below indented quotes.

4 Give yourself at least a one-inch margin on all four sides. Learn to use the margin setting on your machine. Standard paper is eight and a half inches wide and eleven inches long. Set your roll for eleven inches, and when you get near the bottom of the page, watch for the one-inch mark to come up. If your machine has no setting for the bottom margin, mark your paper with a light pencil dot one inch from the bottom.

5 Unless your instructor requests a title page, it is customary to put your name, the date, the assignment, and/or other identifying information in the upper right-hand corner of the first page.

6 Center the title of your paper on the first page. All papers should have a title. Capitalize the first word and all other important words in the title. Do not put quotation marks around your own title; do not underline your own title.

7 If you have more than one page, staple the pages together. It might be a good idea to invest in a stapler. Do not pin, fold, or tear corners in an effort to fasten the pages together; they will come undone anyway.

8 Number your pages, starting with page two, in the upper right-hand corner.

9 Use a uniform indentation for paragraphs. If your machine has no paragraph setting, count five spaces in for each new indentation. Handwritten papers should have paragraph indentations of at least half an inch.

10 Clean copy should have no errors, but nobody is perfect. If you find an error at the last minute, paint it out with correction fluid, put the page back into your machine, and type the correction. If there isn't time for that, make a neat correction on the clean copy. Draw one (and only one) line through the error and write the correction above it in ink.

This glossary is provided as a handy reference to terms you may encounter as you study composition. Some of the terms have been used in *The Writer's Work;* others will be encountered in dictionaries, as part of the explanations of words; in language books; in articles and essays on language and composition; in writers' marketing guides; in stylesheets; and occasionally in letters from editors to writers.

Absolute A modifier, the absolute looks like a reduced "with" phrase: "She stared out the window, [with] *her head in her hands.*" "[With] *The fuse having been set for one minute,* we ran for the bunker." "[With] *The job done,* she took a break." In formal writing, absolutes may have pronoun subjects: "*She* [not "her"] *being late,* we went on without her." The absolute gets its name because it has no connective and because it modifies the whole idea in the main clause instead of any single word in it. Other terms for *absolute* are *ablative absolute, absolute construction, absolute phrase, nominative absolute.*

Absolute degree Words like "unique," "total," "incomparable" describe a condition beyond comparison; thus, they are absolute. Some readers object to expressions like "more unique," "most incomparable." See *Comparison* below.

Accent In dictionaries, words are marked with primary and secondary accent marks to show which syllables to stress: *'re cord* places the accent on the first syllable; *re cord'* places the accent on the second syllable; *'dig ni fy* places a primary accent on the first syllable and a secondary accent on the last syllable. See also *Acute accent* and *Grave accent* below.

Acute accent A diacritical mark (´) used in some dictionaries to show primary stress: *de ter'*. The acute accent is also used in many words of foreign origin (cliché, exposé, olé, resumé); when you use such a word in a composition, ink in the acute accent.

Active voice A verb is in the active voice when its subject is the actor in the sentence: "The dog *chased* the rabbit." "Three young people *found* an apartment." "Time *dragged*." See *Passive voice* below.

Adjective An adjective describes, limits, changes, or in some other way modifies a noun or pronoun: " *a red* apple"; "*young* women"; "*enthusiastic* crowds"; "He is *strong*." Adjectives identify who, which, what kind, or how many. See also *Modification* and *Modifier* below.

Adjective clause A clause used like an adjective: "This is the dog *that bit the mailman.*" "Give the money to those *who need it.*" Begin an adjective clause with a relative pronoun or the subordinators "where," "when," or "why": "This is a time *when we must work together.*" "There must be some reason *why these things happen.*"

Adjective phrase A phrase made up of more than one adjective: "She always seems so *cool, serene,* and *regal.*" Or, any of several other kinds of phrases (*prepositional phrase, participial phrase, infinitive phrase*) "The girl *on the horse* is giving the orders." "This is a day *to remember.*"

Adverb Chiefly a verb modifier, but the adverb can also modify adjectives and other adverbs: "Walk *slowly.*" "She is *very* smart." "They move *quite stiffly.*" Adverbs indicate time (now, then, yesterday), place (here, there), manner (carefully, stupidly), and degree (scarcely, seldom).

Adverb clause A clause used like an adverb: "*When the lights go out,* head for the door." In addition to time, place, manner, and degree (see *Adverb* above), adverb clauses can be used to show cause, comparison, concession, condition, and purpose: "*Because it is raining,* you must stay in." "He is older *than you are.*" "*Although it is expensive,* she uses a lot of it." "*Unless it rains,* I'll work outside." "I'll turn up the volume *so that you can hear the music.*" Start adverb clauses with subordinate conjunctions (see below).

Adverb phrase A group of words composed of several adverbs: "*Slowly, quietly,* and *steadily,* they eased the canoe into the river." An adverb phrase can also be a prepositional phrase used to modify a verb, adjective, or adverb: "*In the morning,* we go fishing." "The tree stands *near the shore.*" "It is too soon *after surgery* for you to get up." "Your speech is short *on information.*"

Affixes Prefixes and suffixes added to roots to form new words: the prefix *ex-* plus the root *port* produces "export." The suffix *-ful* plus the root *hand* produces "handful." See *Prefix* and *Suffix* below.

Agreement Correspondence of singulars and plurals. If the subject of a sentence is a singular word (one item), readers expect the verb to be singular too. A pronoun referring back to a singular subject should also be singular. If the subject is plural, the verb and any pronouns referring to the subject should be plural. In formal writing, the concept of agreement produces sentences like these: "*Each* of the girls *has her* own desk." "*Everybody* in the men's theater group *is doing his* own act." See "Agreement" in Chapter 10.

Antecedent A word or words a pronoun refers to. A problem of "pronoun reference" means that the pronoun does not clearly refer to its antecedent. In "The ship sails the ocean in the moonlight; *it* looks like a dream," the writer intends the pronoun "it" to refer back to "ship," but because "it" is closer to "ocean" and "moonlight," the reference is ambiguous and the writer's idea fails to get through. See "Pronoun Reference" in Chapter 10.

Anticipatory construction An anticipatory construction appears in an inverted sentence or clause in which the subject comes after the verb: "*There is* a dog in the garage." "*There are* several kinds of apples." "*There are* in the opera elements of drama and dance"—the verb in this sentence, "are," anticipates the subject, "elements of drama and dance."

Appositive A word that identifies a following or preceding noun: "My dog, *a retriever,* brings me the newspaper each morning." "*A retriever,* my dog brings me the newspaper each morning." The appositive is usually set off with commas, but some very common appositives are so familiar that writers use them without intending to create emphasis and without setting them off with commas: "my friend Al," "my brother Rod."

Article A kind of noun modifier. The indefinite articles are "a" and "an." The definite article is "the." In modern grammar, articles are sometimes called *determiners* (see below). In general, use "an" [not "a"] before words beginning with vowel sounds: "an apple," "an hour."

Auxiliary verbs Verbs, sometimes called *helping verbs,* used with main verbs to create tense and other aspects of verbs. The auxiliaries include all the forms of "to be" ("am," "is," "are," and so on) and the forms of "do," "have," "shall," and "will." In addition, there is a group called *modal auxiliaries* containing "can," "could," "may," "might," "must," "should," and "would." With these auxiliary verbs, writers create verb phrases like "is running," "do speak," "may have flown," "should have been watching," and so on.

Base clause The main clause in a sentence. The base clause, also called the *independent clause,* is the part of a sentence that can stand alone: "When the sun rises, *the rooster begins to crow.*" "The rooster begins to crow" is a base clause; it could be written as a separate sentence. In sentence-combining problems, the base clause is the top sentence; it is the one to which all the others attach.

Breve A diacritical mark (◡) used to indicate a "short" vowel: hĭt, măt. A vowel is "long" when it says its own name: i = eye, o = oh, and so on. Any other pronunciation of the vowel may be considered short, as marked with the breve, except for pronunciations marked with other diacritical marks (see below).

Caret A proofreader's symbol (∧) for adding to a line of print. Use the caret on clean copy to insert short omissions, to add additional words, or to make corrections. The caret goes below the line, and the insertion is added above the caret. See inside the back cover for the use of the caret in typed papers.

Case Case is related to the form or function of nouns or pronouns, based on their use in a sentence. Nouns and pronouns may be subjects (*subjective case,* also called *nominative*) or objects (*objective case*), or they may show possession (*possessive case*). See "Pronouns as Subjects and Objects" in Chapter 10.

Clause A group of words containing a subject and a verb; every sentence must have at least one clause. A simple sentence is a clause by itself. A sentence may have more than one clause. A clause may be only part of a sentence: "They knew who she was." This sentence has two clauses: "They knew" and "who she was." Since each clause has its own subject and verb, writers must be sure to see that there is agreement within and between clauses. You need to distinguish between *clauses*—which have subjects and verbs (She sleeps *as it rains*)—and *phrases*—which do not (She sleeps *as often as possible*). There are four kinds of clauses: *independent clauses, adjective clauses, adverb clauses, noun clauses.*

Collective noun A group noun: "army," "generation," "minority," "crowd." Collective nouns are usually treated as singulars, even though they identify more than one person: "The *crowd was* shrieking *its* approval." See "Group Words" in Chapter 10.

Colloquial Language used as in conversations. "Colloquial" is frequently used in dictionaries to label expressions acceptable in spoken English but unsuitable for formal written English. "Colloquial" is equivalent to "conversational"; and it is a style not only acceptable but preferred for much writing today—except the most formal. Colloquial writing is likely to be in the first person, may address the reader as "you," and may use contractions and punctuation to imitate speech patterns. See Chapter 2, "Personal Writing," for examples of colloquial writing.

Common noun Any noun except those that are actually names of persons, places, or things (these are called *proper nouns*). Common nouns are rarely capitalized (dog, ship, man, novel) except when they begin a sentence. Proper nouns are always capitalized (Fido, the *Queen Mary,* Oliver, *Roots*). The common noun names a class or group; the proper noun names a specific individual.

Comparative degree Most adjectives and adverbs can show degrees of comparison (fast, faster, fastest; slowly, more slowly, most slowly). The middle degree of comparison (faster; more slowly) is the comparative. In formal writing, use the comparative to express comparison between only two items: "He is the *better* [not "best"] of the two players." Avoid common errors like the double comparative (more better; more slowlier) and the faulty comparative (more good; more soft) and comparing the incomparable. See *Absolute degree* above and *Comparison* below.

Comparison Refers to the degrees of modification of adjectives and adverbs. The degrees of comparison are *positive* (fast; slowly), *comparative* (faster; more slowly), and *superlative* (fastest; most slowly). A few modifiers have no comparison, at least in formal writing. Some readers object to "more unique," "deader," "fullest," and so forth, on the grounds that degrees of uniqueness, deadness, or fullness are illogical. But in informal writing, most readers will accept a sentence such as "That old church was the fullest it's ever been on the day the President gave the benediction." See *Absolute degree* and *Comparative degree* above.

Complement Traditionally, a term for nouns and pronouns in the object position after a "being" or linking verb: "My friend Myrna is a *surgeon.*" Another term for this kind of verb complement is *predicate nominative.* Today, language and composition books use the term *complement* loosely, to mean anything that receives the action of the verb or completes the sense required by the verb. Thus, direct objects, indirect objects, and predicate adjectives may be included in the term *verb complement.*

Complex sentence A sentence containing at least one subordinate clause. "Our canary sings when it feels well" is a complex sentence. "Our canary sings" is the main (independent) clause. "When it feels well" is a subordinate clause—a modifying clause, not a complete sentence.

Composition The art of formulating, organizing, shaping, and developing writing. In contrast with free writing, composition presupposes that a writer has a purpose, and a plan for carrying it out. To compose means to put together writing (or oral language) to achieve an effect on the reader. See Chapter 1, "The Composing Process," and *Rhetoric* below.

Compound Two or more items linked together to form a sentence element. For example, there may be *compound subjects* (Jack and Jill), *compound verbs* (swimming and sailing), *compound objects* (to the doctor or the nurse). When two sentences or two base clauses are joined with one of the coordinate conjunctions, the result is called a compound sentence; "He sang, and his wife applauded."

Compound noun A noun composed of more than one word: "hubcap," "lay of the land," "old-timer." Some compound nouns are spelled as one word, some as more than one word, some as hyphenated words. Compound nouns may have irregular plurals: "mothers-in-law," "sergeants-at-arms."

Compound-complex A sentence containing two independent clauses and one subordinate clause. See *Complex sentence* above.

Conjugation A list of all the possible forms of a verb in all the tenses, moods, and voices, with all the pronouns: "I sing," "you sing," "he sings," "she sings," and so on. The word can also be used to refer to less than the full display of the verb: a conjugation in the present tense, or a conjugation of the passive voice, for example. See the list of principal parts of troublesome verbs under "Verbs" in Chapter 10.

Conjunction A connecting word. There are several kinds of conjunctions: *coordinate* (and, but, or); *correlative* (either-or, neither-nor); *subordinate* (after, if, since, when).

Conjunctive adverbs A connective. Conjunctive adverbs are similar to coordinate conjunctions because they connect full sentences: "I once had a cat; *however*, it ran away." The conjunctive adverbs are:

also	indeed	nevertheless
besides	in fact	next
consequently	instead	otherwise
furthermore	likewise	still
however	meanwhile	then
incidentally	moreover	therefore
		thus

Connective See *Conjunction* above.

Coordinate The term *coordinate* means "equal in order"; it contrasts with *subordinate,* which means "lower in order." Coordinate clauses are clauses of equal importance to the writer: "*Old men snore,* and *babies gurgle in their sleep.*" Each of these clauses could be written as a separate sentence; both are independent clauses. Conjunctions that join coordinate clauses (and, but, for, nor, or, so) are called *coordinate conjunctions.* In contrast, one idea is more important than the other in a subordinate construction: "The men will have to keep working until all the material is gone." The main idea here (The men will have to keep working) is the important one. The other idea (until all the material is gone) has been reduced to a modifier; it is lower in order than the first idea. Other terms for this subordinate construction are *independent clause* for the part that could stand alone and *dependent clause* for the part that "depends on" the other for its existence. In a coordinate construction there are two independent clauses. Neither of them requires the other; each could stand alone: "The men will have to keep working; the new material will arrive soon."

Correlative conjunction Correlative conjunctions operate in pairs: "either-or," "neither-nor," "not only-but also," "both-and."

Cumulative modifier See *Nonrestrictive* below.

Dangling modifier A modifier "dangles" when it seems to have nothing to modify: "*Feeling fine*, the weather turned balmy." Rephrase to make clear to the reader what is "feeling fine": "Because the weather had turned balmy, I was *feeling fine*." See "Misplaced Parts" in Chapter 10.

Declarative sentence A declarative sentence makes a statement of fact, "declares" an assertion: "It is raining outside." "The experiment lasted a year."

Declension A list of all the forms of a pronoun ("I," "we," "me," "us," "my," "mine," and so on). A declension shows number (singular and plural), case (subjective, objective, possessive), and person (first, second, third).

Degree See *Comparison* above.

Demonstrative pronouns The demonstrative pronouns are "this," "that," "these," and "those." They are used like adjectives or definite articles: "this house," "that dog."

Dependent clause A group of words containing a subject and a verb but not a complete thought: "They don't know *where you will be tomorrow*." Dependent clauses begin with relative pronouns and subordinate conjunctions (see below). There are three kinds of dependent clauses: *adjective clauses, adverb clauses, noun clauses*.

Determiner In modern grammar, a word that places, limits, or "slots" a noun or nominal (see below) rather than amplifying or describing it: "*a* catastrophe," "*either* alternative," "*that* hurdy-gurdy," "*their* reasons." Determiners include:

a	no	this	my
an	one	these	your
any	some	what	his
each	the	whatever	her
either	that	which	our
every	those	whichever	their
neither			

Diacritical mark A mark that shows how to pronounce a word. Diacritical marks are used in most modern dictionaries. In some cases, writers must give diacritical marks to show the pronunciation of words, particularly foreign words. See *Acute accent, Breve, Dieresis, Grave accent, Macron, Schwa, Tilde,* and *Umlaut* in this glossary. See also inside the back cover for forms of diacritical marks in typed papers.

Dialect A language pattern differing from a speech pattern that, for the purpose of reference, has been designated "standard." Dialects concern writers because regional speech patterns and "foreign" accents (the patterns and sounds of any language as spoken by someone to whom it is not native) are difficult to reproduce in writing. Listen carefully to the speaker before you try to reproduce his or her dialect; caricatures of dialects are offensive. See also *Standard English* below.

Dieresis A diacritical mark (‥) used to show that a vowel is pronounced as a separate syllable: naïve, coöperation, Brontë. Since few typewriters are equipped with it, most writers ignore the dieresis. But if there is any possibility of a misreading without it, you should ink in the dieresis, especially for foreign words.

Direct object The direct object receives the action of the verb: "I shot the *bear*." "She gave me a *dollar*." Notice that in the second example there seem to be two objects, "me" and "dollar." In this example, "me" is an *indirect object* (see below). See also "Pronouns as Subjects and Objects" in Chapter 10.

Discourse Another word for language. "Discourse" is often used when writers wish to include both oral and written language: "He could produce intelligent *discourse* on any subject without the slightest hesitation."

Double negative See "Dictionary of Usage Problems."

Elliptical construction A sentence structure that omits one or more words. The "understood" subject of many sentences is an elliptical "you": [You] Shut the door." As long as the missing element is clearly implied, there is no problem: "You may be old enough to get married but [you are] not [old enough] to drink." Elliptical constructions are a feature of impressionistic style:

Slung awry by its chain from a thin nail, an open oval locket, glassed. In one face of this locket, a colored picture of Jesus, his right hand blessing, his red heart exposed in a burst spiky gold halo. In the other face, a picture by the same artist of the Blessed Virgin, in blue, her heart similarly exposed and haloed, and pierced with seven small swords.

JAMES AGEE AND WALKER EVANS, *Let Us Now Praise Famous Men*

Epigram An especially well-worded thought. An epigram makes a memorable saying because of its effective wording:

A foolish consistency is the hobgoblin of little minds adored by little statesmen and philosophers and divines.

RALPH WALDO EMERSON, "Self Reliance"

Epigrams are frequently based on antithesis:

Man proposes but God disposes.

THOMAS À KEMPIS, *Imitation of Christ*

They are very often satiric:

Here lies our sovereign lord the king, whose word no man relies on;
he never says a foolish thing nor ever does a wise one.
EARL OF ROCHESTER

Epigraph A motto or inscription on a monument or building, or an opening or illustrative quote at the beginning of a book or chapter or essay. Each chapter of *The Writer's Work* begins with an epigraph.

Etymology The science of tracing the origin and development of a word; a branch of linguistics. The etymology of a word shows the changes in meaning and the various influences that have gone into the present meaning of a word. The best authority on word histories is the *Oxford English Dictionary*, but any good modern dictionary will give a summary etymology of a word. For example, the etymology of "nice" shows that the word comes to us from the Middle English word for "foolish," which came from the Old French word, *nisce,* for "stupid," which came from the Latin words *nescius*, meaning "ignorant," and *nescire,* meaning "not knowing."

Expletive In language study, either the word "there" or the word "it" in an *anticipatory construction* (see above): "*There* were several writers at the convention." "*It* is cold in here." The expletive has no grammatical function: "It" is not the subject in the second example; "There" is not an adverb in the first example. In more general usage, an expletive is a curse or profane oath.

Formal language The language used for writing to an audience of well-educated readers on serious or technical subjects. For such readers, writers conform to the conventions and traditions of print more than in any other writing situation. If writing can be thought of as a continuum, with the loosest, freest, most informal kind of writing at one end (graffiti, free writing) and the most carefully controlled, technical writing at the other end (scientific reports, legal documents), we can say that the more writing moves in the direction of this tightly controlled end of the continuum, the more formal it becomes. See *Standard English* below.

Fragment See *Sentence* below.

Gender Distinction according to sex or the lack of it. Many nouns and pronouns have gender; they are identified by the terms *feminine, masculine,* or *neuter.* A few words have incongruous genders: sailors sometimes speak of ships as feminine; different nations speak of their country as masculine or feminine (fatherland, motherland).

Genitive The Latin grammar term for *possessive.*

Gerund An *-ing* form of a verb used like a noun. "*Fishing* is fun." "What you need is more *jogging.*"

Gerund phrase A phrase containing a gerund plus any modifiers or objects: "*Speaking too rapidly* is one of the signs of nervousness." "I am fond of *opening presents.*" In formal writing, use possessive nouns and pronouns with gerunds: "The question at issue was the *children's praying* in school." "They want *his singing the anthem* to close the show."

Grammar The terms and concepts with which linguists describe a language, such as the eight parts of speech, are the grammar of the language. Grammar is distinct from *usage,* the conventions and traditions about words and expressions that let a writer know, for example, what language may be suitable for formal writing. "Tough guy" is a noun composed of the modifier "tough" and the root word "guy"—this is *grammatical* information. Whether you should use the term "tough guy" in a formal paper about prison inmates is a *usage* question requiring consideration of purpose, audience, and so on.

Grave accent A diacritical mark (`) used in English to differentiate certain words that, although spelled like other words, have different meanings and pronunciations ("learnèd" and "learned" or "belovèd" and "beloved"). The grave accent indicates that the *-ed* syllable is fully pronounced. The grave accent is also used in French: *à la carte, à la mode, chère, crème de la crème.* When you use such a word in a composition, ink in the grave accent.

Idiom Language characteristics peculiar to a language group. An idiom usually cannot be explained in terms of rules of grammar or even the denotations of its words; the idiomatic expression is simply "characteristic" with a given language group. British speakers of English, for example, use "ring up" to mean "call on the phone," but Americans do not use the expression in that way; "ring up" is idiomatic for British speakers but not American.

Imperative A sentence that orders or requests: "Shut the door." "Please turn down the heat." "Halt!" The subject (always "you") is not expressed in an imperative sentence.

Indefinite Several sentence elements are called *indefinite,* meaning "not specifying a particular person or thing." The *indefinite articles* are "a" and "an"; some of the *indefinite pronouns* are "anybody," "anyone," "everyone," "one," "someone"; some of the *indefinite adjectives* are "any," "few," "several," "some." See also *Determiner* above.

Independent clause See *Base clause* above.

Indirect object An indirect object shows to or for whom or what the action of the verb is received: "We gave *her* a new car." In the example, "car" is the direct object; it directly receives the action of the verb "gave." But "her" is the indirect object; it indicates *to whom* the car was given.

Infinitive The "to" form of a verb (to go, to walk, to speak). The infinitive can be used like a noun, as in *"To be* or not *to be,* that is the question." It can also be used like a modifier: "These are the bicycles *to be sold* at auction."

Inflection Refers to the fact that many languages indicate changes in meaning by changes in the forms of words. English is not a highly inflected language, but we do have some inflections: for example, plurals, possessives, subjects and objects, verb tenses, degrees of modifiers.

Informal language See *Formal language* above.

Intensive pronouns The *-self* pronouns when they are used for emphasis with (to intensify) a noun or pronoun: "The dog *itself* can easily jump that fence." "You did it *yourself.*" When these *-self* pronouns are used as complements, they are called *reflexive*: "He gave himself a shock when he touched the wires."

Interjection An exclamation: "Oh!" "Ouch!" "Wow!" An interjection need not have an exclamation point: "I thought, *oh,* if I could only get away from here . . . ."

Interrogative pronoun A pronoun that asks a question (what, which, who, whom, whose): "What are your reasons for wanting to become a writer?"

Intransitive verb A verb that cannot take an object: "He *sleeps* during the day." "They *left* an hour ago." Note that a verb can be intransitive in one sense (They *left* an hour ago) and transitive in another (They *left him* in the station). A transitive verb is one in which the action of the verb "transfers" or "carries over" to an object.

Inverted order The normal order for an English sentence is subject-verb-complement: "A sign—appeared—above the door." Inverted order reverses normal order: "Above the door—appeared—a sign." See *Anticipatory construction* above.

Irony Irony is one means of saying one thing while implying another, often opposite, thing: "He tried on a garish flowered shirt and iridescent walking shorts and said he hoped it would soften his corporate image. I assured him that it did." Here, the author seems to be calmly and seriously agreeing with the man in the garish shirt, but because the shirt is described as garish and because of the image of iridescent walking shorts, the reader knows the outfit will do more than "soften" a corporate image. The irony is in the conflict between what is said and what is implied about the way the man looks. Irony is a form of understatement, and careful use of irony can add much to your writing. But too much irony may sound as though the writer is working hard to be humorous. There is also the danger that irony will slip into sarcasm—never appropriate in formal writing.

Irregular verb A verb that does not form its past tenses or past participle with a suffix like *-ed*: for example, "swim" (swam, swum) or "drink" (drank, drunk). See the list of irregular verb parts under "Verbs" in Chapter 10.

Kernal sentences In modern grammar, those minimal, basic sentences of which our language is composed: "Dogs bark." "The man sees the tree." From these kernel or basic sentences, any sentence in our language can be generated through sentence combining (see Chapter 6).

Linguistics The study of language, including many different branches of study, such as etymology, dialectology, semantics, syntax, and so on.

Linking verbs Linking verbs do not express action; they "link" their subjects to predicate nouns or adjectives. The linking verbs are the forms of "to be," "to become," "to feel," "to grow," "to look," "to remain," "to seem," "to smell," "to sound," "to stay." "She *is* young." "She *appears* young." "She *seems* young." Notice the difference between a linking verb—"This *looks* good"—and an action verb—"He *looks* carefully for mistakes in proofreading."

Macron A diacritical mark (¯) used to indicate the pronunciation of a "long" vowel: cāne, tōne, cūte. See *Breve* above.

Main clause See *Base clause* above.

Mass noun A noun that identifies some commodity or substance we measure by weight, volume, or degree (money, wheat, information). Mass nouns are sometimes called *noncount nouns* to distinguish them from *count nouns.* (We can count one dollar, two dollars, and so on, but not one money, two monies.)

Merged verb See *Particle* below.

Misplaced modifier A modifier that has been accidentally placed near some word the writer does not intend to modify: "There is a pile of clothing for the children *in the basket.*" Rephrase to avoid ambiguity or unintentional humor: "There is a pile of clothing *in the basket* for the children." "In the basket there is a pile of clothing for the children." Modifiers usually gain clarity the closer they are to the word they modify.

Modal auxiliary See *Auxiliary verb* above.

Modification To change or alter. By means of modification, writers can describe, limit, expand, and make clear the relationships among ideas. Note that the basic idea, "I had forgotten," is expanded and clarified through modification in the following sentence:

I had forgotten, in the rage of my growing up, how proud my father had been of me when I was little.
JAMES BALDWIN, *Notes of a Native Son*

Modifier A word or group of words that describes or in some way limits another word or words. Modifiers may be single-word adjectives and adverbs, or phrases and clauses used like adjectives and adverbs. See *Modification* above.

Mood of verbs The "moods" of verbs are *indicative* (for statements and questions); *imperative* (for requests or commands); and *subjunctive* (for expressions of doubt, wishes, probabilities, and conditions contrary to fact). Only the subjunctive is likely to cause writers any problems. See "Conditional Statements" and "Statements of Doubt, Wishes, Probability . . ." in Chapter 10.

Nominal Like a noun. "Nominal" is sometimes used to describe gerunds and noun clauses.

Nonrestrictive An adjective clause is nonrestrictive if it is nonessential. A restrictive clause is essential to tell *how many* individuals are meant or *which ones*. Set off nonrestrictive clauses with commas (see "Punctuation" in Chapter 11). Cumulative modifiers are "add-on" modifiers; they are usually nonrestrictive and should be set off with commas:

George lay back on the sand and crossed his hands under his head and Lennie imitated, *raising his head to see whether he were doing it right.*
JOHN STEINBECK, *Of Mice and Men*

Noun The name of a person, place, thing, or idea (woman, Irene, Texas, dog, tool, freedom). Writers should be careful with nouns used as adjectives (*brick* wall, *school* song, *church* bazaar); avoid making up new adjectives from nouns: "a firefighter invention," "an unusual size shoes," "a literature tradition." Instead, rephrase with a possessive or other form of the word: "a firefighter's invention," "an unusual size of shoes," "a literary tradition."

Noun clause A clause used like a noun: "*What you see* is *what you get.*"

Number Refers to singular and plural.

Object That which receives action, as in *direct object* (see above). There are other kinds of objects, such as object of a preposition, object of an infinitive, object of a participle, object of a gerund.

Objective complement A verb complement after a direct object: "We named him *our leader.*" In this example, "him" is the direct object, and "our leader" is the objective complement.

Paragraph symbol A proofreader's mark (¶) indicating indentation for a new paragraph. You may use the symbol on finished copy, if you don't use it too often (see inside the back cover). "No ¶" indicates that a paragraph indentation should be ignored or is incorrect.

Participle A progressive or perfect form of a verb used like an adjective (*laughing* clown, *broken* promises, *ruined* dreams). When the participle is part of a modifying phrase, you must avoid the problem of the dangling participle. See *Dangling modifier* above.

Participial phrase See *Participle* above.

Particle A preposition or adverb that has merged with a verb: "It's time to close *up* the shop." "Turn *off* the engine." The particle has become part of the verb. Note that the particle is movable: "It's time to close the shop *up*." "Turn the engine off."

Parts of speech In ancient times, scholars hoped to make a science of speech by naming and describing each of the "parts" of language. Traditionally, there are eight parts of speech; *noun, pronoun, verb, adjective, adverb, conjunction,* and *interjection.* The parts of speech get their definitions from *context.* In one context, for example, "punch" is a noun: "She threw a *punch* at him." In another context, "punch" is a verb: "She may *punch* him in the nose."

Passive The term *passive* technically describes only the verb in a passive sentence, but it is customary to define a passive sentence as one that is not an active sentence (see above). A sentence becomes passive when it is transformed so that the direct object appears as the subject: "He drew the pictures" is an active sentence; "the pictures" is the direct object. "The pictures were drawn by him" is a passive transformation of the same sentence; "the pictures" now appears in the subject slot.

Past participle The form of verb used with "have," "has," "had" (have sung, has drunk, had swum). The past participle is used in the "perfect" tenses (present perfect, past perfect, future perfect). See the list of verb parts, under "Verbs" in Chapter 10.

Perfect tense See *Past participle* above.

Person Refers to pronouns used to identify the speaker (I), *first person;* the audience (you), *second person;* and the subject (he, she, it), *third person.* Note that only the third person singular pronouns require *s*-form verbs: "he speaks," "she drives," "it barks." All singular nouns are third person and require *s*-form verbs: "the man speaks," "Sue drives," "the dog barks."

Personal pronouns The personal pronouns are "I," "you," "he," "she," "it," and their plurals; possessives ("yours," "hers," and so on); and objective forms ("me," "us," "them," and so on).

Phrase A group of words without a subject—in contrast with a clause. There are several kinds of phrases: *prepositional, infinitive, participial, absolute.* Informally, a phrase is any group of words or expression: "She used the phrase *God bless you* when anyone sneezed."

Plural More than one.

Positive degree See *Comparison* above.

Possessive Possessive nouns and pronouns can be used to show owner-ship: "*Brenda's* car," "*my* cat." (See "Apostrophe" in Chapter 11.) Note that gerunds are preceded by possessive, not objective, pronouns. See *Gerund* above.

Predicate The predicate is the part of a sentence that makes a state-ment about the subject: "The President [subject] must struggle with the economy [predicate]." The subject is who or what the sentence is about (The President); the predicate tells the reader what you want to say about the subject (must struggle with the economy).

Predicate adjective A modifier of the subject but appearing in the predicate after a linking verb: "She is *pretty*." "The young woman in that position seems very *competent*." Note the difference between a sentence with a progressive verb (She *is talking*) and one with a participle as a predicate adjective (She *is interesting*). The predicate adjective is the one that can be modified by the adverb "very" ("very interesting" but not "very talking").

Predicate nominative See *Predicate noun* below.

Predicate noun A noun in the object slot in a sentence with a linking verb: "The boy is a *lieutenant*." Such nouns are not objects; linking verbs do not take objects.

Prefix A meaning unit added to the beginning of a word: *dis*cover, *re*turn.

PREFIX	MEANING	EXAMPLE
a-	out of, not	atypical
ab-	away from	abdicate
ad-	to, toward	admit
anti-	against	antibody
auto-	self	autograph
com-	with	commit
de-	away, down	deflate
dis-	apart, not	disengage
ex-	formerly, out of	exhale
extra-	out of	extralegal
hyper-	above, very	hyperactive
hypo-	below, under	hypodermic
in-	into, within	insert
in-	not	invalid
mono-	one	monograph
ob-	against, away from	obtuse
non-	not	nonfunctional
per-	through, very	percolate
poly-	many	polygamy
pre-	before	precursor
pro-	before, in favor of	promote
re-	again, back	return
sub-	across	transport
un-	not	unconventional

Preposition Most prepositions are small words of position: "in," "out," "on," "near," and so on. A few other words are also considered prepositions: "during," "except," "since." Prepositions take objects: "to *him*," "for *her*," "between *you* and *me*." See "Objects with Prepositions" in Chapter 10; prepositions are listed there, too.

Prepositional phrase A preposition and its object and any modifiers: "by the boat," "near the great old willow." Prepositional phrases are used as modifiers.

Present participle The *-ing* form of a verb (doing, being, seeing).

Progressive tense The progressive tenses—past, present, and future progressive—are written with the *-ing* form of a verb (is running, was speaking, will be going). See *Gerund* and *Participle* above.

Pronoun A pronoun takes the place of a noun. There are several kinds of pronouns: *personal, demonstrative, indefinite, intensive, interrogative, reflexive, relative.* See "Pronouns as Subjects and Objects" and "Pronoun Reference" in Chapter 10.

Pronoun reference See *Antecedent* above.

Proper adjective An adjective derived from a proper noun (English, Indian, American).

Proper noun The name of a specific person, place, or thing (Jane, Canada, Fido). See *Common noun* above.

Pun A play on words. The pun is an obvious (nonsubtle) form of humor; it relies on similarities in sounds and unexpected applications of meanings:

Our spacemen, Mrs. Lamport fears, are "heading for the lunar bin."
ARTHUR KOESTLER, *The Act of Creation*

Regular verbs Regular verbs form their past and perfect forms by adding *-d* or *-ed* (baked, learned). See *Irregular verb* above.

Reflexive pronoun See *Intensive pronouns* above.

Relative clause A clause beginning with a relative pronoun: "I found the dollar *that you lost.*" In this example, the relative clause is used like an adjective to modify "dollar."

Relative pronouns The relative pronouns are "who," "whose," "what," "that," "whatever," "whom," "whomever," and "which." They may be used to start relative clauses (see above).

Restrictive See *Nonrestrictive* above.

Retained object A direct object in a passive sentence: "They were given a *book* to study."

Schwa A diacritical mark (ə) indicating the pronunciation of a vowel; the schwa looks like an upside down *e*. It is pronounced "uh" like the *a* in "ago" or the *o* in "Dolores" or the *e* in "the."

Second possessive Many pronouns have two possessive forms—the possessive used like an adjective (*my* hat, *her* house) and a second possessive used like a predicate adjective (the hat is *mine*, the house is *hers*).

Rhetoric The art of discovering ideas and selecting words in accordance with purpose, audience, self, subject, and code. Rhetoric is the art of effective writing—writing that has an effect on the reader. Rhetoric is the same as composition (see above).

Semantics The study of meaning; the study not only of what words mean but how they acquire meanings and even what "meaning" means. According to some modern semanticists, writers select words to express the meanings they have in mind, and therefore words do not have meanings but denotations—only people have meanings.

Sentence A group of words expressing a complete thought; a completed relationship between a subject and its predicate. Contrast with *fragment*: an incomplete sentence, an incomplete thought. See *Elliptical construction* above.

Sentence modifier A modifier of the entire idea in a sentence: "He had always been a very excitable person, *causing others to suspect that he was using drugs*."

Series Three or more items in a list: "We ordered hamburgers, cokes, and French fries." See "Use Commas to Separate Three or More Items in a Series" in Chapter 11.

Simple sentence A sentence that consists of one and only one independent clause and no dependent clauses. "Fish swim" is a simple sentence. Note that *simple* has nothing to do with length; the following is also a simple sentence: "Until noon each day, the young man in the sportscar cruised the streets, looking for his friends, looking for girls, looking for anything to do."

Slang Any informal word or expression not yet accepted by educated users of the language; consequently, slang terms are often not in dictionaries. Many slang words are colorful, lively, and suitable for informal writing, but the more formal your writing situation, the less appropriate slang becomes.

Solidus See *Virgule* below.

462

GLOSSARY OF

LANGUAGE TERMS

Split infinitive Placing a word between the word "to" and its verb creates a split infinitive (to quickly go, to really think), a construction to avoid in formal writing.

Squinting modifier A modifier that ambiguously modifies two words: "She told him *seldom* to do any of the hard work." See *Misplaced modifier* above and "Misplaced Parts" in Chapter 10.

Standard English Standard English is frequently defined as the English of educated speakers and writers. Since no two speakers of English speak exactly alike, such a definition creates more problems than it solves. *Standard* is often used to contrast with *nonstandard* or *substandard*. Thus, what many people really mean by standard English is language that follows the rules in their favorite grammar books. You can avoid the issue entirely by not using the term *standard English*. Instead, use the concept of *formal language*, a concept that implies audience, purpose, and the entire complex of decisions a writer must make. Writers who choose to write in formal situations should become familiar with the language expectations of the majority of educated readers (see Chapter 10). It is possible that serious writers might successfully use some "nonstandard" expressions in formal writing; in fact, all language usage is a matter of choice and judgment on the writer's part. Twentieth century writing is moving toward more informality; the question of what is standard or nonstandard may evaporate in time. But writers will always need to decide how they wish to present themselves to readers, what effect they wish to make, and how best to accomplish their writing purpose. See *Formal language* above.

Subject The topic of a sentence, the part of the sentence about which the predicate makes a statement: "*The rats* came in the night and attacked the children." In the example, the subject is "The rats." See *Predicate* above.

Subjective case The case of pronouns (and nouns) used as subjects (I, he, she, they, who); contrast with objective case (see above).

Subjunctive mood See *Mood of verbs* above.

Subordinate Not independent. See *Coordinate* above.

Subordinate conjunction Subordinate conjunctions start adverb clauses (see above):

after	before	until
although	if	when
as	since	whenever
as if	though	where
because	unless	wherever
		while

Suffix A meaning unit attached to the end of a word: event*ful,* dura*tion.*

SUFFIX	MEANING	EXAMPLE
-able, -ible	able to, capable of	portable
-al	act, process of	removal
-ance, -ence	condition, quality of	deliverance
-ant	one who does or is	supplicant
-ate	do or have	dominate
-ful	in abundance	harmful
-ism	belief, doctrine, theory	cubism
-ist	one who does or is	therapist
-ize	become, cause to be	sterilize
-ness	condition of	humanness
-ship	function, status	authorship
-tion	act, process	promotion
-wise	direction, position, manner	clockwise

Superlative degree See *Comparison* above.

Syntax The order of words in a sentence and their relationships to each other. See *Grammar* above.

Tense The aspect of verbs that lets the reader know whether the discourse is in *past, present,* or *future* time.

Tilde A diacritical mark (~) indicating a sound pronounced as if merging an *n* with a *y*: Doña, señor.

Transformation In modern grammar, most of the sentences of a language are generated by combining (transforming) kernel sentences (see above). Thus "The dog will come in when the rain starts" is a transformation of the two kernel sentences "The dog will come in" and "The rain starts." See Chapter 6, "Sentence Combining."

Transitive verb A verb that can take an object. See *Intransitive verb.*

Transposition symbol A proofreader's mark (∩) for transposed letters. You may mark transpositions on finished copy as long as there aren't too many of them. See inside the back cover.

Umlaut A dieresis (··) used to mark certain vowels, especially in German words: *Führer, Düsseldorf, Grösse.* The sound is difficult for English speakers to produce, but you will approximate it if you pronounce *o* or *u* with pursed lips. In formal writing, you should supply the umlaut.

Usage See *Grammar* above.

Verb A part of speech usually expressing action (go, jump, shout); a few verbs, such as the linking and auxiliary verbs (see above), do not express action.

Verbal Verb forms used for other than verb functions. Verbals include *gerunds, infinitives,* and *participles* (see above).

Virgule A slash mark (/), also called a *solidus.* For use of the virgule to mark the ends of lines of poetry in typed papers, see page 287.

Voice Refers to *active* and *passive.* See above.

Word order See *Syntax* and *Inverted order* above.

INDEX

HTC DOWNS-JONES LIBRARY
The writer's work : guide to effective
PE 1408 .M463

3 3081 00023834 6

PE   Memering, Dean   81015
1408
M463 The writer's work

APR 8   5948

PE   Memering, Dean   81015
1408
M463 The writer's work

DOWNS-JONES LIBRARY
HUSTON-TILLOTSON COLLEGE

FORMAT GUIDELINES FOR TYPED PAPERS

IDENTIFICATION
If your instructor doesn't give you another format for identifying your papers, type your name, the course title, the instructor's name, and the date in the upper right-hand corner of the first page.

1″

Kathy Hart

English 110

Professor Mendez

October 3, 1980

5-character indentation for new paragraphs

The Innovative Artist Jackson Pollock

Quadruple-space

TRANSPOSITION SYMBOL
used here to reverse the order of words

For the sake of earning livings, and reputations, painters have always

Double-space

followed the popular trends of their respective periods and concealed their

experimental dabblings in their studio storerooms. At some time earlier,

CARET
with a handwritten insertion above it

1″

innovators had to create the style that established the traditions. The

twentieth century is a time of many such innovators, one of the most prominent

1″

being the pioneer of abstract expressionism, Jackson Pollock. His later works,

and ridiculed by others,

hailed by some, made Pollock a revolutionary figure of modern art. A look at

ACUTE ACCENT

what and how he painted, as well as at the critical reactions to it, is

UMLAUT
(a drawn-in dieresis looks the same as the umlaut)

necessary to understand the impact of Pollock's work.

His creations of the 1940s show not merely a deviation from the conven-

tional rules of painting but a complete and deliberate defiance of them,

behavior that amazed Marc Moiré, the earliest favorable critic of Pollock:

TILDE

Triple-space

BRACKETS
used here to enclose clarifying information the author of the paper has inserted into the direct quote

The most obvious evidence of this rebellion emerges through the sub-

ject matter: there appears to be none. Ten years ago, Künstler and

Fañon experimented briefly with forms as devoid of extrinsic content

Double-space

as Pollock's, but they vitiated the effect by conferring elaborate

titles on their works. Pollock simply tags his with numbers because,

according to Lee Kraener [Pollock's wife], "Numbers are neutral.

They make people look at a picture for what it is--pure painting."

UNDERLINING
used here to signify the use of italics in the original

And that painting should be utterly pure is rebellion of an

unprecedented variety.1

PARAGRAPH SYMBOL

Triple-space

¶ Moiré's astonishment was perhaps to be expected in 1943, but later critics

1″

10-character indentation for all lines of displayed quotes

TRANSPOSITION SYMBOL
used here to reverse the order of letters

NOTE NUMBERS
are typed slightly above the line, with no space between the end of the quote (in this case, the period) and the note number.

LONG QUOTES
If a quote is five or more typed lines long, display it. That is, triple-space above the first line and below the last line of the quote and indent all lines of the quote 10 characters from the left. The quote itself is double-spaced. Note especially that QUOTATION MARKS are used only if, and exactly as, they appear in the original.